Series 2 F

Learning More About
Youth Hunting and Hunter Safety

Handbook/Guide
for Everyone

By Bob Swope

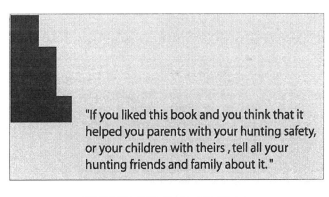

"If you liked this book and you think that it helped you parents with your hunting safety, or your children with theirs , tell all your hunting friends and family about it."

Our Basic Platform

"Our mission statement is we want this book to become the "Bible/Dictionary" for learning more about youth hunter safety and basic hunting fundamental skills. We will continue to help kids, anyone, learn as much as possible about safety at the youth level. Our motto is FAST:

F un

A ction

S kills

T eamwork

1

93002897

Photo Courtesy of My Family

Published and distributed by:
Jacobob Press LLC
St. Louis, Mo.
Tel: (314) 843-4829
E-Mail: jacobobsw@sbcglobal.net

Check our Web site at: www.jacobobpress.com

ISBN 10: 0-9820960-8-9
ISBN 13: 978-0-9820960-8-6
San 257-1862
Copyright 2010

No part of this publication may be reproduced or transmitted in any form or by any means, mechanical or electronic, including photocopying and recording, or by any information storage and retrieval system, without permission in writing from the author or publisher (except the equipment pictures in the book, and other selected pictures to be identified by the author on request).

Printed and Bound by:
No Waste Publishing
Fenton, MO. 63026

Series 2. Book 5
First Edition 2010

This book is the fifth book of the series 2 "Learning More About" books from Jacobob Press. This is volume (edition) one. Every three or four years, or when possible, we will update this book with a new updated volume (version) two.

DEDICATION

This book is dedicated to both my son Rick and his wife Julie. He has been hunting for many years now. He even has his wife Julie involved now. She just recently went out and got her first Elk. I was impressed because as far as I knew she wasn't really into hunting.

AUTHORS ACKNOWLEDGMENTS

My thanks to the following companies and organizations for their help with information and pictures: Missouri Conservation Dept, Damar Corp, World Atlatl Assoc, Missouri Atlatl Association, South County Archers, St. Louis Bow Hunters, Missouri Bow Hunters, Umarex USA, Inc, Bear Archery Products, Keystone Sporting Arms, Daisy Outdoor Products, Easton Archery Co, Gateway Gun Club
The pictures will really help illustrate what I am trying to get across to everyone using this book, help young hunters and beginners learn more about and improve on their basic "hunting & hunter safety" skills.

World Atlatl Assoc, Cahokia 2010

Gateway Gun Club, St. Louis 2010

ABOUT THE AUTHOR

Bob Swope is a long time youth sports coach and teacher. Over the past 42 years of experience working with kids he has spent 25 years coaching, managing, and teaching younger kids (6-14 Yr. olds), both boys and girls in six different sports. His teams are known for their knowledge and use of the fundamentals. He has written twenty one youth sports fundamentals books, covering fourteen different sports or activities over the past eleven years. He brings his experience on training kids. His philosophy is kids will have more fun out there when they know the all the basic fundamentals, and how to apply them to what they are doing, be it sports or hunting. He has taken a team of left over baseball kids, after a draft had been performed, and taken them to a championship and playoffs in just three years using his techniques. This was basically accomplished by teaching them the fundamentals, and getting good knowledgeable, friendly coaches to work on them at practices with the kids. He uses lots of cross training and teaching techniques from one sport and will use them in another when applicable. He is currently a member of the "National Youth Sports Coaches Association." He is a member of the World Atlatl Assoc (WAA), Missouri Atlatl Assoc (MAA), Missouri Bowhunters Assoc, and the National Rifle Assoc (NRA).

* * * * * * * * * * WARNING * * * * * * * * * * * *

If your child or the participant has any physically limiting condition, bleeding disorder, high blood pressure, pregnancy or any other condition that may limit them physically or mentally, you should check with your doctor before participating in hunting, hunter safety activities, or exercises.

Be sure participants are in good physical shape and have been through a certified state hunter safety course and have a licence before going out to hunt.

I can not stress enough that all drills, activities, and exercises in this book should be supervised by an qualified and certified adult. **AUTHOR ASSUMES NO LIABILITY FOR ANY ACCIDENTAL INJURY OR EVEN DEATH THAT MAY RESULT FROM FOLLOWING ANY INFORMATION IN THIS BOOK.**

EXTRA CARE AND CAUTION SHOULD BE TAKEN WITH HANDLING FIREARMS OR SHOOTING DEVICES OF ANY KIND. ACCIDENTS CAN HAPPEN THROUGH CARELESSNESS AND NOT PAYING ATTENTION.

Bob Swope
Jacobob Press LLC
Publisher

TABLE OF CONTENTS

Introduction

My Interest

Several years ago I was asked by a librarian in east Washington State, who liked my writing style, to write a "hunter safety" book for kids and their parents. When I checked into hunter safety books at my favorite book stores, I found they had very little, if any, to choose from. So I decided it was a worthy project. However, when I went on-line I found a bunch of books. It appeared though that they tended to be written in the favor of either adults, or teenagers and up. I have been interested in hunting and fishing since I was a young boy. Not in the usual sense though. My parents were never into hunting or fishing. When I tried fishing, I found it was a lot of fun. I learned from a number of sources. First, in my adult life I had family members and friends who taught me, and my kids (4) how to fish. My older son comes all the way over to Missouri, from Nebraska, to fish with me now when he can find time. He brings his two boys with him sometimes, and we all have a lot of fun.

Firing Firearms

Now, about the hunting. I have never hunted game using a firearm. I always did my hunting with binoculars and a camera. So, you might say what do I know about firearms and hunting. I had never fired firearms before going into the U.S. Army. When we were out on the range firing firearms, some of the instructors could not believe I had never fired a firearm before. It seems I had a natural ability to do it. I fired "expert" at 500 yards right off. No problem! When I seen where my shots were hitting on the target, I made natural corrections and got right into the "bull's-eye." However, I did have on bad experience in the Army, that falls under "hunter safety." I will draw you a mental picture of what happened so that you can understand how accidents happen. To learn how to fire the firearms, they marched us way out by the ocean where the firing range was located. When you fired out at the large bull's-eye targets, they had you get into the "prone" position (lying down on your stomach). There were two soldiers at each target position. One was the shooter, and the other one was the check person who kneeled down next to the shooter.

The check person tapped you on the helmet when the people out at the target waved a white flag that it was OK to fire. Only when you were tapped did you fire, even though it looked like it was OK. When you were done firing all your shots, you pulled the bolt back exposing the loading chamber. Then check person looked to make sure the chamber was empty (You were to only load one 30 Cal.. bullet at a time). When they were sure there were no bullets loaded in the chamber, they tapped your helmet again. This was the signal that you were done and could get up. On this particular day, I fired last. I pulled back the bolt, and my check person tapped my helmet that it was OK to get up. So I closed the bolt so that no sand would get into the chamber, and got up. So later on we were jogging marching the 5 miles back to the barracks. We had to hold our rifles at port arms pointing up. And for some strange reason my bouncing along slipped my grip and I must have accidentally pulled the trigger because I fired a shot off up in the air.

Crazy Circumstances

Well the sergeant called, "Halt," and the whole platoon moved over to the side out of the way. He came over and said who fired that shot, and I told him I did. So he checked my rifle to see if there were any more bullets in the chamber. There wasn't so he told me to report to the first sergeant when we got back. When I went up there I got chewed out pretty good. The only thing that saved me from a "court marshal" was my partners account of what happened. He told them he cleared my weapon when we were done and there were no bullets in the chamber. They never did figure out exactly how it happened, and to this day I'm not even sure. But it did happen, and it was just some kind of crazy circumstances that caused it. It was just a good thing (thank God) that I had the barrel pointing up because there were soldiers all around me on all sides and the shot went up in the air. This why you need to be VERY CAREFUL around firearms of any kind. It's dangerous, and you just never know what kind of crazy thing might happen.

My Thoughts

I think many of you young kids are trying out "hunting" now every year, but not all of you learn all the basic fundamentals you need to know to become a really good hunter. By supplying you with a good, easily understandable, graphically illustrated, fundamental instruction book I can help you have more fun out there because you will feel more like you know more about what you are doing. When I was growing up there were not many instructional books available on any kind of sports or hunting and fishing to help young kids learn about them. So I decided to start writing these books so that hopefully you could learn everything you need to know. The idea is get both mom and dad to come out and maybe get involved, and help you learn at home.

Family Participation

I really never did do much coaching in sports until my own kids started to get involved. When that happened I went down to the park or out in the backyard with them whenever we had time. It did not take me long to see that it was going to be a lot of fun. However, I did take them fishing a lot when we were on vacation up in the high Sierra mountains. We always had lots of fun, and caught more fish than we could even eat. In those days each person could only keep 20 in your possession. The rest you had better eat right away or you would be in big trouble if the game warden caught you violating that rule. You could lose your license and your fish. So we had a lot of big fish fry's. My older son was in the Army, but he never got into hunting. Probably because I didn't. My younger son started hunting around his high school age, and still goes out. Then recently he got his wife involved. They live in Nevada, so everybody hunts it seems. Well this past season my son, his friends, and relatives all put in for tags on Elk. So to get an extra chance, they asked his wife to put in for tags. As I understand it, when the smoke all cleared so to speak, she was the only that got an Elk tag. So they took her out and she got one. My older son is more like me, he hunts with binoculars. When he gets a chance, he goes with his step brother out high in the Colorado mountains hunting Elk or other game. I guess they all like Elk because they are big.

Getting Mom and/or Dad Involved

I have always believed that your mom or dad could have a lot of fun teaching you sports, or hunting and fishing, out in the backyard, park, or target range. I might point out here that not only boys can be successful in hunting. Many girls participate these days, and they have the athleticism to be successfull. I know because I coach many of them every year. Fundamentals can help you girls as well as the boys. On evenings and weekends my two boys and I used to go out to the backyard and practice playing baseball, football, or high jumping for hours. My boys seemed to like it, so we tried to work on their skills every chance we had. They both went on to be quite good in sports. I always felt that because I helped them get started they were just a little better than many of their teammates, and had more fun at whatever sport they were in. Ask your parents to come out with you. You can have fun with them while you both learn about hunting and "hunter safety." It's even fun just reading about the animals or birds you are hunting. Your parents can read this book to you younger kids, and then you can both learn. I think it's a good idea to do some reading once in a while, then you will have at least some idea what to expect when you get out in the woods hunting.

My History

A little history about me. I have coached kids like you in six different sports over a 42 year period. I have managed and coached mostly the younger boys and girls, six to fourteen years old because my thinking is if I can start you out with good fundamentals and techniques, those fundamentals will develop into long term habits for you (muscle memory-core skillls). Most of you kids have been very good at listening to what I had to say. We have fun learning, and those that listened carefully to me were very successful in their sport, whichever one it was. I'm a very good analyist, and so there no reason I can't teach you some things about hunting and "hunter safety" that will be helpful to you.

Some Advice

Some things I would like to mention. Before you do any of these drills, exercises, or activities, make sure you are healthy and in good shape. Make sure your eyesight is good (very important in hunting). Get your eyes checked, then get glasses or contact lenses if you need to. There are a number of reasons for this. First, you need to see what you are firing at, and what's around you in the woods. I have tried to keep all the drills, exercises, and activities as simple as possible and to the point, so they can be accomplished without getting hurt or using expensive equipment. Many times there are things you have around the house that you can use as training aids. As you go through the book you will find these items pointed out to you. However, you will at some point in training need to go out to a target rage and get certified shooting. When working around the house or backyard, make ABSOLUTELY SURE your rifle or weapon (bow) is not loaded. Also if you are practicing "bow and arrow" hunting, don't point it at anyone, only the target. And before you go out in the woods or anywhere hunting or practicing, make sure you are certified in a "hunter safety" course and have the proper license and permit.

Those Who Want to Learn

This book is for all you young kids who think you might want to learn learn more about how to hunt game with a rifle, bow, or other legal weapon. If you just sit around at home all the time and play computer games, I'm sure mom and dad would rather see you get outside more, and getting involved in some type of physical activity like hunting. And if you are maybe afraid of weapons, you can always learn how to do it with binoculars and a camera like I do. At a young age, you may not even know yet what sport you want to get interested in. Well if it's hunting, for pleasure, food, or even competition, then this book is for you. Just about everything you might want, or need, to know is going to be in this book. The terminology, the history, weapons, hunter safety, and how to handle yourself in the woods. There are lots of pictures, charts, and diagrams to show you how it's done. I have found over the years that some of you have a mom or dad that would like to get out there and do something with you. So let them.

However, in this case maybe mom and dad just don't know anything about hunting and shooting devices or how to go about helping you. All of you that are in this situation, tell your mom or dad that with this book they can get out there with you and actually help you learn more about hunting and hunter safety, and be successful at it. Oh yes, I also want to tell you it's great for exercising. Walking around for miles out in the woods can keep you in good condition and healthy. When you are outside for long periods of time, and properly dressed for the weather, your body gets adapted and you will find that you are not sick as much as when you spend most of your time in the house. For all of you kids and parents, here is a book you can use as a guide or reference handbook for learning hunter safety fundamentals, and the techniques of hunting. Take this book with you out to the backyard range, or woods, and use it as you go about learning and having some fun. When you stop and think about it, you and your mom and dad all working together, could become a turning point and a bonding in your lives.

Attitude & Behavior Development

Parents Influence

Most of you boys and girls from the age of *five through eight,* are very impressionable and you are influenced a lot by your mom and dad, whether you know it or not. Also by older brothers and sisters or bigger kids at school. However, don't let your parents or anyone influence you to do something that you know is wrong, just because they do it. Sometimes mom and dad get too involved and carried away in competition events. They start yelling at what they think is a bad call by the officials, things like that. Please don't get caught up in that kind of behavior and attitude. Get mom and dad involved in hunter training with you, whether out in the backyard, the range, or out in the woods. If they see that you are having fun, then that will show them they can have fun working with you. Even just learning to stalk animals and birds with binoculars and a camera can be fun. I have done this many times.

Teamwork

There is a lot of group camaraderie in hunting. Get your best friend, or mom and dad, to join and come out with you to participate in stalking or hunting. I do need to point out though that it can be dangerous. As an example, you may see a group, or a single animal, way off on another hill using your binoculars. And you want to get closer for a shot. So maybe your partner goes off way around to kind of herd them towards you. Some other hunter could accidentally mistake them for game and shoot at them. If they are dressed in "florescent hunter orange" color, that will distinguish them from game, then they have a better chance of not being mistaken for game. If the animal or bird can see them, then they move towards you, and you will get a shot. It has to be teamwork though. You need to know exactly what color they are wearing, and which direction they will circle around from so that you don't accidentally shoot at them. I know there are a number of ways to go about this. One, is have a map with you, covering the area you are hunting in. This way you can go over it and plan your strategy. Another strategy is have a bird call device of some kind. Then when they get in place close to where the animals are, they make a call letting you know about where thet are, and they are ready to try and drive the animal(s) towards you. Also make sure you both have a watch and binoculars, then plan to meet at some spot on the map at a prearranged time.

Hunting Friends

You can also make new friends as hunting partners. Also what is most important for you to realize is you need to develop good sportsmanship and the ability to work with your hunting partner or other hunters. You can be tough against other hunters, but you don't need to hate your competitors. Teamwork can help you both fill your tags if you plan it right. A good teammate, partner, or friend, can be a good influence. It is important though that in hunting you don't want to team up with someone that is wild and crazy, and not conscientious, because they might do things that will get you hurt. Find a partner that is not selfish and easy toget along with. Then if you are together and both see your prey at the same time, prearrange who will take the first shot and following shots. Take turns. Whatever you do, don't go out with a partner that will argue about it all the time. If you both can't work together, find another hunting partner. And quick before they do something that will get you hurt.

Kids Improving Their Hunting Skills

One of the things I have learned is that if learning to hunt is worth all this work and training you are going to put in, then you might as well learn how to be the best you can be at it, and reduce the "danger" factor. Learn to always try your best, and if you don't do well every time, or have any luck, there is always another day, another hunt. I realize this is very hard concept for some of you kids to learn. What I always told the kids on my sports teams was have someone watch you to see what it is you might be doing wrong or need help on. Then that person (coach, parent or instructor) should work with you, over and over, to correct these fundamental problem areas, techniques and skills. I explained to them that if they worked hard they would begin to see that they were improving and getting better and better. Also if you have a good attitude, this will usually be reflected to your hunting partner, and other people around you. In other words it can be contagious to everyone else around you, then everything will be more fun out there.

Kids Attitude

Your attitude towards your mom or dad, hunting partner(s), coaches, trainers, and game officials, will depend a lot on how your mom and dad normally act. You will often reflect their attitude towards other people. Be very aware of what your parents are saying when you are present or nearby. Many times I have seen sports parents and coaches screaming from the sidelines at referee's, officials, or another kid on the team when they make a mistake. Then following that example during practice, you will belittle one of your team mates or the coach without really realizing it. It's wrong! This is really just learned behavior from your mom, dad or coach. You can love your mom or dad, but don't do things like that just because mom or dad was doing it. Here is a concept for all of us, we are not perfect so why should we expect others to be perfect. Think about it, if you need everything to be perfect all the time to function, you have a problem. So please try to get along with your hunting partners and officials. It's very important.

If you are a more competitive person than your hunting partner is, you can help them by being fair with them. You don't always need to be the first to take the shot. Once in a while let them do it. It's a much better attitude to have. Be a leader and encourage your hunting partners rather than belittling them. Like when they shoot first and miss the shot. A little teasing when you are practicing with them is OK as long as it does not bother them, and they know you are only teasing. Some kids are very sensitive though. So know your partner, and whether you can tease them or not. And above all, find this out with a partner before you get out in the woods with them and a loaded weapon. Make sure your partner knows you are only teasing and you are not serious (a common courtesy).

Your good attitude will also help show your partners by example how they can become a better person like you are. On my Nevada youth football team I once had an eight year old boy that was so good at this, he had the full respect of all the other boys on the team. I could even let him run the drills if I had to go over and talk to a parent or one of my coaches for a few minutes. He was like an extra coach on the team. He was that good. Do you know what he is doing now? He coaches and works with young kids in his area on different sports. He is also a very well respected person in the community there where he lives.

Kids Showing Respect

Learn to have respect for your instructors, trainers, and game wardens. They are all trying to help you. The game wardens are there to enforce the rules. Without them some hunters would be hunting illegally out of season, poaching, shooting too many animals, and who knows what else. The number of accidental shooting of other hunters would probably rise also because who would care. It happens to often as it is now even with the rules. Some hunters would just say too bad, they just got in the way of my shot. Ask your mom or dad to follow the rules, and not question the game warden's decisions or advice either. If you are following the rules they will usually leave you alone most of the time. Believe it or not, they are just there trying to help.

FITNESS

Fitness is very important in hunting for the reasons I have already stated. I have had boys come to a summer afternoon or early evening baseball game really dragging their feet, so to speak. And after talking to them, I found out mom's let them go over to a friends house all game day morning at their swimming pool. Swimming is a good workout, but not the day or day before your hunting trip. You need at least one days rest from any heavy exercise before going on a hunting trip, just to let your body recuperate. As training for any sport these days becomes more complex, the trainers, and strength coaches, have found that some of the common exercises actually can be dangerous. So what I have tried to do is find out the latest techniques, and tailor the exercises in this book to fit you kids training and exercising. It takes lots of stamina, and endurance, to stay at the same skill and endurace level all the way until the end of your hunting trip. This means you kids need to have "*cardiorespiratory fitness*" and "*muscular fitness.*" In simple terms cardiorespiratory fitness has to do with your bodies aerobic and anaerobic capacity. Muscular fitness has to do with your strength, power, speed, muscle endurance, and flexibility. Near the end of your hunting trip, you need both a physical and mental advantage going for you so that you can stay focused on getting back to your car, or how to drag your kill back.

To be able to do this you kids need to work on your aerobic, anaerobic, and muscle conditioning constantly. It's not only good for hunting fitness, but in your everyday life. If you are fit, you will feel much better about anything you happen to be doing. When you kids have good muscular fitness you tend to have less injuries. And when you are hurt you tend to heal more quickly. Do not over do it exercising though, but keep at it every day or so, for at least a few repetitions at a session. Hunting takes more stamina and endurance than you would think. Towards the end of a hunting trip you especially need a physical advantage going for you because you are probably going to be tired. To be able to acomplish this you need to work on your endurance constantly. Again not over do it, but keep at it every few days for at least half an hour of conditioning and exercising.

Recovery

Here is an interesting fact. Researchers have found that breakfast cereal and milk are as almost as effective as carbohydate based sports energy drinks for recovery after even a moderate exercising session or a workout. The researchers wanted to understand the relative effects on glycogen repletion and muscle protein synthesis. They found that glycogen repletion, or the replenishment of immediate muscle fuel, was just as good after eating the whole grain cereal, and some aspects of protein synthesis was actually better. Combining "*carbohydrates*" with "*protein*" rather than consuming just one separately will be a big benefit for you after any exercising or workout. Ideally eat the cereal as soon as you get home if you are away, for optimal recovery, but no longer than 30 to 60 minutes after the exercising or workout. Here is another interesting fact the researchers found.

Body mass matters. Researchers found a slight relationship in body size to the amount of recovery food consumed. Larger people benefited from a porportionately larger serving of the recovery food and drinks. Here is something to remember. Gatorade, Powerade, and energy drinks are handy to have right after a workout, but not all of them contain the protein you need. Don't always rely on just the energy drinks. You need to eat something with protein in it right after your workout because the protein speeds up the absorption of the glucose in the sports drink. Lots of young girls have terrible diets. And they wonder why they are tired and listless all the time. Many times it's due to insufficient calories, and insufficient protein runs a close second. The alternative is get the "specialized energy drinks." *XS Energy and Nutrition2GO* are two which take care of that.

Strength Levels

When I was coaching youth football in the 60s and 70s we tried all kinds of techniques to help the kids keep their strength level at or near it's peak. Most participants in competitive sports will go through some type of a short warm up or exercise routine just before the game, to get their muscles loosened up. So even a short little stretching exercise routine before you leave for a hunting trip will keep you loose. We had some boys eat a banana the day before a game to let the vitamins and minerals get into their systems by game time. The idea was make sure these vitamins did not get all sweated out during the game. Now days they have *"Gatorade," "Powerade,"* and *"Pedialyte"* power drinks to take care of that. Another better way is before and after training, you can get sustainable energy from *"XS Energy and Nutrition2GO"* energy drinks. Try them, they also really taste good.

Plenty of Water and Sports Drinks

Staying hydrated during a hunting trip is very important. Many hunters tend to forget that they sweat a lot on a hunting trip, maybe losing as much as 6 to 8 ounces of fluid every 15 minutes, depending on what you are doing. As am example, climbing up and down hills. Make sure to hydrate 2 or 3 hours before you start the trip. Your body's water loss can be even higher in the summer if you hunting in a hot outdoor environment. Nancy Clark, an expert nutritionist, has these recommendations. Bring plenty of water with you on your hunting trip. Then after about every **15 OR 20** minutes of continuous moving or climbing, take a water break and drink a small amount of water, about 5 to 8 ounces. Smaller young hunters may need less water to stay hydrated. Find out what your *"sweat rate"* is. You need to know if you are a moderate or heavy *"sweater."* How you do this is weigh yourself before and after a strenuous hunting trip or workout. Each pound you lose is about a pint (16 ounces) of water loss that you need to replace. Be sure your calculation is accurate, don't forget to factor in how much water you drank before starting, during the trip and your workout.

Sweat Rates

As an example, if you lost 1 pound after an hour long workout, and you drank 16 ounces, your hourly sweat rate is 32 ounces, not 16 ounces. To match that rate you should drink about 8 ounces every 15 minutes. There is some evidence that suggest that both younger and older kids have less developed temperature regulation systems than adults age 18 to 35. This means you should retest your sweat rate once or twice a year. To keep track of all this, get yourself a small pad of paper and start a *"water log."* Nancy says, drinking water is the best choice for a short 1 hour trip or workout. For hunting trips and workouts lasting longer than 1 hour, Nancy suggests using the sports or energy drinks because your body can absorb them into your bloodstream more quickly. They help you avoid dehydration during practice, and aid in your recovery. Also remember that the intensity of your hunting trip or workout will effect hydration. If you are doing a light aerobic session, water is the best fluid. For highly intense, and long hunting trips and workouts, mix in the "energy drinks." See the ***REFERENCE SECTION*** for more information on Nancy Clark's nutrition book.

You younger kids will sweat a lot, especially when you are on a long climbing type hunting trip or doing a longer intense workout. You overheat quicker than us adults. I suggest taking a hand towel with you to use in wiping off from time to time because you will sweat. A suggestion is have mom or dad get you the *"energy drinks (XS Energy, Nutrition2GO) and water,"* to take with you on your hunting trip. Take a bottle of each (water and energy drink) with you when you are at an outside workout session, especially if it's warm or hot out where you are doing this. We had a football coach that had parents cut up oranges, then hand them out for the kids to suck on during the half time break at our football games. This idea helped, but then when they came out with *"Energy Drinks,"* and more research, they found much better ways to handle sustainable energy and hydration.

GENERAL HEALTH

Good Health Habits

It is generally a good idea for you to start out in life with good health habits. What we are talking about is plenty of sleep, a good nutritious balanced diet, with plenty of timely exercise and conditioning. By timely we mean don't over exercise a few hours, or a day, ahead of time before going on a hunting trip. You should be in good physical shape and well rested to hunt. You may feel that it's not necessary, but it is. Lets say you are way out in the woods and kill a deer, how will you get it back to your car. If you need to carry it very far you will find out what I'm talking about. A deer can weigh between (small) 100 lbs and 400 Lbs (large). And you need to be in good shape to even drag it back to your car.

Staying in Shape

Also not being tired or sick will improve your mental outlook, abilities, endurance, and attitude while hunting. Just a few words about dietary supplements, should you decide to use them. **DO NOT** take anything containing *"Ephedra"*. It is illegal to use in high school sports now, and has some very serious side effects. Death being one. So why take a chance? Also stay away from *"Anabolic Steroids."* Steroids can also have bad side effects such as increased irritability, and possible liver or kidney trauma. You kids are not going to be hitting home runs like baseball players, or lifting weights like football players, so you don't have to be strong in that way to be in good shape to hunt. Let yourself develop naturally for the long term.

One more thing to point out, a recent study of teenage girls found that those who drink *Coca Cola* were three to five times more likely to experience bone fractures later on, than girls who did not drink it. Things like climbing up and down hills to locate game, or up in a tree stand is going to take some strong arms and legs. Some times you need all the strength your body can muster, which is enough without needing to worry about bone fractures when you put any kind of stress on your arms or legs. So drink water instead, and don't take the chance. Researchers say the caffeine and high level of phosphoric acid in coca cola alters calcium metabolism, and may cause or aid in bone loss.

Flu and other Diseases

Nothing can be worse than catching a cold or getting the flu while you are on a hunting trip. It's bad enough when it happens at home. You are susceptible to a bunch of different bugs from the common cold to the deadly H1N1 flu virus nowdays. Besides following the CDC recommendation of frequent hand washing before eating or putting your hands into your mouth, what should you do to stay healthy? The Flu is spread through the air. This means stay away from people coughing or sneezing near you. Eat plenty of fruits and vegetables because they contain antioxidant nutrients that build up your immune system. However, they only reduce the risk of getting the flu though, they don't prevent you from getting it. Don't rely only on multivitamins for help, they have not shown to be effective against flu prevention. During flu season get a flu shot. At worst case you will normally only get a mild case of the flu. If you even think you are coming down with the flu, rest a couple of days before going out on a hunting trip. Then see how you feel? Drink lots of hot fluids at the onset of flu symptoms, they impair viral replication, and they have a mild decongestant effect. Elderberry syrup is an age old remedy for viral illnesses. It will shorten the duration of the flu. It is available at many health food stores, supplement outlets, and some pharmacies.

Infectious Diseases & Other Controls

Human Blood Infectious Diseases

Here are some rules for you to follow, with respect to infectious diseases being spread through contact with human blood. This would be when either you, or your hunting partner(s) is bleeding from an accidental cut or wound of some kind. If any one of you notices that one of you is bleeding, you should stop them and handle it immediately. Always cary a first aid kit with one of you. If it's a minor cut or scratch, it should be covered with a bandage, or cover of some kind that won't come off and expose the blood. Hepatitus-B is a serious illness easily transmitted through blood contact. It can be prevented by vaccination, and you are strongly advised to see your doctor about getting vaccinated. HIV is also a blood borne disease to be careful of. I know it won't be easy, but if your clothing has blood on it then it should be changed or at least covered if at all possible. This is so that it can't be spread to one of your hunting partners. All of these precautions should be taken to protect everyone from coming into direct contact with blood that could be infectious. For safety purposes these general rules also apply when you are working with mom, dad, friends, or your trainer out in the backyard or target range. Better to be safe than sorry.

Chronic Wasting Disease (CWD)

CWD is a infectious disease that causes degeneration of the brain in deer, elk and moose. There is no evidence though that CWD effects livestock or humans. It is important to control though because of the potential impacts on deer populations and herd management. One way to keep CWD from spreading is to avoid transporting the tissues containing the CWD infection, such as the brain, spinal cord and other organs from deer, elk and moose taken from other states into your state. Hunters in CWD areas are advised to completely bone out harvested deer, elk and moose in the field and bring back only the meat.

Here are some guidelines of what to transport when hunting out of state:

- Meat that is cut and wrapped (either commercially or privately).
- Quarters or other portions of meat with no part of the spinal column or head attached.
- Meat that has been boned out.
- Hides without the head attached.
- Clean (no meat or tissue attached) skull plates with antlers attached.
- Antlers with no meat or tissue attached.
- Upper canine teeth.
- Finished taxidermy products if carcasses are brought in from out of state with the spinal column or head attached, the hunter should take them to a meat processor or taxidermist as soon as possible and indicate that the animal was harvested from a suspected CWD location. This step will help ensure proper disposal of animal material. If hunters process their own deer, or elk, they should dispose of the remains in a landfill so that other animals are not exposed to carcasses that may be infected.

If you encounter or harvest a deer that has no obvious injuries but is in poor condition, contact local Consevation Department staff and, if appropriate, the deer will be tested for CWD.

Lead in Meat Risk

Hunters, and meat processors, can reduce the lead risk. Recent studies have shown that people who eat venison (deer meat) taken with lead-based ammunition may be exposed to lead bullet fragments in the meat. Removal of the tissue immediately around the wound area will reduce the risk, but likely will not eliminate exposure to the lead. Health officials in Missouri and several other states have reviewed this new information and have concluded that lead in venison (deer meat) is a concern, but not a human health crisis. They note that millions of deer and other big game animals are taken by hunters each year to help control big game populations. However, caution is advised for young children, or women of child bearing age. Children less than 6 years of age are particulary sensitive to leadexposure because of their developing bodies. Concerns for lead exposure also extend to pregnant women and women of childbearing age because they can pass lead to their unborn children.

The selection of ammunition for hunting deer or turkey is a matter of personal choice. Consevation Departments strive to make the most current knowledge available so that hunters can make informed decisions. For those most concerned about this new information, one solution is to use nontoxic ammunition that is available at most ammunition outlets. For more information on lead and venison (deer meat) in Missouri, go to: **mdc.mo.gov/hunt/deer**

Animal Meat Containing Harmful Bacteria

As with any perishable meat, raw or undercooked game meat can contain harmful bacteria such as *Salmonella* and *Escherichia coli*. These bacteria live in the intestinal tracks of game, and cause illness in humans when eaten. Contamination of game is usually related to the manner in which the animal was wounded, dressed, handled, or processed. Improper temperature control, preservation practices (canning, dehydration), cooking, and handling may lead to bacterial outgrowth and foodborne outbreaks in these meats. Therefore, proper handling of game meat from the field to the table is extremely important. Bacteria exists everywhere in nature, in the soil, air, water, and the foods we eat. When the bacteria have nutrients (food), moisture, time, and favorable temperatures, they grow, rapidly increasing in numbers to the point where some can cause illness. Therefore, understanding the important role temperature play in keeping food safe is critical to prevent foodborne illnesses.

Critical Temperatures

Bacteria grow most rapidly in the range of temperatures between 40 degrees F and 140 degrees F, doubling in number in as little as 20 minutes. This range of temperatures is often called the "*temperature danger zone*." Temperatures below 40 degrees F will slow the growth of bacteria, but will not kill them. This obsevation explains why perishable foods such as meat will gradually spoil in the refridgerator. Spoilage bacteria will make themselves known in a variety of ways. As an example, meats may develop an uncharacteristic oder or color and/or may become sticky or slimy. Molds may also grow and become visable. Bacteria capable of causing foodborne illnesses either dont grow, or grow very slowly, at refridgerator temperatures. Always make sure your refridgerator temperature stays below 40 degrees F. Properly handled game meat stored in a freezer at 0 degrees F will always be safe. Freezing slows the movement of molecules, causing the bacteria to enter a dormant stage. However, once thawed, these bacteria can again become active and lead to a foodborne illness.

Cooking Game

Always cook raw game meat to a safe internal temperature. Temperatures of 160 to 212 degrees F reached in baking, roasting, frying, and boiling will destroy bacteria that can cause foodborne illnesses. When roasting game meat, use an oven temperature of no lower than 325 degrees F. Ground meats to an internal temperature of 165 degrees F. Cook game steak and roasts cuts to an internal temperature of 145 degrees F for medium rare, to 170 degrees F for well done. If raw game meat has been processed and handled safely, using the above temperature guidelines will make them safe to eat. And I stress *PROCESSED AND HANDLED SAFELY AND CORRECTLY.*

Nutrition and Diets

Overweight

If you are even slightly on the overweight side be extra careful not to over work or push yourself too hard. Especially when you are on a hunting trip or begin to exercise. Don't worry though because your body will tell you. If there is any question have mom or dad take you to your doctor, then talk to them about it. You only increase your exercise repetitions when you see that you are getting into shape, and can handle it. If you are even just a little overweight it's probably a good idea to have a doctor check you out anyway before starting to do any hunting. Your doctor will give you a better idea of what you can or can't do. You have to be in excellent shape to be out hunting if you are going to be moving up and down hills to get to where the game is located. Being way overweight could be a problem in hunting because people that are way overweight may only like to stay in a blind, or just hide on the ground next to a tree someplace and wait for the game to come to them. If that's you, I want to caution you, people who overweight are at a high risk for heart problems.

Is Overweight a Problem With Kids

Overweight can be a big problem with young kids reaching puberty (around 12 -13 Yrs. old), especially girls. I was just talking to a coach several years ago at a track-meet about my "Track and Field" book. I was trying to sell him on getting a copy of the book. He said, "Can I take a look at it," and I said, "Yes." He thumbed through the pages for several minutes. Then said, "This is a great book for kids to learn about track." Then he looked through it some more and said, "I don't see anything in here about weight and diets though." He asked me if I had any information about "nutrition" and "diets" in my books. And I told him, "Very little."

Then he told me that I should put information in my books about the subject because it's very important to young kids, especially when you are going into *puberty*. He said, "At that point they tend to eat way too much fast food, then their weight balloons up. This makes it very difficult for them to compete in a high energy sports like swimming or running." You may say, that doesn't apply to me because while hunting I won't be doing any swimming or running. But you may need to move around more than you think, to get to where the game is. The more I thought about it, the more I thought he was right on. So now I put this information in all my books. Many of you kids do not watch your nutrition. You are always in a big hurry to get somewhere, or do something. So mom or dad pulls into the fast food restaurant and gets a burger to go. What you get there is NOT the most nutritious food though. Probably has a high fat content. Eat enough of it and, yes you will put on weight.

Advice

What advice can I give you? Here is what I have come up with. After researching the subject, I have decided to basically follow some of the suggestions and recommendations of Nancy Clark, MS, RD. She has a book out called, "Sports Nutrition Guidebook" (See the reference section). But also you need to get mom and dad to help you out at home by following through on what you need to do in order for it to work. I guess I should not say, "You need to go on a diet." What I really mean is you kids getting the proper nutrition. Nancy Clark offers tips to help you fuel yourself for optimal growth and performance, be it sports or hunting. I will try to explain some of her tips to help you with your nutritional needs, but I have to stress that I am not an expert at this. From what I read the critical time is when you reach *puberty*. Your body is going through a change. This is also when your nutritional needs start to change. Adults usually talk about dieting to lose weight. You kids do not need to diet in this way. You just need a variety of healthy foods to keep your bodies growing properly.

Your Weight

Some of you kids are overweight, but even you can improve your health whether you exercise or not, by just eating nutritious foods and being a little more active. However, you kids can damage your health by doing something drastic like deciding to eat only lettuce or skipping meals. I'm sure some of you kids feel you either weigh too much or too little. But remember some kids have large frames and some kids have small frames. Take that into consideration. If you are worried about your weight, have your doctor check your body mass index (BMI). This is a way to estimate how much body fat you have. If your doctor is concerned about your weight they can recommend some goals. They may want you to lose some weight, or gain weight at a slow pace. To do this right it really should be done with your doctor's help. If you need to lose weight, and mom or dad can afford the cost, you can also work with a dietitian who can show you how to reduce calories and carbohydrates safely while still getting the necessary nutrients.

What Can You Kids do?

The best general thing you can do is eat a balanced diet, and get plenty of physical activity. Physical activities can be things like; riding your bikes, shooting baskets above the garage door, running laps out at a track or field, dancing, helping your dad rake the leaves, or even helping your mom clean the house. What you want to limit is your nonactive things like watching TV for long periods of time, or playing computer games all the time. You can try to eat a variety of healthy foods. A balanced diet means you should not eat the same thing every day. Have mom help you eat a mix of foods from different food groups. These would be things like:

- Fruit and vegetables
- Meats, nuts, and other protein rich foods
- Milk and dairy products
- Grains. Especially whole grain foods, like whole grain cereal and breads

Protein helps build your muscles and other body structures. The calcium and vitamin-D helps your growing bones. Vitamins and other nutrients in the fruit and vegetables keep your bodies working as they should. The Fiber helps prevent constipation. The carbohydrates give you energy.

Tips-Here are some of Nancy's tips:

Fluids

Kids need to have fluids while out hunting, at training sessions, or out at the range. And your mom or dad needs to make sure you have these fluids when you are at theses places. Don't depend entirely on yourself to bring them, have mom or dad remind you. The fluids needed are cold water, diluted juice, or a sports energy drink. Any *non stop* physical activity that lasts 30 to 40 minutes will cause you kids to get overheated when compared to an adult doing the same activity. At a given running speed you kids will produce more body heat, sweat less, and gain more heat from the environment than an adult would while doing the same activity. I always like to send kids on a water break between every 30 minutes and an hour, depending on what we are doing and how hard we are working. Coaches, I know it's hard to remember when you are in the middle of a training session, but try not to forget. It's important!

Protein

An adequate amount of protein is very important for you kids in sports. It helps you grow and it builds strong muscles. Athletic kids involved in sports may need .5 to 1.0 grams of protein per pound of body weight per day. As an example, a nine year old who weighs 75 pounds would need about 37 to 75 grams of protein. You kids can easily get this in three glasses of milk (about 30 grams each) plus a small serving of a protein rich food at lunch and dinner. If you do not drink very much milk, and eat meatless pasta dinners often, you are at risk for a protein deficient diet.

Although you kids need an adequate amount of protein, any extra (too much) protein will NOT build bigger muscles. Even strength training, using a light-to-moderate resistance technique that reduces stress on the joints and ligaments, won't bulk up your muscles. At *puberty* it's the hormones that kick in that causes the muscular bulk.

Junk Food

You active kids can meet your nutrient needs with a variety of wholesome foods that are within 1200 to 1500 calories per day. So believe it or not, you actually have SOME room for fatty junk food. Your parents should NOT restrict all the fat you kids might eat. Generally you need a diet where about 30 per cent of the calories are from fat (see the REFERENCE SECTION for sample menus). You may not get enough energy if you eat significantly less fat. The danger is too much junk food snacks might kill your appetite for nutritious meals. This is especially important if you eat too little lunch at school, then devour too many afternoon junk food treats. The ideal thing is for you to eat a second lunch after school instead, to meet your fueling needs.

Calorie Intake

Active kids may need as many calories as their mom or dad do, in fact maybe more. As an example, a six year old boy or girl who weighs about 45 pounds requires about 1800 calories per day. That would be about 40 calories per pound of your weight. Plus you will need about 100-300 more calories if you are involved in sports. An average nine year old at 78 pounds needs about 2500 calories per day. This is 32 calories per pound of your weight, plus the extra calories for sports. A normal growth sign that you are eating enough is that you notice that your training does not stunt your growth when your energy needs are met. If you notice that you seem to be overly fatigued, irritable and lethargic, it's because you are not taking in enough calories.

Weight and Pressures

Many of you young kids are under a lot of pressure to be thin, especially girls. Even in the third grade dieting is common now. A recent California study showed that 30-45 per cent of nine year old girls, and 40-86 per cent of ten year old girls had, or were showing, signs that they had an eating disorder. Athletes in sports that emphasize leanness such as ballet, gymnastics, figure skating, swimming, and running (such as soccer, lacrosse, track), have you kids dieting. This is standard. Pressure to be thin and have the "perfect body" means trouble ahead for you kids. Dieting is a health risk for you kids to develop a full blown eating disorder. You need to have your mom or dad recognize that dieting is not just about eating, it's about feeling not "good enough," having a poor self image, and low self esteem. Make sure you down play people teasing you about your body size as an important part of your worth, instead tell them they need to learn to value and accept there are individual differences in the size of kids.

Don't comment about the size of large children to your friends either because that large person might hear you, and conclude from your comment that they should be thin to be valued and loved. Next thing you know they are dieting. Bad move! And guess whose fault that would partially be? This is very important with you young girls who are coping with body changes during *puberty*. Your efforts to control your weight may lead to a sense of frustration, guilt, despair, and failure. And it can lead to a pattern of unhealthy eating, and a eating disorder. Have your parents watch you closely for your own good. Don't be afraid to ask them to do that for you. It's in your best interest.

Childhood Obesity

These days child obesity is a problem. Although in 2008 the experts say obesity has leveled off. Competitive sports that are directed at only winning games with the best athletes offers only humiliation to overweight kids who long to be fit and be adopted by their peers. Appropriately prescribed and competently supervised strength training can be good for obese children because it gives them a chance to shine and be noticed. They are probably one of the strongest kids in their class. So if you are that person then use that to your advantage. It may work for you, try it!

Planning

Many of you kids often eat poorly because both you and your parents have failed to plan for better choices. On the way to sports practice, do you think ahead and bring bagels and bananas to be eaten in the car? Or do you just take the easy way out and succumb to mom or dad getting you a candy bar or chips from the snack shack? What about fluids? Does your mom or dad MAKE YOU bring your own water bottle? Before workouts and target shooting, have you prepared to eat an early pasta dinner, or do fast food burger's and taco's fill your empty stomach on the way there? Does your mom or dad have juice boxes ready for you? Think about it. Your mom or dad can really HELP you if you let THEM know what YOU need so that THEY can do a little planning for you.

Menus

With her permission, we have reprinted several of Nancy Clark's sample menus in the back of the book in the ***REFERENCE SECTION***. These are just to give you and your parents some ideas. They are not etched in stone. If you are having some eating or weight problems, and can't afford the book, these menus may be helpful. The best thing though is to buy Nancy's book (See the reference section), or check it out at the library. If your are going to be in sports or hunting, you will be glad you did . It is the best book on "nutrition" I have ever seen for kids in any kind of sport.

In Summation

You kids take care of yourself. Don't get caught up in the "I don't have time mode." Take the time to plan ahead, with or without mom or dads help. There is an old saying that says, "Sometimes the best pace to find a helping hand is at the end of your own arm." Want to perform better? Then get plenty of sleep 2 days before a hunting trip. More than 7 or 8 hours sleep a night will make you feel a whole lot better. If you extend your sleep time to 10 hours per day for 2 weeks, studies show that you should see a big difference in your performance and alertness out in the woods.

Hunting History

The Beginning

I'm sure that hunting started as soon as prehistoric man got hungry. It has evolved a long way from then. I think we moved from throwing stones, to hatchets, to spears, to bow and arrows, to crossbows, to guns. Anyway something like that. Hunting was a crucial part of the early man hunter-gatherer societies before the domestication of livestock and the start of agriculture, which begin about 11,000 years ago. Hunting strategies diversified with the development of the bow, about 18,000 years ago. And it diversified again with the domestication of the dog, about 15,000 years ago. There is fossil evidence of spear use, going back about 16,200 years ago. Even when animal domestication became widespread, hunting was a big contributor to the supply of food. It was still prevalent even after the development of agriculture. Supplementary to meat from hunting, other materials used were bone for implements, sinew for cords, and fur, rawhide, leather, and feathers were used as clothing. With the domestication of the dog, ferret, and birds of prey, various forms of animal aided hunting developed including scent hound hunting, sight hound hunting, ferreting, and falconry. These mainly took place in medieval times. Dog breeds were selected for certain tasks during the hunt, they had names like setters, pointers, and retrievers. As time went on, hunting emerged as more of a sport for those in the upper social class.

PICTURE 1

Modern Hunting

With modern firearms weapons came control problems. Hunters were killing more animals than they could use for food. Soon some animals and birds either became extinct or nearly extinct. Rules and hunter safety then came into existence to try and control hunting. Regulation of hunting is now primarily regulated by state law. Additional regulations are imposed through United States environmental law in the case of migratory birds and endangered species. Regulations do vary from state to state, and govern the areas, time periods, techniques and methods by which specific game animals may be hunted. Some states make a distinction between protected species and unprotected species (vermin and varmint's) such as Feral Hogs *(SEE PICTURE 1)*, for which there are no hunting regulations. Hunters of protected species require a hunting license in all states, for which completion of a hunting safety course is sometimes a prerequisite.

Game animals are divided into several categories for regulatory purposes. Typical categories with example species are as follows:

- Big Game: White Tailed Deer, Mule Deer, Moose, Elk, Reindeer (Caribou), Bear, Big Horn Sheep, Pronghorn, boar, Javelina, and other exotic species found in special hunts.
- Small Game: Hare, Rabbit, Squirrel, Raccoon, and Opossum.
- Furbearers: Mink, Pine Martin, Red Fox, Beaver, Bobcat, and Musk Rat.
- Predators: Coyote, Cougar (Panther/Mountain Lion).
- Waterfowl: Ducks, Mallards, Geese, and Canada Goose.
- Upland Game Birds: Turkey, Grouse, Pheasant, Chukar, Dove, and Bobwhite Quail.

Quotas and Limits

Hunting big game usually requires a "tag" for each animal harvested. Tags must be purchased in addition to the hunting license, and the number of tags issued to an individual is usually limited. Where there are more prospective hunters than the quota for that species, then the tags are usually assigned by a lottery. Tags may also be restricted to a specific area, or wildlife management unit. Hunting migratory waterfowl usually requires a duck stamp issued by the Fish and Wildlife Service. The harvest of animals other than big game animals is usually restricted by a "bag" limit and a "possession" limit. A bag limit is a maximum number of specific animal species that a hunter can harvest in a single day. A possession limit is a maximum number of a specific animal species that can be in an individual's possession at any time. Some regulations for big game hunting often specify a minium caliber or muzzle energy for firearms. The use of lead ammunition can be limited or banned because of environmental and health concerns.

Hunter Ethics and Safety Rules Implemented

For the safety of the hunter, bystanders, and the game or birds, "hunter safety" rules were implemented. However, according to the National Safety Council, hunting is a safe activity. In fact, hunting results in fewer injuries per 100,000 participants than do many other sports, including cycling, bowling, golf and tennis. However, as with any activity, you should always use good judgement and take responsibility for your actions. Deer and Turkey hunters (Missouri) should follow safe, ethical hunting practices. In fact these rules would apply to any hunter. These include:

- Always be sure of your target and beyond before you shoot.
- If you hunt from a tree stand, make sure you always wear a safety harness. Annually, serious accidents occur when the hunter falls from the tree.
- Always make sure your equipment is in good working condition before you leave on a hunting trip. And make sure your firearm is properly sighted in.
- Clean and properly care for your game.
- If you hunt on private land, always be sure to obtain permission from the landowner, and respect their property as if it was your own. Scout the areas where you plan to hunt ahead of time so that you know where the boundaries, houses, roads, fences and livestock are located on the property. And remember, permission is required to enter private land.
- If you do not kill your deer or turkey instantly, always make every effort to find the wounded animal.
- Always pick up all your litter including spent ammunition. Leaving the area better than the way you found it is a sign of thanks for the privilege of hunting there.
- If you are involved in a firearms related accident, the law requires that you identify yourself and render assistance. Failure to do so is a class 'A' misdemeanor.
- Always report observed violations of the law to a conservation agent or local sheriff as soon as possible.
- Always know and obey all wildlife laws.
- Develop your skills and knowledge, and share them with others.
- Always know and follow the rules of gun safety.
- Make every effort to retrieve and use all game.
- Always respect the rights of all hunters, non-hunters and landowners.
- Respect the land and all wildlife.
- Always be sensitive to others when displaying harvested game.
- And most of all remember, hunting is not a competitive sport.

SECTION 1

Hunting & Hunter Safety

Explanation

Hunting is shooting game for food, sport or game population thinning. To accomplish this you will need a firearm, bow, or some other type of hunting device. It's legal in most states to hunt big game animals, small game animals, upland game birds and waterfowl as long as you have a license and have passed a hunters safety test. You can hunt certain small game animals classified as varmint's or non-game in many states without a license. Most all of the states specify what you can and can not use to hunt these different types of game. "Hunter safety" is part of hunting. Most states will require you pass a hunter safety test to get your license and permits. Check with your states hunting laws and regulations before you ever go out on a hunting trip.

Spaniel & Pheasant

What Can Be Used for Hunting

We will cover each of the legal, depending on what state you are in, hunting firearms and devices such as rifles, shotguns, muzzleloaders, air rifles, bows, crossbows, slingshots and atlatls. For each of these hunting devices we will cover; the popular firearms or devices, what ammunition is used, handling of the device, how to load and unload, maintenance, and the hunter safety code for each device.

Hunting and Hunter Safety Fundamentals

How to Conduct Yourself While Hunting

Basically follow the ethics and safety rules shown on page 23, use the basic fundamentals, and above all follow the "10 Commandments" of firearm safety (most popular). Following these will eliminate many accidents and tragedies. In most states you will need to complete a "hunter safety education class" before you can purchase your first hunting license, or get a permit.
The fundamentals you need to know are:

- Firearm Safety
- Gun & Devices Storage Safety
- Firearms Purchase/Laws Safety
- Handling & Harvesting Safety
- Trapping Safety
- Physical Conditioning

- Clothing Safety
- Gun Clubs and Range Safety
- Safety When Attacked by Game
- Tracking, Stalking, Waiting Safety
- Disabled Safety

Learning the Fundamentals

The first step is signing up, or taking an on-line, hunter safety education class. Most everything you need to know will be covered, and there will be a knowledgable person either where the class is given or on-line, to answer any questions you may have. And I must tell you young kids that you don't need to be an adult or a rocket scientist to learn and pass a hunter safety course. Much of it is just common sense. There are many types of classes available for different types of firearms and other hunting device owners, from women's hand gun classes to youth classes. Some of theses classes go into specific scenarios that you run into while out hunting. Our focus will be on boys and girls from 6 to 18 years old. Although you adults can learn from this book also. We will start with rifles first *(PICTURE 2)* because they are probably the most common of the firearms used in hunting big or small game.

PICTURE 2

Other Considerations

Before we go into the firearms and hunting devices, there are other fundamental things to consider also such as; what clothing to wear, gun and shooting device storage and care safety, belonging to clubs and firing ranges for practice, firearm purchase and laws, handling and harvesting game, transporting game, being attacked by game, trapping, and conditioning

Firearm Safety

General Gun Safety

Following the "10 Commandments" of gun safety at all times will promote general gun safety. Even though you can hunt with a handgun, we are not including it in this information because hand guns are not usually used in outdoor game hunting, mostly only rifles, shotguns, muzzleloaders and pneumatic (air) powered guns. Observing these fundamental "10 Commandments" for firearm safety will eliminate many accidents and tragedies:

Firearm 10 Commandments

1. ALWAYS keep your gun pointed in a safe direction *(SEE PICTURE 2)* while carrying.
2. ALWAYS treat every firearm as if it were loaded.
3. ALWAYS make sure the firearm is unloaded, and the action is open, except when actually hunting or preparing to shoot.
4. ALWAYS be sure the barrel and action are clear of obstructions and that you have the proper ammunition for the firearm you are carrying.
5. ALWAYS be sure of your target before you pull the trigger.
6. NEVER point a firearm at anything you do not want to shoot. And ALWAYS avoid all horseplay with a firearm.
7. NEVER climb or jump over an obstacle while carrying a loaded firearm.
8. NEVER shoot at a flat, hard surface or water.
9. ALWAYS store firearms and ammunition separately.
10. ALWAYS avoid the use of alcohol and other drugs just before or during shooting.

Clothing Safety

What To Wear

What you wear for hunting can provide more safety for you. Tests have been conducted and conclusively demonstrated that fluorescent (hunter) orange was by far the most easily seen and recognized bright, unnatural color against a natural woods type background. Over the last 50 years, hunter orange has proved to be an enormously effective deterrent to mistaken-for-game accidents. So this is the clothing color you should be wearing most of the time *(PICTURE 3)*. Deer are apparently color blind, they can't tell orange from green. It even shatters the illusions influenced by "easy blur."

Camouflage   **Hunter Orange Vests**
PICTURE 3

There are other clothing safety issues, but this color on your jackets and vests is the most effective hunter safety rule you can follow, except in special cases against special game. Any clothing you wear should be made of a soft, noise resistant material. Being on the ground means you will come in contact with branches, undergrowth, briers, or other natural objects that may cause noises when brushed up against. Wearing quiet clothing will reduce any unwanted sounds that might "spook" your target.

Other Colors

Other colors are for those special hunts. In those cases it is important that the clothing be camouflaged with patterns that blend in naturally with the terrain to be hunted *(SEE PICTURE 3)*. This would apply when you hunting out in open range, or way back in the high mountains where there are not many other hunters around, and you don't want the game to see you coming from long distances away. Like you may want to wear white if you are hunting in the arctic where everything is snow covered. Camouflage is OK out in a boat waiting for waterfowl. Other hunters can usually see you are out in a boat, and ducks might get spooked if you are covered with fluorescent orange.

Keeping Warm and Dry

When you out hunting, which is usually in the winter when it is cold outside and the weather is not so good, you need to be warm and dry. Choose clothing that accomplishes that. You need a hat, gloves, and the proper boots for the terrain you are hunting, and the weather you are in. And depending on where you are hunting and whether it's on water or raining, you need to have waterproof clothing.

Gun and Hunting Devices Storage & Care Safety

Storage At Home Safety

This is a big hunter safety issue. Believe it or not, most firearms are stored unsafe. Leaving a loaded gun around the house where there are kids is just asking for trouble. Kids are inquisitive, and guns seem to fascinate them. Consider the benefits of a gun safe, gun locks, or a locking cabinet *(SEE PICTURE 4)*. Or even a combination of these.

Here are some facts from the "National Safety Council" to consider:

In 1999, 3,385 children and youth ages 0-19 years old were killed with a firearm. This includes homicides, suicides, and unintentional injuries. This is the equivalent to about 9 deaths per day, which is a figure commonly used by journalists. Of the 3,385 deaths here is the breakdown:

- 214 Unintentional
- 1,078 Suicides ■ 1,990 Homicides
- 83 for which the intent could not be determined
- 20 due to legal intervention

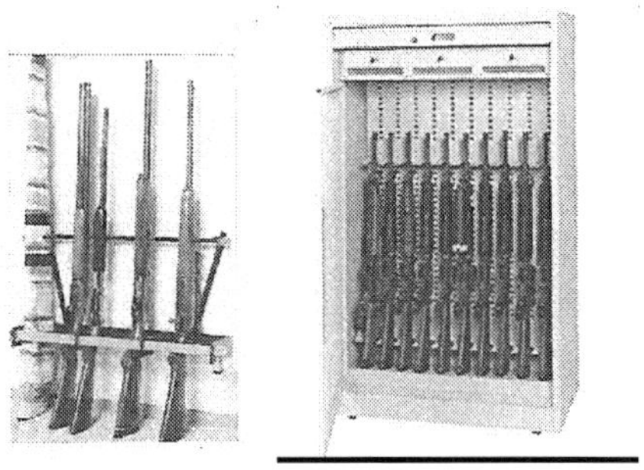

Of the total firearms related deaths here is the breakdown:

- 73 were of children under five years old
- 416 were children 5-14 years old
- 2,896 were 15-19 years old

Lock Racks   Cabinets
PICTURE 4

If you have a hunter, or anyone, in your house that has a firearm, weapon, or shooting device that is nor stored under lock and key, these are 3,385 reasons to have them get them stored under lock and key. And I suggest you take care of this immediately. If a "gun safe" or "cabinet" is too expensive for you, put it on a credit card, pay a little each month. When you do get one, hide the key. And always store the ammunition in another separate place under lock and key. Whatever it takes! But do it. Then sit down and have a talk with all the people in your house, explaining the dangers of loaded weapons. It may just keep your kids around to reach adulthood. If you keep a gun out handy in case you are worried about someone breaking into your house then get a can of "wasp spray" and spray them in the eyes, instead of using a gun on them. It has a 20 - 30 foot range.

Transportation Storage Safety

Your firearms and shooting devices need to be stored in a safe place in your vehicle while traveling back and forth to wherever you are going to be hunting. Most hunters travel in pick up trucks. They make heavy lock "safe's" that fit in the beds of trucks. There are also companies that will build locking storage boxes **(SEE PICTURE 5)** into the entire bed of your truck. By using these, you will keep your weapons safe from damage, or being stolen. When you are in a boat, on your way to a waterfowl hunt, keep all firearms unloaded, and put a trigger lock on them so that if they accidentally fall over, they don't fire and injure your hunting partners in the boat.

PICTURE 5

Picture Courtesy of Delmar Corp

Firearm and Hunting Devices Maintenance Safety

Regular cleaning and keeping up with necessary repairs is important! If you want to be a hunter and hunt, do what it takes to learn how to keep your firearms safe, accurate, make them last longer and hold their value. These are things like cleaning then oiling your rifle or shotgun, and waxing your bow string. And by the way, always check and double check your rifle or shotgun to make sure they are not loaded, before you start working on them. If you NOT going to do the maintenance yourself, then take the weapon into a pro shop and have regular maintenance and check-ups done. If you are going to keep hunting, this will pay off in the long run.

Gun Clubs and Firing Ranges Safety

Gun Clubs

If you get into hunting you may end up in a gun club *(SEE PICTURE 6)* if you really like hunting. Many of them feature public lines for rifles, shotguns, and pistols. They also have ranges

PICTURE 6

available for match activities and training rentals. Their matches are usually available to the public. Most do NOT, however, rent or loan firearms for use on the public lines. They emphasize safety at their facilities. They have rules published on the site, they have "Rangemaster's" and "Range Safety Officers" that monitor all activities. If you are new to shooting, you will find that the controls they use will guide you into safe gun handling habits. If you are an experienced hunter, but new to the range, you will be able to relax and enjoy yourself, knowing that they are keeping a close eye on the new shooters. Membership is open to the public, but there will be prepaid fees.

Firing Ranges

Many young kids get their target practice by going out and setting bottles and cans on a fence post someplace, and then do what is referred to as "plinking." But just as hunters, you kids that go out plinking have certain responsibilities. First you need to ask permission to shoot on private property. Then you need to pick up the targets when you are finished shooting, and you need to be

Public Line Range

Wilderness Outdoor Range
PICTURE 7

concerned about safety. The big problem that greatly concerned landowners is plinker's who shoot at glass bottles, then leave the broken and shattered pieces laying around where they could injure livestock or damage tires. Most states have commercial shooting ranges, shooting clubs and unmanned Department shooting ranges *(SEE PICTURE 7)*. These designated shooting ranges are set up with the proper safety control measures which range users must adhere to (see the "10 commandments" on page 25). These measures are simply a set of rules to be followed while handling firearms. These rules differ very little from the "10 commandments." Firing on a designated shooting range should be a planned activity allowing many shooters an opportunity to practice firing their weapon *(SEE PICTURE 7)*.

Here are a few additional safety rules that apply to any range:
1. Keep the action open, muzzle pointed down range or in a safe direction, and the firearm unloaded until you are up on the firing line, and the range has been cleared for loading and firing.

2. ALWAYS wear proper, adequate eye and ear protection.

These general safety rules apply to both indoor and outdoor ranges:
1. Know and obey all range commands and signs. Know where others around you are at all times. Shoot only at authorized targets.
2. Designate someone to act as the "range officer" when none are present or assigned.
3. ALWAYS open, unload and secure firearms during cease fires.
4. DO NOT handle firearms or stand at the firing line when others are down range.
5. Smoking, eating or drinking while on the firing line is prohibited.
6. ONLY those firearms authorized on a given range facility will be allowed.
7. All firing will be done from designated firing lines or positions.

There are a number of Department Wildlife management areas (such as in Oklahoma) that have been designated unmanned shooting ranges. They vary from an earth berm as a backstop *(SEE PICTURE 7)* to shooting benches and target stands.

While using Department (State) shooting facilities, specific rules and information should be noted and are posted as you enter the area. The first sign you should see states:

> USE AT YOUR OWN RISK. USERS
> MUST HAVE AN (Name of the State)
> HUNTING LICENSE UNLESS EXEMPT.

The second sign nearest the unmanned shooting range will have specific rules which include:

> # RULES
> 1. Shooting hours sunrise to sunset only.
> 2. No glass of any kind permitted on the range.
> 3. No fully automatic weapons allowed.
> 4. Remove all targets and debris when finished.
> 5. No alcoholic beverages.
> 4. Always practice safety on the range.

Surrounding the Department (State) shooting ranges are designated impact areas where no one is allowed. These safety zones are posted and marked with 12' x 14" fluorescent orange signs stating:

> # DANGER
> STAY OUT.
> SHOOTING RANGE ZONE

Firearms Purchase /Laws Safety

Firearms Purchase
Numerous municipal, state and federal statutes control the use, ownership, transportation, purchase, sale and legal use of firearms. Most states require a permit to purchase a firearm, but some do not. In almost all states a permit is required to purchase and carry a concealed handgun, but there are states that allow you to purchase, but not carry a concealed firearm. In some states an eligibility certificate or pistol permit is required to purchase a handgun. Both of these documents are usually valid for a 5 year period, they allow unlimited purchases, and will wave the long gun waiting period. The best thing to do is check out the laws in your state before you go in to purchase a rifle or other type of firearm.

The Law
A gun law is a law that applies to firearms. Restrictions on gun purchase and ownership vary greatly both by country and type of firearm used. In the United States the laws will vary from state to state. It is the responsibility of each individual hunter or gun owner to be aware of what is legal and what is not. A license is required to possess, import, or sell firearms. In the United States, most federal gun laws are spelled out in one of the following:
- National Firearms Act (1934)
- Gun Control Act (1968)
- Firearms Owner's Protection Act (1986)
- Brady Handgun Violence Prevention Act (1993)
- The Omnibus Crime Control Act (1994)

In addition to federal gun laws, most states and some local jurisdictions, have imposed their own firearms restrictions. The "right to keep and bear arms" is a feature of the second amendment to the United States Constitution, but by international standards we have only a few restrictions on the possession of firearms.

The issue of gun law has become a political and/or controversial issue in many societies. There are many differing views on how gun laws should be set up in a society. There is a typical disagreement over whether guns should be prohibited in the interest of public safety, or whether gun ownership by the general public improves safety and should be allowed. This debate gets fueled by the black market sales of firearms, illegal firearm manufacturing, over the border purchases, witness intimidation, self defense as a right, use of deadly force in self defense, accidental shooting, victims rights, use of firearms in killing sprees, criminal use of firearms that were originally legally purchased, use of stolen firearms by criminals, alternatives to firearms, and hunting vs self defense use.
However, remember that the constitution allows us to have a firearm. You hunters are not the big problem though, it's carelessness, misuse by criminals, and people that are mentally ill.

Handling and Harvesting Game Safety

Areas of Concern
There are three basic areas of concern when processing or harvesting wild game.
- Initial Handling
- Transporting
- Care in the Kitchen (Cooking)

Initial Handling

Initial handling of wild game (animals & birds) after the kill is very important. If it's not done right, you could transmit a disease to other game or other states, such as Chronic Wasting Disease (CWD). This occurs in deer, elk and moose. CWD has not been found in Missouri's deer herd. However, it has been found in nine other states, including Kansas, Illinois and Nebraska. If you are going to hunt deer, make sure to check with the "Dept. of Fish and Game" or the "Conservation Dept." in your state to find out if their deer herd has it. One way to keep CWD from spreading is to avoid transporting the tissue containing the CWD infection, such as the brain, spinal cord and other organs from deer, elk, and moose taken from other states into your state. Hunters in CWD areas are advised to completely bone out harvested deer, elk and moose in the field and bring back only the meat. Here are some guidelines of what to transport when hunting out of state.

1. ONLY meat that is cut and wrapped (either commercially or privately).
2. Quarters or other portions of meat with no part of the spinal column or head attached.
3. Meat that has been boned out.
4. Hides without the head attached.
5. Clean (no meat or tissue attached) skull plates with antlers attached.
6. Antlers with no meat or tissue attached.
7. Upper canine teeth.
8. Finished taxidermy products if carcasses are brought in from out of state with the spinal column or head attached, the hunter should take them to a meat processor or taxidermist as soon as possible and indicate that the animal was harvested from a suspected CWD location. This step will ensure proper disposal of animal material. If hunters process their own deer or elk, they should dispose of remains in a landfill so that other animals are not exposed to carcasses that may be infected.
9. If you encounter or harvest a deer that has no obvious injuries, but is in poor condition, contact your local game department staff and, if appropriate, the deer will be tested for CWD just to be safe.

Transporting Harvested Game

The big safety concern with transporting harvested game is the introduction of disease into healthy environments. Chronic Wasting Disease (CWD) can cause harm to big game, while the avian flu is a damaging disease for migratory birds. Areas with documented cases of CWD are popping up all over the country, and many states are adding language to their state regulations concerning transportation of wild game to aid in the containment of these and other diseases. Read the initial handling guideline above, and contact your state department of game before you do any transporting. This way you will know what you can and can't do.

Transporting Harvested Game Through the Woods

Moving game through the woods can be very difficult, and even dangerous. Be sure to wear "hunter orange" clothing while moving your harvest (even if your state doesn't require it), and consider putting orange on the animal itself for extra protection. Keep the animal low to the ground, even if it means pulling it through heavy underbrush. It's important to make yourself easily seen as you move your harvest through the woods.

Permits to Transport Harvested Game

Every state requires a permit to transport harvested game. With these permits come specific tagging and transportation requirements. Before moving a carcass, you must tag it with a completed field tag that includes your name, address, hunting licence number, date and time of the kill. This tag must be written in ink and stay on the carcass until it has been presented to an official game check station. If you don't have an official field tag, you can make one, as long as it has all the required information. If you are unable to attach the tag at the site where you killed the deer, you must attach it as soon as you reach an area where you can do so, like your home, hunting camp or vehicle. In this case, the completed tag must be in your possession while you move the game. Your state might require the carcass to be kept in the county where it was killed until it has been taken to a game check station. It must be checked in within 24 hours of the kill, though some states have a longer 72 hour requirement.

It is usually required that the person who made the kill also takes the game to the check station. After you have transported your game to a game inspection station in some states, the official will band your harvest with a metal band, which must remain on the animal the entire time it is in your possession. That includes when you keep antlers or horns, and on game mounts. While transporting game birds, bear in mind that the head or a fully feathered wing must remain intact and attached to the bird. In some states pheasants and grouse must have a wing, head or foot attached. One thing to consider when transporting game birds is to not freeze more than two birds together in one package. Freezing numerous birds makes it very difficult for inspectors to identify the species and gender of each individual bird.

Take Notice
Each State has it's own laws detailing how the harvest can be moved, and how to do it while reducing the risk of spreading disease. Make sure you know what the law says in your state before going out on a hunting trip.

Respectful Ways to Transport Harvested Game
Hunters appreciate the luck of other hunters. All you need to do is drive by any game check-in station and your sure to see hunters gathered around, telling stories of the hunt and standing proudly by their harvest (kill). Non-hunters, though they may understand the thrill of the hunt, might not want to see scores of vehicles parading through town with dead, bloody animals strapped to their trunks or roof. Even so, hunters must check-in their harvest with the option of a variety of locations. Some stations are even in the middle of complexes, surrounded by department stores and restaurants. In an effort to be respectful, not only to the animal but also to the public, some states have incorporated transportation language into their regulations. For example, New Jersey requires hunters to be discreet when transporting game by rinsing away excess blood and gore.

The state also requests that hunters position the game so the field-dressed side is facing the vehicle and not the public *(SEE PICTURE 8)*, and to push the tongue of the dead animal back into it's mouth. One of the easiest ways to respectfully transport harvested game is to simply cover the game with a tarp. Not only does this keep the animal hidden from sensitive eyes, but it also protects the game from dirt and road grime, as well as the elements outside. For checking purposes, regulations information is usually available where permits and licences are sold, and on the Internet.

PICTURE 8

Care in the Kitchen (Cooking)
Hunters need to be careful harvesting game such as deer and game birds if they are going to bring it home for

cooking. Preparation starts right after shooting the animal or bird. First do not handle deer or other wild animals that appear sick or act abnormally. Generally the animal you shoot will not need to be bled out because enough blood vessels will be severed by the bullet. However, if it has been shot in the head, neck or spinal cord, it should be bled. This from the Department of Natural Resources (DNR) when processing wild game. Follow these precautions:

- When handling, always wear heavy rubber or latex gloves when field dressing wild game.
- If intestinal contents contact meat, consider the meat contaminated, cut off and discard affected area.
- Proper carcass care in the field is vital to preserve wild game. Big game animals should be field dressed immediately to cool the carcass, and then hung by the head to allow the body cavity to drain thoroughly. In warm weather carcass cooling can be hastened and maintained with bags of ice. For big game animals, ice bags can be placed directly into the body cavity. Unlike venison, bears are marbled with fat and can spoil quickly at temperatures above 40 degrees. Venison can survive for several days at temperatures as high as 50 degrees as long as the carcass is kept our of the sun and protected from flies. Placing the carcass into a cheesecloth game bag or applying a liberal application of black pepper to the body cavity will discourage fly contamination.
- Wash your hands with soap and water before and after handling meat. Sanitize equipment and work surfaces thoroughly.
- Thoroughly clean equipment and work areas; then sanitize with a 50/50 solution of household chlorine bleach and water after processing. Wipe down counters and let them dry; soak knives for one hour.
- Dispose of hide, brain and spinal cord, eyes, spleen, tonsils, bones and head in a landfill or your normal garbage pick up.

Safety Practices When Cooking Wild Game

The Michigan Department of Community Health recommends proper food safety practices when cooking venison, as well as any other meat or poultry. Thoroughly cooking meat is important to reduce the likelihood of any bacterial disease. All meat, including venison, should be cooked until the meat is no longer pink and the juices run clear. If cooked according to the guidelines and chart below, the likelihood of any disease transmission to individuals consuming this meat is extremely small.

- Use a meat thermometer to cook meat to proper internal temperatures (minimum 165 degrees for all types of meat from ground or fresh venison, 170 degrees for the breast of game birds and waterfowl, and 180 degrees for the whole bird), which helps ensure harmful bacteria are killed and meat is not overcooked. The color of meat is an unreliable indicator of doneness.
- For jerky, steam, boil or roast meat to 165 degrees F using a meat thermometer prior to dehydrating. Dry at 130 degrees to 140 degrees F until thoroughly dry. Jerky is properly dried when it cracks on bending but doesn't break.

Recommended Minimum Internal Cooking Temperature For Venison and Poultry	
Type of Meat	Temperature (°F)
Ground Venison, Sausage, Bologna	165°
Fresh Venison (Chops, Steaks, Roasts)	165°

Game Birds/ Waterfoul
    Breast
    Whole Bird
	
	170°
	180°

Safety Practices When Cooking Wild Game Birds

Game birds offer much variety in flavor and should be cared for just as carefully as big game animals. First remove the entrails and crop as soon as possible after shooting. This allows the air to circulate in the body cavity and aids in cooling the carcass quickly and thoroughly. If the weather is hot, the birds should be placed individually in plastic bags and put on ice. Whatever you do, avoid piling warm birds in mass. Here is more specific information to follow:

- Plucking or picking is a matter of personal preference. Some hunters like to pick the feathers while the bird is warm. Others say a thoroughly chilled bird is easier to pluck. The trick in plucking birds, warm or chilled, is to pick only a few feathers at a time rather than a handful. In plucking, remove coarse feathers first, then the smaller feathers as you proceed. Pinfeathers can be removed with the tip of a small knife and the forefinger. A mixture of melted paraffin and boiling water (3/4 of a pound of paraffin to 7 quarts of water) brushed over the bird, and allowed to harden will remove the down. And it is important to have the water hot before adding the paraffin. Paraffin added to cold water can produce a film on the surface, which could lead to an explosion. Birds can also be dipped in the paraffin mix. When you remove the paraffin coating the down comes off. Repeat if needed. Some hunters prefer to singe the bird: however, the bird has a nicer appearance if paraffin is used. The pinfeathers also come out easily using paraffin. So, if you plan to roast a bird, use the paraffin method.

- Scalding the birds by dipping in hot water (145 degrees Fahrenheit) also helps remove the feathers. This relaxes the muscle tissue around each feather so that the feather can be easily removed. However, if birds are held for several hours or frozen before plucking, then scalding may break down the fatty tissue in the skin, resulting in difficult plucking and tears in the skin. Some birds pick easier than others. Immature birds will generally have pinfeathers (especially early in the season) and more tender skin. If you want to serve birds whole, you probably should pick them. One general rule may be to pluck the larger, more perfect birds, and skin those that are smaller or badly shot up.

The large tendons that run up into the shank can be easily removed at this time if you haven't removed the feet yet. Cut through the skin of the leg 1-1/2 inches above the hock joint *(SEE PICTURE 9)*. Don't cut the ten dons. Lay the bird at the edge of a table or thick cutting board with the cut just above the edge. The leg should project over the edge. Press the leg down sharply with the side of the hand. The bone should snap at the joint. Tendons should come away with the foot. If they tear away from the feet, remove one by one with a skewer or tweezers. Fishy tasting ducks or other waterfowl that feed on aquatic vegetation, and animals probably should be skinned.

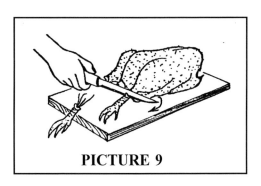

PICTURE 9

Other Game Bird Safety Issues

There are some other safety issues with game birds. Such as what to look for before you dress a game bird, what to look for during and after dressing a game bird, and diseases. What game birds are we talking about:

- Turkey
- Pheasants
- Grouse
- Guinea Fowl
- Partridge
- Quail
- Duck
- Geese
- Doves
- Pigeons

What to Look for Before you Dress a Game Bird

- Species, age and overall appearance: What is it, a Pheasant, a Partridge? Does it look like an old bird? Does it look like it's in bad shape, spots with feathers missing, that sort of thing.
- Parasites (External): Does it have a heavy infestation of lice and ticks? This means the meat may be of poor quality, and there is a likelihood of tick borne disease such as Lyme Disease or Q Fever. And be especially careful to not get bit by the tick while handling.
- External injuries: If the bird has bruises, lacerations, broken leg, wing, or neck, these are a bad sign. This could mean the bird will have poor meat quality, the meat will not preserve well and there is a likelihood of disease causing bacteria.
- Gangrenous: This is a sign not to dress the bird.
- Dermatitis: This is also a sign not to dress the bird.
- Cannibalism: Any sign of this also means don't dress the bird.

All of these may be signs of a sick or diseased bird. DO NOT dress it, instead I Suggest you put it in a plastic bag, contact your local Department of Conservation, or Fish and Game Department, and ask them where to take it so that they can check it out for you.

What to Look for During and After Dressing a Game Bird

- Skin: is underskin gelatinous and soft, is there fluid or blood under the skin. This is a sign to stop and not to continue to dress the bird.
- Feathers: feathers come off easily, feathers are sparse, feathers have a helicopter appearance. This is another sign to stop and not to continue to dress the bird.
- Underskin, Visceral and Muscle Fat: it is gelatinous, is it firm or does it have cheese like appearance, it is discolored (blood tinged), and is there excessive fat. These are all indicators of the type of diet the bird had, maybe a disease, or the availability of food. This could also mean it had a diet deficient in essential nutrients, and a diet high in protein.
- Meat: look for firmness, free of blood spots, free of parasites, accepted color, free of odor, and the meat has good size. These are good signs. Is the meat discolored, this is a bad sign. Does it have Sarcosporidiosis hemorrhagic spots (small red spots). This is a bad sign.
- Internal Organs: What do they look like as best as you can tell, take note of anything abnormal. These would be the liver, the kidney, the lung, the spleen, the crop, gizzard and intestine, and it's reproductive organs.
- Overall Appearance: plain and simple, does it look like it's a normal bird as best as you can tell. If you have other birds, compare them. One the same size that looks very different from the rest is a clue.

Game Bird Diseases of Public Health Importance

- Colibacillosis (Escherichia coli): all types of game birds may have this. It is a foodborne pathogen (a specific agent such as a bacterium).
- Salmonellosis (Salmonella spp.): all types of game birds may have this. It is an important foodborne pathogen (a specific agent such as a bacterium).
- Erysipelas (Erysipelothrix rhusiopathiae): Turkeys can have this. It is rare in water fowl. It is a foodborne pathogen (a specific agent such as a bacterium). It is found in the meat and internal organs.
- Botulism (Clostridium botulinum): Type E is of concern. No lesions seen in water fowl. More common in aquatic birds. Signs are flaccid paralysis. It is a foodborne pathogen (a specific agent such as a bacterium).
- Pseudotuberculosis (Yersinia pseudotuberculosis): Turkeys can have this. It is a foodborne pathogen (a specific agent such as a bacterium). It is found in the meat, internal organs.

All of these may be signs of a sick or diseased bird. DO NOT continue to dress it, or handle it, instead I Suggest you put it in a plastic bag, secured, then contact your local Department of Conservation, or Fish and Game Department, tell them what you suspect and ask them where to take it, or what you can do with it, so they can check it out for you.

Safety When Attacked By Game

I have heard it said that you may be more safe from being attacked by game while out hunting in the field than you are driving down to the supermarket. Wild animal attacks do happen but they are fairly rare. And they are probably because the person being attacked did something to allow the attack to happen in the first place. And they are usually because the person being attacked not understanding wild animals. Most wild animals will go out of their way to avoid you if they hear or see you coming, and that includes snakes. The animals or reptiles of most concern are bears, wild boars (hogs), and snakes. But lets also look at potential problem animals like cougars, bobcats, lynx, coyotes, wolves, deer, and moose. To avoid having problems with wild animals, here are "*The Basic Eight Common Sense Rules*" to follow:

- NEVER approach a wild animal or reptile.
- NEVER threaten, run towards, or tease a wild animal or reptile.
- NEVER cause a wild animal or reptile pain, or abuse it.
- NEVER attempt to pet any wild animal or reptile, but especially large ones.
- NEVER try to hand feed a wild animal or reptile, attempt to take care of it if it is injured.
- If you unexpectedly meet a wild animal or reptile on the trail, ALWAYS back off slowly while facing it. Then slowly move away from the animal allowing it to run from you if it's cornered.
- NEVER turn and run from a wild animal because it's probably faster than you. If you run it may consider you a source of food and attack.
- ALWAYS talk softly in a monotone when you encounter the wild animal or reptile, then back away very slowly, and don't make any sudden moves.

We will look at the animals separately, or together depending on how closely they tend to react to humans. Each one has certain special traits that you need to remember.

Bears

Bears are big and dangerous, so beware of them if possible. Best thing to do is leave the area when you see one. One hunter carries a cowbell, and uses it when necessary. The noise seems to keep the bears away. They will usually attack if cornered with no way out. They are short tempered, so take them as a serious threat when seen in the wild. However, what do you do if you encounter a bear in the field, or you know they are in the area. Here are some suggestions to avoid a problem:

- ALWAYS keep your camp site clean, with your garbage disposed of, and fresh food placed out of reach. One suggestion is throw a rope over a heavy limb, pull the food up at least 12 feet out of reach, and use a solid container. When bears stand up they can reach up high *(SEE PICTURE 10)*. A good place for your food is in the trunk of your car, although I have seen a video of a bear tearing apart a car to get inside, but NEVER have food in your tent.

PICTURE 10

- ALWAYS try to travel with others. The more people along, the less likely an attack will happen, but remember it's still possible.
- ALWAYS make plenty of noise, especially if you are alone unless you are hunting. Use the cowbell I mentioned, singing, talking, clapping your hands and so on. This is most important in thick forests, where you have seen fresh bear tracks or signs.
- ALWAYS keep your eyes open for bear tracks, freshly killed animals, and if you smell a musty strong odor be extremely cautious. Avoid streams during salmon spawning, and be extra careful around berry patches and thick brush.
- NEVER go near a fresh kill of any kind, because a bear may be near and want to guard their hard earned meal.
- If you do see a bear, leave the area very slowly and DO NOT run. The bear may associate this with game (their dinner) and chase you from instinct. And NEVER get between a moma bear and her cubs.
- NEVER feed a bear just so that you can get a good picture, or you can get closer to them. This is not very smart and very dangerous.
- And if you do come face to face with a bear, NEVER make direct eye contact with them, because they may take that as a stare down threat.
- ALWAYS remember to make noise, use a bell, scream, clap your hands, or sing.
- NEVER go near or approach a bear at any time. Keep in mind not to run or try to climb a tree, because the bear can run and climb faster than you.
- Black bears may back off if you challenge them, but if you are attacked you should yell, scream, fight, and be aggressive. Again, it just depends on the individual bear as to whether they will back off or not.
- The "Bear Management Office in Yellowstone Park" suggests you back away and try to make yourself inconspicuous when you encounter any bear. They further add that if you are facing a grizzly bear, stand your ground. Then if they hit you, fall down and play dead no matter what they are doing to you.

When you are attacked by a bear:
- Immediately drop to the ground and make yourself as small as you can by rolling into a ball.
- Clasp your hands over the back of your neck and remain still (if you are wearing a backpack keep it on to protect your neck and head.

Cougars

They are a very large member of the cat family, and while their attacks are rare they do happen. According to the "*Canadian Ministry of Environment,*" it seems they may be attracted to children due to their higher pitched voices, smaller size (food source size maybe), and irregular movements. It is suspected that cougars are not able to properly identify children as humans and they may think youngsters are prey. Our neighbors up north (Canada) suggest:
- Have your children play in groups, the more the safer.
- Keep your eyes on your kids at all times when in cougar territory.
- If you have a dog, keep it near your children. The dog can see, smell, and hear the cougar way before we can, so it will act as an early warning system.
- When you are in cougar territory, keep a radio or portable TV. playing to create noise.
- Keep your kids close to you during the hours of darkness.
   Many cougar attacks could be prevented by following the same above basic guidelines when moving out in the field around cougars. Make noise, stay in groups, and so on.

Never turn your back on a cougar, and always remain upright. Additionally, do everything you can to make yourself look larger. Do not try to hide or roll up into a ball, because neither one will work effectively against a cougar. And if you are attacked, fight back as hard as you can with whatever you can pick up and throw at them to show you are not prey. Most cougar attacks are the result of normal predator (they are after prey) behaviors by them and so are somewhat predictable, but remember there are exceptions.

Moose

Moose might be neat to photograph and watch, but a few years ago a man was killed by a moose on the grounds of a University. Moose are not usually considered to be serious threats to attack by most people, but they have the potential to seriously injure or kill you because of their size. In Alaska, moose are the "biggest attack threat," in some areas. In addition to the *basic eight common sense rules,"* (Page 36) keep these rules in mind:

- NEVER get between a cow and her calf.
- NEVER allow your dog to chase a moose or harass it.
- Never corner a moose around houses, trees, or fenced in yards, because they may attack you out of fear.
- If a moose does attack you, immediately ball up and cover your head. Then stay as still as you can and make no quick movements.
- Keep in mind that if the animals hump is standing up and it's ears are back, it may be ready to attack you, or is at least scared and unpredictable as to what it will do next. If that happens, try to make your self appear larger than you are by raising your arms and extending your fingers, but make no quick movements.

Wild Boar (Hogs)

In some areas these animals are becoming a problem. Many times they will be in packs, but not always. They are a wild animal, and they have been known to be fearless with a bad temper. They have razor sharp tusks that can cut you up pretty good. They will usually charge with their head down and swing their head to cut you. And they are not always small, some big boars will weigh up around 200 pounds. And when they hit you it will be like one of these NFL 300 pound lineman hitting you at a full run. They are very fast so don't try to outrun them. If you are attacked in daylight, look for a close by tree or something big to get behind or climb. And do it quick when you make a break because as I said, I've seen them charge, and they are extremely fast. If it's at night I've heard that sometimes shooting them with a camera startles them, and the light scares them off. Basically take the same preventative action as stated in the "basic eight common sense rules" on page 36.

Bobcats and Lynx

These are smaller members of the cat family. They are usually somewhat inactive during the winter months. The lynx is a little bit larger than the bobcat, but the bobcat is considered to be the more aggressive of the two. It is possible to encounter either animal up in the northern states. But remember most attacks are simply scratches and clawing's. However, each one has been known to go for the throat of a victim during an attack. So, protect your face and throat if you are attacked by either one of theses cats. Take the same preventative action as stated in the "basic eight common sense rules" on page 36.

Deer

Both buck's and doe's will attack humans under certain conditions. If they get into a fenced yard and cornered, and feel threatened, they will attack, and with all those antlers bucks can do some damage. Also they have sharp hoves which can cut you. The best time to stay away from doe's is when they have baby fawn's. The best time to stay away from bucks is during the "rut" (breeding time for deer). It goes by day length and moon phases. This can be from late October to the middle of November up in the north. Down south it could be from November to January depending on the moon. They can be bad tempered during this season, so it's best to know when it's that time of the year when you are out in the woods. Be alert and observant, and give buck's with antlers a wide berth unless you are hunting them. If you are attacked, remember they will try to knock you down then gore you or try to stomp on you. So, protect yourself from being knocked down. If there is cover, get behind a tree or big rock where they can't get at you with those antlers and sharp hoves. Generally speaking, take the same preventative action as stated in the "basic eight common sense rules" found on page 36.

Wolves and Coyotes

These animals get a bad reputation, mostly because of the media attention they get. It used to be almost impossible to read an outdoor adventure book that did not have a vicious wolf attack at some point in the story. Basically it's untrue though. Most hunters and people that know about wolves will tell you that a wolf will never attack a healthy human unless they have been cornered. However, I'm sure that if they felt threatened, or they were starving and you encountered them, they would attack. Strong healthy wolves and coyotes do not attack humans unless there is no other option for them, because they generally fear humans. If you are attacked by one of these animals and injured, you should clean the injury with soap and water, then disinfect it. It may be a gorge, cut, crushing of a bone, or scratches that you will be treating.

So there could be a lot of blood loss, remember your first aid and stop the bleeding first. If you have a bite, it may be deeper than you suspect, and the most serious aspect of the wound may be the risk of infection. Infection is common from animal claws and teeth, which are dirty and have bits of decayed meat on them. There may also be trauma from being dragged, thrown, pulled, or from an impact with an object such as a rock. If you receive an injury from one of these animals, always seek medical attention as soon as possible. And besides the danger from the wound, there is also a possibility of rabies. So get checked! Generally speaking, take the same preventative action as stated in the "basic eight common sense rules" found on page 36.

Snakes

If you are going to be in the woods hunting, hiking, or just strolling you will probably encounter a snake at some time. These animals also get a bad reputation, mostly because of the media attention they get. It used to be almost impossible to read an outdoor adventure book that did not have someone getting bitten by a snake somewhere in the story. When you think of snakes, the first thing that comes to mind is that they might be poisonous. Actually though less than 10 percent of the snakes in the world are dangerous to humans. So even if you are randomly bitten, the odds are it will not be from a poisonous snake. However, if you are bitten, or you are with someone that has been bitten, most doctors suggest you do the following:

- ■   DO NOT let the injured person drink any alcohol.
- ■   DO NOT cut the wound in any manner (which used to be suggested).
- ■   DO NOT attempt to suck the poison out (this used to be done by mouth and is not suggested).

- DO NOT use a tourniquet (this also used to be suggested, but not now).
- DO wash and clean the bite with soap and water, immobilize the bite, treat for shock, and immediately seek medical attention. Statistics show that less then one half of one percent of people bitten by a poisonous snake will die from the bite, even if left untreated.

If you leave the snake alone, they will probably leave you alone. Generally speaking, take the same wild animal preventative action as stated in the "basic eight common sense rules" found on page 36.

Tracking, Stalking, Waiting for Game Safety

Safety of the Hunter

Safety of the hunter is important when stalking, tracking or waiting for game. First you need to be in good physical condition to travel up and down hills and mountains, depending on where you are hunting." See *the section on conditioning and exercising*." It can be dangerous when crawling around on the ground to get closer to your prey, watch out for snakes. I recommend you carry a snake bite and first aid kit with you. Also to get close enough for a shot, don't forget to CAMOU-FLAGE your rifle and scope." It's not that hard to do. And don't forget to use binoculars to get a better close up pre-look at the game. To keep safe, basically you want to follow the "10 Commandments" on page 25.

General Safety Rules for Tracking, Stalking or Waiting

These are some of the basic safety rules to follow:
1. ALWAYS keep your finger off the trigger and out of the guard until the instant you ready to fire.
2. ALWAYS keep the safety on until ready to fire; however, the safety should never be a substitute for safe firearm handling.
3. ALWAYS know how far your bullets or arrows will travel when fired
4. NEVER take a shot at animals or birds on top of ridges or hillsides.
5. NEVER climb a tree or ladder with a loaded firearm, bow or crossbow.
6. NEVER jump a ditch or cross difficult terrain with a loaded firearm, or a nocked arrow.
7. ALWAYS use the two-hand carry whenever possible because it affords you the best muzzle control.
8. ALWAYS carry arrows in a protected cover or quiver.
9. If you accidentally fall, make sure you disassemble the gun and check the barrel from the breech end for obstructions. Check other shooting devices for dirt, mud, or snow in the firing mechanism parts. And ALWAYS carry a field cleaning kit.
10. ALWAYS make sure you know where your hunting partners are at all times.
11. NEVER swing your gun or bow out of your safe zone of fire. Know your safe carries when there are other hunters to your sides, in front of you, or behind you.
12. When hunting, ALWAYS wear daylight fluorescent orange so that you can be seen from a distance or in heavy cover.
13. Control your emotions when it comes to safety. If you lose control of your emotions you may do something carelessly. Show discipline, rehearse in your mind what the safe actions should be. Show restraint and pass up shots which have the slightest chance of being unsafe.
14. Follow all basic safety rules for bows on pages 155 and 156.
15. Follow all the basic safety rules for crossbows on pages 176 and 177.
16. Follow all basic safety rules for slingshots and atlatls on pages 184, 195 and 196.

17. Follow all basic safety rules for firearms on page 25.
18. ALWAYS tell someone (communicate) where you are going hunting and when you plan to return. If you are going to move from one area to another, advise someone.

General Safety Rules for Waiting on the Ground, in Tree Stands and in Blinds

If you are down on the ground waiting for game to come to you, or up in a tree stand *(SEE PICTURE 11),* follow the general rules for stalking and tracking on pages 40 and 41 that apply.

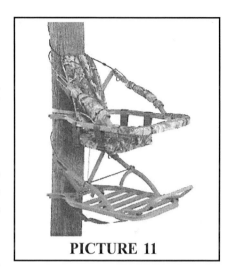

PICTURE 11

In Tree Stands
In addition, follow these basic safety rules that apply to tree stands.

1. ALWAYS wear a safety belt. If your stand collapses, a safety belt will prevent you from falling. Also DON'T leave much slack in the belt. One or two feet will allow you to turn 360 degrees, and if a fall occurs, you will only fall one or two feet.
2. ALWAYS use a cord or rope to raise and lower all equipment from the stand, keep your hands free for climbing. Keep equipment on the opposite side of the tree from which you are climbing, so if you do fall, you won't fall on your equipment. ALWAYS inspect your stand. Check for loose rotten boards, loose nuts and bolts, and replace worn chains or straps.
3. Practice setting up your stand. Be familiar with the workings of the stand before you go into the woods. Before using manufactured stands, ALWAYS read the instructions and warnings. ALWAYS tell a dependable person (communicate) where you are hunting and when you plan to return. If you are injured and can't get out of the woods, then someone will know where to look for you. And it's also a good idea to take a cell phone with you.
4. ALWAYS pick a mature tree on which to secure your stand. DO NOT use a tree that is rotten, or has dead limbs that may fall on the stand. Clear the tree of any limbs that could cause a fall, but get permission before you start clearing. If you are not allowed to cut limbs, use cords to tie them back.
5. If the weather turns bad, return to the ground. High winds can make stands unstable. Rain, snow or sleet can cause you to slip. DON"T fall asleep. This is a common cause of accidents. If you do get drowsy, leave the stand and walk around to wake up.
6. The higher you are in the stand, the further you might fall, DON"T panic though. Immediately try to determine the injuries you have. Check for spinal cord injuries by wiggling your feet and legs. If you suspect you have this type of injury, DON"T move.
7. If you are hurt in a fall and are bleeding, first try to stop excess bleeding, Check for broken bones. If you think you have any, support them with splints if possible. Carry a survival kit with you at all times. In the kit include matches, string, candy bars, a whistle and any other items that will make an overnight stay more comfortable.
8. If you told someone (communicate) where you are and when you are expected to return, help should be on the way. Hunting safely from a stand depends on what you do before you hunt. Being prepared is the best way to prevent tree stand accidents.

Waiting on the Ground for Turkeys

In addition, follow these basic safety rules that apply to waiting on the ground for turkeys to come to you:

1. ALWAYS wait for the turkey to come to you. DON'T try to track or stalk a turkey, they have excellent eyesight and they will spot you coming from a long distance. Let the turkey do the walking!
2. Make absolutely sure you see a turkey with a beard before pulling the trigger.
3. When calling a turkey in, NEVER use a gobble call on a spring hunt because it increases your odds of getting accidentally shot.
4. ALWAYS dress defensively and wear full camouflage from the top of your head to the tip of your toes. Wearing only partial camouflage may leave just enough exposed to look like parts of the turkey. NEVER wear white, blue, or black, including undergarments, to hunt spring turkeys as those colors are associated with wild turkeys and can contribute to hunter-mistaken-for-game accidents.
5. When calling in a turkey, sit still with your back against a big tree, to hide you from the turkeys and stalkers.
6. ALWAYS assume any call or footsteps are from another hunter. DON'T shoot until you see the whole turkey and know it's sex.
7. If you see another hunter, talk to them clearly (communications), and DON't move. NEVER wave or use a turkey call to alert another hunter.
8. Turkeys are tough. You need to get close (30 yards or less is best). Then go for a clear head or neck shot. DO NOT try to shoot them in the body or when they are flying.

PICTURE 12

9. On turkeys, smaller shot, No. 4, 5, and 6, work better than larger shot, due to the denser shot patterns.
10. NEVER wear turkey colors, they are red, white, and blue (Kind of patriotic aren't they).
11. ALWAYS wear hunter orange when going in or out of the woods to hunt, and when walking around in the woods.
12. When still waiting for a turkey in camouflage, put a hunter orange band on a tree near you *(SEE PICTURE 12)*.
13. If you shoot a turkey or carry a decoy, wrap it in hunter orange.
14. Any movement you make while on the ground must occur when the turkey is behind a tree or other obstacle.
15. You may NOT use dogs to help you take a turkey.

Waiting for Game in a Ground or Box Blind

Use the basic "10 Commandments" safety rules on page 25 while in the blind. In addition follow these basic rules that apply to waiting in a ground or box blind for game to come to you.

1. While waiting NEVER lean a gun against the wall where it could fall over, go off, and fire if it has accidentally been left loaded, and with the safety off.
2. ALWAYS place the blind on the ground downwind from where the target game will be so that the game won't smell you. And just to be safe, use anti-smell techniques to mask your smell.
3. ALWAYS plan your "field of fire" ahead of time so that you don't accidentally shoot any other hunters with blinds in the area, or that may cross in front of you.
4. It may be a good idea to place your blind at the edge of a tree line overlooking a meadow or grazing area *(SEE PICTURE 13)*, especially if you are alone, because this way other hunters may not be as likely to come up from behind you.

5. If another hunter does come up close to you, or in your "field of fire," call out in a loud clear voice who, and where, you are (communication).

6. If you are in an elevated box blind *(SEE PICTURE 14)*, follow the same safety rules as on page 41 for tree stands as you would if you were located up in a tree stand.

7. Mark all sides of your blind with a wide strip of hunter orange. This way other hunters coming into the area will see your blind and know where you are, but turkeys will not. They will only see the orange as a shade of grey area.

PICTURE 13

Waiting for Game out in a Waterfowl Blind *(SEE PICTURE 15)*,

1. You are in a high risk group for hypothermia because of the proximity to water, wind and changing weather conditions. Stay warm and avoid hypothermia.

2. ALWAYS wear wool clothing or clothing that stays warm when wet, like some fleece products. Bring extra clothes in a waterproof bag.

3. If you fall in, go home. Or, take a break and change into some warm, dry clothes.

4. Control wind and wetness by using waterproof shells, jackets, waders and boots.

5. Bring a variety of high energy and high sugar content food bars for quick energy and calories.

6. ALWAYS wear a hat of some kind. Most warmth escapes through your head.

PICTURE 14

PICTURE 15

7. Your extremities are very important. It's not fun to hunt with cold feet, hands, or head. ALWAYS bring chemical hand warmers for emergencies.

8. When you are planning a waterfowl hunt, DON'T forget to check to be sure the boat is in good working condition, with enough gas for the trip, and equipped with the proper number of personal floatation devices and other safety gear.

9. Make sure that everyone on the boat has a properly fitted, coast guard approved, life jacket or float coat.

10. NEVER stand up in a unsecured boat to shoot.

11. ONLY shoot when you are at a naturally comfortable angle.

12. ALWAYS be aware of dogs with you in the boat, as well as your other partners. And be extra careful with your gun because as with a ground blind everyone is in close quarters.

13. ALWAYS unload a shotgun when moving from position to position in a boat.

14. ALWAYS put your unloaded shotgun in a secure case. This keeps the shotgun cleaner and will remind you to unload the shotgun before moving in the boat.

15. Floating gun cases will earn their keep when a boat tips over, and they go into the water.

16. If you have kids along with you in the boat, bring along some coloring books to keep them quiet and occupied in between game sightings.

17. Waterfowl hunting can be safer and more enjoyable if you ALWAYS plan ahead and make safe practices part of your water based hunting trip. Safety is always most important.

When You Are Stalking Game by Wading in Water

1. Take time to see what's happening around you before you wade right into the water.

2. ALWAYS read any "warning signs" in the area. Study them all, and take them seriously.

3. Check conditions of the water beforehand. Ask someone if the water is rising, falling or steady. Ask other people nearby, if any, what they have already observed (communicate). Information like this is critical when you are miles from a dam and can't hear sirens.

4. Heed your natural warning instincts. Assume any unusual noise coming from a dam is a signal to leave the water.

5. ALWAYS monitor the water level. Use stationary rocks or logs as water level gauges and check them often, especially when you are far from a dam. Other signs of rising water; the sound of rushing water changes pitch, birds and fish become more active, plant material from inundated shore lines float downstream, water moves faster and becomes cloudy.

6. ALWAYS have an escape route planned. No matter where you wade, ALWAYS have an escape route through shallow water in mind.

7. Carry a wading staff. Fast water can sweep you off your feet. A sturdy stick, wading staff or ski pole helps you maintain at least two points of contact with the streambed.

8. ALWAYS accept help. If you are stranded or struggling, you are in danger, If someone offers help, take it. If nobody offers, ask them for help (communicate).

9. Recognize your limits. DON'T exceed the limits of your strength, agility and endurance. A tired wader traversing rising water and slick rocks is inviting tragedy.

10. If water overcomes you, get rid of the equipment. Grandpa's gun or your favorite hunting vest mean nothing if you don't live to use them again. Jettison gear if a free hand or less weight could save your life.

11. If you are swept away, float on your back, draw your knees up to your chest, and point your feet downstream. This position protects your head from rocks and other obstructions. Use your arms to steer into slow or shallow water, remain calm and keep your head above water at all times.

12. If you are in deep water, swim with the current and diagonally across it. If at all possible avoid using all your strength to fight the current. Conserve energy by moving downstream, then only stand when you are in slow, shallow water. Respect your tailwaters. Use common sense when wading, and you will live to enjoy it again and again.

Trapping Safety

If you are going to be trapping or attempting to trap fur bearing animals you must first get a certificate of trapper education, then you get a permit and a trapping licence in most states. Before you go out trapping, check the Conservation or Hunting and Fishing Department in your state for all the regulations and rules. Trapping is generally not a dangerous activity, but there are risks related to weather, drowning, animal bites, and disease. Also trapping can be a rigorous activity. Do be aware of your physical limitations, and stay in shape. Develop safe attitudes. And make safe behavior a habit. You can trap, by the way, in conservation areas, but you need a special permit. Following are some of the rules, issues and risks involved in trapping safety that we will explain:

- ■ Hypothermia ■ Frostbite ■ Drowning ■ Carrying a Map and Compass
- ■ Survival During Trapping ■ Traveling To and From Trapping Areas
- ■ Setting Large Body-Gripping Traps ■ Firearm Safety That Applies to Trapping
- ■ Contracting Diseases ■ Being Bitten or Injured ■ Making Yourself Visible
- ■ Traveling on Ice-Covered Lakes, Ponds, Rivers, and Streams

Hypothermia

Hypothermia is the leading cause of death among people who enjoy outdoor recreation. Cold weather, wind, and water can lead to a loss of body heat. When your body temperature starts to drop, hypothermia sets in. The three signs of hypothermia are: (1) Shivering, (2) Becoming confused, (3) Being clumsy. You can prevent hypothermia by wearing warm, dry clothing. Wool clothes are a good choice because wool insulates even when wet. Use hip boots or waders, plus long-sleeved rubber gloves when trapping in water.

Frostbite

Frostbite occurs when ice crystals form in your body's cells. It's a common injury to your cheeks, ears, nose, toes, and fingers. Symptoms include white to grayish yellow skin, and an intense cold, numb feeling. Pain and blisters may also be present. To protect your frostbitten skin from further injury, drink warm fluids, put on more clothes, or wrap up in blankets. The frozen area can be soaked in warm water (102 to 105 degrees F). And NEVER rub frostbitten skin, contrary to popular belief it doesn't work. In fact rubbing will cause further injury.

Dangers Relating to Drowning

It is a good idea to wear an inflatable personal floatation vest when trapping around water. When wading in streams, it is best to travel upstream *(SEE PICTURE 16)*. If you use a boat or canoe follow all safety regulations, and take a boating safety course.

PICTURE 16

Carrying a Map and Compass

It is easy to get lost if you are in unfamiliar territory. When you are looking for animal signs and places to set traps you may not be paying close attention to landmarks and trails. The following are some rules to go by:

- ALWAYS carry a compass and a map of area you are trapping.
- Many trappers and hunters carry a global positioning system (GPS) unit. If you do carry a GPS, make sure you know how to use it BEFORE you go out trapping.
- Still carry the compass for a backup.

Survival During Trapping

Although many people trap alone it is best to use a buddy system for any outdoor activity. This way if you are injured or sick your buddy can assist you, or go for help. Wireless phones are good to have along, but don't totally depend on them because you may be out of range, or find yourself with a dead battery when you need the phone the most. Here are some basic rules to follow:

- ALWAYS tell your family exactly where you are going and when you plan to return.
- A trapper should know how to start a fire. If you find yourself in a hypothermia situation it may be difficult to start a fire with out a firestarter, so make sure you have one with you.

Traveling To and From Trapping Areas

Trappers need to be careful when traveling to and from trapping areas. You need to learn to wear your seatbelt.

- ALWAYS wear a seatbelt when traveling to and from trapping areas. You may need to pull off the road in a rough place. Also you may be watching fields and other habitats when you are supposed to be watching the road, then tumble down an embankment. If you are tumbling around loose in the vehicle you can't control, you are going to get hurt.

• Hunters often say that driving to and from hunting and trapping locations may be more dangerous than the hunting or trapping activity itself.

Setting Large Body-Gripping traps

Some traps, such as large body-gripping traps used for beaver, can be dangerous to a trapper who doesn't know how to use them. If you are accidentally caught in a large trap you need to know how to release yourself, which may be difficult if you can't use one of your arms. You can drown or die from hypothermia if you get caught in a large trap set underwater.

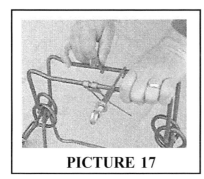

PICTURE 17

• ALWAYS use a safety gripper when setting large body-gripping traps *(SEE PICTURE 17)*.
• When setting large body-gripping traps, trappers should ALWAYS carry setting tongs and a length of rope with a loop in the end. And keep it in a pocket where you can easily reach it with one hand. If you are caught, thread the rope through the ends of the springs. Put your foot in the loop and use your free arm to pull the loose end. This releases pressure on the springs.

Firearm Safety that Applies to Trapping

Many trappers carry firearms to shoot the animals caught in their traps. If you are going to be in trapping, take a hunter education course to learn about firearm safety. Practice safe habits around firearms at all times. Following are some specific rules:

• When shooting at an animal in a trap be careful about ricochets off the trap or rocks.
• ALWAYS look beyond your target when shooting a firearm.
• Keep the muzzle under control and pointed in a safe direction.
• Treat every gun as if it is loaded.

See page 25 for additional firearm safety rules and suggestions.

Contracting Diseases

General trapping precautions to follow to protect against diseases include:

• Wear protective gloves, eye protection, and protective coveralls when handling carcasses or scat.
• Wash hands and arms thoroughly with soap and water after handling animals.
• Clean and disinfect knives, skinning boards, cutting surfaces, and other equipment with a solution of 1.5 cups household bleach in 1 gallon of water.
• Avoid sick animals, or ones that DO NOT act normal.
• DO NOT drink untreated water from lakes or streams.
• Cook all wild game thoroughly.

Being Bitten or Injured

This section pertains to bacteria, parasites, and viruses that cause infection and disease. Wild animals can carry a number of diseases that are infectious to humans (zoonotic diseases). Some diseases are specific to one or a few species of furbearers, while other diseases affect many species. Wildlife diseases transmittable to humans or domestic pets should be of concern to anyone who regularly encounters or handles wildlife. Infectious diseases can be caused by numerous organisms and may spread by direct and/or indirect contact with infected animals. Trappers can also be exposed to parasites that infect wild animals. Follow the recommended precautions to protect

yourself from potential hazards. If you become ill make certain your doctor is aware of your trapping activities. Recognize and manage the risks for being bitten or injured by wild animals:
- If bitten by an animal you should wash wounds thoroughly with soap and water, apply bandages, and immediately seek medical attention.
- Keep the animal confined if possible, or kill it without damaging the head so that local authorities can examine it for rabies.

Making Yourself Visible
Trappers should make themselves visible to hunters by wearing hunter orange clothing. Trappers have occasionally been wounded by hunters who failed to see the trapper, or by hunters who fail to properly identify their target (communication). This is also helpful if you are lost, injured, or sick.

Traveling on Ice-Covered Lakes, Ponds, Rivers, and Streams
Avoid traveling on ice-covered streams and rivers where water currents can cause weak spots. Carry a walking staff to help you check for ice conditions in front of you as you travel. If you fall through the ice try to climb out by facing the direction you came from when the ice gave way. You should build a fire immediately when you reach shore unless you are close to shelter or your vehicle.

Disabled Safety

Some people might think that because you are disabled that you can't hunt. Not true! I know Missouri has special hunts for persons with disabilities. In 2009 they had 10 special hunts exclusively for persons with disabilities. They are not through the regular managed deer hunt application process though. For information in Missouri on who qualifies and how to apply, call the specific hunt location during normal business hours between July 1 and Aug. 15, or by Oct.1. You can get the dates and locations through the "Missouri Conservation Department." They cover Disabled Hunting with muzzleloaders, regular rifles, shotguns, and crossbows. In Missouri these are deer hunts. Different states have different types of disabled hunts. I even seen one that was offering a bear hunt.

Wheelchair Hunting
This seems to be very popular. Probably because they make all types of all-terrain wheelchairs *(SEE PICTURE 18)*. They come with all types of equipment. You can get them with accessories like a gun rack, a mobile blind, and a fishing pole holder. You can even get them with all kinds of tires for all kinds of terrain. Some have big balloon tires to give you a nice smooth ride on rough terrain. I've seen them with special accessories like dirt treads, and you can even get chains for them in snow along with replacement skis on the front, or standard front castor wheels. They have special target shooting ranges for hunters in wheelchairs. It could be using either a rifle, pistol, air pistol or shotgun. The targets can be either paper, card or electronic for rifle and pistol, or for a shotgun the target is called a "bird."

PICTURE 18

Wheelchair Accessible Hunting

Special wheelchairs and adaptive equipment, nonprofit clubs and other organizations for the disabled, and state regulations that accommodate the needs of the disabled, all make the great outdoors more accessible than ever now for disabled hunters, and even trappers. If you are deciding whether hunting is the right activity for you, here are some things to consider:

- Should you use a manually or electronically powered wheelchair? A manual wheelchair might be the right choice if you have good upper body strength. However, if you experience pain or are easily tired, an electronic chair might be a better choice.
- Would an off road or all terrain wheelchair make your hunting experience any better? If it would, make sure the tires and wheels are tough enough to handle the terrain.
- Look into all the many kinds of adaptive equipment available now, such as gun rigs, trigger adapters, and duck blinds. You can find them on-line.
- If you are interested in finding out more about the hunting options available, the internet is a great resource. You will find links to laws and permits there that affect the disabled on a state by state basis.
- You will also find there a lot of clubs on the internet, and organizations that are dedicated to making wheelchair hunting an enjoyable experience for you. As an example, they will design, coordinate and arrange hunting adventures for you as well as fishing.

General Disabled Hunting Safety

If you decide to get into disabled hunting or trapping, you need to check out all the rules before you go out on a hunting trip. First thing, check with your states "Conservation Dept." or "Hunting and Fishing Dept." They will send you all types of brochures with basic rules and regulations and other information in them. They will also tell you where to get permits and licences. Since your situation is unique, you need to be sure you know all the safety precautions. And you can have a "Disabled Hunter Companion" to help you while hunting. Follow all the firearm safety "10 commandments" found on page 25. In addition here are some "TIPS" and things to consider:

- Make sure you leave a trip plan with a family member before you leave.
- You are required to wear fluorescent hunter orange as well as any person that accompanies you. You may bring another person with you to assist. However, that person may not hunt or possess a weapon. They are only there to assist.
- Practice safe firearms or trap handling at all times. Respect the safety zones around buildings and developed areas at parks. Be sure of your target while shooting and beware of the area behind your target. Campgrounds or parks may be closed, but hikers may wander into the area and create a danger.
- ALWAYS follow the "leave no trace" outdoor ethics when you leave, with regard to shell casings, food, drinks, or anything else you brought with you.

Wheelchair Hunting Safety

If you hunting in a wheelchair, follow all the general safety precautions, rules, and regulations for the weapon you are using. In addition follow these additional rules, "TIPS," and suggestions:

- Remember, you are in a wheelchair. So stay on the trail and areas that your wheelchair can safely handle. Even if you have an all-terrain wheelchair, they could accidentally go down a slope and crash, or tip over, and throw you out.
- Remember, you are allowed to have a "Companion" person with you to assist. So use them, and let them scout out ahead of you in rough terrain before you enter.

■ And while carrying a firearm with you in the wheelchair, make sure it's unloaded, safety on, and not pointed at anyone until you get to your hunting area. Then when you do get there make sure you actually have a target, and are ready to fire.

Other Disabled Hunting Requirements

You are allowed to hunt if you are disabled in another way, and not in a wheelchair, such as heart trouble and in a "walker." Below are some of the typical qualifications and provisions for Disabled Hunting Permits and Licenses:

From the State of Wyoming (they have some good rules):
Section 4. "*Disabled Hunter Permit Qualifications*" says; any person having a physical or visual disability as attested in writing by the applicant and certified by a licenced physican, optometrist, or ophthalmologist on a form provided by the Game Department, may be issued a Disabled Hunter Permit if the person:

(a) Is permanently unable to walk without the use of, or assistance from, a wheelchair, scooter, or walker;

(b) Is restricted by lung disease to the extent the person's forced expiratory volume for one (1) second, when measured by a spirometer, is less than 35 percent (35%) predicted, or arterial oxygen tension is less than 55 mm/Hg on room air at rest;

(c) Has a cardiac condition to the extent the person's functional limitations are classified in severity as Class III or Class IV, according to standards established by the American Heart Association and defined in section 3 of this regulation;

(d) Has a permanent, physical impairment that prevents the person from holding or shooting a firearm or bow in hand;

(e) Has central visual acuity that permanently does not exceed 20/200 in the better eye with corrected lenses, or the widest diameter of the visual field is not greater than 20 degrees; and/or,

(f) Can produce to the Department written proof that the last official certification of record of the United States Department of Veterans Affairs or any branch of the Armed Forces of the United States shows the person to be at least 65 percent physically disabled.

Section 5. "*Disabled Hunter Permit Provisions*" says:

(a) The disabled hunter shall:
1. Only take animals in accordance with State statutes and Commission rules and regulations;
2. be in possession of the Disabled Hunter Permit in the field while taking animals;
3. Possess a valid hunting licence issued under authority of title 23, Commission rules and regulations, unless exempt by statue from the need to posses a valid hunting licence.

(b) The disabled hunter shall not:
1. Discharge a firearm or other legal hunting device from a motor vehicle except as other wise provided in accordance with the Commission's regulation Chapter 38, "Hunters with a Qualifying Disability Authorized to Shoot from a Vehicle;"
2. Discharge a firearm or other legal hunting device from a watercraft (except a sinkbox), including those propelled by a motor, sail and wind, or both; except when the motor has been shut off, the sail furled, or both; and progress has ceased. The watercraft may be drifting as a result of current or wind action, beached, moored, resting at anchor, or propelled by paddle, oars, or pole. A watercraft under power may be used to retrieve a dead or wounded animal, but a firearm shall not be discharged while the watercraft is under way;

3. Transfer the Disabled Hunter Permit to another person or allow another person to use the permit.

(c) The disabled hunter shall submit an application on a form provided by the Department. The application shall be completed in full and shall bear the applicant's and the physician's, optometrist's, or ophthalmologist's printed name, address and signature on the application that certifies the applicant meets the qualifications of a Disabled Hunter as specified in section 4 of this regulation. Disabled Hunter Permits shall be issued to qualified applicants by the Department's License Section, Regional Offices or designated Department personnel.

(d) The same person shall not be issued a Disabled Hunter Permit and a Disabled Hunter Companion Permit.

Section 6. "*Disabled Hunter Companion Permit*" says:

(a) The Department shall issue Disabled Hunter Companion Permits in accordance with this section.

1. The applicant for a Disabled Hunter Companion Permit shall be at least 14 years of age.

   2. The applicant for a Disabled Hunter Companion Permit shall do so on a form provided by the Department.

   3. The form shall contain all of the following information and shall be signed by the applicant and the Disabled Hunter:

      (a) The applicant's name, address, and telephone number;

      (b) The Disabled Hunter's name, signature, date, address, and telephone number;

      (c) The Disabled Hunter's hunting license number, if a license is required by statute, and type of hunting license;

      (d) The Disabled Hunter's permit number as issued by the Department; and,

      (e) The Disabled Hunter's sportsperson identification number.

Section 7. "*Disabled Hunter Companion Permit Provisions*" says:

The Disabled Hunter Companion Permit shall be valid for the calendar year in which it was issued, unless the Department revokes the permit.

(a) The Disabled Hunter Companion shall:

1. Be in possession of the Disabled Hunter Companion Permit in the field while taking a wounded or retrieving an animal killed by the Disabled Hunter;

2. Only take a wounded animal in accordance with state statute and Commission rules and regulations, and shall not take an animal under the authority of a Disabled Hunter Companion Permit that has not been wounded by a Disabled Hunter and for which a license is required for the Disabled Hunter;

3. Be in possession of the Disabled Hunter's license and carcass coupon while taking any animal that has been wounded by the Disabled Hunter for which a carcass coupon is required or while retrieving such animal killed by the Disabled Hunter, and shall detach, and date the Disabled Hunter's carcass coupon prior to leaving the site of a kill when a wounded animal is dispatched;

4. Not transfer the Disabled Hunter Companion Permit to another person or allow an otherperson to utilize the permit; and,

5. Be accompanied by the Disabled Hunter to the location where the Disabled Hunter wounds the animal that requires the Disabled Hunter Companion to pursue and dispatch the wounded animal.

(b) Game birds or game animals taken, tagged, or retrieved by a Disabled Hunter Companion on behalf of a Disabled Hunter shall become part of the Disabled Hunter's bag or possession limit and do not count against the Disabled Hunter Companion's bag or possession limit.

(c) Any person who is in possession of a Disabled Hunter Companion Permit, but is not a licensed and permitted hunter for Grand Teton National Park or the National Elk Refuge, and is accompanying a Disabled Hunter who is hunting in Grand Teton National Park or the National Elk Refuge, shall be exempt from the Park Permit and National Elk Refuge Permit requirements, but shall be required to meet the hunter safety card requirement.

(d) A person may obtain more than (1) Disabled Hunter Companion Permit, but each permit shall be issued for only (1) Disabled Hunter.

Section 8. *"Revocation or Denial of a Disabled Hunter Permit or Disabled Hunter Companion Permit"* says:

(a) The Department may deny or revoke a Disabled Hunter Permit or Disabled Hunter Companion Permit for the following reasons:

1. The Department can not verify all information and documentation provided by the applicant for the Disabled Hunter Permit or Disabled Hunter Companion Permit;

2. The applicant made false statements on the application to secure a permit;

3. The permittee is convicted of violating any provision of the title 23, Wyoming statute, or any Commission rule or regulation governing the taking of wildlife while exercising any privilege of the permit;

4. The Disabled Hunter Companion while assisting the Disabled Hunter allows the Disabled Hunter to violate any provision of title 23, Wyoming statutes, or any Commission rule and regulation governing the taking of wildlife; or,

5. The permittee no longer qualifies as a Disabled Hunter as defined in this regulation.

(b) Any person who has a Disabled Hunter Permit Application or Disabled Hunter Companion Permit Application denied by the Department may appeal the Department's decision to the Chief Fiscal Officer in accordance with Commission rules and regulations.

(c) Any person who has a Disabled Hunter Permit or Disabled Hunter Companion Permit revoked by the Department may appeal the Department's decision to the Commission in accordance with Commission rules and regulations.

Section 9. *"Fees For Disabled Hunter Permit and Disabled Hunter Companion Permit"* says:
There shall be no fee for the Disabled Hunter Permit. The fee for the Disabled Hunter Companion Permit shall be $5.00.

Section 10. *"Making False Statements to Obtain a Permit"* says:
Any person that makes a false statement on the application to obtain a Disabled Hunter Permit or Disabled Hunter Companion Permit or any physican, optometrist, or ophthalmologist who makes a false statement on an application in order that a person might fraudulently obtain a Disabled Hunter Permit shall be in violation of this regulation and such violation shall be punishable as provided by Title 23, Wyoming statutes.

Section 11. *"Proof of Permit"* says:
Permits issued in accordance with this regulation shall be in the possession of the individual in whose name the permit has been issued and shall be immediately produced for inspection on request of an officer authorized to enforce this regulation.

Section 12. *"Savings Clause."* says:
if any provision of these regulations is held to be illegal or unconstitutional, such a ruling shall not affect other provisions of this regulation which can be given effect without the illegal or unconstitutional provision; and, to this end, the provisions of these regulations are severable.

Disabled Trapping Safety

You can be disabled and trap. However, in most states you must take a trapper education coarse, then get a permit and license. And in some states if you are 40% Military Disabled it's free. For trapping safety, follow all the wheelchair safety rules and suggestions on page 76. And if you are carrying a firearm follow the "10 commandments of firearm safety" found on page 24 and 25. In addition, follow the safety rules for any of the other weapons you might be using. Here are a few additional rules to follow:

■ When you are out checking your trap lines, let your "Companion" or helper check out traps in dangerous places like creeks with high or steep banks.

■ Make sure you are using the suggested type and kind of trap for the animal you are trapping. Make sure you don't accidentally get caught in your trap while trying to set it.

■ Make sure you understand and are following all the rules for trapping in your state BEFORE you go out trapping.

Conditioning & Exercising

Nobody ever thinks of conditioning as part of hunter safety, but it is! If you are way back in the mountains somewhere hunting and you kill a big game animal, and you are out of shape, you are going to be in big trouble trying to drag it or carry it out back to your car on your back. Or just trying to drag a big buck out of heavy woods will tire you out quick if you are not in shape. There are a number of ways to get in shape. You can go to a gym, or just do it at home yourself. We will first give you a quick stretch out warm-up, then a complete routine for long term conditioning. Long term conditioning will keep you in good health for most of your life. I still do these after 50 or more years, and I'm still in pretty good shape.

Quick Warm-Up Routine (No.1)

This is a little quick warm up routine you can use to get warmed up and your muscles stretched out. It doesn't take too long, and you will be glad later on that you did this.

The Routine

1. Start by doing 10 jumping jacks to get your muscles warmed up.
2. Next slowly do 6 "seated hamstring/quadriceps stretches.
3. Next slowly do 3 pelvic stretches on each side, holding for 3 seconds.
4. Next slowly do 6 push forward pull back ankle stretches.

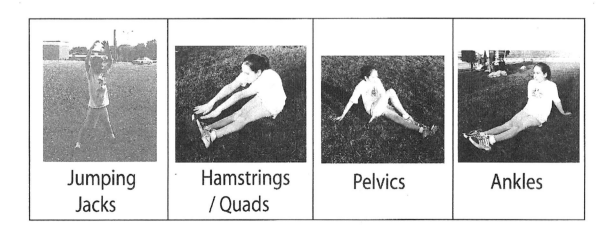

| Jumping Jacks | Hamstrings / Quads | Pelvics | Ankles |

5. Next slowly do 3 front quadriceps stretches on both thighs, leaning forward and holding for 3 seconds.
6. Next slowly do 6 rear shoulder stretches, holding for 3 seconds.
7. Next slowly do 3 front shoulder stretches on each shoulder, holding for 3 seconds.
8. Last find a wall and slowly do 3 calf stretches on each leg, holding it 3 seconds.

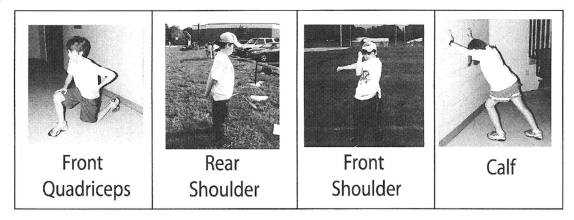

Front Quadriceps | Rear Shoulder | Front Shoulder | Calf

How does conditioning help

Modern sports training and conditioning is advancing all the time. In this book we will follow the latest recommended exercises, training techniques, and tailor them for the younger kids. Over the past several years researchers and physicians have identified exercises that are commonly used that can, in some cases, be potentially harmful to your body. These exercises can be modified though to eliminate the undesirable characteristics. This book will now use the safer alternatives. I will break them down into the fundamental categories, and how they relate to what you want to learn. We will use picture figures, and charts as much as possible, to eliminate some of the confusion for you. So bear with us those of you that are older and have already been through all this. This book was written basically as a "reference" book for younger hunters and beginners to use when conditioning long term for hunting trips. You can take the book right along with you out to the backyard, park or wherever you ate training, to look at for reference purposes.

I suggest that as a hunter if you are not very interested in exercising and training, then try to make a game out of it. Get mom or dad to come out and do these exercises with you. For instance say something to them like, "I bet I can do this better than you," or "I bet you can't beat me down to the fence." Then try to do the exercise faster or better than your mom or dad. This will keep you interested. If mom or dad can't come out to help, then get an older brother or sister, or one or two of your friends to come over and do the exercises with you. Get into exercising at home. It can be fun, and it is good for your overall health. You will need to be well conditioned to hunt or trap in rough terrain areas. These exercises will also condition you to get into the habit of lifetime exercising.

Warm up and Stretching

This is the start of the complete routine. You need to warm up before doing any flexibility, stretching, strengthening, or other exercises. Before starting, you can *slowly* "jog" around the yard or do "jumping jacks," for about one to three minutes to get your muscles warmed up. Warming up raises your body temperature several degrees while rushing blood deep into your muscles and connective tissues. It also reduces the chance of ligament strains, muscle tears, and general soreness. A warm up is required before you start any of these stretching, flexibility, or strength exercises. The shorter time is for you five to eight year olds. The longer time is for you 12 year olds and up. Adjust the time accordingly with all ages in between. Start stretching with the upper part of your body first, and end up with the lower part of your body last.

NOTE: When doing the all the stretches you need to inhale and exhale deeply and slowly two or three times (Breaths) while your body is in the stretching position. This is a yoga technique. By breathing deeply in and out, it lets you stretch out farther. Then after vigorously stretching and exercising, unless you are going to the strengthening or other exercises next, be sure to do a "*COOL DOWN*" routine, instead of just stopping cold. Or do your cool down after the strengthening or other exercises have been completed.

DIAGRAM 1

Warm-Up No.1 - Jumping Jacks

From the standing position put both feet together and both hands down at your sides. The first move is jump up slightly kicking both feet out to the side while raising both arms up together over your head. For the next move you jump up slightly and bring both of your arms back down to your sides while bringing both feet together. Then you repeat this over and over with a constant jumping motion for one to three minutes. You can increase how long you do them each week as you get stronger if you like *(SEE DIAGRAM 1)*.

Exercise No.1- Neck Stretch

This stretching exercise is for the neck muscles. It is for all hunters and trappers because many times you are twisting and turning your head to take a look. From the standing po-sition, put your hands down at

FIGURE 1

your sides, turn to the right and put your chin on your right shoulder. Hold for two in and out breaths, then relax. Next move your head back to center, then put your chin on your chest. Hold that position for two in and out breaths, then relax. Then turn to the left, and put your chin on your left shoulder. Hold that position for two in and out breaths, then relax. Repeat this at least five times, for all three of the positions. After you have been doing these every day for awhile, you can increase the number slightly for extra work if necessary *(SEE FIGURE 1)*.

FIGURE 2

Exercise No. 2- Fingers Stretch

This stretching exercise is for the fingers. Most hunters and trappers can use this ex-ercise because they use their fingers to pull triggers or traps. It keeps them steady. From the standing position, put both your feet out about shoulder width apart. Than put both arms straight out in front. Next, with your fingers spread and pointing straight out, squeeze your fingers together in a fist, then extend them back out. Then keep squeezing and extending them over and over for about five seconds. Now while you are still squeezing your fingers in and out, move both arms overhead for about five seconds. Next while still squeezing in and out, raise both arms out to your sides for about five seconds. Now while still squeezing in and out, repeat all three positions three times *(SEE FIGURE 2)*.

Exercise No. 3- Wrist Stretch

This stretching exercise is for the wrist muscles. All hunters and trappers can use this stretch to help steady firearms and handle traps. From the standing position, put both your feet out about shoulder width apart. Then put both arms straight out at your sides. Next, with your fingers spread slightly apart, pointing straight out, roll or rotate both hands in a circle at the wrist joint with fingers spread, go as far down and around as you can. Do this while deep breathing, then relax your hands back down at your sides. After relaxing for about five seconds repeat at least five times *(SEE FIGURE 3)*.

FIGURE 3

Exercise No.4- Forearm Extensor Stretch

This stretching exercise is for the forearm extensor muscles. All hunters and trappers can use this stretch because you will use your forearms some way in handling firearms and traps. From either a standing or sitting position, put your right arm straight out in front of you with your palm facing down. Then keeping the right hand rather stiff, take your left hand and grasp the back of your right hand and push it downward so that the hand is twisted a little towards the right. You should feel the stretch on the top side of the right forearm. Hold that position while doing your breathing, then let go and bring your arms back down. Relax for ten seconds in between each stretch. Repeat this at least five times for each arm *(SEE FIGURE 4)*.

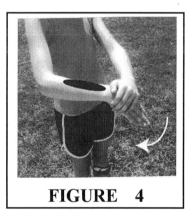

FIGURE 4

Exercise No.5- Forearm Flexor Stretch

This stretching exercise is for the forearm flexor muscles. All hunters and trappers can use this stretch because you will use your forearms some way in handling firearms or traps. From either a standing or sitting position, put your right arm straight out in front of you with your palm facing down. Then take your left hand and grasp the fingers of your right hand, and pull it back so that the fingers are pointing upwards. You should feel the stretch on the underside of your right forearm. Hold that position while doing your breathing, then let go and bring the arms back down. Relax for ten seconds between each stretch. Repeat this at least five times for each arm *(SEE FIGURE 5)*.

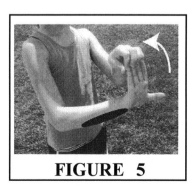

FIGURE 5

FIGURE 6

Exercise No. 6- Triceps Stretch

This stretching exercise is for the triceps and rotator cuff muscles. All hunters and trappers can use this stretch because you will use your triceps in handling firearms and traps. From the standing position, put your right hand behind your head, and touch the top of the opposite (Left) shoulder blade. Hold the elbow of your right hand using your left hand. Then gently push down on your elbow, pushing your right hand down your back. Hold that position while doing your breathing. Then totally relax for six seconds in between each stretch. Then switch arms, put your left arm behind, touch the top of your right shoulder and push down. Repeat this five times for each arm *(SEE FIGURE 6).*

FIGURE 7

Exercise No. 7- Biceps Stretch

This stretching exercise is for the biceps muscles. All hunters and trappers can benefit from using this stretch because you will use your biceps in some way. From the standing position, with your back to a wall and feet shoulder width apart, reach back and place both hands behind you against a wall at about shoulder height. Next bend both knees down until you feel the stretch in your front biceps area of your upper arm and shoulders. Hold that position while doing your breathing, then raise your knees back up to the starting position, put your arms down and relax for ten seconds between each stretch. Then repeat this at least five times *(SEE FIGURE 7).*

FIGURE 8

Exercise No. 8- Rear Shoulder Stretch

This stretching exercise is for the anterior and medial deltoid, and pectoral major muscles. All hunters and trappers can benefit from using this stretch because they use their shoulders in handling firearms and traps. From the standing position, with your legs apart, put both your arms straight down behind your back. Then grasp both hands together at the fingers. Next push down and rotate your shoulders up, keeping your arms straight. Hold that position while breathing, then totally relax your arms and shoulders for four seconds in between each stretch. Repeat five times *(SEE FIGURE 8).*

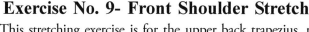

FIGURE 9

Exercise No. 9- Front Shoulder Stretch

This stretching exercise is for the upper back trapezius, rhomboids, and posterior deltoid muscles. All hunters and trappers can benefit from using this stretch because they use their shoulders in some way. From the standing position, with legs apart, put your left arm straight out to your right across your chest. Next make a fist and bend your right arm up towards your chin. Hold that position while you do your breathing, then bring both arms back down and totally relax for four seconds in between each stretch. Next switch and put your right arm out to your left. Then bend up your left arm and hold while doing your breathing. Repeat this at least five times for each arm *(SEE FIGURE 9).*

Exercise No. 10- Side Torso Stretch

This stretching exercise is for side torso, upper back, and rib cage. All hunters and trappers can benefit from using this stretch because they use their torso in some way. From the standing position, put both your feet about shoulder width apart. Then put your right hand on your right hip. Next put your left arm straight up towards the sky and make a fist. Then keeping your arm as straight as possible, move it over to the right until it touches the top of your head. Next twist your wrist so the knuckles are pointing to the right. Then bend your whole upper body to the right, and hold that position while doing your breathing. Put your arms down at your sides and relax for ten seconds between each stretch. Then switch and stretch the other side. Repeat at least five times with each arm *(SEE FIGURE 10)*.

FIGURE 10

Exercise No. 11- Waist & Stomach Stretch

This stretching exercise is for the waist and stomach muscles. All hunters and trappers can benefit from using this stretch because they use their waist and stomach in some way. From the standing position, with legs about shoulder width apart, put both arms straight out at your sides. Then twist your entire torso 90 degrees to the left, hold there while doing your breathing, then back to facing front. Now twist 90 degrees to the right and hold while doing your breathing. Then put your hands down at your side, and relax for ten seconds. Repeat this at least five times to each side *(SEE FIGURE 11)*.

FIGURE 11

Exercise No. 12- Seated Pelvic Stretch

This stretching exercise is for the lower back, obliques, and gluteus maximus (butt). All hunters and trappers can benefit from using this stretch because they use their pelvis in some way, especially hunters waiting in tree blinds. From the sitting position, put your left leg straight out in front with your toes up. Next put the right leg over the left, just back of your knee, with your toes pointed outward. Then put your left elbow on your right knee, with the hand on your right hip. Next put your right arm out to the side, and slightly back for balance. Turn your head to the right, then hold that position while doing your breathing. Then put your arms down and totally relax for ten seconds in between each stretch. Now switch legs and repeat at least five times to each side *(SEE FIGURE 12)*.

FIGURE 12

Exercise No. 13- Hip Extensor Stretch

This stretching exercise is for the hip extensor muscles. All hunters and trappers can benefit from using this stretch because they use their hips in some way, especially hunters waiting in tree blinds. From the lying position, head up, put your left leg straight out in front with toes down. Next lift your right leg up, keeping it as straight as possible, with your foot flat. Grasp your right leg with both hands behind the knee and pull back towards your head. Hold that position while doing your breathing, then put your leg

FIGURE 13

down. Now totally relax for about ten seconds in between each stretch. Switch, then lift up your left leg and repeat the pull. Repeat this at least five times with each leg *(SEE FIGURE 13)*.

Exercise No. 14- Upper and Lower Back Stretch

This stretching exercise is for the upper and lower back muscles. All hunters and trappers can benefit from using this stretch because they use their lower back in some way, especially hunters in the prone position. Lying on your stomach, spread your legs to hip width, and put the tops of your feet on the floor. Rest your chin on the floor, then bend your elbows and put your forearms on the floor with palms down. As you inhale press your forearms against the floor and raise your chest and head. Keep your pelvis and thighs against the floor. Hold that position while doing your breathing, then as you exhale lower your head slowly back to the floor. This stretches your lower back *(SEE FIGURE 14-A)*. Now totally relax for about ten seconds in between each stretch. For the upper back do the same thing except this time instead of raising up on your elbows, use your palms against the floor to push all the way up *(SEE FIGURE 14-B)*. This stretches your upper back. Repeat this at least five times for either your upper or lower back, but not both. Do the lower one day and the upper on another day.

A

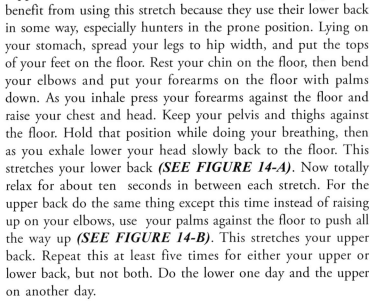

B

FIGURE 14

Exercise No. 15- Seated Hamstring Stretch

This stretching exercise is for the "hamstrings," and quadriceps muscles. All hunters and trappers can benefit from using this stretch because they use their hamstrings when climbing hills or tree blinds. From the sitting position put both legs together out in front of you. Toes should be pointing straight up. Keeping your knees down to the floor or ground, reach forward and touch your toes with both hands. Hold that position while you do your breathing, lean back, put your hands out at your side, totally relax for ten seconds. Repeat five times *(SEE FIGURE 15)*.

FIGURE 15

Exercise No. 16- Thigh Stretch

This exercise is for the front thigh quadriceps muscles. All hunters and trappers can benefit from using this stretch because they use their thighs in some way when climbing tree blinds or creek banks. From the kneeling position, put your right leg out in front of you. Next put your right hand on your right thigh, and your left hand on your left waist. Put a towel or pad under the down knee for protection. Keeping your back straight shift your weight to your front leg. Then lean forward until you feel a stretch in the front of the hip and thigh of the leg you are kneeling on. Hold that position while doing your breathing, then lean back and totally relax for six seconds. Then switch legs and stretch the other thigh. Repeat five times with each leg *(SEE FIGURE 16)*.

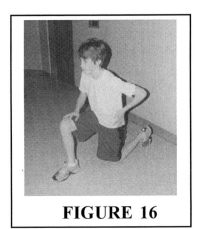

FIGURE 16

Exercise No. 17- Straddle Groin Stretch

This exercise is for the inner thigh groin muscles. Hunters and trappers can benefit from using this stretch because they use their groin muscles in some way, especially hunters when climbing hills or tree blinds, and trappers climbing creek banks. From the sitting position, put both legs way out to the side in front of you, toes up, keeping your knees down and straight. Next grasp both hands together at the thumbs, then keeping your arms straight, lean forward, and reach way out in front. While doing this, try to keep your back straight. Hold that position while doing your breathing. Then lean back and totally relax for ten seconds in between each stretch. Repeat this five times *(SEE FIGURE 17).*

FIGURE 17

Exercise No. 18- Abductors Stretch

This exercise is for abductors in the inner thigh. Hunters and trappers can benefit from using this stretch because they use their legs and thighs in many ways while hunting and trapping. From the standing position, put your right arm down at your side, and extend your left leg to the top edge of a chair, bench or some other stationary item. Whatever the item is, the leg has to be as straight out to the side as possible. Then push lightly down, with the left hand just above the left knee. Hold that position while doing your breathing. Then put the leg down and totally relax for ten seconds, in between each stretch. Now put your right leg up, push down, and hold while doing your breathing. Repeat five times for each leg *(SEE FIGURE 18).*

FIGURE 18

Exercise No. 19- Knee to Chest Stretch

This stretching exercise is for the knee, and lower back muscles. All hunters and trappers can benefit from using this stretch because they use their knees in many different ways while hunting and trapping. From the lying position face up, put your right leg straight out front, with toes up. Pull your left leg up tight to your chest, with both hands grasped together just below your knee. Hold that position while doing your breathing. Then put the left leg down and totally relax for ten seconds in between each stretch. Repeat this five times for each leg *(SEE FIGURE 19).*

FIGURE 19

Exercise No. -20 Calf Stretch

This stretching exercise is for the calf muscles. All hunters and trappers can benefit from using this stretch because they use their calf muscles, especially hunters climbing tree blinds, and trappers climbing banks. Stand in front of a wall and stagger your left foot in front of your right foot, with both heels flat on the floor. Next lean forward and put both of your hands against the wall, then bend the leading front leg down until you feel the pull in your

FIGURE 20

59

right leg calf. Remember you have to be far enough away from the wall so that you can feel the pull. When you feel the pull hold that position for about three seconds. Then stand up and relax for about ten seconds. Now lean back against the wall and stretch the calf on your left leg for three seconds. Repeat this three times for each leg *(SEE FIGURE 20)*.

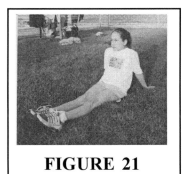

FIGURE 21

Exercise No. 21- Ankle Stretch

This exercise is for ankle area muscles. Hunters and trappers can benefit from using this stretch because they use their ankles in many ways while hunting and trapping. From the sitting position put both your feet, relaxed toes up, out in front of you with feet together. Arms out at your sides for balance. Next keeping your legs flat to the floor or ground, roll both ankles forward, pushing your toes downward. Hold that position while you do your breathing, then relax your feet back to the starting position (up). Next, keeping your heels flat to the floor, roll both ankles back towards your head, with your toes pointing up. This is a hard pull towards your head. Hold that position while breathing. Relax your feet for ten seconds between each stretch. Next with both feet together, roll them around in a circle. Repeat five times for each position *(SEE FIGURE 21)*.

Coordination & Agility

These drills are designed to teach you how to move around in the woods and rough terrain. They will also help you improve your balance and agility as you move around in the woods, stalk game, and get in and out of creeks, and just about anything else you do that takes coordination or agility. If you will do these drills every few days, you will notice your coordination and agility improving.

Coordination

Activity No. 1 Crossover Foot (Carioca)

The Basics are

This is called the crossover foot, side to side, or "carioca" exercise activity. This is agility and coordination "*core training*" to keep you from tripping over your feet while on the move. What it will do for you is amazing, believe me. It's very widely used in almost all sports now. The feet have to keep crossing over each other, from in front to behind. It's an old football drill, but it works great for coordination and agility training in any sport *(SEE FIGURE 22)*. All hunters and trappers should work on this because they can benefit by being very coordinated while out

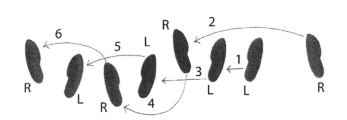

FIGURE 22

hunting, moving through dense brush, climbing hills, climbing tree blinds, or even getting in and out of boats to go duck hunting.

Practice

Get mom or dad to come out in the backyard with you, or down to the park, where there is lots of thick grass. Thick grass will give you some cushioning if you accidentally fall at first. Or you can even do this indoors. Have mom or dad stand in front of you, and both of you face each other, at about two or three yards apart. Have mom or dad do the same steps you are going to do, except they will start out to their right (a mirror image). Start out by both of you walking through this slowly until you learn how to move your feet, then speed up little by little. Start with your feet apart, then step to the left with your left foot. Next step to the left, with your right foot crossing over the top of your left foot. Then step again to the left, with your left foot crossing behind your right foot. Next step again to the left, with your right foot crossing behind your left foot. Then step again to the left, with your left foot over the top of your right foot. Then keep repeating this combination of steps to the left, over and over, for about ten to twenty yards. Then stop and reverse these steps, going first to your right with your right foot, then with your left foot over your right, and so on, back to where you started. The better you get, speed the process up faster and faster. After a few weeks, you should be able to do this at a full run. A "*TIP*." Put your arms straight out to your sides at first while moving, for balance. Keep working with mom or dad because you can learn how to do this if you are having trouble. Do this drill for five to ten minutes at a practice.

Body Agility

Activity No. 2- Running Backwards

The Basics are

This is called the running backwards agility skill. This will help you just getting a better feel of the backwards and twisting movements for getting around in dense woods and underbrush, and when you need to quickly change directions. It will definitely help your body balance. All hunters and trappers need to work on this activity because it helps your change of direction agility no matter where you are.

FIGURE 23

Practice

Find a very large backyard, a big area in a park with thick grass, or you can do this drill indoors in a big gymnasium. It's better outside in the grass though. The reason I am suggesting thick grass as a choice is it will cushion your fall a little if you accidentally fall backwards a lot when starting out. Get mom or dad to come out and help you, then both you line up side by side about two or three yards apart, with at least about 30 yards of clear space behind you. Then both of you start running backwards while pumping your arms up and down *(SEE FIGURE 23)*. Do this for about 30 yards then stop, turn around, and repeat the drill for about 30 yards back to where you started. Usually you will fall down the first few times you try this activity. If either of you (mom or dad) fall down, laugh and make a joke out of it. A "TIP." The secret for keeping your balance is raising your knees high while pumping your hands up and down as fast as you can.

Once you can run fast for the 30 yards, and not fall down, your interest level will go up because you can do something your friends may not be able to do! When you do become good at this, then you can change the activity a little to make it harder. An alternative way to do this is run backwards about ten yards, have mom or dad blow a whistle, then you turn around without stopping, and run forward. Keep doing this, and change directions every ten yards. This is one of the best skill activities for kids, that I have seen, that will really improve your changing direction coordination and agility, and keep you from tripping over your own feet if you accidentally get turned around or stumble. You should do this drill for at least five minutes at a training session.

Rollover Agility

Activity No. 3- Shoulder Roll & Rollout
The Basics are
This is a little different kind of shoulder roll than the one they use in football. It's more like just before you hit or make contact with the ground, you turn sideways and roll over on the fleshy part of your shoulder and upper arm (either one). This is also good body "core training" in case you trip over a log or branch while stalking out in the woods. The one arm is brought more into the stomach area, so you don't accidentally stick out your arms to break the fall. Next you tuck your head in a little towards your chest before you make contact, roll on over on your back, then keep on rolling over and over in the same direction until you slow down enough to come to a stop *(SEE FIGURE 24)*. The last roll should bring you over on your stomach, then you just push up and get up.

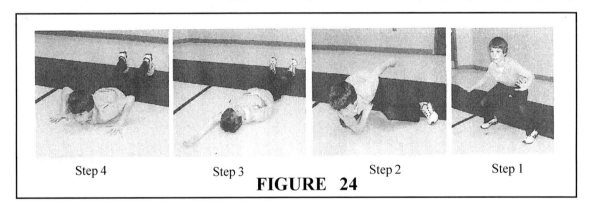

Step 4   Step 3   **FIGURE   24**   Step 2   Step 1

Practice
Find a very large backyard, a big area in a park with thick grass, or you can even do this drill indoors in a big gymnasium. The reason I am suggesting thick grass as a choice to work on is because it will cushion your hands a little as you move around. A "**TIP.** " The trick to this technique is as soon as contact is made with the ground you have to quickly start your roll. If you hit down solid on your shoulder there is a good chance you are going to mess it up pretty good. After practicing this for a week or two from a fixed standing start I would start with a very short run up to get moving, then dive out and turn the shoulder for the roll, just to get a better feel of it. Until you have practiced this for awhile, find a couple of exercise pads to land on before you go out to the grass. For you younger five year old kids, it's a good idea for you to wear elbow pads, knee pads, and wrist guards for this exercise at the beginning, just in case your coordination is not too good and you accidentally fall on an arm or elbow. When you have the pads and guards on it tends to give you a sense of safety. Do at least five of these at a training session to start with.

Strength Activities

These drills are designed to build up your strength. For most of you they are for your arms, and legs. They are not to build you into a muscle bound weight lifter type, but just enough to tone up your muscles so that you will be a little stronger. You need strength for hunting and trapping mostly in your upper body and legs. Rifles are heavy, and creek banks are sometimes very steep, and hard to get in and out of when setting or checking a trap line. Many of you young kids these days just sit around at home a lot, and don't have a lot of chores to do as kids did years ago, like out on a farm. And because you have very little to do with your arms or legs like pitch hay or carry heavy buckets of milk like kids used to do, your arms and legs are sometimes weak. It is important that you do some of these drills every day or two. But before you do make sure you stretch out the muscles in the part of your body that you are strengthening. If you get tired and quit for a week or two weeks, then these activities probably won't help you very much.

NOTE: Make sure you follow all breathing instructions for each activity (*a Yoga technique*). Because there are different parts of your body that need strengthening, we will break this down into the upper back, lower back, chest, shoulders, arms, and legs. For a good light weight training program, a utility bench and a lightweight barbell set for kids would be great if your mom and dad can afford it. If not, at least get a dumbbell set. They are not too expensive. In fact you could find some work (odd jobs) around your neighborhood and save enough to get a set of dumbells for yourself. Start with 3.3 or 4 pound lightweight dumbbells at five years old, and work up to 6.6 or 7 pound dumbbells later as you get stronger. Your upper body needs to be strong enough to hold up the heavier firearms for an extended period of time waiting to make your shot. If your arms, and legs are weak then you are eventually going to run into trouble out on a hunting trip, especially you younger beginner hunters and trappers.

UPPER BACK

Activity No. 4- Dumbbell Rowing

The Basics are
This exercise is pulling your hands up and down in a rowing type motion while using a dumbbell. This is good for strengthening the back of the arm muscles, the upper back, and the shoulder arm socket area. It is especially useful in holding and aiming rifles, and carrying big traps out to a trap line *(SEE FIGURE 25)*.

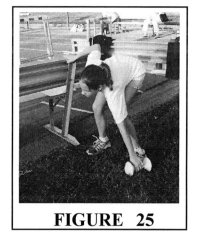

FIGURE 25

Practice
Stretch out your shoulders, torso, biceps, triceps, and hamstring muscles before you do this strengthening. Hold a dumbbell in your left hand, with the palm facing in, and to the left end of a utility bench, table or couch. Make sure the dumbbell is heavy enough for you to feel the pull on your muscles. It will depend on how old you are as to what the weight needs to be. Trial and error use will determine the weight. Put your right hand on the top of the bench, table or couch, for support. Next bend forward at the hips until your back is parallel to the ground and arched, with your knees bent slightly. Your left arm with the dumbell should hang down. While in this position you pull the left arm up under your arm pit until your elbow is pointing down. Then you lower the dumbbell slowly back down. You should feel a slight pull along the right outside of your back. This is working the Latissimus Dorsi muscles (Lats) along your back. Then turn around, switch the dumbbell to your right hand, and repeat this process. Take a deep breath just before you start to pull up, then let it out slowly as you let the dumbbell back down. Five year olds should only do about five of these with each arm. As you get a little older and stronger you can increase the reps and weight

LOWER BACK

Activity No. 5- Straight Leg Deadlift

The Basics are

This exercise is lifting up dumbbell's from the floor, by using your back and straightening up your legs. It is useful for all hunters and trappers to strengthen your lower back and legs. This will give you hunters more strength for climbing hills and tree blinds, and trappers more strength for getting in and out of creeks with steep banks, and lifting up heavy traps *(SEE FIGURE 26)*.

FIGURE 26

Practice

Stretch out your hamstrings and lower back before you do this strengthening. Stand straight up with a dumbbell in each hand, with your palms facing your stomach. Your knees should be bent, with your legs about shoulder width apart. Next lower the dumbbells by bending over, using only your back and NOT your arms. Keep the dumbbells close to youir shins, and your head should be looking up and not down. Then raise up, bringing the dumbbell's up, by straightening your legs and using your back. While doing this your hips should be moving forwards. Take a deep breath just as you start to bend down, then let it out slowly as you come back to the straight up position. Five year olds can start out with about five of these lifts, then increase the number later as they get stronger and older

Activity No. 6- Back Extension (Superman)

The Basics are

This exercise is laying down, extending both the hands and the legs, then raising the feet and the hands up slightly off the floor or ground and holding this position. It is also useful for all hunters and trappers to strengthen your lower back, legs, and it tightens up your stomach muccles. This will also help hunters get up quickly from a prone position if necessary *(SEE FIGURE 27)*.

FIGURE 27

Practice

Stretch out your lower back and stomach muscles before you do this strengthening. Lay down on your stomach on a floor or flat surface, with both arms straight out in front of you. Face your palms down, and your legs straight out behind you. Next pull in your abdominal muscles, like you would be creating a small space between your stomach and the floor or ground. Lift both arms and legs, just a few inches up off the floor. Hold that position for about five seconds. While doing this, you need to stretch out in front and in back as much as you can. Then lower the arms and legs slowly. Take a deep breath just as you lift up your arms and legs, then let it out slowly as you lower them. Start out doing about five of these, then increase the number a little each time as you get older

CHEST

Activity No. 7- Chest Press

The Basics are

This exercise is for pressing, or pushing, up dumbbell's in each hand. This helps you build up your upper body chest strength. It is useful upper body strength for shooting rifles, and setting heavy duty traps *(SEE FIGURE 28).*

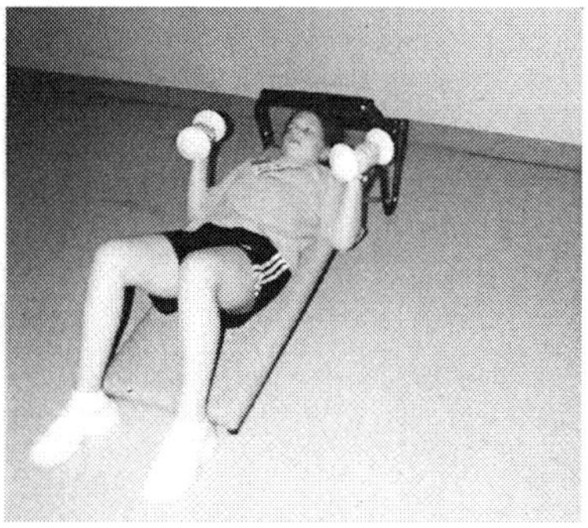

FIGURE 28

Practice

Stretch out your biceps, triceps, and front shoulders before you do this strengthening. Lay down on some type of utility bench, or even on a mat, on your back with a dumbbell in each hand, and with your feet on the floor, knees bent Then push both of your arms up directly over your shoulders, with your palms facing forward, and arms extended. Next bring the dumbbells back down slowly to your sides, with your elbows just a little lower than your shoulders. Then push the dumbbells back up again. While doing this you should pull in your stomach abdominal muscles, but don't push your back into the flat surface. All during the press, your shoulder blades should not raise up off the bench.

Start out with five year olds doing only about five of these, up through 12 year olds doing about ten. Take a deep breath before you push the dumbbells up, then let it out slowly as you bring your arms back down. Nine to 12 year olds that do not have a dumbell set, you can substitute the barbell weight for the equivalent dumbbells weight. I don't advise the barbells for you younger five to eight year old kids because it might be too much weight for you to handle. You can use the barbells when you get older. You can also do more repetitions once you get older.

Activity No. 8- Shoulder Front Raise

The Basics are

This is lifting up dumbbell's one at a time in each hand, from a hanging down position to a straight out in front position. It is useful for shooting rifles while standing. Extra shoulder strength will also help climbing tree stands *(SEE FIGURE 29)*.

Practice

Stretch out your front and rear shoulders, and your triceps before you do this strengthening. Stand straight up, with your feet about shoulder width apart, and with a dumbbell in each hand. Your arms should hang straight down, turned with the palms facing your stomach in front of youir thighs. Pull in your abdominal muscles, and have your knees relaxed. Next raise your right arm straight out in front of you, to about shoulder height, hold it there for five seconds, and then slowly lower it back down to the arm hanging down position. Take a deep breath just before you raise your arm, hold it for about three seconds, then let it out slowly as you lower your arm. Next you repeat the process with your left arm. Start out with five year olds doing about five of these with each arm, up through 12 year olds doing about eight with each arm. You can do a few more of these once you get a little older and stronger .

FIGURE 29

LEGS, TOES, ANKLES

Activity No. 9- Toe Raise

FIGURE 30

The Basics are

This exercise is raising way up on your toes and holding that position for a few seconds, to strengthen the lower legs, toes, and ankles. This is for all hunters and trappers because at some time you will need leg strength in hunting and trapping *(SEE FIGURE 30)*.

Practice

Stretch out your ankles and calf muscles before you do this strengthening. Stand up straight with your feet about shoulder width apart, and arms out at your sides for balance. Then raise up on your toes as high as you can go. Hold that position for five seconds. Then come slowly back down to the starting position. Five year olds start out only doing about five of these, with 12 year olds doing about eight. Increase the number of reps by a few as you get older and stronger. Take a deep breath before you start to push up, then let it out slowly as you come back down.

Activity No. 10- Cone Jumping

The Basics are

This exercise is standing at one end of a line of cones, then jump hopping with your feet together over each cone through to the end of the row. This is for all hunters and trappers because hunters will use their leg and toe strength in climbing hills and tree stands, and trappers climbing steep creek banks *(SEE FIGURE 31)*.

FIGURE 31

Practice

Stretch out your ankles, calf, and lower back muscles before you do this strengthening. This is another alternative drill to strengthen your thigh and leg muscles. This is safer for you younger kids than running up and down stairs or steps. This should help give you more leg and toe strength for climbing. First get a set of 9 inch tapered orange cones that are available in many stores now. And they are not that expensive. Set them out in a row, spaced at about 18 to 24 inches apart, depending on your age and size. Stand at one end right in front of the first cone, and face the row. Now hop, landing with both feet together, over each cone all the way through to the end of the row. This is a *"core training"* drill. The object is for you to jump up as high as you can, and go all the way through to the end of the row as quickly as you can . Now on the way back turn around and hop back all the way through, landing on both feet each time. Focus on going through each time jumping higher and faster than you did the time before. Try to do at least two sets of down and back every other day if possible. Then you will start to notice after several week just how much quicker and stronger you are becoming.

THIGHS, QUADS, HAMSTRINGS, BUTTOCKS

Activity No. 11- Wall Sits

The Basics are

This exercise is to strengthen the quadriceps (front thigh), and also the hamstrings, gluteal (buttocks), and back muscles. Basically it's leaning against a wall then sitting half way down then back up with your back against the wall. This is for all hunters and trappers because at some time or another you will be using these muscles in hunting and trapping *(SEE FIGURE 32)*.

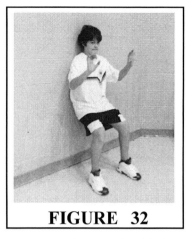

FIGURE   32

Practice

Stretch out your calf, quads, lower back, hamstrings, hips, thighs and buttocks muscles before you do this strengthenig. Stand up against a wall, put both feet about shoulder width apart and about 1-1/2 feet out in front of you. Put both hands up, out to the front, palms up, then your back slides down the wall until your thighs are parallel to the floor. Take a deep breath before you slide down the wall, then hold the down position for at least ten seconds. You should slide down the wall far enough, to feel a tightening in your front and back thigh muscles. Then as you straighten back up to the starting position, you slowly expel the air, then you relax for about ten seconds. Start out by doing about three to five of these. If you are a large boy or girl, still carrying a lot of baby fat, you may not be able to do that many. In that case start out with the most you can easily do, without struggling too much, then increase the number as you get older and stronger .

Activity No. 12- Half Squats
The Basics are

This is another exercise is to strengthen the quadriceps (front thigh), hamstrings, gluteal (buttocks), and back muscles. It's standing up, feet apart and squatting only half way down. This is for all hunters because it will help you climb hills and tree stands, and trappers climbing up steep creek banks *(SEE FIGURE 33)*.

FIGURE   33

Practice

Stretch out your calf, thigh, quads, lower back, and buttocks muscles before you do this strengthening. Stand, with both hands on your hips, and feet slightly apart. Next squat halfway down, keeping your balance. Take a deep breath before you squat, and hold that position for at least five seconds. Keeping your back straight, you should lean forward just far enough to feel the tightening in your front and back thigh muscles. Then as you straighten back up to the starting position, you slowly expel the air. Start out by doing about three to five of these. If you are a large boy or girl, still carrying a lot of baby fat, you may not be able to do that many. In that case start out with the most you can easily do, without struggling too much, and increase the number as you get stronger.

KNEES
Activity No. 13- Knee Bend Pulls
The Basics are

This exercise is a exercise is to strengthen your knees. Basically it is laying down on your stomach, then pulling up your leg against a resistance band. This is for all hunters and trappers because at some time you will use your knees in some way while moving and turning *(SEE FIGURE 34)*.

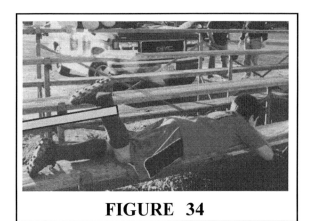

FIGURE 34

Practice

Stretch out your calf, knee, thigh and buttocks muscles before you do this strengthening. The exercise is going to be a little harder to accomplish because you will need mom or dad to find a resistance type stretch band for you. And will need another person to help out. Ideally, you also need an exercise bench in order that you can hold onto the front bar(s), and not slip backwards. The bench also gives you place for the non exercising foot to pull against. The right kind of stretch band is not easy to find. The cheapest, and maybe the best place, is on the "InterNet". Knees are probably at, or near, the top of the list for sport injuries. This means that if you can get set up to do this exercise, it will be a big help and maybe keep you injury free. And you need your knees to be in good shape to be traveling around in rough terrain.

Lay down on your stomach on top of a bench to do this exercise. Then hold on to the bars or the front of the bench with both hands. Attach the stretch band behind you to something permanent. Next slip the free end of the band around your right ankle. Then take a deep breath before you pull your leg up, then hold the up position for at least five seconds. Then as you lower your leg to the starting position, you slowly expel the air. If you can't afford an exercise bench, but you can get a band, you can still get set up to do this exercise. In that case, what you do is cut off two broom stick handles about nine inches in length. Then find a place out in a backyard corner with plenty of grass and space around it.

Drive the stakes about 4 inches into the ground, and about 12-14 inches apart. Now lay down on your stomach, reach out and hold on to the handles with each hand. Next extend both feet out behind you, with your toes pointed down. Then have the helper get down behind you on their knees, moving their left knee up against the sole of your left foot for support. Next the helper puts your right ankle through the other end of the stretch band, and holds the other end stationary. Now you can go ahead and pull up with your right leg. Start out by doing about three to five of these with each leg . You can increase the number of pulls as you get older and stronger.

Cool Downs after Exercising

Explanation

After your body gets all heated up it tries to cool itself down after a rigorous workout. So make sure you do *"cool downs"* after doing any strenuous exercises or drills. Cool downs can be as simple as slowly just walking around the yard, or pedaling very slowly and relaxed on an exercise bicycle, for at least 3 - 5 minutes. Or it could be just a slowed down, and relaxed, version of the strenuous exercise you just finished. Remember the more intense your exercise pace was, the more gradual your cool down pace should be. Step it down gradually. Another thing to point out is, don't get "chilled" right after a strenuous intense exercise routine, by being someplace where the temperature is cool. Such as outside when it's 50 or 60 degrees. Experts say the ideal temperature to cool down in is 68-72 degrees.

Conditioning and Exercising Summation

By this point I know a lot of you hunters and trappers are thinking what does all of this conditioning have to do with hunting or trapping. You are probably saying to yourself, "I don't need to be doing all that stuff because I'm just going to be walking around out in the woods." And that may be true for a lot of you, but what about you hunters and trappers that go way out to territory where it's rough terrain and far away from anyone out in the "boonies." How are you going to drag that big trophy elk *(SEE FIGURE 35)* back to your car. My son went out elk hunting one time a few years ago with his step brother, WAY back in the mountains in Colorado. And they were up at elevations of maybe 8,000 to 10,000 feet. His step brother does this a lot, so he stays in shape for it, but my son does not. He was telling me about all the places they were, and what they went through.

FIGURE 35

And they were hours and hours away from getting back to the truck. What if my son's step brother fell and got hurt, or they got a big trophy elk. I don't know how my son could have easily got his brother or an elk out of the mountains in the rough country where they were. And then to further complicate things the air is thinner, and it's harder to breathe. Imagine even you and a buddy dragging a 700 to 1,000 pound elk out of the mountains. Even a cow can weigh from 500 to 800 pounds, that's 250 to 400 pounds apiece. I don't think so! So you better be in shape. The alternative is to field dress your kill on the spot, package it up and carry it out on your back. And this is still going to take a lot of energy to pack out that much meat.

SECTION 2. Firearms

Explanation

This whole section is an introduction into firearms. There are many types of firearms used in hunting. We will cover the more popular types of firearms that are used in hunting. This breaks down to "rifles," "shotguns," "air rifles" and "muzzleloaders." We will start with rifles because they are the most common and popular type of firearm used in hunting. We will give some insight into choosing a firearm, taking care of it, storing it, transporting it and safety while using it. For youth and beginning hunters we will try to keep it as simple and basic as we can.

Rifles

Types of Rifles

This is an introduction into hunting with rifles. They are the most popular firearm for hunting. There are a number of special types, but it really comes down to five, "bolt action," "lever action," "pump action," "semi-automatic," and "pneumatic (air)." Hunters have been debating for a long time over a very simple question: what type and/or caliber gun will serve a hunter the best? There is no simple answer for this question, everyone has slightly different features they feel they need. Above all, you need to be comfortable and familiar with your chosen firearm. First what are you going to use it for, deer, elk, bear, or wild boar? That will have a lot to do with your choice. In tough economic times it may just come down to cost. What can you afford. Then you need to decide whether the areas where you will probably hunt are going to be in dense type woods or brush, from a wood line on the edge of a clearing, a blind, or a tree stand.

Bolt Action Rifles

These rifles are probably the most popular firearm for big game hunting (deer) as opposed to small game (rabbits). Depending on who you talk to, each one has it's strong points as to why it is the best one to use, and why it is better than another rifle for a particular big game animal. We are going to list what may be, according to some experts, the top 9 in this category, and not listed in any particular order.

1. **Winchester Model 70**

    There are several versions of this rifle. The pre-64, post-64, and the classic. Available features include a simple adjustable trigger, detachable or non-detachable box magazine with or without hinged floorplate, and a 3 position safety on the bolt

2. **Ruger Model 77**

    The original M77 was replaced by the M77 Mark II in 1989, and it is made in several versions. Features include a Mauser type extractor, non-detachable box magazine with hinged floor plate, and integral scope mounts. Older models had adjustable triggers. The Mark II models have a 3 position bolt mounted safety.

3. Savage Model 110

It is not the most attractive rifle ever designed, but it has a well deserved reputation for strength and accuracy. One of the reasons for it's accuracy is the barrel locknut, which many call ugly. Features include an adjustable trigger, detachable or non-detachable box magazine (which varies by model), and a 3 position thumb safety. A feature called "Accutrigger" is available on newer models.

4. Browning A-Bolt

The A-Bolt (which was replaced by the A-Bolt II in 1994) was made in a variety of variations and grades, is a comfortable, well-made, attractive, and unique rifle *(SEE FIGURE 36)*. Features include glass bedding (bedded at the recoil lug and at the rear of the receiver), adjustable trigger, a short 60 degree bolt throw, an ergonomically designed bolt knob, detachable box magazine on the hinged floor plate, and a bolt lock thumb safety. They come in a left hand or right hand version.

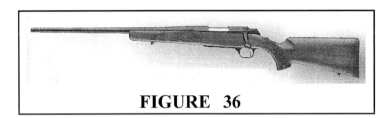

FIGURE 36

5. Remington Model 700

The model 700 is an enduring rifle, and maybe the most popular American bolt-action rifle of all time, despite it's trigger safety problems. It is available in many variations and grades. Features include an adjustable trigger, detachable or non-detachable box magazine with or without a hinged floorplate (depending on the model), and a side mounted thumb safety.

6. Sako 85

This rifle is now sold in the USA by Beretta, and they have been well respected for years. Features include a very slick action with a fairly short bolt throw, which can mean quick follow up shots. It's currently available in a number of variations, the 85 is a fine rifle which comes in a number of action lengths, probably more than any other commercially produced sporting rifle.

7. Mossberg 4x4

The 4x4 is made in a variety of models, available in 6 calibers from .25-06 to .338 chamberings. Features include Mossberg adjustable LBA trigger, a drop box magazine, and many types of stocks from wood to synthetics.

8. Weatherby Vanguard

Like the Mark V, the Weatherby Vanguard rifle is made in a variety of models, and in more chamberings than the Mark V. It was built to be a less expensive option for those who wanted the Weatherby name, but didn't have the cash for the Mark V. It's features include an adjustable trigger, guaranteed accuracy, non-detachable box magazine with a hinged floorplate, and a side mounted thumb safety.

9. Tikka T3

Tikka is a subsidiary of Sako of Finland, and so automatically enjoys the prestige that the Sako name has, but the T3 has been criticized for being built using many manufacturing

71

shortcuts. I guess what is important is does it perform, and the T3 seems to perform. It has been praised for it's smoothness, and features an adjustable trigger and integral scope mounts. It also has a removable box type magazine.

Lever Action Rifles

These rifles are "traditional" when it comes to deer hunting, especially the old flat sided Winchester and Marlin rifles chambered for 30-30 Win. However, these are not the only lever action rifles that have enjoyed success with big game hunters. Other designs have proven themselves useful and popular. We are going to list what some experts say may be the top 7 in this category, and not listed in any particular order.

1. **Marlin Model 336**

    The Marlin model 336 is one of the most successful lever action rifles in history, and deservedly so. Whether chambered for 30-30 Win or the harder hitting 35 Rem, the 336 provides a strong, smooth, well designed action in a rifle that is a pleasure to carry and shoot. Features include side ejection and a solid top, which allow for easy, solid scope mounting above the bore.

2. **Winchester/USRAC Model 94**

    When it was last being built, the model 94 was probably the most recognized lever action rifle in the world still in production with widespread use *(SEE FIGURE 37)*. While not as inherently smooth or strong as the Marlin Model 336, the model 94 has a loyal following, and has done the job for many years. Some common complaints though include the open top receiver which makes scope mounting inconvenient. They feature chamberings from 30-30 Win to 480 Ruger. Manufacture of these rifles was discontinued in 2006.

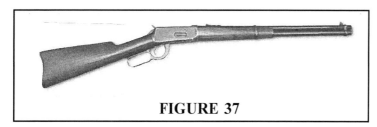

FIGURE 37

3. **Ruger Model 96/44**

    This is called a sweet little rifle. And though it looks like the old model 44, the 96 has a detachable rotary magazine instead of the tubular magazine found on it's semi-automatic predecessor. Features include side ejection and solid top receiver for scope mounting. Users say this is a very smooth and accurate gun, and excellent for close-cover brush hunting. It is chambered for the 44 Rem magazine.

4. **Savage Model 99**

    Though it is now discontinued, the Savage 99 is a rifle that broke the mold for lever action rifles. The rotary magazine (later a detachable box magazine) allows for the use of pointed bullets, unlike the tubular magazines often found on lever action guns. The action is both strong and smooth, with a wide and hand filling receiver rather than the tall and slim style found on the Marlin 336 and Winchester 94.

5. **Marlin Model 1894**

    This model is a bit different than Marlin's other lever action guns, but they are just as good. Instead of the round bolt found on their other models, the 1894 has a flat sided bolt that sits flush with the receiver, featuring a solid top and side ejection for proper scope mounting. It has 3 chamberings: 357 Mag/38 special, 41 Rem Mag, and 44 Rem Mag/44 Special. Of these nothing less than the 44Mag is recommended for big game.

6. **Browning BLR**

This model, introduced in 1971, is their offering to lever action lovers, and it has gained quite a following with some hunters. The rotating bolt allows for positive lockup, and side ejection makes scope mounting easy. The detachable box magazine also makes it a standout rifle. It has chambering from 22-250 through 450 Marlin.

7. **Marlin Models 1895 & 444**

The Marlin big-bore lever action rifles are just as good as the smaller 336, and they should be, since they are simply scaled up versions of the same gun. They are chambered for 45-70 (Model 1895) or 444 Marlin (Model 444), these guns pack a wallop, and will handle tougher game than their smaller ancestors. These full-grown lever action guns are some of the most dependable and accurate knocker-downers available. Just right for wild bore.

Slide (Pump) Action Rifles

For those of you that love pump shotguns, this rifle is for you. Hunting deer with a rifle can be awkward, because most rifles operate differently than your favorite old shotgun going for game birds. Remington has long offered the only commonly available choice.

1. **Remington Model 7600**

For those of you that are fans of slide action rifles, also known as pump guns, Remington is the only choice for hunting deer and big game *(SEE FIGURE 38)*. They are faster operating than bolt actions, these pump guns are often preferred by hunters who use pump shot guns. The 7600 is the only commonly available pump rifle out there that we could find, although I know must be more. The 7600 comes in calibers from 243 through 30-06. Older variations include Models 76 and 760.

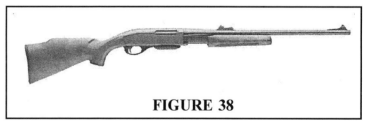

FIGURE 38

Semi-Automatic Rifles

These rifles have gained a bad reputation in some circles, mainly through lack of understanding them. Automatics have a valid place in the hunting world, and are much faster and easier to use than other types of rifles. One hunter said he spent his first 20 years of deer hunting using a semi-automatic, and in so doing learned just how good and dependable an automatic deer rifle can be. And as a plus is they have a reduced recoil. We are going to list what may be the top 5 in this category, and they are not listed in any particular order.

1. **Remington Model 7400**

The Remington semi-automatic rifles are probably the most popular big game rifles of their kind. For a long time they have been the most affordable automatic deer rifle, they have held their ground through various models such as the 74, 740, and 742. Some hunters are not a big fan of Remington autoloaders, but a lot of hunters are, and they have taken a lot of game over the years. The model 7400 is available in calibers from 243 through 30-06.

2. Ruger Model 44 (44 Carbine)

This is the model that one hunter used for 20 years of deer hunting. He puts it at the top of his list. Although it is no longer manufactured, it is included because of his long and pleasant history with this rifle. With it's shorter handy carbine length and the hard hitting 44 Rem mag cartridge, this is an excellent gun for hunting in brush at ranges out to 100 yards or so.

3. Browning BAR

Since it was introduced in 1967, the Browning Automatic Rifle (BAR) has set the standard for autoloading centerfire hunting rifles. It is known for it's excellent accuracy and dependability, the BAR also lives up to Browning's reputation for high quality and usability. For decades, it was the only commercial automatic chambered for magnum cartridges. It is available in calibers from 243 through 338 Win Mag.

4. Ruger Model 99/44 Deerfield

When Ruger discontinued the model 44 in 1986, it left a vacuum in the rifle world. No rifle compared with model 44 carbine as a fast, hard-hitting brush gun. 14 years later, Ruger again produced a semi-automatic carbine in 44 Rem Mag, but of an entirely new design *(SEE FIGURE 39)*. Similar in looks and size, the action is different and not as scope friendly, but it will hit just as hard.

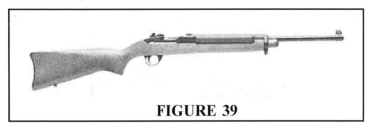

FIGURE 39

5. Benelli R1

The Benelli R1 semi-automatic rifle was introduced in 2003. However, it does not have much of a reputation of any kind yet, but Benelli is a respected name, well known for their excellent autoloading shotguns. Initial reviews of this odd looking rifle sound promising though. It is available in 30-06 and 300 Win Mag.

Pneumatic (Air) Rifles

Air guns are not new. Air gun technology has existed since the 15th century. Today air gun hunting has increased a little in popularity for pest control and small game hunting. These are a good rifles to use for pest control, on undesirable varmint's, or rodents. It can also be used for small game hunting during the legal hunting season. When selecting a gun for hunting, use pellets, and look for high velocity ammunition (at least 700 FPS in a .22 caliber, or 950 FPS in a .177 caliber). We are going to list what may be the top 9 in this category, and not necessarily in any order.

1. Diana RWS Model 34

This is RWS's most popular and affordable air rifles. It has accuracy, power and style all combined into this gun. It features a full size hardwood stock, adjustable trigger, automatic safety, and a finely rifled barrel. The .177 caliber is capable of a 1000 FPS velocity. For hunting use .177 Caliber hunting pellets ammunition.

2. Diana RWS Model 350 Magnum

This is probably the most popular high power air rifle. This is what you use for long range pest control. It features spring-piston action, single stroke barrel cocking, a hardwood stock, fully adjustable sights, and a finely rifled steel barrel. It comes in .177 caliber or .22 caliber.

The .177 caliber is capable of a 1250 FPS velocity, and the .22 caliber is capable of 1050 FPS velocity. For your best all around performance, use RWS Super Mag pellets ammunition.

3. RWS Model 460 Magnum

This is probably the highest powered commercially manufactured air rifle. This is what you use for long range pest control with hard hitting. It features spring-piston action, under level single stroke barrel cocking, a hardwood stock, fully adjustable sights or scope mounting, and a finely rifled steel barrel. It comes in .177 caliber. The .177 caliber is capable of a 1350 FPS velocity. For your best all around performance, use RWS Super Mag pellets ammunition.

4. Gamo Hunter Elite Model

This is Gamo's higher power Hunter Elite .177 caliber air rifle. This is what you use for longer range pest control with hard hitting. It features a break barrel single cocking system, automatic cocking safety, second stage adjustable trigger, manual safety, a hardwood stock with a ventilated rubber pad for recoil absorption, and a 3-9x50 precision, illuminated reticle scope. The .177 caliber is capable of a 1200 FPS velocity with PBA, 1000 FPS with lead.

5. Gamo Hunter Extreme (The Beast) Models

This is Gamo's ultimate higher power Hunter Extreme .177, and .22 caliber air rifle. This is what you use for longer range pest control with hard hitting. It features a break barrel single cocking system, automatic cocking safety, second stage adjustable trigger, manual safety, a hardwood stock with dual interchangeable barrels, and a 3-9x50 illuminated center glass scope. The .177 caliber is capable of a 1650 FPS velocity with PBA, 1250 FPS with lead pellets. The .22 caliber is capable of a 1300 FPS velocity with PBA, 950 FPS with lead pellets.

6. Beeman R1 Model

This is the "Elegant Workhorse" of the Beeman air rifle line. This is the fastest .177 Beeman airgun available. It has a muzzle velocity of 950 FPS. It comes in three calibers, .177, .20, and .22. To truly harness the power, the .20 caliber is recommended. This is a rifle for handling any varmint situation. It features the Beeman "R" series trigger. Recognized as one of the finest available on a sporting rifle. It has an automatic cocking safety. For those that like a shorter barrel, a carbine model is available in .177 and .20 calibers.

7. Ruger New Explorer Model

This is Ruger's newest model, specially designed for youth and small framed adults *(SEE FIGURE 40*. It comes in .177 caliber only. It has a muzzle velocity of 500 FPS, fully adjustable rear sight with two green fiber-optic elements, a stylish thumb-hole stock with vent holes in a raised cheekpiece, light weight, 4-1/2 pounds, an automatic anti-beartrap safety, a two stage non-adjustable trigger, and a smooth firing behavior.

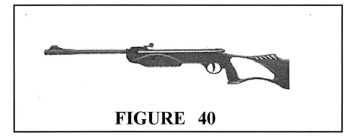

FIGURE 40

8. Walther Talon Magnum Model with Nitro Piston

This is Walther's finest high power .177 caliber air rifle. This is what you use for small game and varmint control. It features a break barrel cocking system, a Crossman Nitro Piston, automatic safety, muzzle brake for extra cocking leverage, synthetic stock, a 3-9x32 scope and mount. The .177 caliber is capable of 1400 FPS velocity with hyper-velocity pellets, and 1200 FPS velocity with lead pellets.

9. **Crossman NPSS Digital Camo Model**
This is Crossman's American Muscle, short stroke, gas nitro piston, .22 caliber air rifle. This is what you use for pest control with hard hitting, close range shooting. It features a break barrel single cocking system, two stage adjustable trigger, a bull barrel, carbon fiber stock, and a 3-9x40AO scope with mil-dot reticle. The .22 caliber is capable of a 1000 FPS velocity.

Help In Choosing Your Rifle

Helpful Information

When talking about rifles, it's good to understand how they are sized. They go by barrel sizes which is called the caliber or bore size. We have added a Table No.1 with the popular calibers, their metric equivalent and the typical bullet diameter. The data is taken from the *Wikipedia Free Encyclopedia*. We have also added a Table 2 with the recoil for some of the common caliber rifles young hunters might use. This data is taken from *Chuck Hawks Rifle Recoil Table*. If you are a small hunter, this may give you a rough idea of what to expect. Another way to reduce the recoil is use low recoil type ammunition. It is also a good idea to use a "recoil pad" on the rifle butt, and "hearing protection" while you are beginning to get used to your rifle.

TABLE 1 Common Calibers and Metric Equivalents

Caliber	Metric Equivalent	Typical Bullet Dia. (In./mm)	Caliber	Metric Equivalent	Typical Bullet Dia. (In./mm)
.17	4.4 mm	0.172 (Rem HMR)	.28	6.8 mm 7 mm	.284 (REM) 7.213 mm
.177	4.5 mm	.177 (Lead) .175 (BB)	.30	7.62 mm	.308 (30-06, 7.62 NATO)
.22,.218, .219,.221, .222,.224	5.5, 5.56 5.7 mm	.223 -.224 (22LR, .223 Rem, 5.56 NATO)	.44	10.8 mm	.427-.430 (REM)
.24	6 mm	.243 (WIN) 6mm (REM)	.45	11.4 mm	.458 (45-70 GOV)
.27	6.8 mm 7 mm	.277 (WIN) 7.035 mm			

TABLE 2 Common Rifle Recoil Data

Cartridge	Recoil (FT-LBs)	Cartridge	Recoil (FT-LBs)
.17HMR	0.2	.270 WIN	17.0
.22 LR	0.2	.280 REM	17.2
.22 WMR	0.4	.30-06 SPFD	20.3
.22 Hornet	1.3	.308 WIN	17.5
.243 WIN	8.8	.44 REM	11.2
.25-06 REM	12.5	.45-70 GOV	23.9

Handling Your Rifle

Explanation

We will cover handling your rifle out in the field and at home. When we talk about handling, we mean when you are just carrying. We will talk about firing and shooting later in this section. Note: We are not going to cover pistols. We will go over hunting game with your rifle later in the book.

Handling In the Field Position

There are several ways to handle or carry a gun so that it is never a threat to other hunters, yet it is ready for instant use. A good position is to grip the small of the stock in the trigger hand and cradle the barrel in the crook of the other arm *(SEE FIGURE 41-A)*, except NOT when another hunter is walking next to you on the muzzle side. Another position is the shoulder carry *(SEE FIGURE*

41-B), except NOT when another hunter is walking single file behind you. Another position is the muzzle down carry *(SEE FIGURE 41-C)*, except NOT when another hunter is walking single file in front of you. Still another carry, and maybe the best because it gives better control of the muzzle, is to hold the fore end in one hand and the small of the stock in the other *(SEE FIGURE 41-D)*, except NOT when another hunter is walking next to you on the muzzle side, or single file in front of you.

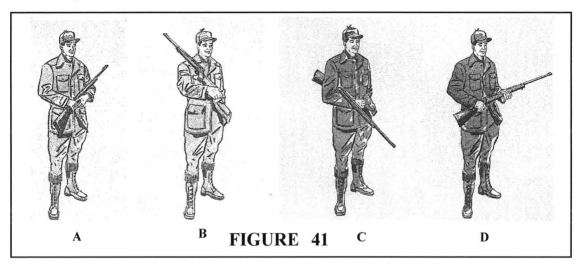

A   B   **FIGURE 41**   C   D

Pictures Courtesy of the National Rifle Assoc. (NRA) Circa 1957

In all carries the standard rules apply:
  1. Safety is ON.
  2. Your finger is OUTSIDE THE TRIGGER GUARD.
  3. The muzzle is ALWAYS IN A SAFE DIRECTION, AND UNDER CONTROL.

Handling At Home
When handling a rifle, shotgun, muzzleloader, or air rifle at home whether just sitting and holding it or working on it:

  ■ First ALWAYS make sure it is unloaded.
  ■ ALWAYS point the muzzle away from you or any one else nearby.
  ■ When sitting lay it across your lap with your hands away from the trigger *(SEE FIGURE 42-A)*.
  ■ If you are cleaning it or repairing it, put it on a weapon holder of some kind and pointed away from you or anyone nearby *(SEE FIGURE 42-B)*.

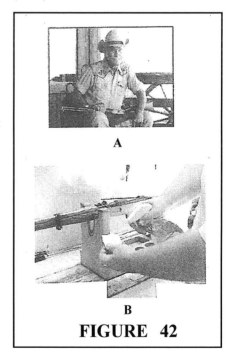

A

B

FIGURE 42

Firing Your Rifle

Firing Rifles In the Field
There are several stable ways to fire rifles out in the field so that it is never a threat to other hunters. First thing, before firing check the area for other hunters, and observe what's behind your target. There are four basic standard positions to fire from, prone, standing, sitting, and kneeling. Leaning, and from high seats and vehicles that are stopped and not running are alternate positions. You also need to know how to sight and aim, and pull the trigger.

What's Behind Your Target

Find out what's behind your intended target. There are state maps for their hunting areas, showing what is in these areas like state parks, firing ranges, hunting clubs, or homes. Know which nearby area your hunting partners might be in. Use Tables 3 and 4 to see approximately how far your ammunition will actually travel in the air. These are not exact, but they will give you an idea how far they will go at line of sight. The tables will not work though for shooting up in the air at an angle. The information we do have is compiled from other sources like ammunition companies, hunting clubs, hunting associations, hunting organizations and the internet, using their information. Once you have an idea what is behind your target, act responsibly and choose not to fire if their is any question about safety in your mind.

Getting Ready to Fire

Get familiar with your gun, know what it's capable of doing. If you have never used the gun before, read the manual ahead of time. If you bought your gun used, go on line at the manufacturers web site and print out a manual. Most guns have a manual on-line that you can print out. If not, buy one from the manufacturer. It will be worth the money. So, before you shoot the gun, especially a new gun:

FIGURE 43

■ Be sure you have followed the instructions for assembly, if required. Conversely, do not disassemble the gun beyond the point the manufacturer recommends.

■ Be sure you understand how the action works and how to properly load and unload your rifle.

■ Be sure you know where the safety mechanism is and how it works here is just one of several types *(SEE FIGURE 43)*. Check your manual!

■ Be sure you understand the steps involved in cleaning your gun. Before loading the gun, make absolutely sure that the inside of the barrel is free of dirt or other objects. Even a small obstruction can result in a serious injury. Never try to remove an object from the barrel by loading another cartridge or shell in behind it and then firing. You could lose a hand or fingers doing this.

■ Be sure you know what the proper ammunition is for your new gun. Ammunition must be the same caliber or gauge as that marked on the firearm, or recommended by the manufacturer. Unfortunately not all firearm barrels are marked. If it is not, then check with the manufacturer or a gun shop to be sure of what ammunition can be used in your particular firearm.

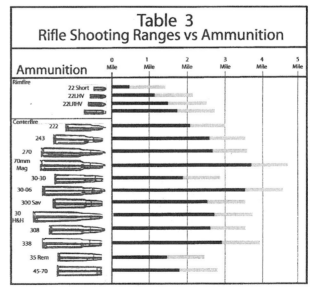

Table 3
Rifle Shooting Ranges vs Ammunition

NOTE: ■■■ = Maximum range at sea level
          ░░░ = Maximum range at 12,000 feet altitude

78

The wrong ammunition could blow up and cause a serious accidental injury. It's a good idea to carry only the proper ammunition for the gun you are shooting. As an example, a 20 gauge shotgun shell will pass through the chamber of a 12 gauge shotgun chamber and lodge in the barrel. So whenever you head out to hunt, check the pockets of your hunting vest or coat to be sure you are carrying only the ammunition specifically intended for the gun you are using.

Table 4
Air Rifle Shooting Distance vs Ammunition

Ammunition / Caliber	0 Yards	10 Yds	20 Yds	30 Yds	40 Yds	50 Yds	80 Yds	100 Yds	500 Yds	1000 Yds	1 Mile
Gammo Pellets .177 Red Fire			1200 FPS MV								
.177 Raptor			1200 FPS MV								
Crosman .177 Destroyer			1000 FPS MV								
Daisy .22 Precision Max			800 FPS MV								
Beeman .22 Crow Magnum											
Predator Inter'nl .22 Predator											
RWS .177 Super-H					1000 FPS MV						
BB's .177 Round Ball			400-600 FPS MV								
.22 Round Ball			400-600 FPS MV								
Shot Shell			400-600 FPS MV								

NOTE: These are the approximate maximum range distances for some of the leading air rifle pellets taken from Velocity Press, www.loadammo.com, and other internet testing data. FPS = Feet Per Second, MV = Muzzle Velocity, ▬▬▬ = Effective Range, ▒▒▒ = Leave Clear Behind Target

After Loading

We will cover more information on ammunition in the section on "Loading and Unloading," and "Ammunitions." After you have loaded your rifle, check the distance to your target, and know what lies beyond your target. Are you within the range of your gun? Have an idea before you leave, or take a copy of our distance tables out hunting with you. Check out our tables for rifles and air rifles *(SEE TABLES 3, 4)*. As you can see in the tables, your shells go a long way past your intended target, especially if you miss the target with your shot. You need to be aware of where your hunting partners, and people living nearby, are located for miles in all directions. When you are sure of your target and what's beyond, then go ahead and sight in on the target, unlock the safety, try to stay relaxed, then pull the trigger. (some the distance information for rifles is taken from "Field & Stream" magazine data. And some information for Air rifles is taken from Gamo and Beeman Data).

Positions for Firing

There are a number of different firing positions you can get into before firing *(SEE FIGURE 44)*. The basic positions are:

- Standing
- Prone
- Sitting
- Kneeling
- Leaning
- High Seats and Vehicles

Standing With a Rifle

The most common position is facing slightly to the right (if right handed) and keep your body upright. Keep your left arm under the fore end of the rifle, with you elbow tucked in or out *(SEE FIGURE 44)*. It's whichever position is more comfortable to you. It may change from firearm to firearm. Using a sling will help stay steady in the standing position *(SEE FIGURE 45)*. But you want to use a military type strap sling. The padded hunting slings may be good for carrying on your back, but they are not as good for shooting. I used the strap when I was in the Army, and as I remember it helped me a lot with the M1 rifle (9.5 pounds). If you have no stick for support, try to lock your arm against your chest and rest the rifle on your hand. When using stick(s) they

Kneeling   Sitting   Standing   Prone

FIGURE 44

FIGURE 45

should be in the perpendicular *(SEE FIGURE 46)* to increase stability. And as a suggestion, try not to remain in the standing position for too long.

Prone

Angle your body to the left axis of the rifle (if right handed) and keep as much of your body in contact with the ground as possible *(SEE FIGURE 44)*. It may be more comfortable to bring your right leg up if you are lying flat to the ground, rather than back and in line with the target. If one is available, use a bipod mount, or put a soft rest (sand bag) under the front hand or under the rifle fore end. Shoot off your elbows only where there is no other choice. When you are using a secure rest (if right handed) pull the rifle firmly into your shoulder with your right hand, and bend your left arm bent across the chest so that the hand supports the right elbow or the toe of the stock, which forms a stable triangle of support.

Sitting

When sitting, either cross your legs or dig your heels into the ground with your legs apart *(SEE FIGURE 44)*; face slightly to the right (if right handed). Rest both of your elbows on the inside of your knees and use a stick (or extended bipod) to steady the rifle fore end if possible.

Kneeling

If you are right handed, kneel down sitting on the right heel of your right foot, with your right knee on the ground *(SEE FIGURE 44)*. Rest your left elbow on your left knee, while keeping your other elbow under the rifle or locked against the body. Use a stick (or extended bipod) to steady your front hand or the rifle where possible.

Leaning

Use a soft rest under your left hand, or the rifle fore end if leaning on something like a wall. If a tree or post is being used, never rest the rifle barrel against it. It is usually more steady to lean your body against the tree and use a stick (or better two sticks) to support the rifle fore end *(SEE FIGURE 46)*.

High Seats and Vehicles

A soft pad can be made from some material and taped over a shooting rail like a seat back. Or a soft pad, bean bag, or sand bag can be used on the vehicle roof or fitted to the vehicle frame.

Shooting Your Rifle

Sighting and Aiming

Almost all rifles come equipped with some type of "iron sights." This term refers to the standard front and rear sight combination. This usually comes in the form of a post or blade on the top, front end of the barrel or slide, and either an open (block) or closed (aperture or peep) at the top rear of the slide or receiver. Lining up the front straight bar and rear parts so that they produce the proper "sight picture" will result in the bullet striking the target right where you intend it to hit *(SEE FIGURE 47)*. You will find most rifle sights are adjustable for elevation, so that you can end up with the same proper sight picture on a target that is far away. Also some sights are adjustable for windage (side-to-side) to counter the effects of wind on your shot. The down side for these sights are that most beginning hunters are not going to get properly sighted into their target with them. Too many adjustments, too many problems, plus you may miss your target a lot. In fact you would probably spend more money on ammunition trying to sight them in than you would on an economical scope.

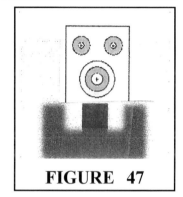

FIGURE 47

The other type of sight is called a "scope." This is the best way to go. And they are adjustable *(SEE FIGURE 48, Basic Scope Shown)*. Once your scoped rifle has been bore sighted for 100 yards, then go to a rifle range and see how it fires, which should offer at least a 25 or 100 yard firing position. Then start at the 25 yard position. Put up a large paper target like an "NRA" 100 yard small bore rifle target, which has a large black bulls-eye. Bring some sand bags to rest either the rifle or your forearm on the hand holding the front of the rifle. Load one round into the chamber and get ready to shoot. Put the cross hairs on the center of that big black bulls-eye, and make your adjustments.

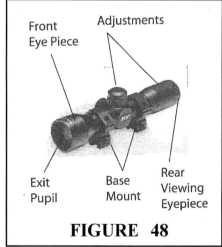

FIGURE 48

Picture Courtesy of Keystone Sporting Arms

Now here is a neat little exercise just before you shoot. Close your eyes for 10 seconds then open them. Did the crosshair drift off the center of the target while your shooting eye was closed? If it did it means that your muscles are under tension trying to keep the rifle on the target. The view from your scope should look something like *FIGURE 49*. Shift your position slightly until you can close your eyes and find that the rifle is still aimed directly at the point of aim when you open them. Now your muscles are properly relaxed and you are in position to do your best shooting. Go through this routine before you fire every shot. Take your shot, then go out and look at your target or retrieve it, then see where your shot went compared to where you aimed.

FIGURE 49

Once you get pretty good at 25 yards, then go out and put up a 100 yard target. The one I hear is good is the "Outers Score Keepers Target" *(SEE FIGURE 50)*. It has a center bulls-eye and 4 smaller bulls-eyes, one in each corner. It's also overlaid with 1" grid lines , which makes it easy to see how far your bullet holes are from the point of your aim. Take 3 shots then check your bullet holes. No need to go out to measure, instead use a spotting scope or some good binoculars. This will save you a lot of steps out at 100 yards. Now estimate the center point of impact for the 3 bullet holes. If you shot well, they should be within about a 3 inch (or smaller) circle some where on the target.

FIGURE 50

This is how you get to know your rifle. Be sure to refer to and read your owner's manual for specific directions on how to adjust your scope. The manual will go over sighting in the weapon. Rifle scope's are more expensive than shotgun scope's. One of the better lower cost 4x scopes are the "Leupold" scopes. Owners say they hold up pretty good, better than some of the others. And believe me there are a bunch of them. Best thing to do is get a demonstration then try it out yourself. One more thing to suggest. Get a good pair of binoculars to check your target and to look for and scout your game, DO NOT use your scope to spot for game.

Pulling the Trigger

Firing you gun by pulling the trigger is not as simple as it sounds. It really depends on what type of game you are shooting at and what kind of gun you are using. The best way to get the feel for the correct trigger pull is to practice. This is called "dry firing." It's practicing at home with an empty gun. Actually this is crucial to success in the field or on the shooting range. It really depends on which rifle you are using. Almost each rifle has a some special type of trigger that they say is better than on other rifles. Basically, rifle triggers are ment to have a slow, gentle squeeze. In most rifle shooting situations, including most hunting, precise shot placement is more important than trigger pulling speed. Instead of pulling a rifle trigger back suddenly, you gradually add pressure at the same rate to the trigger, with the sights correctly aligned, until the rifle fires. This keeps the rifle pointed steadily at your target and helps avoid flinching.

Trigger Types

There are a number of trigger pulling types, but basically there are three types of rifle triggers:

- Single Stage
- Two Stage
- Set Triggers

Single Stage

Most triggers on sporting, and target rifles today are single stage triggers. They ideally have no movement before releasing at their set weight, and when they fire they move only far enough rearward to release the sear. This type of trigger is great for achieving a surprise break. The feel of the perfect trigger is compared to that of breaking a glass rod. Most triggers supplied on brand new guns today are single stage triggers, but they are not properly adjusted when you get your rifle.

Two Stage

The two stage trigger *(SEE FIGURE 51)* is most common on military rifles and is supposed to be safer than a single stage trigger. The two stage trigger has a long initial movement. The shooter pulls the trigger back to take up this slack until a sharply increased resistance is felt (that is the first stage). Then the actual surprise break that will fire the rifle is begun, and from that point on the two stage trigger operates like a single stage trigger. Air rifles generally have a two stage trigger.

Set Triggers

The set trigger allows the shooter to have a greatly reduced trigger pull (the resistance of the trigger) while maintaining a degree of safety in the field. There are two types: "Single set" and "Double set." A single set trigger is usually one trigger that may be fired with a conventional amount of trigger pull weight, or may be set by usually pushing forward on the trigger. This takes up the creep in the trigger and allows the shooter to enjoy a much lighter trigger pull. The double set trigger accomplishes the same thing as the single set trigger, but uses two triggers; one sets the trigger and the other fires the rifle. Set triggers are most likely to be found on customized rifles and competition rifles where a lighter trigger pull is beneficial for accuracy. Some air rifles use them.

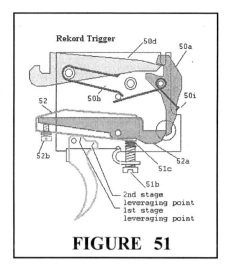

FIGURE 51

Taking Care Of Your Rifle (Maintenance)

Now, lets say you just got your rifle. The next step is taking care of it. In other words, maintenance. This is all part of "*hunter safety*". If your rifle fails because of a malfunction due to the lack of maintenance, you or someone near you could get hurt. First, be absolutely sure your weapon is UNLOADED. When the season is over, or after being used, it is recommended that you disassemble your weapon, clean it, re-lubricate it, oil the stock, then return it to it's storage place. Before you start to clean, check your owners manual that came with the rifle, for maintenance instructions. If you bought a used weapon, and don't have a manual, check on the internet for one. I randomly checked and found several that are free that you can just print out. Or contact the manufacturer for a manual. If you need to pay for it, they are not very expensive, it's worth the money.

Cleaning And Lubricating

There are a number of slightly different ways to clean and lubricate your firearm. You can break most of them down to the stock, the action, and the barrel. Check the barrel. Should any powder or dirt accumulate, they can be easily removed. Most manufacturers say push a patch moistened with a good solvent, made for firearm cleaning, through the barrel from the muzzle end. Next soak a bronze or brass brush with the solvent and run it through the barrel several times, using long even strokes. Push the clean patches through in the same manner until the last patch comes out clean. Then push a lightly oiled patch through the length of the bore. Use a wire brush soaked in solvent to remove any powder or dirt residue from the trigger assembly, the bolt, extractors, receivers, and all other operating parts. Place a thin film of high-pressure gun grease around the pivot pins and other moving parts inside of the receiver and action, and on the front curved frame surfaces that mate with the fore end (forestock). Wipe all parts dry, oil lightly with gun oil preservative, and re-assemble.

Cleaning And Oiling Stocks

There are a number of slightly different ways to clean and oil your rifle stock. You can break most rifles down to just the stock. Remove any accumulation of dirt or other debris from the stock with a clean cloth. If it's a wood stock, you may want to periodically oil it with "Milsek Furniture Cleaner" and polisher. It will make the stock look better than brand new.

NOTE:

We will show some general diagrams for the different types of rifles. This is so that you can familiarize yourself with the general part names of the different parts of the rifle, and see where they are located.

Bolt Action

Typical Basic Parts Location:

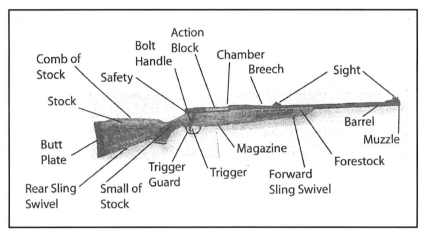

Lever Action

Typical Basic Parts Location:

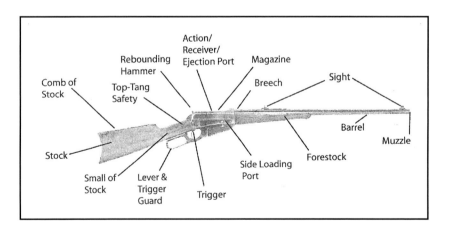

Pump Action

Typical Basic Parts Location:

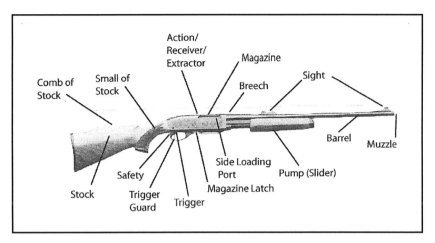

Semi Automatic Action

Typical Basic Parts Location:

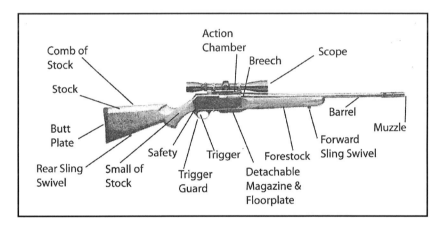

Pneumatic (Air)

Typical Basic Parts Location:

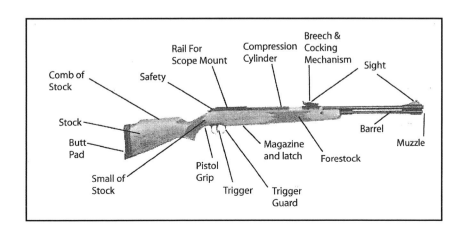

Rifle Storage

Storage is also a big part of rifle safety. Putting rifles in a safe place (UNLOADED) for storage is extremely important. Many hunters just put their rifle up high in a closet someplace, thinking nobody will bother it there. But little kids are very inquisitive! They are fascinated by firearms. It's not uncommon for them to go find your rifle while you are not home, get it down, and attempt to see how it works, or just play with it. And often during play they point it at a brother, sister, or friend and pull the trigger. If you forgot to UNLOAD it, someone will get injured or killed. So what you need to do is put all your rifles in a cabinet or safe, and under lock and key. And you should never store the ammunition in the same place as the rifle, even if they are under lock and key. And your kids should never know where the key is. Also see basic "Gun and Shooting Device Storage" on page 26.

Cabinets and Safe's

There are a number of slightly different types of Safe's and cabinets to store your firearms in. I like the ones with metal doors and no glass front *(SEE FIGURE 52-A)*. This way small, inquisitive kids can't see what's inside. They are not all that expensive. You can find them on the internet for $100 to $150. Wood cabinets are nice and they look pretty, but someone could see guns inside, break the glass and get in *(SEE FIGURE 52-B)*. If you can't afford a safe or cabinet, at least put a trigger lock on all your firearms. They are not that expensive either. You can get them for about $10 to $20 each. Also I

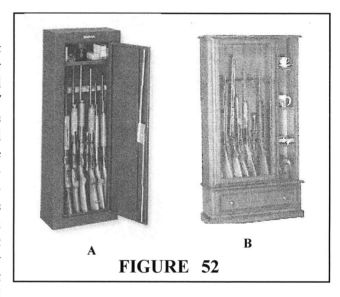

FIGURE 52

suggest a small safe somewhere in another part of the house to store you ammunition in. Don't put it in the same place as the firearms. This is just one more level of safety.

Loading and Unloading Your Rifle

Explanation

Loading and unloading your rifle can be dangerous. Much caution should be taken. We advise you to get out the manual on your firearm and read the section very carefully where it shows you how the do this. Each type of rifle can be a little different. We will give you the basics of doing this just to give you a general picture. The manuals go into great detail, and we don't have room in this handbook to cover every possible little detail for every rifle.

Loading and Unloading Rifles

There are different types of "actions" for rifles. Basically you have "bolt action," "lever action," "pump action," and "semi automatic action." Each one is a little different. One big problem with unloading is a shell getting stuck somewhere down the barrel. And then when you check it for safety reasons, you don't notice it. As an example, you pull back the bolt, and a shell in the chamber comes out, so you think it's unloaded. That happened to me in the Army. The shell came out, and I did not notice that a shell was stuck or wedged somewhere down in the barrel. So later

86

on while jogging back to the barracks from the rifle range it became unlodged and slipped down into the chamber because I was carrying the rifle at "port arms" (at about straight up and down). Then somehow my finger hit the trigger, because I was NOT holding the rifle correctly, and the rifle fired up in the air. I was just lucky it didn't hit anyone next to me. Not that this would happen to you while you are hunting, but it shows how a strange little series of events can accidentally happen and possibly cause a serious injury.

Loading a Bolt Action Rifle

Here are a couple of safety measures to take before you attempt to load your bolt action rifle:

1. Never attempt to load your rifle with ammunition that does not meet the cartridge designation stamped on the barrel. Only use clean, dry, factory loaded ammunition which conforms to the industry standards.

2. Before loading your rifle always check the bore and chamber to be sure they are free of grease, oil, or any other obstruction. Always be sure the chamber is empty, the bolt is open, and the "safety" is on SAFE. And always make sure your hands are NOT near the muzzle of a loaded rifle.

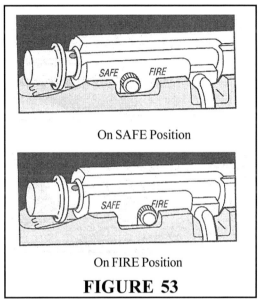

On SAFE Position

On FIRE Position

FIGURE 53

Note: Remember some rifles are single shot and have no magazine while others have a multi-shot magazine. Also never put a slide button safety, or any safety, half way between the SAFE and FIRE positions just before you start to load *(SEE FIGURE 53)*. Because unless it's all the way forward or all the way to the back, you can not be sure if it's on SAFE or FIRE. And accidents happen as I have previously explained!

Loading a Single Cartridge

Many rifles can be loaded with a single cartridge, provided the magazine is empty. To put in a cartridge, open the bolt and put the safety on SAFE. Next put the cartridge, bullet end towards the muzzle, directly into the chamber *(SEE FIGURE 54)*, pushing down with your thumb.

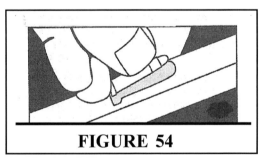

FIGURE 54

Rifles with a Tubular Magazine

Here is a warning: 1. Never add a cartridge to a partially loaded tubular magazine. The rifle will not function properly unless the inner magazine tube is locked securely in place. First open the bolt by lifting the bolt handle and pulling it all the way back. Then, with the safety on SAFE, keeping your fingers away from the muzzle, turn the rifle upside down and unlock the inner magazine tube by turning the knurled locking end plug *(SEE FIGURE 55)*. Next pull the inner tube out until the loading port is open. Then insert the cartridges, the bullet end

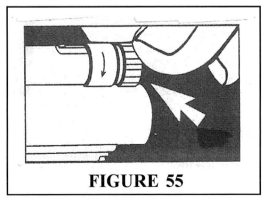

FIGURE 55

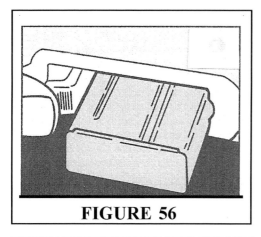

FIGURE 56

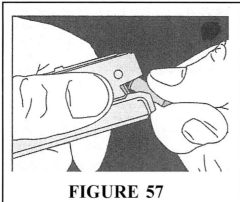

FIGURE 57

towards the muzzle *(SEE FIGURE 54)*. When you have loaded up to the magazine capacity (12 cartridges for 22 Win. Mag. Rimfire, and .17 Hornady Mag. Rimfire models); 25 for short, 19 for long, or 17 Long Rifle cartridges for the model 981T, then slide the inner tube back in place, turning it slightly to ease passage over the loaded rounds. DO NOT force the tube down. Next rotate the knurled locking end plug to the locked position. Note: the inner tube will not lock in place if the number of cartridges you load exceeds the manufacturers stated magazine capacity.

Rifles with a Clip Magazine

To load a clip magazine, first open the bolt by lifting the bolt handle and then pull it all the way back. Then with the safety on SAFE, remove any magazine in the rifle by pressing the release button as shown *(SEE FIGURE 56)*. Now insert up to seven cartridges into the magazine. As you load them, push the cartridges down and rearward *(SEE FIGURE 57)*. Next replace the loaded magazine, and make sure it locks in place.

Unloading a Bolt Action Rifle
Rifles with a Single Cartridge
To unload a single cartridge rifle, first put the safety on SAFE, then while pointing the rifle in a safe direction, open the bolt and eject the loaded cartridge from the chamber. Then just to be safe, point the muzzle up in the air, to let any loose cartridges fall back down into the chamber, then open and close the bolt several more times.

Rifles with a Tube Magazine
To unload a rifle with a tubular magazine, cycle the action over and over by opening and closing the bolt, until the ejection of cartridges coming out stops. When the last cartridge has been ejected, the bright orange plastic follower will be visible in the feed throat. Note: The inner magazine tube MUST be locked in place to unload the rifle. Caution: Completely open and close the bolt several more times to be certain that both the chamber and the feed mechanism are empty.

Rifles with a Clip Magazine
To unload a clip magazine, first open the bolt by lifting the bolt handle and then pull it all the way back. Then with the safety on SAFE, remove the clip magazine by pressing the button. Then only reinsert the clip again when you are ready to shoot. Finally, inspect the interior of the receiver visually, then leave the bolt in the open position.

Unloading if the Rifle Fails to Fire
Misfires: If you squeeze the trigger and the cartridge does not fire, remain in your shooting position and count to 10. Then operate the bolt to eject the misfired cartridge from the rifle.
Underpowered Shot: An underpowered shot is usually if the ammunition is fresh, clean, and factory loaded. However, if you hear an unusual sound or low report, you should stop shooting immediately and proceed as follows:

Warning No. 1: Because the bullet may actually still be in the barrel, you must unload completely and then, with the bolt removed *(SEE FIGURE 58)*, use a cleaning rod from the breech end to see if there is any obstruction. If there is, it should be removed by a qualified gunsmith. Otherwise, personal injury or damage to the rifle could result. DO NOT remove bolt prior to ensuring that the rifle is unloaded.

Warning No. 2: DO NOT attempt to load another cartridge until you have ensured that the chamber and the barrel are clear of the obstruction.

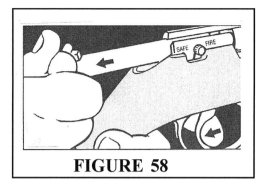

FIGURE 58

Loading a Lever Action Rifle

Warning: Here is a safety measures to take before you attempt to load your lever action rifle. Before loading or firing, always check the bore and chamber to be sure they are free of dirt, grease, oil, or any other obstruction. With the action open, and the hammer block safety on SAFE *(SEE FIGURE 59)*, look through the barrel to see if there is any obstruction, if there is, it must be removed before firing. Otherwise personal injury or damage to the rifle could result.

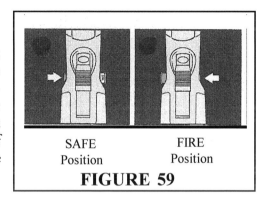

SAFE   FIRE
Position   Position
FIGURE 59

Loading a Single Cartridge

Many rifles can be loaded with a single cartridge. However, the lever action rifle needs to have the safety button on SAFE, the rifle empty, and the lever open. Then place a single cartridge with the bullet forward, in the ejection port, and onto the carrier *(SEE FIGURE 60)*. Now return the lever to the closed position. The cartridge will be fed directly into the cham-

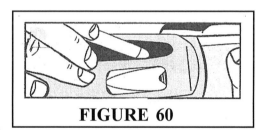

FIGURE 60

ber and the rifle will be cocked and ready to fire when the hammer block safety button is moved to the fire position. Two Warnings on loading:

Warning No. 1: Never attempt to load your rifle with ammunition that does not meet the cartridge designation the rifle. On some rifles it is stamped on the barrel, and on others it is not. Use only ammunition suitable for a tubular magazine rifle. Clean, dry, factory loaded ammunition which conforms to industry standards is recommended.

Warning No. 2: Regarding ammunition: Some pointed and full metal jacket round nose bullets which are on the market can chain fire other cartridges in a tubular magazine during recoil causing severe injury and damage to the rifle. Hornady Lever Revolution ammunition has a soft pointed plastic tip, and can be used safely in your rifle. If you are uncertain about the safety of using a particular cartridge in your rifle, contact the ammunition or bullet manufacturer.

Unloading a Lever Action Rifle

To unload a lever action rifle, first put the hammer in the half cock position and the hammer block safety button on SAFE *(SEE FIGURE 59)*. Next, keeping your fingers away from the trigger, and with the gun pointed in a safe direction, manually eject all cartridges by opening and closing the lever, until you are sure the magazine and chamber are empty *(SEE FIGURE 61)*. The lever must

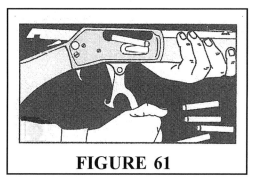

FIGURE 61

be completely closed and then fully opened to ensure proper feeding and ejecting of all cartridges. Then, with the lever in the open position (bolt to the rear), inspect the chamber, carrier and magazine carefully to be sure there are no cartridges left in the rifle.

Warning No. 1: During the unloading process, be sure the hammer block safety button is on SAFE *(SEE FIGURE 59)*, because each time the lever is completely closed (bolt closed), your rifle is cocked and ready to fire. Keep your fingers away from the trigger and be sure the gun is pointed in a safe direction during unloading.

Unloading if the Rifle Fails to Fire

Misfires: If you squeeze the trigger and the hammer falls, but the cartridge does not fire, remain in your shooting position with the gun pointing in a safe direction. Then count to 10. Next open the action. Underpowered Shot: An underpowered shot, or "squib," can usually be detected because you hear an unusual sound or low report, you should stop shooting immediately and proceed as follows:

Warning No. 1: Because the bullet may actually still be in the barrel, you must unload completely and then, with the action open, use a cleaning rod to see if there is any obstruction. If there is, it should be removed by a qualified gunsmith. Otherwise, personal injury or damage to the rifle could result.

Loading a Pump (Slide) Action Rifle
Loading a Single Cartridge

To load a single cartridge into a pump action rifle, first point the rifle in a safe direction. Next engage the safety by pushing in the button so that the red band does NOT show *(SEE FIGURE 62)*. Now pull the fore-end (the pump) fully rearward to open the action. Next put one cartridge of the correct caliber through the ejection port and into the chamber *(SEE FIGURE 63)*. Now push the fore-end (the pump) forward to close the action. The rifle is now loaded and ready to fire. To fire the rifle, push the safety button in from the other side until the "red" band shows. Now you are ready to fire.

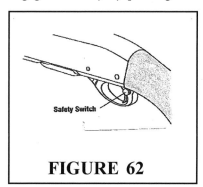

Safety Switch

FIGURE 62

Loading a Magazine and the Chamber

To load the magazine into the chamber of a pump action rifle, first point the rifle in a safe direction. Next engage the safety by pushing in the button so that the red band does not show *(SEE FIGURE 62)*. Now pull the fore-end (the pump) fully rearward to open the action. Next put one cartridge of the correct caliber through the ejection port and into the chamber *(SEE FIGURE 63)*. Now push the fore-end (the pump) forward to close the action. Next push the magazine latch forward and pull the magazine from the receiver. Now put four cartridges of the correct caliber, one at a time, into the magazine. Keep the bullets aligned toward the chamber *(SEE FIGURE 64)*. Next put

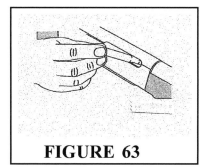

FIGURE 63

the magazine back into the rifle, then make sure it is fully latched into position. The magazine and the chamber are now fully loaded. To fire the rifle disengage the safety button until the red band shows. Now the rifle is ready to fire.

Unloading a Pump (Slide) Action Rifle

To unload a pump action rifle, first point the rifle in a safe direction. Next engage the safety button to the SAFE position by pushing it in. The red band will NOT show. Now push the magazine latch forward, and pull the magazine from the rifle. Next pull the fore-end slowly rearward until the front end of the shell is even with the ejection port. Now lift the front of the shell outward and remove from the ejection port. Next remove all the cartridges from the magazine *(SEE FIGURE 65)*. When it is empty replace the magazine in the rifle and open the action.

WARNING: Now check the chamber and the magazine to make sure there are no cartridges anywhere still in the rifle.

Loading a Semi-Automatic Action Rifle
Loading a Single Cartridge

To load a single cartridge into a semi-automatic action rifle, the hammer has to be cocked. To cock the hammer the slide needs to pulled all the way rearward. If there is no cartridges in the magazine, the slide will remained locked in it's rearward position. Immediately push the safety to it's ON position *(SEE FIGURE 66)*. The safety is ON when it protrudes fully on the right side of the rifle (the slide handle side). Next put a cartridge into the ejection port, bullet end towards the muzzle.

Then press the lifter latch. This will release the slide (which is attached to the bolt) and the bolt will chamber the cartridge and lock. Next, holding the rifle upside down, and using a cartridge *(SEE FIGURE 67)*, depress the lifter latch and then the lifter in one smooth motion. As the lifter is depressed the rear end of the magazine can be seen. Using the thumb of your right hand, push the cartridge fully into the magazine until the base of the cartridge is held by the inside end of the magazine release button.

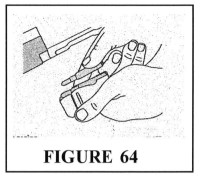

FIGURE 64

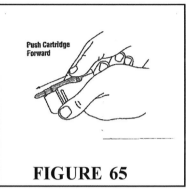

Push Cartridge Forward

FIGURE 65

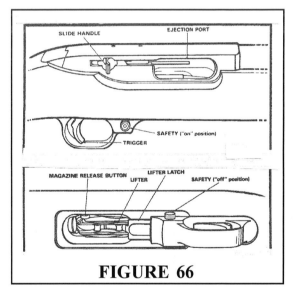

SLIDE HANDLE   EJECTION PORT

SAFETY ("on" position)

TRIGGER

MAGAZINE RELEASE BUTTON   LIFTER LATCH
LIFTER   SAFETY ("off" position)

FIGURE 66

A maximum of 4 cartridges can be loaded into the magazine this way. And don't forget, there is one cartridge already in the chamber. The rifle is now fully loaded and ready to fire. To fire the rifle, push the safety button to the "off" position. Now you are ready to fire. DO NOT touch the trigger though until you are actually ready to fire. Each time the trigger is pulled a cartridge is fired and then, automatically, an empty cartridge case is extracted and ejected, and a new cartridge is chambered. This continues until all the cartridges are fired. After the last shot has been fired the slide will remain locked open. Always move the safety to the "ON" position as soon as the firing sequence is completed.

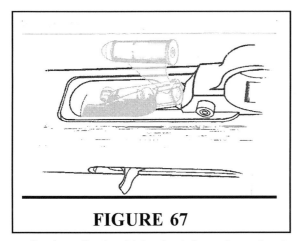

FIGURE 67

WARNING No.1: Ejection of fired cases. When firing make sure that bystanders are well clear of you and standing a safe distance in the rear. Empty cartridges are ejected to the right side of the rifle with some velocity, and could cause some injury to any person who is standing too closely alongside of you. Left handed shooters should be particularly cautious concerning ejected cartridge cases and should wear shooting glasses to avoid the possibility of injury from the ejected cartridge cases and particles of powder. All shooters should wear suitable shooting glasses when firing this rifle. Actually the rifle should be fired from the right shoulder to avoid this problem.

WARNING No.2: Handling. Do not load the rifle until you are ready to use it, and unload it immediately when you have completed shooting. Do Not chamber a cartridge until you are in the immediate area where you plan to shoot. Always put the safety in the SAFE position before chambering a cartridge, and never carry the rifle loaded with the safety in the FIRE position. When the safety is off, the rifle is in the fire mode. So any accidental little blow or jar may be a sufficient force to actuate components of the firing mechanism, and may cause a chambered cartridge to discharge. Such a discharge can occur with or without the trigger being directly struck or touched. A shooter should always be alert to the possibility of accidental discharge regardless of the position of the safety. The only SAFE rifle is one in which the bolt is open and the chamber and magazine are empty.

WARNING No.3: Loading. Be certain the primer of each cartridge is seated flush with, or below, the surface of the cartridge case base. A primer discharged by the impact of the closing breech mechanism can result in a premature discharge of the cartridge with possible serious injury to the shooter and those nearby. Also DO NOT attempt to force the slide handle to close over a cartridge. If a cartridge does not chamber readily, check the bore and chamber to be certain they are free of obstructions. If they are clear, and a cartridge does not chamber readily, then check the cartridge to be certain it is the proper caliber, and of the correct dimensions, for the rifle.

Loading a Magazine

Loading a cartridge directly into the chamber can be eliminated if you want to only load a magazine. To load just the magazine, the slide should be released so that it is fully forward before a cartridge is loaded into the magazine. If an attempt IS MADE to load the magazine while the slide is in it's rearward position, the slide will "slam" forward as soon as the cartridge is pressed against the lifter latch.

Unloading a Semi-Automatic Action Rifle

To unload a semi-automatic action rifle, first point the rifle in a safe direction. Next engage the safety by pushing it to the on position *(SEE FIGURE 66)*. If the safety can not be moved to the "ON" position it may be because the hammer is not cocked. However, there is no need to cock the rifle in this situation. If this happens instead turn the rifle upside down *(SEE FIGURE 67)* and press the magazine release button with your thumb. Then one at a time the cartridges can be removed from the magazine.

WARNING No.1: When emptying the magazine be certain every cartridge is removed. However, DO NOT trust your "feel." Visually inspect and be certain the magazine follower is visible.

WARNING No.2: Emptying the magazine does not prevent the rifle from being fired. Check the chamber after emptying the magazine to be certain the chamber is also empty.

Unloading if the Rifle Fails to Fire or Malfunctions

First avoid and minimize "jams" and "malfunctions" by keeping your rifle clean and oiled. The slide needs to be fully rearward so that it locks in place at the end of the stroke. Locking the slide prevents it from moving forward and possibly jamming the cartridge if it was not thrown clear of the receiver. NOTE: The slide can not be locked in it's rearward position when there are cartridges, even just one, still in the magazine.

Misfires: If you squeeze the trigger and the hammer falls, but the cartridge does not fire, remain in your shooting position with the gun pointing in a safe direction. Then count to 10. Next open the action.

Underpowered Shot: An underpowered shot, or "squib," can usually be detected because you hear an unusual sound or low report, you should then stop shooting immediately and proceed as follows:

WARNING No.3: Because the bullet may actually still be in the barrel, you must unload completely and then, with the action open, carefully use a cleaning rod to see if there is any obstruction. If there is, it should be removed by a qualified gunsmith. Otherwise, accidental personal injury or damage to the rifle could result.

Loading a Pneumatic Air Rifle

First, you need to realize there are basically two types of ammunition. There are pellets and there are BB's. The pellets are similar to bullets, and the BB's are round like small ball bearings. Note: Loading all air rifles is not exactly the same.

Loading a Single Pellet into an Air Rifle

To load a single pellet into an pneumatic air rifle, first put the rifle on SAFE *(SEE FIGURE 68)*. Make sure you are only using the manufacturers recommend size of ammunition (pellet). Next point the rifle in a safe direction. Now pull the bolt all the way back *(SEE FIGURE 69)*. Place one pellet, nose forward *(SEE FIGURE 70)*, in the loading port (breech). Next, lightly push the pellet into the barrel by closing and locking the bolt. DO NOT jam the bolt forward though because this will damage your rifle. Now be sure the bolt is closed before firing. If it is not closed and fully locked, air may remain in the rifle and the pellet may not be discharged.

Loading BB's into an Air Rifle (BB Gun)

To load BB's into the BB gun air rifle, first open the bolt *(SEE FIGURE 68-A)* by pulling the handle back. Next put the trigger safety to the "ON" position *(SEE FIGURE 68-B)*. Follow that

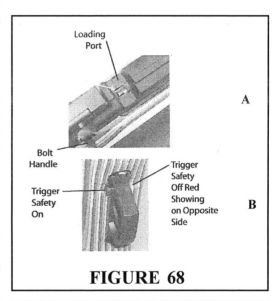

FIGURE 68

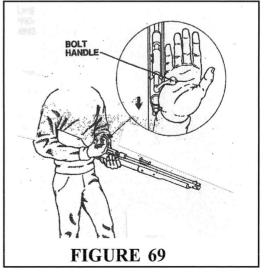

FIGURE 69

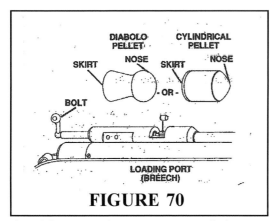

FIGURE 70

by pumping your rifle. Do that by pulling the lever outward for a full stroke then return. **NOTE**: The bolt must be open to pump the rifle. For greater safety the manufacturer recommends that the bolt remain open while pumping and that you only close the bolt when the barrel can be pointed in a safe direction.

With the muzzle pointed in a safe direction, pump the gun the desired number of times up to 10. By the way more power means a greater chance of serious injury. **NOTE**: DO NOT pump the gun more than 10 times. Muzzle energy increases that are produced by more than 10 pumps will damage your rifle.

CAUTION No.1: Be sure you grasp the pump handle firmly as you close the lever to prevent it from snapping back and causing a possible injury. Also be very careful to keep your fingers out of the cocking mechanism when closing the lever. There are three" pinch points" to be careful of *(SEE FIGURE 71)*.

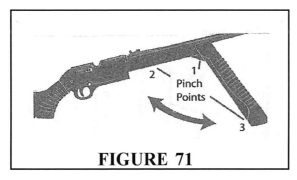

FIGURE 71

WARNING No.1: DO NOT open the bolt, then close the bolt, and then pull the trigger before pumping. This procedure can result in a loaded gun, and a projectile being propelled from the gun during pumping. Instead, recock the bolt by opening the bolt and put the trigger safety to "ON" before pumping.

Filling The Magazine : To fill the magazine, find the loading door which is located on the left side of the receiver on the rifle *(SEE FIGURE 72)*. Next push the door down and fill the magazine with approximately 50 BB's. DO NOT overfill or the feed system may not operate properly. Now, with the bolt handle back and BB's in the magazine, raise the muzzle of the gun up 45 degrees to 90 degrees. When raising the muzzle, make sure the front sight is pointed upward since the gun may not feed properly if it is on it's side *(SEE FIGURE 73-A)*. A BB can be seen on the magnetic tip by looking into the loading port *(SEE FIGURE 73-B)*. If a BB does not feed into the magnetic tip when the muzzle is raised, shake the gun slightly. Now, push the bolt

FIGURE 72

handle fully forward and the BB is in the firing position. **NOTE**: Be sure the front sight is pointed upward when raising the muzzle to insure proper feeding.

CAUTION No.2: Always view the BB when closing the bolt and loading port.
WARNING No.2: BB's feed from the magazine by gravity which requires that the muzzle be raised. NEVER assume the chamber or magazine is empty, even if the gun does not fire a projectile, always check.

Unloading a Pneumatic Air Rifle

To unload the pellet in the air rifle, first put the rifle on "SAFE" *(SEE FIGURE 74)*. Next pump the rifle 8 times, then point it in a safe direction. Now take it off of "SAFE" and fire the rifle. Another way to unload your rifle is don't reload the rifle. Instead put the safety on "SAFE." Then with the rifle upside down, the bolt in the open position, insert a cleaning rod into the muzzle end of the barrel and gently push the jammed pellet into the pellet loading port which is forward of the bolt *(SEE FIGURE 75)*. However, don't try to reuse the pellet again. If for some reason you are unable to un jam your rifle, most manufacturers will let you return the rifle and they will un-jam it for you. And usually free of charge, especially if it's within the warranty.

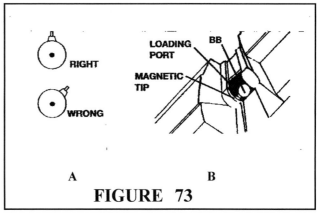

FIGURE 73

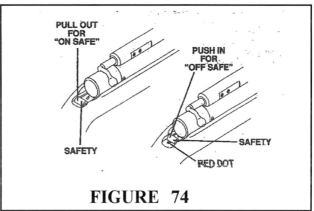

FIGURE 74

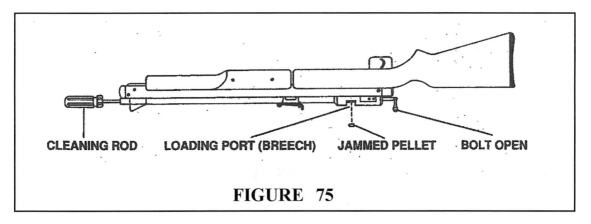

CLEANING ROD   LOADING PORT (BREECH)   JAMMED PELLET   BOLT OPEN

FIGURE 75

Unloading (Emptying) a BB Gun Magazine

To unload BB's in a BB gun air rifle, first open the bolt, then put the safety to the "ON" position *(SEE FIGURE 68-B)*. Next open the magazine door, cup your hand over it and tilt the rifle fully to the left side. Now shake the gun until all the BB's are removed. Then remove any BB's from the loading port *(SEE FIGURE 73-B)*.

Unloading Your BB Gun in Case it Malfunctions or Jams

First open the bolt then immediately put the safety in the "ON" position. If bolt is not completely closed, DO NOT try to close it until after opening it by pulling the bolt handle all the way back. The gun will not fire a projectile when the bolt is completely open. At this point the bolt is closed, then pump the gun up 10 times, and try to fire it again. If projectile still does not fire, follow these steps carefully:

1. Open the bolt. 2. Put trigger safety to "ON." 3. Clear the barrel by running a cleaning rod through from the muzzle end *(SEE FIGURE 75)*. Be careful not to damage the bolt tip by pushing the rod through too hard. When it comes out, do not try to reuse the BB or pellet. 4. Repeat operating steps. Make sure a BB or pellet is fed into the firing position. If after following the firing procedure again the projectile still does not fire, then return the gun to the manufacturer to find the problem.

Summation For Loading and Unloading all the Rifles

Make sure you check your rifle manual before you attempt to load or unload your rifle. This is because your rifle may be slightly different than the one we show (a basic rifle). Follow all the directions for loading and unloading, and make double sure you are loading the correct size of ammunition for your rifle. The information we have is in general, and only here to give you an idea how to load and unload in case you don't have a manual or even a clue how it operates. You can in most cases go on line, download a manual for your exact rifle model, and print it out for the rifle you have, and in most cases it is free.

Ammunition for Your Rifle

Explanation

Now that you understand a little better of how to handle, load and unload your rifle, you need to have some idea of what ammunition to use. We will NOT cover every possible ammunition that can be used in your rifle. There is just too many types of ammunition sources out there, especially for rifles to try and cover them all. We will basically use "Federal" or "Hornady" for our ammunition information, unless otherwise stated. We will NOT mention special target ammunition. We will try to cover the more common ammunitions used in game hunting. We will also use popularity as one of our targets as well as commonality. As an example, if you are going out deer hunting what would you be more likely to use, and which types of rifles use what type of ammunition. You would not want to use a big game rifle and ammunition if you are only mostly going out to hunt Squirrels or rabbits. Depending on what ammunition it was, you might blow them to pieces. In other words "overkill." Bare that in mind as you read on through the section.

> NOTE:
> We will try to chart this out for you in a tables to make it a little easier for you to overview and link the firearm or hunting device, ammo, and game all together, for a quick overview. This will give you a general idea of what firearm or device, ammo, animal or game bird is generally in what class . There are more rifles in the different classes, but we are going to only list the more common and popular firearms or devices in the class. The information we are showing comes from the manufacturers stated information, which may or may not be true. Muzzle velocity on firearms is shown only to give you some idea of the ammunitions force coming out of the barrel.

Rifle Ammo Types

There are a lot of ammo types for rifles because there are more types of rifles out there than any other type of hunting firearm. The main thing to remember is first look on the barrel of your rifle *(SEE FIGURE 76)* where they tell you what caliber to use by stamping it. However, if your rifle is NOT marked and there is any question then consult your manual, a gunsmith, or the company that manufactured your rifle. The wrong ammunition could blow up and cause a serious injury. Many of these companies have a "hot line" for questions. We will break this section down into the different types of rifles, ammo used for the different sizes of game, and whether it commonly used in short range or long range situations.

Our point is to let you know what rifles are recommended for shooting some of the more common types of game animals or birds. A good choice of ammunition will have adequate killing power for your intended quarry, not too much, but not too little either. Your rifle should have enough power to insure a humane kill if you do your part. If your favorite caliber is not mentioned, then look for something similar.

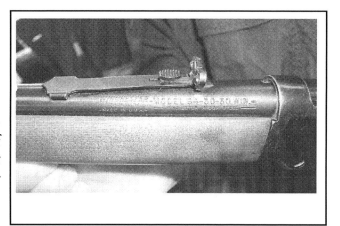

If a cartridge with similar capabilities is included, you can conclude that your favorite ammunition must also be a satisfactory choice. Winchester, Federal, and Hornady have come up with a rating system to divide game animals into four categories. Winchester and Federal list a numerical value from 1 through 4 for their rifle ammunition. Hornady HITS are more precise for individual cartridges, but also indicate similar game weight classes. These numbers are supposed to be a general guide for the appropriate hunting application (game weight) of the various loads for centerfire rifle cartridges. They call this the "CPX Rating System for Hunting Cartridges." CPX stands for "Controlled eXpansion Performance." We put this info in some handy little tables for you in this section for a quick overview.

CPX RATING TABLE

CPX CLASS	ANIMALS COVERED IN THIS CLASSIFICATION
CPX1 This class calls for bullets that will expand very rapidly or fragment on impact. Hornady V-Max, Remington Power Lokt are examples.	Composed of Small Game: Varmits, and small predators that weigh up to 50 pounds. Typical examples are species like sand rats, prarie dogs, woodchucks, marmots, coyotes, javelina. It also includes squirrels, and rabbits.
CPX2 This class calls for bullets that have controlled expansion which are best for this class. Hornady Interlock, Remington Core- Lokt, Winchester Power Point are examples.	Composed of Intermediate Size Game: Generally light framed animals with relatively thin skin and light muscles and bones. Typical examples are species like Deer, antalope, sheep, goats, black bear, boar, feral pigs, some north american caribou. They typically weigh about 51 to 300 pounds.
CPX3 This class calls for bullets that are designed for delayed, controlled expansion and deep penetration which is best for this class. Hornady InterBond, Remngton Core- Lokt, Winchester fail safe, partition gold are examples.	Composed of Large Size Game: Generally large framed, heavy animals with tough skin, heavy muscle tissue and bones. Typicals examples are species like elk, moose, alg, zebra, kudu, eland, brown bear, some north american caribou, lions, tigers, grizzly, brown and polar bears. They typically weigh about 301 to over 1000 pounds.
CPX4 This class calls for expanding bullets that are heavily constructed which is needed for this class. A-Square Dead Tough, Barnes X-Bullet, Trophy Bonded Bear Claw are examples.	Composed of Extra Large Size Game: Generally thick skin game. Typical examples are cape buffalo, hippo, rhino, and elephant. It also includes Asian and Australian wild water buffalo, guar, and american bison. They typically weigh about 1000 pounds up to 12,000 pounds.

TABLE 5 RIFLES FOR SMALL GAME & VARMINTS								
MFR ↓ Muzzel Velocity MV (FPS) →	Ammunition Caliber					Barrel Length	Game Class	Relative Cost
	.22 (Short) HV-HP	.22 (Long) LR	.22 WMR (22 Mag)	.17 M2	.17 HMR			
	1045	1500	2000	2000	2550			
BOLT ACTION RIFLES								
	Where to Take the Shot on Game [1]					22 Inch	CPX1	Exp
Remington Model 5- 22 LR	Anywhere on Body Up To 25 Yds.	Anywhere on Body Up To 85 Yds.	Head Shots Only Up To 125 Yds	Anywhere on Body Up To 85 Yds.	Head Shots Only Up To 165 Yds			
Cricket 22 Cal. Youth	Anywhere on Body Up To 25 Yds.	Anywhere on Body Up To 85 Yds.	Head Shots Only Up To 125 Yds	Anywhere on Body Up To 85 Yds.	Head Shots Only Up To 165 Yds	16-1/8 Inch	CPX1 (Only Mice, Rats, Small Birds for SR)	Very Rea
Winchester Wildcat, Model CMZ 453	Anywhere on Body Up To 25 Yds.	Anywhere on Body Up To 85 Yds.	Head Shots Only Up To 125 Yds	Anywhere on Body Up To 85 Yds.	Head Shots Only Up To 165 Yds	20.9-21 In.	CPX1	Exp
Ruger Model 10/22, 77 22 Cal.	Anywhere on Body Up To 25 Yds.	Anywhere on Body Up To 85 Yds.	Head Shots Only Up To 125 Yds	Anywhere on Body Up To 85 Yds.	Head Shots Only Up To 165 Yds	18.5-24 Inch	CPX1	Exp
Savage Model Mark II, 93R 22 Cal.	Anywhere on Body Up To 25 Yds.	Anywhere on Body Up To 85 Yds.	Head Shots Only Up To 125 Yds	Anywhere on Body Up To 85 Yds.	Head Shots Only Up To 165 Yds	20.75-22 Inch	CPX1	Rea
Marlin Model 883, 925, 917 22 Cal.	Anywhere on Body Up To 25 Yds.	Anywhere on Body Up To 85 Yds.	Head Shots Only Up To 125 Yds	Anywhere on Body Up To 85 Yds.	Head Shots Only Up To 165 Yds	22 Inch	CPX1	Mid
LEVER ACTION RIFLES								
	Where to Take the Shot on Game [1]					22-24 Inch	CPX1	Exp
Marlin Model 5, 39A 22 Cal.	Anywhere on Body Up To 25 Yds.	Anywhere on Body Up To 85 Yds.	Head Shots Only Up To 125 Yds	Anywhere on Body Up To 85 Yds.	Head Shots Only Up To 165 Yds			
Henry Model H001, Golden Boy- 22 Cal.	Anywhere on Body Up To 25 Yds.	Anywhere on Body Up To 85 Yds.	Head Shots Only Up To 125 Yds	————	Head Shots Only Up To 165 Yds	18.25-20.5 Inch	CPX1	Very Rea
Winchester Model 9422, 9417- 22 Cal.	Anywhere on Body Up To 25 Yds.	Anywhere on Body Up To 85 Yds.	Head Shots Only Up To 125 Yds	Anywhere on Body Up To 85 Yds.	Head Shots Only Up To 165 Yds	20.5-22.5 Inch	CPX1	Mid
Ruger Model 96 22 Cal.	Anywhere on Body Up To 25 Yds.	Anywhere on Body Up To 85 Yds.	Head Shots Only Up To 125 Yds	Anywhere on Body Up To 85 Yds.	Head Shots Only Up To 165 Yds	17-19 Inch	CPX1	Mid
Browning Model BL-17, BL-22- 22 Cal.	Anywhere on Body Up To 25 Yds.	Anywhere on Body Up To 85 Yds.	Head Shots Only Up To 125 Yds	Anywhere on Body Up To 85 Yds.	Head Shots Only Up To 165 Yds	20-24 Inch	CPX1	High Mid

Abbreviation Definitions:
HV-HP = High Velocity, Hollow Point, Rea = Reasonable, Mid = Mid Range, Exp = Expensive, Mag = Magnum, WMR =Winchester Magnum Rimfire, HMR = Hornady Magnum Rimfire, M2 = Mach 2, FPS = Feet Per Second
NOTE [1] : With what ammo to take a head shot with to keep from blowing a small animal to pieces.

Small Game Animals (CPX1)

Small game animals are usually rabbit, squirrel, fox, and small varmint's *(SEE TABLES 5-7)*. The rifles we will cover are the "bolt action," the "lever action," the "pump action," the "single shot" (any action), the "autoloading action," the "youth" (any action), and the "pneumatic (air) rifle" types. Some important suggestions. Are you just going out to shoot varmint's and small pests, or are you going out for game to eat such as rabbits and squirrels. If you notice on the "game" tables, some say "head shots only at xxx yards." This is because the bullets have such a high muzzle

TABLE 6   RIFLES FOR SMALL GAME & VARMINTS

MFR ↓ Muzzel Velocity MV (FPS) →	Ammunition Caliber					Barrel Length	Game Class	Relative Cost
	.22 (Short) HV-HP	.22 (Long) L, LR	.22 WMR (22 Mag)	.17 M2	.17 HMR			
	1045	1500	2000	2000	2550			
PUMP ACTION RIFLES								
	Where to Take the Shot on Game [1]							
Henry Model H003T, H003 TM- 22 Cal.	Anywhere on Body Up To 25 Yds.	Anywhere on Body Up To 85 Yds.	Head Shots Only Up To 125 Yds	—	—	19.75-20.5 Inch	CPX1	Mid
Remington Model 572 BDL- 22 Cal.	Anywhere on Body Up To 25 Yds.	Anywhere on Body Up To 85 Yds.	Head Shots Only Up To 125 Yds	—	—	21 Inch	CPX1	Mid
SINGLE SHOT (ANY ACTION) RIFLES								
	Where to Take the Shot on Game [1]							
Henry Acu- Bolt Model 22 Cal.	Anywhere on Body Up To 25 Yds.	Anywhere on Body Up To 85 Yds.	Head Shots Only Up To 125 Yds	—	Head Shots Only Up To 165 Yds	20 Inch	CPX1	Rea
H & R Ultra Hunter Model 22 Cal.	Anywhere on Body Up To 25 Yds.	Anywhere on Body Up To 85 Yds.	Head Shots Only Up To 125 Yds	Anywhere on Body Up To 85 Yds.	Head Shots Only Up To 165 Yds	20-22 Inch	CPX1	Rea
Dakota Model 10 22 Cal.	Anywhere on Body Up To 25 Yds.	Anywhere on Body Up To 85 Yds.	Head Shots Only Up To 125 Yds	Anywhere on Body Up To 85 Yds.	Head Shots Only Up To 165 Yds	23 Inch	CPX1	Exp
NEF Sportster Model 22 Cal.	Anywhere on Body Up To 25 Yds.	Anywhere on Body Up To 85 Yds.	Head Shots Only Up To 125 Yds	Anywhere on Body Up To 85 Yds.	Head Shots Only Up To 165 Yds	20 Inch	CPX1	Very Rea
Savage Mark Mark 1 Model 22 Cal.	Anywhere on Body Up To 25 Yds.	Anywhere on Body Up To 85 Yds.	Head Shots Only Up To 125 Yds	—	Head Shots Only Up To 165 Yds	21 Inch	CPX1	Rea
Stevens Model 30G, 30-TD, R 22 Cal.	Anywhere on Body Up To 25 Yds.	Anywhere on Body Up To 85 Yds.	Head Shots Only Up To 125 Yds	—	Head Shots Only Up To 165 Yds	20-24 Inch	CPX1	Rea
T/C Contender G2 Model 22 Cal.	Anywhere on Body Up To 25 Yds.	Anywhere on Body Up To 85 Yds.	Head Shots Only Up To 125 Yds	Anywhere on Body Up To 85 Yds.	Head Shots Only Up To 165 Yds	23 Inch	CPX1	Mid
Winchester 1885, Low Wall- 22 Cal.	Anywhere on Body Up To 25 Yds.	Anywhere on Body Up To 85 Yds.	Head Shots Only Up To 125 Yds	Anywhere on Body Up To 85 Yds.	Head Shots Only Up To 165 Yds	24 Inch	CPX1	Exp

Abbreviation Definitions:
HV-HP = High Velocity, Hollow Point, Rea = Reasonable, Mid = Mid Range, Exp = Expensive, Mag = Magnum, WMR =Winchester Magnum Rimfire, HMR = Hornady Magnum Rimfire, M2 = Mach 2, H&R = Harrington & Richardson, NEF = New England Firearms, T/C = Thompson/ Center, FPS = Feet Per Second
NOTE [1] : With what ammo to take a head shot with to keep from blowing a small animal to pieces.

velocity or energy that if you use a body shot up close you may blow the animal apart which is not going to leave much eatable meat. Remember this when using air rifle pellets, if the game you are hunting is to eat then use the non lead pellets to avoid getting lead poisoning. In addition, "*HORNADY*" makes special ammunition called "Varmint Express." This ammunition is designed around the hard hitting performance of their V-Max ™ bullet. The bullets profile and sharp point tip combine for a higher ballistic coefficient, which translates into pinpoint accuracy, even in long range, lower velocity situations. Ask your local ammunition or arms dealer about the "V-Max" ammunition. Here is a way to test your own rifle at different range distances. The experts say shoot at a bar of "Ivory Soap," which very closely simulates the flesh and meat of small game. This will

TABLE 7 RIFLES FOR SMALL GAME & VARMINTS

MFR ↓ Muzzel Velocity MV (FPS) →	Ammunition Caliber					Barrel Length	Game Class	Relative Cost
	.22 (Short) HV-HP	.22 (Long) L, LR	.22 WMR (22 Mag)	.17 M2	.17 HMR			
	1045	1500	2000	2000	2550			
AUTOLOADING ACTION RIFLES								
	Where to Take the Shot on Game [1]							
Marlin Model 60SS, 795 22 Cal.	Anywhere on Body Up To 25 Yds.	Anywhere on Body Up 85 Yds.	———	Anywhere on Body Up To 85 Yds.	———	18-19 Inch	CPX1	Very Rea
Remington Model 597 LSS 22 Cal.	Anywhere on Body Up To 25 Yds.	Anywhere on Body Up 85 Yds.	Head Shots Only Up To 125 Yds	Anywhere on Body Up To 85 Yds.	Head Shots Only Up To 165 Yds	20 Inch	CPX1	Very Rea
Ruger Model 10/22DSP, K10/22T, 10/17 RBR	Anywhere on Body Up To 25 Yds.	Anywhere on Body Up 85 Yds.	Head Shots Only Up To 125 Yds	Anywhere on Body Up To 85 Yds.	Head Shots Only Up To 165 Yds	18.5-20 In.	CPX1	Rea
Savage Model 64 FSS 22 Cal.	Anywhere on Body To 25 Yds.	Anywhere on Body Up 85 Yds.	———	Anywhere on Body Up To 85 Yds.	———	21 Inch	CPX1	Rea
YOUTH (ANY ACTION) RIFLES								
	Where to Take the Shot on Game [1]							
Henry Mini Bolt Model 22 Cal.	Anywhere on Body Up To 25 Yds.	Anywhere on Body Up 85 Yds.	———	———	———	16.25 Inch	CPX1	Rea
Marlin Model 915Y, 915YS 22 Cal.	Anywhere on Body Up To 25 Yds.	Anywhere on Body Up 85 Yds.	———	———	———	16.25 Inch	CPX1	Very Rea
Savage Cub Model 22 Cal.	Anywhere on Body Up To 25 Yds.	Anywhere on Body Up 85 Yds.	———	———	———	16 Inch	CPX1	Very Rea
Savage Mark 1, 1-GY, 1-FVT 22 Cal.	Anywhere on Body Up To 25 Yds.	Anywhere on Body Up 85 Yds.	———	———	———	19-21 In.	CPX1	Very Rea

PNEUMATIC (AIR) RIFLES

MFR Muzzel Velocity MV (FPS) →	Ammunition Caliber					Rifle Length	Game Class	Relitive Cost
	.20 Cal. Pellet	.25 Cal. Pellet	.22 Cal. Pellet	.177 Cal. Pellet	.177 Cal. Pellet			
	700	725	1000+	1350	1600			
	Where to Take the Shot on Game [1]							
Gamo Hunter Extreme .177, .22 Cal.	———	———	Anywhere on Body Up To 30 Yds.	Head Shots only Up To 60 Yds.	Head Shots only Up To 60 Yds.	41.75 to 48.5 Inch	CPX1	Mid
RWS 460 Mag 22, .177 Cal.	———	———	Anywhere on Body Up To 30 Yds.	Head Shots only Up To 60 Yds.	Head Shots only Up To 60 Yds.	43.25 to 45 Inch	CPX1	Mid
Ben. Sheridan .20, .22, .25 Cal.	Head Shots only Up To 60 Yds.	Head Shots only Up To 60 Yds.	Anywhere on Body Up To 30 Yds.	———	———	36.5 to 48.25 Inch	CPX1	Rea
Beeman R1 Carbine .177, .20, .22	Head Shots only Up To 60 Yds.	———	Anywhere on Body Up To 30 Yds.	Head Shots only Up To 60 Yds.	———	40.25 to 46.5 Inch	CPX1	Exp
Crossman NPSS .22 Cal.	———	———	Anywhere on Body Up To 30 Yds.	———	———	43.875 Inch	CPX1	Mid

Abbreviation Definitions:
HV-HP = High Velocity, Hollow Point, Rea = Reasonable, Mid = Mid Range, Exp = Expensive, Mag = Magnum, WMR =Winchester Magnum Rimfire, HMR = Hornady Magnum Rimfire, M2 = Mach 2, FPS = Ft. Per Second
NOTE [1] : With what ammo to take a head shot with to keep from blowing a small animal to pieces.

100

TABLE 8	RIFLES FOR DEER & INTERMEDIATE GAME									
MFR ↓ Muzzel Velocity MV (FPS) →	Ammunition Caliber							Barrel Length	Game Class	Relative Cost
	.30-30 Win 150 Gr	.30-06 Spfd 180 Gr	.243 Win 100 Gr	.270 Win 130 Gr	.308 Win 150 Gr	7mm Rem Mag 150 Gr	.44 Rem Mag 240 Gr			
	1960	2340	2700	2600	2300	2470	1760			
BOLT ACTION RIFLES — Where to Take the Shot on Game										
Winchester Model 70	Anywhere on Body Up To 100 Yds.	Anywhere on Body Up To 200 Yds.	Anywhere on Body Up To 100 Yds.	Anywhere on Body Up To 200 Yds.	Anywhere on Body Up To 300 Yds.	Anywhere on Body Up To 300 Yds.		22-26 Inch	CPX2	Exp
Remington Model 700	Anywhere on Body Up To 100 Yds.	Anywhere on Body Up To 200 Yds.	Anywhere on Body Up To 100 Yds.	Anywhere on Body Up To 200 Yds.	Anywhere on Body Up To 300 Yds.	Anywhere on Body Up To 300 Yds.		20-26 Inch	CPX2	Mid
Savage Model 110	Anywhere on Body Up To 100 Yds.	Anywhere on Body Up To 200 Yds.	Anywhere on Body Up To 100 Yds.	Anywhere on Body Up To 200 Yds.	Anywhere on Body Up To 300 Yds.	Anywhere on Body Up To 300 Yds.		20-22 Inch	CPX2	Mid
Ruger 77, K77 Models	Anywhere on Body Up To 100 Yds.	Anywhere on Body Up To 200 Yds.	Anywhere on Body Up To 100 Yds.	Anywhere on Body Up To 200 Yds.	Anywhere on Body Up To 300 Yds.	Anywhere on Body Up To 300 Yds.	Anywhere on Body Up To 100 Yds.	18.5-24 Inch	CPX2	Mid
Browning A-Bolt Model	Anywhere on Body Up To 100 Yds.	Anywhere on Body Up To 200 Yds.	Anywhere on Body Up To 100 Yds.	Anywhere on Body Up To 200 Yds.	Anywhere on Body Up To 300 Yds.	Anywhere on Body Up To 300 Yds.		20-26 Inch	CPX2	Exp
Kimber Model 84M	Anywhere on Body Up To 100 Yds.	Anywhere on Body Up To 200 Yds.	Anywhere on Body Up To 100 Yds.	Anywhere on Body Up To 200 Yds.	Anywhere on Body Up To 300 Yds.	Anywhere on Body Up To 300 Yds.		22 Inch	CPX2	Exp
Weatherby Vanguard Model	Anywhere on Body Up To 100 Yds.	Anywhere on Body Up To 200 Yds.	Anywhere on Body Up To 100 Yds.	Anywhere on Body Up To 200 Yds.	Anywhere on Body Up To 300 Yds.	Anywhere on Body Up To 300 Yds.		24 Inch	CPX2	Rea
LEVER ACTION RIFLES — Where to Take the Shot on Game										
Winchester Model 88, 94, 1800's	Anywhere on Body Up To 100 Yds.	Anywhere on Body Up To 200 Yds.	Anywhere on Body Up To 100 Yds.	Anywhere on Body Up To 200 Yds.	Anywhere on Body Up To 300 Yds.	Anywhere on Body Up To 300 Yds.	Anywhere on Body Up To 100 Yds.	18-24 Inch	CPX2	Exp
Marlin 336, 1894	Anywhere on Body Up To 200 Yds.	Anywhere on Body Up To 200 Yds.	Anywhere on Body Up To 100 Yds.	Anywhere on Body Up To 200 Yds.	Anywhere on Body Up To 300 Yds.	—	Anywhere on Body Up To 100 Yds.	20-24 Inch	CPX2	Mid
Ruger Model 96/44	—	—	—	—	—	—	Anywhere on Body Up To 100 Yds.	18.5 Inch	CPX2	Rea
Savage Model 99	Anywhere on Body Up To 200 Yds.	Anywhere on Body Up To 200 Yds.	Anywhere on Body Up To 100 Yds.	Anywhere on Body Up To 200 Yds.	Anywhere on Body Up To 300 Yds.	—	—	24 Inch	CPX2	Mid
Browning B78, BLR	Anywhere on Body Up To 200 Yds.	Anywhere on Body Up To 200 Yds.	Anywhere on Body Up To 100 Yds.	Anywhere on Body Up To 200 Yds.	Anywhere on Body Up To 300 Yds.	Anywhere on Body Up To 300 Yds.	Anywhere on Body Up To 100 Yds.	20-22 Inch	CPX2	Exp
Henry Big Boy, 30/30	Anywhere on Body Up To 200 Yds.	—	—	—	—	—	Anywhere on Body Up To 100 Yds.	20 Inch	CPX2	Mid
Mossberg Model 464	Anywhere on Body Up To 200 Yds.	—	—	—	—	—	—	20 Inch	CPX2	Rea
Puma 10, 12, 44, M-92 Models	—	—	—	—	—	—	Anywhere on Body Up To 100 Yds.	20-24 Inch	CPX2	Rea

Abbreviation Definitions:
Spfd = Springfield, Rea = Reasonable, Mid = Mid Range, Exp = Expensive, Win = Winchester, Mag = Magnum, FPS = Feet Per Second, Cal. = Caliber, Gr = Grains

give you a rough idea of the pellet penetration, at various distances, in game such as Rabbits and Squirrels.

Intermediate Size Game Animals (CPX2)

The most popular intermediate size game animal young beginning kids are most likely to hunt is deer. So our table is going to be directed towards the ammunition to use with the more popular

101

TABLE 9 RIFLES FOR DEER & INTERMEDIATE GAME											
MFR ↓	Ammunition Caliber									Barrel Length	Game Class	Relative Cost
Muzzel Velocity MV (FPS) →	.300 Win Mag 150 Gr	.30-06 Spfd 180 Gr	.243 Win 100 Gr	.270 Win 130 Gr	.280 Rem 140 Gr	.308 Win 150 Gr	7mm Rem Mag 150 Gr	—	—			
	3000	2340	2700	2600	2700	2300	2470	—	—			
PUMP (SLIDE) ACTION RIFLES												
	Where to Take the Shot on Game											
Remington Model 7600	—	Anywhere on Body Up To 100 Yds.	Anywhere on Body Up To 200 Yds.	Anywhere on Body Up To 200 Yds.	Anywhere on Body Up To 200 Yds.	Anywhere on Body Up To 300 Yds.	—	—	—	22 Inch	CPX2	Exp
Browning BPR Model	Anywhere on Body Up To 100 Yds.	Anywhere on Body Up To 200 Yds.	Anywhere on Body Up To 100 Yds.	Anywhere on Body Up To 200 Yds.	—	Anywhere on Body Up To 300 Yds.	Anywhere on Body Up To 300 Yds.	—	—	20-24 Inch	CPX2	Mid

MFR ↓	Ammunition Caliber									Barrel Length	Game Class	Relative Cost
Muzzel Velocity MV (FPS) →	.44 Rem Mag 240 Gr	.45-70 Govt 300 Gr	.30-06 Spfd 180 Gr	.243 Win 100 Gr	.223 Rem 55 Gr	.300 WSM 180 Gr	.270 WSM 150 Gr	.308 Win 150 Gr	7mm WSM 140 Gr			
	1390	1600	2340	2400	2500	2570	2700	2300	2540			
SEMI - AUTOMATIC RIFLES												
	Where to Take the Shot on Game											
Ruger 44, M14 Models	Anywhere on Body Up To 100 Yds.	Anywhere on Body Up To 100 Yds.	Anywhere on Body Up To 200 Yds.	Anywhere on Body Up To 200 Yds.	Anywhere on Body Up To 200 Yds.	Anywhere on Body Up To 200 Yds.	Anywhere on Body Up To 200 Yds.	Anywhere on Body Up To 300 Yds.	Anywhere on Body Up To 300 Yds.	16.25 To 22 In.	CPX2	Mid To Exp
Remington Woodmaster, 750, 7400	—	—	Anywhere on Body Up To 200 Yds.	Anywhere on Body Up To 200 Yds.	—	—	Anywhere on Body Up To 200 Yds.	Anywhere on Body Up To 300 Yds.	—	18.5 - 22 In.	CPX2	Mid
Browning BAR Short Track	—	—	—	Anywhere on Body Up To 200 Yds.	—	Anywhere on Body Up To 200 Yds.	Anywhere on Body Up To 200 Yds.	Anywhere on Body Up To 300 Yds.	Anywhere on Body Up To 300 Yds.	22 To 24 In.	CPX2	Exp
Ruger All Weather	—	—	—	Anywhere on Body Up To 200 Yds.	—	—	—	—	—	18.5 Inch	CPX2	Mid
Benelli R1	—	—	—	Anywhere on Body Up To 200 Yds.	—	Anywhere on Body Up To 200 Yds.	Anywhere on Body Up To 200 Yds.	Anywhere on Body Up To 300 Yds.	—	24 Inch	CPX2	Exp

Abbreviation Definitions:
Spfd = Springfield, Govt = Government, Rea = Reasonable, Mid = Mid Range, Exp = Expensive, Win = Winchester, Mag = Magnum, WSM = Winchester Short magnum, Rem = Remington, FPS = Feet Per Second

rifles that beginners are more likely to use. Although you could probably kill a deer with the smaller caliber ammunition such as .22, .177, .20, or .25 caliber, it may take a beginner more than one shot to bring the deer down. If it's a big buck, and you only wound them, you are obligated to hunt them down and not let them roam around wounded out in the woods to die. So this means you need to use a higher power ammunition and try to kill the deer if possible with one well placed shot. For the ammunition to use in the CPX2 game class *SEE TABLES 8-9, 18*. We will cover the "bolt action," the "lever action," the "pump action," and the "semi-automatic action." Some important suggestions. Are you just going out to shoot the deer for sport, head and antlers, or are you going out for the meat. If you are going out with the intention of just going for the head and antlers to mount on a wall, then think about this idea. Have the meat processed. Then donate it to the poor and hungry near where you live. If you want to use the meat, you may want to consider a "head or shoulder shot only up to 200 yards." This would be to guide you in what ammunition to use to outright kill the deer with one shot, and keep the deer hide free of any bullet holes. Or it may say, "Anywhere on body up to 200 yards," this is when you want to preserve the head and antlers.

Transporting Rifles

We have already been through some of this. See "Transportation Storage" for firearms safety on page 27.

Following are the rest of the "Hunter Safety" rules to follow for transporting rifles:

General Safety of the Hunter

Safety of the hunter as well as the equipment (firearms-Other Devices) is important. First thing is CHECK on the laws in your state because other states may be different. The next thing to consider is whether they are concealed or being carried (transported) in the open where they can be seen by the public. Some states have a BAN on carrying a concealed weapon, some don't. However, in some states when you do so, you may be arrested and charged with disorderly conduct, on the grounds that the display threatens the public peace or safety. So make sure you understand what you can or can't do in your state. In almost all places, except for law enforcement or private security personnel, carrying firearms is prohibited in public buildings schools and taverns. ALWAYS look for the signs because where you can't carry a firearm is almost always posted in a big sign. A New York law requires mandatory trigger locks on all firearms and provides for test firing of new pistols on order to provide ballistic "fingerprinting" information to be stored in a computer data bank. There are a few *general* transporting rules to follow for your own safety:

1. Whatever vehicle you are in, if you are carrying any kind of firearm, ALWAYS make sure it is unloaded.
2. If it's in your car, keep it stored in a reasonably secure container with a lock. As an example, a heavy, locked, safe compartment that sits in the back of a pickup truck. And make sure the device and ammunition are stored in separate places.
3. If you are carrying any kind of firearm device, ALWAYS make sure you have a license to carry, and the firearm is registered.
4. NEVER leave your vehicle unlocked with a gun in it. Gun racks may look cool, but they are NOT the safest way to transport your guns if you will be leaving the vehicle.

Transporting While Driving

Be sure to check the local laws of the places you are visiting. Basically follow the general transporting safety rules on page 32. There are a few other safety suggestions:

1. They make special built in metal box safe's *(SEE PICTURE 5)* for transporting firearms or shooting devices in pickup trucks. Damar Corp, Colorado, makes a real nice unit for your pickup truck.
2. Firearms should NOT be displayed in truck window gun racks because the display may provoke anti-hunter sentiment. It's also an invitation to thieves.

Transporting While In a Boat

Many hunters use small craft to reach their favorite hunting spots. Hunting safety includes respecting basic boating principals. The "10 Commandments of Firearms Safety" also apply. Hunters should take a few boating safety precautions to insure their wellbeing and a successful outing while in the boat:

1. ALWAYS let someone else know where you will be hunting, and file a boat plan.
2. ALWAYS check the weather before venturing out on a trip. Anticipate poor weather and return home early.
3. Avoid alcohol use while hunting from a boat, or traveling in the boat to your hunting spot. Alcohol effects operator reaction times, impairs decision making, and accelerates heat loss, which promotes cold weather type injuries.
4. Avoid wearing waders while onboard a boat. If you accidentally fall overboard with a pair of waders on, their added weight, when filled with water, can make rescue nearly impossible.
5. Every person on the boat should be wearing a "Personal Flotation Device" (PFD). If you fall overboard in cold water, your first reflex will be to grasp. A PFD will help keep your head above the water surface and prevent inhalation of water. A brightly colored PFD will make

you more visible to other hunters. If you do accidentally fall overboard, reenter the boat from it's stern (rear) to prevent capsizing.

6. NEVER enter a boat that has the motor running.

7. Stay with your boat if it capsizes, most capsized boats will still float and you can climb up on their hull to get out of the cold water.

FIGURE 77

8. ALWAYS check the capacity plate of the boat, and distribute the weight evenly within the boat. Hunt ing gear can be heavy and the boats used by hunters are often small. Smaller boats are easier to capsize.

9. ALWAYS remain seated while hunting, tending to decoys, or handling a dog. If movement is required on a small boat, stay low in the center of the craft and consider the changes you are making to the boats center of gravity *(SEE FIGURE 77)*.

10. ALWAYS stow any loaded firearm with it's safety on and the muzzle pointed outboard.

11. ALWAYS keep firearms unloaded and cased in your boat after dark.

12. If shooting is conducted from the boat, establish zones of fire and avoid shooting across the path of another shooter.

Transporting While Flying

You can take your firearm with you, but you may only take guns, ammunition, gun parts, and other hunting weapons in your checked luggage. None of these items are allowed in your carry-on. Here are the transporting in an aircraft general safety rules in more detail:

1. ALWAYS check with the airline or travel agent to see if ammunition is permitted in checked baggage on the airline you are flying with. If ammunition is permitted, it must be declared to the airline at check in.

2. Small arms ammunitions for personal use must be securely packed in fiber, wood, metal boxes, or other packaging specifically designed to carry small amounts of ammunition. ALWAYS ask about limitations or fees, if any, that apply.

3. Compressed air guns (BB guns), including paintball markers, must be carried in checked luggage without the compressed air cylinder attached.

4. Firearms carried as checked baggage must be unloaded, packed in a locked, hard-sided container, and declared to the airline at check-in.

5. Gun powder including black powder and percussion caps are not permitted in "carry-on" or "checked" baggage.

6. You should remain present during the check in screening of firearms and ammunition, and provide the key or combination to the security officer if they need to open the container. If you are not present, and the security officer must open the container, the airline will make a reasonable attempt to contact you; if they cannot, it will not be placed on the plane.

7. You MUST securely pack any ammunition in fiber (such as cardboard), wood or metal boxes, or other packaging specifically designed to transport ammunition. You cannot use firearm magazines/clips for packaging ammunition unless they completely and securely enclose the ammunition (by securely covering the exposed portions of the magazine, or by securely placing the magazine in a pouch, holder, holster or lanyard).

8. Ammunition may be carried in the same hard-sided case as the firearm, as long as you pack it as described above.

9. Most airlines will let you take one bow with a quiver and arrows as "checked" baggage, but not as a "carry-on."

10. Most airlines will let you take an uncocked crossbow packed in a hard-case as "checked" baggage, but not as a "carry-on."

11. Most airlines will let you take slingshots and atlatl's packed in a case as "checked" baggage, but not as a "carry-on."

Ammunition Ignition Powered Rifle Hunter Safety Rules

For basic rifle hunter safety follow the "10 Commandments" found on page 26.

Air Powered Rifle Safety Rules

For air powered hunter general rifle safety rules follow the "10 Commandments" general firearm rules on page 26. However, there are additional hunter safety rules that apply only to air powered rifles *(SEE FIGURE 78)* because they operate different than other types of rifles, and require some of there own special safety rules:

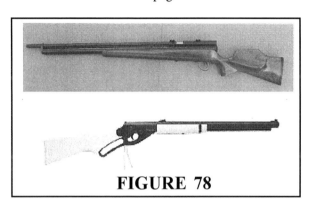

FIGURE 78

1. For CO2 powered guns, the containers must be kept at temperatures below 120 degrees F; at temperatures above this level, the pressure begins to increase very rapidly, and can cause the container to fail, and cause increased leaking through the seals. Then the gun may not fire correctly. Adults and children should carefully read and understand all instructions that come with their gun.

2. For their own safety, children using the BB guns and pellet guns must be supervised by an adult.

3. Adults and children should carefully read and understand all instructions that come with their BB air gun, and understand the proper safe use of them.

4. Their is no way to see if a BB air gun is loaded unless it has a bolt. So the gun needs to be checked to see if it is cocked, by trying to open the cocking lever to see if the spring has been cocked. If the lever is hard to open, the gun is uncocked. If it opens freely, it is cocked and loaded. If it's loaded it could also accidentally fire, so keep it pointed away from your face and body.

5. Keep a firm grip on the lever of a BB gun when cocking. The lever could slip, slam shut, and possibly cause an injury.

6. ALWAYS be sure of your target backstop. A backstop is something used to stop a bullet, BB or pellet. Hills, wood, a pile of sand or a man-made bullet trap can be used to stop a bullet. However, they must be free of any hard objects that would cause a ricochet.

7. ALWAYS be sure the barrel is free of obstructions. Make sure there is no mud, snow or dirt in the barrel after laying it down in the ground. If it's new, you must clean it before using it the first time.

8. The rifle should be on safe at all times when NOT actually being fired.

9. When out on the range, NO ONE may cock or load an air powered rifle until the command has been given.

10. When out on the range, NEVER go downrange when the range is not clear. Rifles may not even be touched while someone is downrange.

11. When out on the range, the BB gun must be left in the quarter cocked position so that the range safety officer can see that the gun is NOT cocked.

Shotguns

Explanation

This is an introduction into shotguns. Shotguns are different from rifles in that they shoot shells loaded with shot (small round balls) or sabot slugs which are similar to bullets. The sabot slug basically packs more hitting power out at longer distances (for deer). Shells loaded with shot spread out in a pattern which is ideal for up close shooting of game birds and waterfowl. Here is an interesting fact. Some areas do NOT allow rifles for hunting large game animals such as deer because of the danger of the bullet traveling much farther. So what has happened is many shotguns have been adapted for hunting larger game. This is where buckshot comes in for the bigger pellets. Generally, there are four standard shell lengths, the standard 2-3/4 inch, the 2-3/4 inch magnum, the 3 inch magnum, and the 3-1/2 inch magnum. You can decide power levels and charge weight, even within the same shell size. As an example, there are "dove loads" which are usually #8, #7-1/2, or #5 and #6 for Squirrels and rabbits. They have a low brass base and a mild recoil, in a standard 2-3/4 inch shell. Having a variety of ammunition makes the shotgun a very adaptable firearm, which spans shotguns for sporting hunting purposes all the way to law enforcement and military usages for them.

Shotguns for real young 5 or 6 year old kids can be very dangerous. I think young beginning kids should only go out hunting varmint's, small game animals, small game birds, waterfowl, or go out "plinking" using a single shot shotgun with an adult or someone to supervise them until they get older. We just don't think it's such a good idea for young kids to be out with a shotgun all by themselves, and especially a group of young boys. Too many possible problems and the possibility of an accident. Shotguns may be OK for Coyotes of Foxes, but they are overkill for a small rats or mice where an air rifle will do fine.

> NOTE:
> We believe young kids can get into the double barrel type shotguns when they get older, and have more experience. At close distances, which is usually the case with young kids, double barreled shotguns will blow away small birds. Some small birds barely get up to half a pound in weight. Some of the bigger birds still only weigh 6 or 7 pounds.

Types of Shotguns

The shotgun is the preferred firearm to use for hunting Turkeys, Game Birds, and Waterfowl. There are a number of special types, but it really comes down to four basic types for game hunting:

- The "Single Shot"
- The "Pump (Slide) Action"
- The "Semi-Automatic"
- The "Double Barrel"

Hunters have been debating for a long time over a very simple question; what type and/or gauge (caliber) gun will serve a hunter the best? There is no simple answer for this question, just like in rifles, everyone has slightly different features they feel they need. Above all, you need to be comfortable and familiar with your chosen shotgun. First what are you going to use it for, turkeys, game birds like pheasants, waterfowl, small animals, or varmint's? That will have a lot to do with your choice. And in tough economic times it actually may just come down to cost. What can you afford? Then you need to decide whether the areas where you will probably hunt are going to be in dense type woods or brush, from a wood line on the edge of a clearing, a blind, a tree stand, or out in a boat. Some guns favor a certain type of habitat, and that can affect your choice of firearm. Shotguns come in a wide variety of bore sizes, ranging from .22 inch (5.5 mm) up to 2 inch (5 cm). As an example: the internal diameter of a 12 gauge shotgun barrel is therefore equal to the diameter of a lead weighing 1/12 of a pound, which is .729 inches. A popular gauge for shotguns is 12 gauge. Some companies make shotguns in many gauges though. They make them in 10, 12, 16, 20, 28, and 410. A 10 gauge shotgun is almost exclusively used in goose hunting, but 12 gauge shotguns also make good goose guns. At the other end of the scale the smaller, lighter weight, .410 has little felt recoil, and some say it is a perfect "starter gun" for young beginner hunters. It is a perfect gun for small game such as grouse and rabbit. The trouble with the 16 and 28 gauge shotguns is that they are not common enough for the ammunition to be readily available. The reason the 12 gauge is so popular is it is versatile. It can be used with birdshot and 2-3/4 inch shells to hunt for small and upland game. It can be used with 3 inch long, or magnum 3.4 inch long shells to hunt turkeys or waterfowl. It can be used with slugs or sabots to hunt big game out 100 yards or farther. 12 gauge ammunition is comparatively cheap and readily available. One problem with the 12 gauge shotgun is it is heavy. The 20 gauge is also very popular. It is generally lighter in weight than the 12 gauge, has less kick, and the ammunition is widely available. So you might consider it instead of a 12 gauge. On this page *(SEE TABLE 10)* is a table showing gauge vs bore diameter:

Table 10 Gauge vs Bore Size									
Gauge	Bore Dia.	Gauge	Bore Dia.	Gauge	Bore Dia.	Gauge	Bore Dia.	Gauge	Bore Dia.
1	1.669"	8	.835"	15	.677"	22	.596"	29	.543"
2	1.325"	9	.802"	16	.662"	23	.587"	30	.537"
3	1.157"	10	.775"	17	.650"	24	.579"	31	.531"
4	1.052"	11	.751"	18	.637"	25	.571"	32	.526"
5	.976"	12	.729"	19	.626"	26	.563"	.410 [1]	.410
6	.919"	13	.700"	20	.615"	27	.556"		
7	.873"	14	.693"	21	.605"	28	.550"		

Note:
[1] .410 is not really a gauge, except by convention. It is the actual diameter of the bore in decimal inches.

Chokes for Shotguns

You can't talk about single shot shotguns without talking about chokes. For those of you that don't know what a choke is or what it does, we will explain. A choke is a screw in device that goes into the barrel muzzle of the shotgun. It restricts the size of the barrel at the muzzle. You can get different barrel restrictions by just screwing in a different choke. Why would you want to do this? It increases the percentage of shot that hit the target, it squeezes the pattern down and doesn't let the shot spread out as far after they leave the barrel. To see what the pattern is for your shotgun, you

Table 11 Percentage of Shot Inside 30 In. Circle			
Choke Type	20 Yards	30 Yards	40 Yards
Cylinder	80%	60%	40%
Skeet	92%	72%	50%
Improved Cylinder	100%	77%	55%
Modified	100%	83%	60%
Improved Modified	100%	91%	65%
Full	100%	100%	70%

Table 12 Std. Choke Constriction (Inches)		
Choke Type	Gauge	
Designation	10/12/16/20	20/410
Cylinder	.000	.000
Light Skeet	.003	.003
Skeet	.005	.005
Improved Skeet	.007	.007
Improved Cylinder	.010	.009
Light Modified	.015	.012
Modified	.020	.015
Improved Modified	.025	.018
Light Full	.030	.021
Full	.035	.024
Extra Full	.040	.027
Super Full	.050	———

need to do a pattern test. One way to measure this is to shoot at a 40 inch square piece of paper placed on a target at 40 yards out. Then after shooting, retrieve the target and draw a 30 inch diameter circle around the highest concentration of pellet holes in the paper. Then count the holes. As an example, if the ammo you are using is loaded with 1-1/2 ounces of No. 2 steel shot, it contains about 156 pellets. If you count 94 pellet holes, your gun placed about 61 percent of the charge into the 30 inch circle *(SEE TABLE 11)*. Looking at Table 11 you see that the charge is delivering a "modified" performance. From one of the best choke manufacturer's Briley, check out **TABLE 12** to see the constriction.

Single Shot Action Shotguns

These are shotguns that hold only one shell at a time. They are probably the least expensive type of shotgun available, and this is mainly because you only get one shot before you have to open the breech and reload a new shell before it can be fired again. They come in a number of actions. It just depends on which type you like. These types of guns are great for inexperienced young beginning kids as they tend to be safer with only one shot at a time.

We are going to list what may be the top 10 shotguns in the single shot category, and they are not listed in any particular order, nor are they all the cheapest, but they are affordable.

1. **Winchester Model 37 .410**
   There are several versions of this shotgun. It is out of production now. The model 37 is better than the 37A or the 370. Is made better. You can still find them used if you look for them on line. This is a good shotgun for a young beginning hunter. Not as much recoil as a 12 gauge.

2. **Savage Model 94 .410**
   These are out of production now. They are hard to find though anywhere. An excellent shotgun if you can find a used one. This is a good shotgun for a young beginning hunter. Not as much kick (recoil) as a 12 gauge.

3. **Rossi Model S41 410 .410**
   These are nice shotguns, and they are in production now. They are imported by Rossi from Brazil, so I'm not sure how good the quality is, but they are not too expensive. This would be a good shotgun for a beginning hunter. Not as much kick as a 12 gauge.

4. **Winchester Model 37 or 37A 20 Ga.**
   There are several versions of this shotgun. It is out of production now. The model 37 is better than the 37A or the 370. Is made better. You can still find them used if you look for them on line. The model 37 is a good shotgun for a young beginning hunter. The 37A is a good second choice, and may be more available. Not quite as much kick (recoil) as a 12 gauge.

5. **Savage/Stevens Model 94 20 Ga.**
   This is a good single shot shotgun for a young beginning hunter. It is out of production now. You may still be able find them used, although it may be harder, if you look for them on line. Also a good intermediate choice for a young teenager. Not quite as much kick (recoil) as a 12 Ga.

6. **H & R "Topper" SB1288 Model 20 Ga.**
   This is a good single shot shotgun for a young beginning teenage hunter *(SEE FIGURE 79)*. Should be readily available. Features include a modified choke and walnut stock. Also a good intermediate choice for a young teenager. Not as much kick (recoil) as a 12 gauge.

7. **Remington Spartan Model 100 20 Ga.**

This is a good single shot shotgun for a young beginning teenage hunter. Should be readily avail able. Features include multiple choices of chokes.

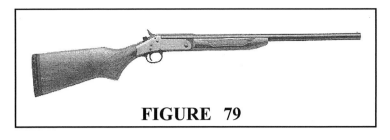

FIGURE 79

Also a good intermediate choice for a young teenager. Not quite as much kick (recoil) as a 12 gauge.

8. **H & R "Topper Deluxe" SB1118 Model 12 Ga.**

This is a good single shot shotgun for an older beginning teenage hunter. Should be readily available. Features include a walnut stock. Also a good intermediate choice for a young adult beginning hunter. A little more kick (recoil) than the .410 or 20 gauge.

9. **Winchester Model 37 "Red Letter" 12 Ga.**

This is a good single shot shotgun for an older beginning teenage hunter. Out of production, but you should be able to find a used one on line. Also a good intermediate choice for a young adult beginning hunter. A little more kick (recoil) than the .410 or 20 gauge.

10. **Remington Model 37 "Red Letter" 12 Ga.**

This is a good single shot shotgun for an older beginning teenage hunter. Out of production, but you should be able to find a used one on line. Multiple chokes available. Also a good intermediate choice for a young adult beginning hunter. A little more kick (recoil) than the .410 or 20 gauge.

Pump (Slide) Action Shotguns

Pump action shotguns are usually the most reliable of the repeating shotgun. They have been around for a century or more, and their simplicity and reliability gains them many fans each year. They have advantages over semi-automatics, because they are lighter and less expensive. The disadvantages are more recoil kick and manual operation. I'm going to list what may be the top 7 shotguns in the pump-action category, and they are not listed in any particular order, nor are they all the cheapest, but they are affordable. I am only listing .410, 20 Ga. and 12 Ga. Because these are a better choice for young beginners, and their ammunition is more readily available:

1. **Benelli Super Nova Model 37 20 Ga.**

Some hunters that have these think they are great. This is a good shotgun for a young beginning teenage hunter. Some kick (recoil), but not as much as a 12 gauge.

2. **Browning BPS Model .410, 20 Ga. or 12 Ga.**

This shotgun has a reputation for long lasting durability. It has many features that other shotguns in this category don't, like dual machined steel action bars, and a forged and machined steel receiver. It also has straight down shell ejection, making it ideal for right or left handed hunters. This is a good shotgun for a young or intermediate (age wise) level hunter. Not as much kick (recoil) with the .410 or 20 Ga. More kick with the 12 gauge.

3. Ithaca Model 37 20 Ga. & 12 Ga.

These are nice shotguns apparently because they stay in demand. They have bottom ejection, but it's hard to load when you want to chamber just one shell. Here is a feature that makes me nervous, the safety is on the trigger guard and located right behind the trigger. However, that has not kept hunters from buying them. Most models have a steel receiver, but it's aluminum on the "ultra light" models. The 20 Ga. is a good shotgun for a young beginning teenage hunter, and the 12 Ga. may be better for older teenagers and adults.

4. Mossberg Model 500, 535, 590, 835 .410, 20 Ga., 12 Ga.

These are nice shotguns apparently because they stay in demand *(SEE FIGURE 80)*. However, they have been known to occasionally malfunction. Some of their features are a tang-mounted ambidextrous safety, but they are usually plastic and tend to break. Young hunters may want to think twice about getting one of these because of the potential problems. If a

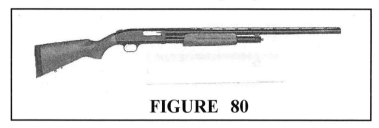

FIGURE 80

shotgun is going to have problems, it's probably going to be with less experienced hunter. If you are going to get one, the .410 and 20 Ga. would be for a young beginning teenage hunter, and the 12 Ga. may be better for older teenagers and adults.

5. Remington Model 870, 887 .410, 20 Ga., 12 Ga.

The 870 has been around for about 50 years. It may be the most accessorized shotgun of all time. However, poor quality control has plagued recently built 870s, but overall they remain popular. The 870s steel receiver is good for strength, bad for weight. The worst feature of all repeaters is the safety location; it's in the trigger guard, and behind the trigger. Also you need to be careful which shells you feed your 870s. Check with a gun shop! The 887 is too new to know much about yet. The model 870 .410 and 20 Ga. would be for a young beginning hunter with a little experience. The model 870 12 Ga. would be for older teenage hunters or adults.

6. Winchester Model 1300 & SXP 12 Ga.

The 1300 has been Winchester's main pump shotgun in recent years, but was discontinued in 2006. It's an average sort of pump shotgun, and never gained the popularity of the Remington 870 or the Mossberg 500. It's features are a alloy receiver, and crossbolt safety in front of the trigger guard. Reliability reports vary for the 1300, but many hunters like it. It would be an intermediate level choice for an older teenager or adults. It will have more kick (recoil) than a .410 or a 20 Ga. The SXP (super X pump) is Winchester's latest offering in a long line of pump shotgun models. It has a Benelli Super Nova similar type design. But it's too new to have a reputation yet, or know it's reliability.

7. Older Winchester Models 12 and 1897

The 1897 model was popular in it's day. More than a million were built before it was discontinued in 1957. This model featured an exposed hammer (and thus had no other safety) and side ejection. For many years, the premier Winchester pump gun was the model 12. Originally was chambered in a 20 Ga. It's features are a crossbolt safety in front of the trigger. It was built in many configurations, which included 12, 16, 20, and 28 Ga. The model 12 in a 20 Ga. or a 12 Ga. would be for an older teenager or adult.

Semi-Automatic (Autoloading) Shotguns

Semi-automatic shotguns have been around for many years now. Many hunters favor them. Although they are not as reliable as pump or slide action shotguns, they are still very reliable. They have reduced recoil which will make them easier for younger kids to use compared to other actions. Two of the best at reducing the recoil action are the Browning Golds and Beretta 390-391 series gas operated shotguns. A felt recoil proves nothing, and no action reduces it better than a gas operated semi-automatic. Bruised shoulders are cumulative. We will look at what may be the top 7 semi-automatic shotguns in this category, not in any special order or price range:

1. **Benelli Super Black Eagle Model**

   These semi-automatics use an inertia system, rather than gas, to operate the action. It will handle shells from 2-3/4" to 3-1/2," and there are no gas ports to keep clean. Benelli's have a good reputation, and a unique style for a shotgun that blends angles with curves. It features include a crossbolt safety located behind the trigger.

2. **Beretta Model 391**

   These are gas operated shotguns. They are built in a variety of variations, including one that handles the blonky 12 Ga. 3-1/2" magnum shells which indicates this action is quite versatile. It has good looks and the reliability that Beretta shotguns are know for. It features a crossbolt safety located in front of the trigger in the trigger guard, which is a better location (easier to use) than behind the trigger. They also feature an Aluminum receiver for lighter weight. The AL391 Urika, introduced in 1999 may be the finest autoloader ever built. The 20 Ga. is a good shotgun for a young beginning teenage hunter, and the 12 Ga. may be better for older teenagers and adults.

3. **Browning Gold Model**

   Browning has a long and excellent reputation for fine guns, and the gold model is no exception *(SEE FIGURE 81)*. It's self regulating so it can handle both light and heavy loads without ad

   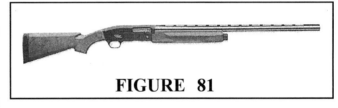

   FIGURE 81

   justment. It's also a good looking shotgun, which doesn't hurt it's reputation at all. It's also available in a 3-1/2" version that will shoot lighter loads. It features include a magazine cutoff, which can be handy, and a crossbolt safety located behind the trigger. Supplied choke tubes come in 3 variations, Full, modified, and improved cylinder. The 20 Ga. is a good shotgun for a young beginning teenage hunter, and the 12 Ga. may be better for older teenagers and adults.

4. **Franchi Model 612 & 620**

   This company makes some fine autoloaders. Both of these models have an user-adjustable gas system, so they handle hot loads as well as lighter ones. They feature an Aluminum receiver, a magazine cutoff, and a crossbolt safety located in front of the trigger. Their 712 and 720 models are similar, but have a non-adjustable gas system. The 912 is their non-adjustable 3-1/2" magnum version. They also make a model 48, a long-recoil-action similar to the early Browning autoloaders, which have a crossbolt safety located behind the trigger. The 20 Ga. is a good shotgun for a young beginning teenage hunter, and the 12 Ga. for adults.

5. **Mossberg Model 935**

   This model is chambered for a 3-1/2" 12 Ga. magnum, and uses a self regulating gas system. This gun was developed for use with 3" and 3-1/2" shells, so don't expect it to function with dove loads. It comes in 12 Ga. only. It is only available in synthetic stocks. The safety is centered on the rear of the receiver for ambidextrous thumb operation. Supplied choke tubes for this model are either premium X-factor or Ulti-Full on turkey models. The 12 Ga. may be better for older teenagers and adults.

6. **Remington Model 1100 & 11-87**

   The 1100 has been around a long time, and it's still going strong. It's not clear why because the newer 11-87 is an improvement on it. The big disadvantage of the 1100 is it's use is limited to only the shells it's designed for (2-3/4" or 3"). On the other hand the 11-87 can handle lighter loads along with 3" long magnums. Both come in a variety of sub-models. The safety is a crossbolt behind the trigger. The even newer gas operated 105CTi has hi tech features, but it's big drawback is going to be the price. The 20 Ga. is a good shotgun for a young beginning teenage hunter, the 12 Ga. may be better for older teenagers and adults.

7. **Winchester Super X2 Model**

   This is a gas operated autoloading shotgun. Some versions are self regulating, while some specialized models may include interchangeable gas pistons for use with different loads. The 3-1/2" magnum version will handle everything from hotter 2-3/4" shells on up. It features a crossbolt safety located behind the trigger. It appears to only come in a 12 Ga. The 12 Ga. may be better for older teenagers and adults rather then the younger kids.

Double Barrel Shotguns

Double barrel shotguns have been around for many years now. They were invented in Britain. Most all of the double barrel shotguns built today use the familiar break open design. And fundamentally they are similar to the break-action single shot guns with which most kids learn how to shoot. The side by side (SxS) barrels *(SEE FIGURE 82-A)* open when a top lever is pressed to the side and the barrels pivot down around a hinge pin, which opens the action and exposes the breetch end of the barrels for loading or unloading. Most double barrel shotguns come with a choice of chokes.

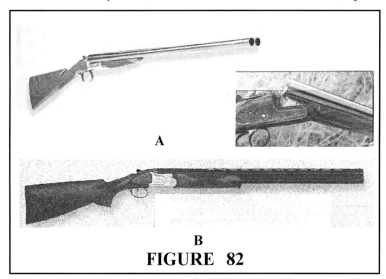

A

B

FIGURE 82

Then you have the over-under (O/U) double barreled shotguns *(SEE FIGURE 82-B)*. Their action can be either the boxlock or sidelock type. The stack barrel is made to balance and swing just as well as a side-by-side. Some of the O/Us advantages include a single sighting plane, short overall length, and excellent balance. They have a single trigger, and offer a very fast second shot, faster than an autoloader.

Side-By-Side

We will look at what may be the top 5 double barreled, side-by-side (SxS) shotguns in this category, not in any special order or price range (they are expensive though):

1. **AyA Model 4/53**

   These are classic Spanish side-by-side double barreled shotguns. They are not for young kids for several reasons. One, they are very expensive ($3000 to $4000) to be in the hands of a young hunter. And two, they can be dangerous for an inexperienced hunter to handle. However, they do come in 20 Ga. and 12 Ga.

2. **SKB Model 385 and 485**

   These are classic side-by-side double barreled shotguns made in America. Both models are discontinued now. They are not for young kids for several reasons. One, they are very expensive ($2500 to $3000) to be in the hands of a young hunter. And two, they can be dangerous for an inexperienced hunter to handle. However, although rare they do come in 20 Ga. and 12 Ga. if you can find them. The 20 Ga. is a good shotgun for a young beginning teenage hunter, and the 12 Ga. may be better for older teenagers and adults.

3. **Weatherby Athena D'Italia**

   Weatherby sells this model, but it is imported from Italy with an old English side-by-side design. One of it's features is it has a double trigger. I have only seen these for sale in a 28 Ga. which is harder to find the ammunition for.

4. **H & K Fabarm Classic Lion**

   This model is sold by H & K, but it's an old English classic design side-by-side, double barreled shotgun. One of it's features is it has a double trigger. I have only seen these for sale in a 12 Ga. I don't know if they were made in a 20 Ga.

5. **Ruger Gold Label Model**

   The Gold Label side-by-side double barrel shotgun is American Made *(SEE FIGURE 83)*. Ruger has revived this classic, but without all the gingerbread frills. I think this model is going to be popular. One hunter used one recently hunting Quail in a Souther California brushy mountain area. Here is his comments: "The quick mounting characteristics, snap-shooting qualities and light weight paid off." They bagged their Quail. The gun he was using was set up in an Improved Cylinder/Modified choke configuration. Only available in 12 Ga.. model.

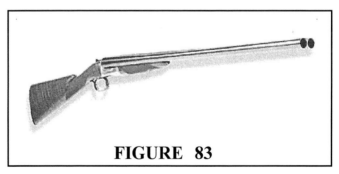

FIGURE 83

Over/Under

We will look at what may be the top 7 double barreled, over/under (O/U) shotguns in this category, not in any special order or price range (they are expensive though):

1. **Beretta Model 686 and 687**

   These are classic Italian over/under double barreled shotguns. They are not for young kids for several reasons. One, they are very expensive ($1600 to $3000) to be in the hands of a young hunter. And two, they can be dangerous for an inexperienced hunter to handle.

However, they do come in 20 Ga. and 12 Ga. The 20 Ga. is a good shotgun for a young beginning teenage hunter, and the 12 Ga. may be better for older teenagers and adults.

2. **Browning Citori Lightning Model**

These are classic over/under, double barreled Browning shotguns. Both the Lightning and Lightning grade IV have some nice features. Their features include Ventilated Rib barrel, single selective trigger action, Hammer ejectors, top-tang barrel selector/safety, walnut stock, and three different "invector-plus" choke tubes are available. And get this, they come in .410, 20, and 12 Ga. with a recoil pad on the 12 Ga. The .410 or 20 Ga. is a good shotgun for a young beginning teenage hunter, and the 12 Ga. may be better for older teenagers and adults.

3. **Franchi Alcione Model**

These are classic Franchi over/under, double barreled shotguns. They have some nice features that make them ideal for handling and performance. Their features include a barrel selection button on the trigger, it can fire either barrel independent of the other; recoil is not necessary to reset the hammer to fire the second barrel. They have interchangeable barrels, easy to open action, and they feature a exclusive "no catch" slip-pad recoil pad. When closing the action it automatically sets the safety to the "safe" position. They come in 20 and 12 Ga. The 20 Ga. is a good shotgun for a young beginning teenage hunter, and the 12 Ga. may be better for older teenagers and adults.

4. **Weatherby Athena**

This shotgun does have some fine craftsmanship, but it does have some drawbacks; the chamber
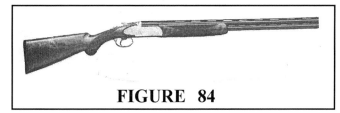

FIGURE 84
is only 2-3/4", it only comes in a 28 Ga. and ammunition will be harder to find. The 28 Ga. is a good shotgun *(SEE FIGURE 84)* for a young beginning teenage hunter, if you can deal with the drawbacks.

5. **H & K Fabarm Silver Lion Model**

This model is designed as a youth model. It has some nice features. They include milled solid steel or lightweight alloy receiver to give shooters choices for balance, pointability, and ease of carry. And they have a leather covered rubber recoil pad. They come in 20 Ga. and 12 Ga. The 20 Ga. is a good shotgun for a young beginning teenage hunter, and the 12 Ga. may be better for older teenagers and adults. This could be a good choice, they are still what I consider expensive, but priced right for what they are.

6. **B. Rizzini Aurum and Artemis Models**

This is an imported, serviced in the USA, double barrel over/under shotgun. The Aurum features include a case hardened, box lock action, automatic ejectors, single selective trigger, full side ribs, ventilated top rib, and a walnut stock. The Artemis has similar features to the "Aurum." Both models can be found in .410, 20 Ga. and 28 Ga. All of these models would be a good shotgun for a young beginning teenage hunter, but ammo will be hard to find for the 28 Ga.

7. **SIG Aurora High Grade Models TR20, TR40, TR25, TR45**

This is an imported, serviced in the USA, double barrel over/under shotgun. The features include a Machined alloy steel boxlock, automatic ejectors, ventilated rib barrels, strong-tapered bolt lockup, single selective trigger, manual safety and barrel selector, and a safety system that only allows firing when action is fully closed. Available in 20, 28, 12, and .410 gauges. The 20, 28, and .410 gauges are a good shotgun for a young beginning teenage hunter, and the 12 Ga. may be better for older teenagers and adults. Of note, the 28 Ga. ammunition may be harder to find and more expensive.

Help In Choosing Your Shotgun

Helpful Information

When talking about shotguns, it's good to understand how they are sized. They go by barrel sizes which is called their gauge. We have added a Table No. 10 on page 105 with the different gauges and their bore size. The other thing you young kids may want to consider when getting your first gun is the recoil (kick) it has. We have added another Table 13 give you some idea of the recoil (kick) to expect from the different gauge shotguns you might use. This data is taken from *Chuck Hawks Rifle Recoil Table and other Internet Data*. Another way is use the low recoil RST type shotshells. If you are a small hunter, this may give you a rough idea of what to expect. It may be a good idea to use a "recoil pad" on the rifle butt, "hearing protection" and "eye protection" while you are beginning to get used to your shotgun.

TABLE 13	Shotgun Recoil Data										
Gauge	Shell Length (Inches)	Shot Oz.	@ Muzzle Velocity (FPS)	Gun Weight (Lbs)	Recoil Energy (Ft-Lbs)	Gauge	Shell Length (Inches)	Shot Oz.	@ Muzzle Velocity (FPS)	Gun Weight (Lbs)	Recoil Energy (Ft-Lbs)
.410	2.5	1/2	1200	5.5	7.1	16	2.75	1-1/8	1240	7.0	27.6
.410	3.0	11/16	1135	5.5	10.5	12	2.75	1	1180	75	17.3
28	2.75	3/4	1200	6.0	12.8	12	2.75	1-1/8	1200	75	23.0
20	2.75	7/8	1200	6.5	16.1	12	2.75	1-1/4	1330	75	32.0
20	2.75	1	1220	6.5	21.0	12	2.75	1-1/2	1260	75	45.0
20	2.75	1-1/8	1175	6.5	25.0	12	3.0	1-5/8	1280	75	52.0
20	3.0	1-1/4	1185	6.5	31.0	12	3.0	1-7/8	1210	8.75	54.0
16	2.75	1	1220	7.0	21.5	10	3.5	2-1/4	1210	10.5	62.9

Note: FPS = Feet per second

Handling Your Shotgun

Explanation

We will cover handling your shotgun out in the field and at home. When we talk about handling, we mean when you are just carrying, or on the couch at home. We will talk about firing, shooting, and loading/unloading later in this section. Note: We are not going to cover pistols.

Handling In the Field Position

There are several ways to handle or carry a gun so that it is never a threat to other hunters, yet it is ready for instant use. A good position is to grip the small of the stock in the trigger hand and cradle the barrel in the crook of the other arm *(SEE FIGURE 41-A)*, except NOT when another hunter is walking next to you on the muzzle side. Another position is the shoul-

FIGURE   85

der carry *(SEE FIGURE 41-B)*, except NOT when another hunter is walking single file behind you. Another position is the muzzle down carry *(SEE FIGURE 41-C)*, except NOT when another hunter is walking single file in front of you. Still another carry, and maybe the best because it gives better control of the muzzle, is to hold the fore end in one hand and the small of the stock in the other *(SEE FIGURE 41-D)*, except NOT when another hunter is walking next to you on the muzzle side, or single file in front of you. If your shotgun has a sling studs and incorporates sling swivels, there is a new way to carry it hands free on your back like a backpack. It's called the "Outlaw Sling" *(SEE FIGURE 85)*. This lets you do a lot of things not possible using the old standard way.

In all carries in the field or at home the standard rules apply:

1. Safety is ON.
2. Your finger is OUTSIDE THE TRIGGER GUARD.
3. The muzzle is ALWAYS IN A SAFE DIRECTION, AND UNDER CONTROL.

Handling At Home

When handling your shotgun at home whether just sitting, holding it or working on it:

- First ALWAYS make sure it is unloaded.
- ALWAYS point the muzzle away from you or anyone else nearby.
- When sitting lay it across your lap with your hands away from the trigger *(SEE FIGURE 42-A)*.
- If you are cleaning it or repairing it, put it on a firearm holder of some kind and pointed away from you or anyone nearby *(SEE FIGURE 42-B)*.

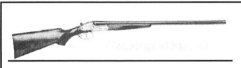
Single Barrel

Double Barrel
FIGURE 86

Shotgun Hunter Safety

As with any firearm, certain safety rules must be observed because shotguns are not toys. The shotgun is a legal hunting firearm to use mostly for small game, varmint's, upland game birds, waterfowl, turkeys and deer, but not big game animals like bear and elk. They come in different types such as single and double barrels as we have previously gone over *(SEE FIGURE 86)*. And because they are different they have some of their own special safety rules. Generally follow the "10 Commandments" firearms rules found on page 26, plus the rules below.

General Shotgun Precautions

Following all the safety rules at all times will make shotgun hunting a more pleasant experience for you:

1. ALWAYS keep your finger off the trigger. For some reason it's a natural tendency for some hunters is to put their finger on the trigger when they hold a shot gun. Shotguns are especially dangerous because the shot spreads out when they fire. The only time your finger should touch the trigger is at the instant you plan to shoot.
2. When NOT actively shooting, keep the gun unloaded with the action open. Whenever you pick up a shotgun, develop the habit of opening the action and checking the chamber to verify that the gun is unloaded.
3. ALWAYS know your shotgun(s). Familiarity with your guns basic parts, and how they function, is a prerequisite for safe shooting.

116

4. DON'T depend on the gun's safety. The safety is a mechanical device, and it can break. The safety is NOT a replacement for safe gun handling.

5. ALWAYS make sure the gun and ammunition match. If there is any question about compatibility between the gun and ammunition, DON'T shoot. The gauge of the shell must match the gauge of the shotgun.

6. DON'T carry shells of mixed gauge. Whenever you are through shooting, immediately remove unfired shells from your clothing. The wrong size shell in the chamber is dangerous.

7. ALWAYS check your gun for barrel obstructions. They can cause the gun barrel to burst. If you accidentally stumble and jam the barrel into the ground, unload and check the barrel for mud or snow before you shoot.

8. ALWAYS protect your eyes and ears when shooting or you are around shooters. Guns make noise which can detrimentally affect your hearing.

Firing Your Shotgun

Firing Rifles In the Field

There are several stable ways to fire rifles out in the field so that it is never a threat to other hunters. First thing, before firing check the area for other hunters, and observe what's behind your target. There are five basic standard positions to fire from, prone, standing, sitting, kneeling and leaning. However, most of the time you may be standing or sitting in a boat. You also need to know how to sight, aim, and pull the trigger.

What's Behind Your Target

Find out ahead of time what's behind your intended target(s). There are state maps for their hunting areas, showing what is in these areas like state parks, firing ranges, hunting clubs, or homes. Know which nearby area your hunting partners might be in. Use Tables 14 as a guide to see approximately how far your ammunition will actually travel in the air. These are not exact, but they will go at line of sight. The tables will not work though for shooting up in the air at an angle. The information we do have is compiled from other sources like ammunition companies, hunting clubs, hunting associations, hunting organizations and the internet, using their information. Once you have an idea what is behind your target, act responsibly and choose not to fire if their is any question about safety in your mind.

Getting Ready to Fire

Get familiar with your shotgun, know what it's capable of doing. If you have never used the gun before, read the manual ahead of time. If you bought your gun used, go on line at the manufacturers web site and print out

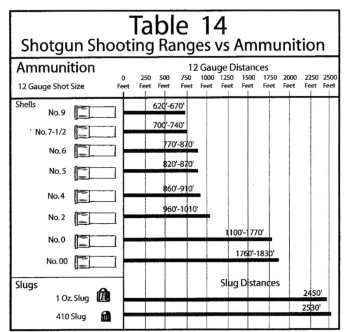

NOTE: These are the approximate maximum horizontal distances for the leading pellets of shotstrings fired from a 12 gauge shotgun.

a manual. Most guns have a manual on-line that you can print out. If not, buy one from the manufacturer. It will be worth the money. So, before you shoot the gun, especially a new gun follow the same steps as getting ready to fire a rifle on page 78.

After Loading

We will cover more information on shotgun ammunition later in this section where we cover "Loading and Unloading," and "Ammunitions" for shotguns. After you have loaded your rifle, check the distance to your target, and know what lies beyond your target. Are you within the range of your gun? Have an idea before you leave, or take a copy of our distance tables out hunting with you. Check out our distance table for shotguns *(SEE TABLE 14)*. As you can see in the table, your shells go a long way past your intended target, especially if you miss the target with your shot. You need to be aware of where your hunting partners, and people living nearby, are located for miles in all directions. When you are sure of your target and what's beyond, then go ahead and sight in on the target, unlock the safety, try to stay relaxed, then pull the trigger. (the distance information for rifles is taken from "Field & Stream" magazine data.

Positions for Firing

There are a number of different firing positions you can get into before firing *(SEE FIGURE 44)* on page 80. The ones you will probably use the most are "standing" or "sitting" in a boat.

Shotgun Field Etiquette and Manners

In any situation, etiquette is just good manners. In shooting, good etiquette introduces another element of safety. Practice proper shotgun shooting etiquette in the field and you will be a safe and popular hunting partner.

1. NEVER shoot across another hunter.
2. DON'T interfere with another hunter's dog.
3. NEVER take your gun off safety until the game has flushed.
4. DON'T shoot at low flying birds: you may inadvertently hit a dog or another hunter.
5. You should ALWAYS wear hunter orange.
6. ALWAYS maintain a "straight line" when hunting with others.
7. If you DON'T know where your hunting partners are, don't shoot.

Shooting Your Shotgun

Sighting and Aiming

See "sighting and aiming" in the rifle section on page 81. However, most of this information would apply when you might be deer hunting with your shotgun over a longer distances. Most shotgun hunters will be hunting upland game birds and waterfowl. This will be stand up shooting where you will need *trap shooting* practice to get better at it. It's not your normal type sighting and aiming. Basically it's bring your gun up, lead the target and fire.

Pulling the Trigger

See "pulling the trigger" in the rifle section on page 82. However, most of this information would apply when you might be deer hunting with your shotgun over a longer distances. Shotguns are a little different than rifles because triggers may be single or double. Which is better for young hunters? There is one big difference. The pull length with a single trigger always remains the same, but if you have a double trigger the pull is longer with the front trigger than the rear trigger. This does bother some hunters. So it may be better for young beginning hunters to use a single trigger shotgun. One less problem or lesson to learn while shotgun hunting. However, the double trigger does seem to have an advantage worth considering. When flushing birds such as quail, a double barrel shotgun with two triggers comes in handy when a second bird flushes and you can get a shot off on them without needing to break down to reload. You just need to remember to move the barrel selector switch right after the first shot.

Wingshooting

Wingshooting

Here are some tips from an expert to help you become a better wingshooter. One of the biggest mistakes is lifting their head from the stock as they fire. The other big mistake is stopping their swing as the trigger is squeezed. Basically this can be cured by working on your focus, and dry firing. Keeping your cheek glued to the stock as the gun fires is an absolute must because failing to do so will cause you to shoot over the target. Stopping your swing just as you pull the trigger will cause you to shoot behind your target. So just learn to keep your head down, and pull the trigger as the muzzle swings through the target. Two ways to get training are go to a nearby gun club and get an experienced shooter there to instruct you in trap shooting, or go to the "Remington Shooting School." You can find a location and schedule by calling 1-800-742-7053.

Gateway Gun Club Trap Shooting

Taking Care Of Your Shotgun (Maintenance)

Lets say you just got your shotgun. The next step is taking care of it. In other words, maintenance. This is all part of "*hunter safety*". If your shotgun fails because of a malfunction due to the lack of maintenance, you or someone near you could get hurt. First, be absolutely sure your gun is UN-LOADED. When the season is over, or after being used, it is recommended that you disassemble your gun, clean it, re-lubricate it, oil the stock, then return it to it's storage place. Before you start to clean, check your owners manual that came with the gun, for maintenance instructions to fit your gun. If you bought a used weapon, and don't have a manual, check on the internet for one. You can usually print them out for free. Or contact the manufacturer. for a manual. They are not very expensive.

Cleaning And Lubricating

There are a number of slightly different ways to clean and lubricate your shotgun. You can clean them basically the same standard way as a rifle *(SEE PAGES 83-84)*. A couple of "*TIPS*." Get a bore light so you can see better down the barrel. Use "Prolix" to clean with instead of using just any handy gun oil. And last get a "Outer Fowl Out Kit." This is the ultimate in cleaning; it is an automatic electro chemical process that takes from 1/2 to 2 hours depending on how dirty the bore is, and it works with all kinds of firearm not just shotguns.

NOTE: We will show some general diagrams for the different types of shotguns. This is so that you can familiarize yourself with the general part names of some of the different parts and location. Of course if you have a manual, it will show you exactly where the parts are on your particular shotgun.

Single Shot Action
Typical Basic Parts Location:

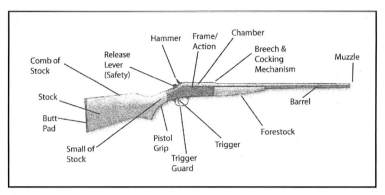

Pump (Slide) Action
Typical Basic Parts Location:

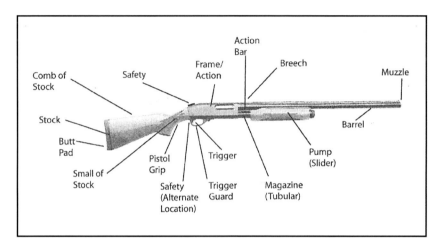

Semi Automatic Action
Typical Basic Parts Location:

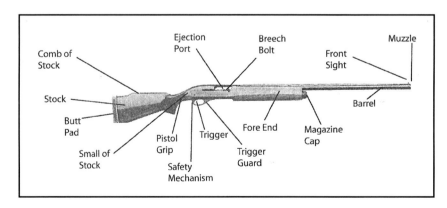

Double Barrel- Side by Side
Typical Basic Parts Location:

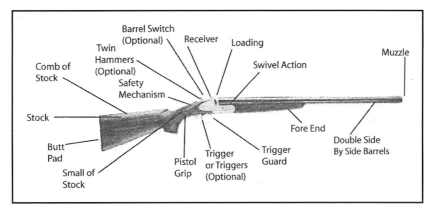

Double Barrel- Over/Under
Typical Basic Parts Location:

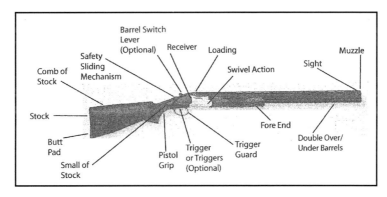

Shotgun Storage

General storage for shotguns is the same as for rifles *(SEE PAGES 26, 27, 86)*. Basically it's under lock and key in a cabinet or safe. The closed door safe may be better because it is out of the sight of young inquisitive and prying eyes.

Transporting Your Shotgun

Transporting shotguns is basically the same as for rifles *(SEE PAGES 27, 102-104)*. Basically it's under lock and key, and out of sight, in your truck or van. Minimum is in the trunk of your car with a trigger lock. If it's in plain sight you need to worry about theft. Keep that in mind if it's on a gun rack behind the front seat of your truck.

Loading and Unloading Your Shotgun

Loading Shotguns
There are five different types of shotguns. Basically you have the "single shot," the "pump (slide) action," the "semi automatic action," the "side by side double barrel" and the "over under double barrel." Loading each one is similar in some ways, but still a little different. The biggest problem will be, is it loaded. If it is and you don't realize it, there is a lot of danger if it accidentally fires. Shotgun blasts spread, which could really accidentally injure someone. We will give you the basics just to give you a general picture. The manuals go into great detail, and we just don't have room in this book.

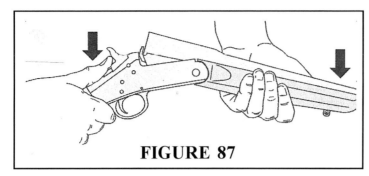

FIGURE 87

Loading the Single Shot

First make sure the hammer is forward in the un-cocked position, then open the action *(SEE FIGURE 87)*. Now look through the bore to make sure there are no obstructions in the barrel. Next observe the cartridge designation stamped on the barrel.

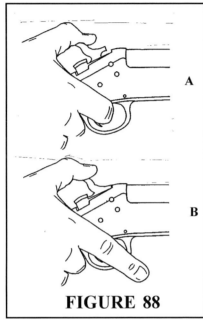

A

B

FIGURE 88

Then place the proper cartridge in the chamber and close the action with enough force to make sure it is securely in place, and can not be opened without pressing the release lever. NOTE: You will hear a distinct "click" when the action locks closed. Insure that the action is closed and locked before proceeding. While you avoid contact with the trigger, raise the firearm up and place the buttstock securely against your shoulder. Next pull the hammer fully to the rear to the cocked position. You are fully loaded. All you need to do is take careful aim and pull the trigger to fire the shotgun.

WARNING NO.1: DO NOT dry fire your shotgun because damage could occur to the barrel and/or the firing pin.

Should you decide to not fire after cocking the hammer, carefully lower the gun from your shoulder and keep the muzzle pointed in a safe direction. Then carefully hold the hammer back securely with your thumb and pull the trigger *(SEE FIGURE 88-A)*. Now, slowly let the hammer move forward approximately 1/4 of an inch, then release the trigger *(SEE FIGURE 88-B)*. Continue to guide the hammer down until it is fully forward *(SEE FIGURE 89)*. We suggest you practice this procedure with an empty firearm to get familiar with it.

UN-COCKED HAMMER

TRANSFER BAR

FIRING PIN

FIGURE 89

Unloading the Single Shot

Some single shots have an "automatic ejection" feature which ejects both fired and unfired cartridges when the action is opened. To eject a fired casing or an unfired round of ammunition from the gun, first point the muzzle in a safe direction and make sure no one is in the ejection path. Then press the release lever and open the gun fully *(SEE FIGURE 87)*. The empty casing or unfired round will automatically be ejected from the gun. Using extreme care, fired or unfired cartridges can be caught as they are ejected from the chamber. However always handle live ammunition carefully to avoid accidental discharge.

WARNING NO.2: In case of a misfire, keep the gun pointed in a safe direction and wait one minute before opening the gun.

Loading a Pump (Slide) Action Gun

Before loading, move the safety button fully rearward *(SEE FIGURE 90)* to the "ON" (SAFE) position. During loading, NEVER allow your fingers or any objects to contact the trigger, and keep the muzzle pointed in a safe direction at all times. Next depress the action lock lever *(SEE FIGURE 91)* then open the action by pulling the fore end completely rearward. Check to be certain that the ammunition selected is the same type of cartridge as designated on the left side of the barrel. If you wish to load the gun with the maximum number of shells, or fire single shots, load the first shell through the ejection port located on the right side of the receiver *(SEE FIGURE 92)*. The shell can be inserted directly into the chamber on top of the elevator. Then close the action by moving the fore end completely forward. Be sure to leave the safety "ON" (fully rearward) until you are ready to shoot. The gun is now fully loaded, and will fire if the safety is moved to the "OFF" (FIRE) position and the trigger is pulled.

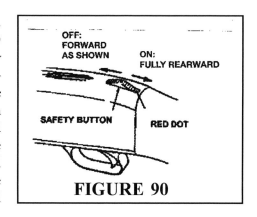

FIGURE 90

Loading the Pump Magazine

Load the magazine tube by turning the gun so that the trigger guard is facing up and the action is closed. Now push the front end of the shell into the magazine tube until the rim of the shell snaps past the cartridge stop *(SEE FIGURE 93-A, B)*. NEVER attempt to exceed the magazine capacity for your model of shotgun.

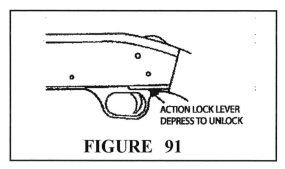

FIGURE 91

WARNING NO.1: Handling ammunition in poorly ventilated areas may result in exposure to lead and/or substances know to cause birth defects, reproductive harm, and/or other serious physical injury. Have adequate ventilation at all times. And wash your hands thoroughly after exposure.

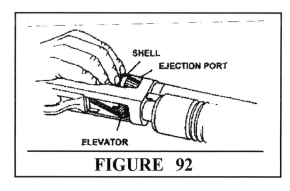

FIGURE 92

Unloading a Pump Action Gun

First move the safety button to the "ON" (SAFE) position, and keep the muzzle pointed in a safe direction while unloading the gun. Then depress the action lock lever *(SEE FIGURE 91)* and pull the fore end rearward, slowly, until the live shot shell is completely withdrawn and visible in the ejection port. Then remove shot shell by hand. Continue to pull the forearm rearward to release the next shot shell into the elevator. Now turn the gun so that the ejection port faces downward to allow the released shot shell to drop out through the ejection port. Next push your fore end completely forward, closing the bolt without a shell being chambered.

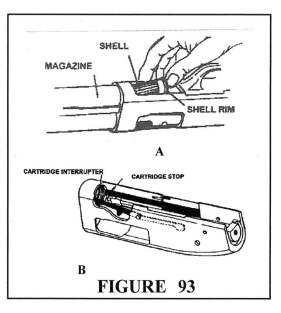

FIGURE 93

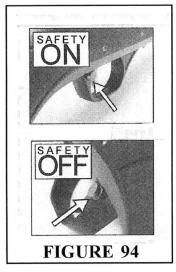

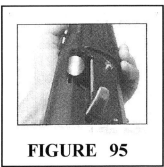

FIGURE 95

CAUTION NO.1: Turn the gun over so that the trigger guard is positioned upward and the gun remains pointed in a safe direction. Now, insert your right thumb into the opening in the bottom of the receiver and depress the cartridge stop on the right side to release shot shells one at a time *(SEE FIGURE 93)*. Repeat this until all shot shells are removed from the magazine tube.

CAUTION NO.2: Depress the lock action lever and pull the fore end completely rearward. Now visually and physically inspect the chamber, elevator and magazine tube to be certain the gun is completely unloaded. Now leave the action open, rearward position and the safety button fully rearward in the "ON" (SAFE) position.

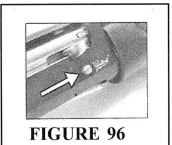

FIGURE 94

Loading a Semi Automatic Shotgun

First move the cross trigger block safety to the "ON" (SAFE) position *(SEE FIGURE 94)*. Keep the muzzle pointed in a safe direction while loading. Make sure the ammunition you are using is the correct size and gauge as marked on the barrel. Next visually inspect the chamber and barrel for obstructions by pulling back the bolt until it locks back. NOTE: If the bolt will not lock back then push the carrier stop button rearward then retry locking the bolt rearward. The chamber and barrel should be free of oil and grease as well as obstructions *(SEE FIGURE 95)*.

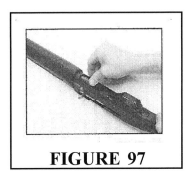

FIGURE 96

After inspection, release the bolt by depressing the carrier latch button *(SEE FIGURE 96)*. Next turn the gun upside down so that the barrel is pointing towards the ground and you are looking at the carrier latch. Now depress the carrier latch and insert up to five -2-3/4 inch cartridges or five 3 inch cartridges or four 3-1/2 inch cartridges into the magazine tube. NOTE: If there is a plastic spring cap in the magazine tube then all the capacities are decreased by one round *(SEE FIGURE 97)*.

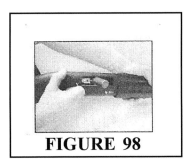

FIGURE 97

Unloading a Semi Automatic Shotgun

Make sure the cross trigger block safety is in the "ON" position, and your fingers are away from the trigger. Draw back the bolt until a cartridge is ejected or the bolt has traveled fully rearward. If there was no cartridge in the chamber, nothing will be ejected. Now slide the bolt back forward until it is fully closed. Repeat the drawing back of the bolt while depressing the carrier stop button until no more rounds are ejected from the gun. The bolt will lock back when the last round is ejected *(SEE FIGURE 98)*. Now lock the bolt in the rearward position. NOTE: You must move the carrier stop button rearward for the bolt to lock in the rearward position. With the bolt locked back, visually inspect the chamber to be sure that it is empty. You should also look down into the receiver through the ejection port and verify that the magazine tube is empty *(SEE FIGURE 99)*.

FIGURE 98

If for some reason the cartridge in the magazine tube will not rise up into the chamber after repeated attempts to manually cycle the gun, perform the following steps:

1. Manually close the bolt.
2. Turn over the gun so that the trigger guard is facing you (upward). Depress the carrier latch button *(SEE FIGURE 96)* and then depress the carrier latch.
3. With the same finger that you are depressing the carrier latch with, depress the shell latch. The shell latch is located on your left hand side with the gun in the upside down position. It is a piece of metal that should be holding the round in the magazine tube. The cartridge should slide up and out of the gun with your guidance.

    NOTE: The cartridge is under spring tension. Repeat this process until the magazine tube is empty. Now turn the gun over and lock the bolt back and verify that the gun is empty. If you had to follow the procedure for a cartridge that was not being released from the magazine tube, make sure the gun is empty and let a qualified gunsmith inspect the gun before you load or use the gun again.

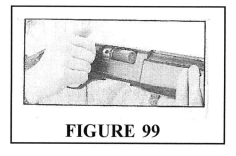

FIGURE 99

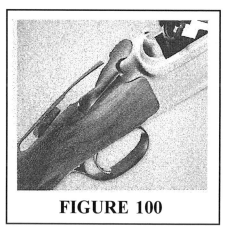

FIGURE 100

Loading a Side by Side Double Barrel Shotgun

First move the manual safety to the "ON" (SAFE) position by pushing the slide button rearward with your thumb until it stays in place *(SEE FIGURE 100)*. Keep the muzzle pointed in a safe direction while loading, and keep your fingers out of the trigger guard and away from the triggers at all times. Make sure the ammunition you are using is the correct gauge and length for your gun as marked on the barrel. However some guns are not marked. In that case, check with the manufacture or a gun dealer. Next open the breech of the gun *(SEE FIGURE 101)* by holding the gun with one hand grasping the buttstock immediately behind the receiver tang, and the other hand firmly grasping the fore end.

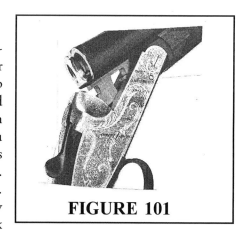

FIGURE 101

Now with the thumb of the hand grasping the buttstock, push the top lever to it's extreme right position. Then applying downward pressure with the hand grasping the fore end of the gun, ease the muzzle down until movement of the barrels stops with the breech now fully open *(SEE FIGURE 101)*. Next, visually check each bore for obstructions. If there are none, start loading your ammunition. Now place a shot shell of the proper size, and

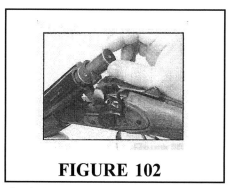

FIGURE 102

desired type into the chamber of each barrel intended to be fired *(SEE FIGURE 102)*. Next close the breech with your hands in the same position as when you opened it. Do this by applying upward pressure with the hand grasping the fore end, and ease the muzzle up until movement of the barrel stops with the breech fully closed. Next visually check the manual safety slide button to make sure it is in the "SAFE" position. Now visually check the top lever to make certain it is in the closed position *SEE FIGURE 100)*. Now your shotgun is loaded and ready to fire.

WARNING: If the manual safety is not in the "SAFE" position, the gun is ready to fire. So, DO NOT touch the triggers until you are absolutely ready to fire the gun.

Unloading a Side by Side Double Barrel Shotgun

First make sure the gun is pointed in a safe direction, and your fingers are out of the trigger guard and away from the trigger(s). Next move the manual safety to the "ON" (SAFE) position by pushing the slide button rearward with your thumb until it stays in place *(SEE FIGURE 100)*. Now open the breech. Then remove any unfired shot shells from the chambers of both barrels. Next visually check each bore for obstructions. If there are none, your gun is safely unloaded. If there are obstructions, they need to be cleared.

Clearing Barrel Obstructions

Push a shotgun bore cleaning tool through the bore from the breech end of both barrels until the end of the tool comes out at the muzzle. If for any reason an obstruction can not be easily cleared, stop, and contact the manufacturers authorized service center or a qualified gunsmith to take care of the problem. DO NOT try to do it yourself.

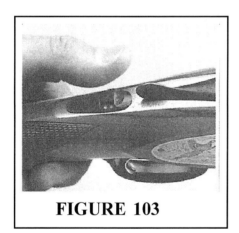

FIGURE 103

Loading an Over & Under Double Barrel Shotgun

First move the manual safety to the "ON" (SAFE) position by pushing the slide button rearward with your thumb until it stays in place. When it is you should see the letter "S" fully exposed on the tang directly in front of the top edge of the safety *(SEE FIGURE 103)*. Keep the muzzle pointed in a safe direction while loading, and keep your fingers out of the trigger guard and away from the trigger at all times. Make sure the ammunition you are using is the correct gauge and length for your gun as marked on the barrel. Now select the barrel you want to use by pushing the barrel selection button to the right or left.

Pushing the button to the left, exposing one red dot, will select the bottom barrel to fire first. Pushing the button to the right, exposing two red dots, will select the top barrel to fire first. Next unlock the action by pushing the top lever to the right, then open the breech of the gun by holding it the same way as the "side by side" gun, then putting downward pressure on the barrels. When loading, insert one or two shot shells. If you are loading just one shot shell, make sure the barrel selector is positioned to fire only that barrel. When your shells are loaded in the chamber, keeping your fingers out of the trigger guard and away from the trigger (one), close the action the same way as the "side by side" gun. Now your gun is loaded and ready to fire.

Unloading an Over & Under Double Barrel Shotgun

First make sure the gun is pointed in a safe direction, and your fingers are out of the trigger guard and away from the trigger. Next move the manual safety to the "ON" (SAFE) position by pushing the slide button rearward with your thumb until it stays in place *(SEE FIGURE 100)*. Now open the breech. Then remove any unfired shot shells from the chambers of both barrels. Next visually check each bore for obstructions. If there are none, your gun is safely unloaded. If there are obstructions, they need to be cleared.

Clearing Barrel Obstructions

Push a shotgun bore cleaning tool through the bore from the breech end of both barrels until the end of the tool comes out at the muzzle. If for any reason an obstruction can not be easily cleared, stop, and contact the manufacturers authorized service center or a qualified gunsmith.

Misfires

If you pull the trigger and the gun does not fire, keep it pointed in a safe direction and wait 30 seconds. Then, open the action carefully, remove and examine the loaded shot shells. If the shot shell primer is dented, but did not fire, DO NOT reuse the shot shell. If the primer is not dented, check to see if the barrel selector is set correctly for the proper barrel. If the gun still fails to fire, contact the manufacturer. If you experience a light or "squib" load, always check to make sure the barrels are clear of any obstructions before you attempt to reload.

Summation for Loading and Unloading all the Shotguns

Shotguns can be very dangerous. So, make sure you check your shotgun manual before you attempt to load or unload your shotgun. This is because your shotgun may be slightly different than the one we show (a basic shotgun). Follow all the directions for loading and unloading, and make double sure you are loading the correct size of ammunition for your shotgun. The information we have is in general, and only here to give you an idea how to load and unload in case you don't have a manual or even a clue how it operates. You can in most cases go on line, download a manual for your exact shotgun model, and print it out for the gun you have, and in most cases it is free.

Ammunition for Your Shotgun

Explanation

Now that you understand a little better of how to handle, load and unload your shotgun, you need to have some idea of what ammunition to use. We will NOT cover every possible ammunition that can be used in your shotgun. There is just too many types of ammunition sources out there, especially for shotguns, to try and cover them all. We will basically use "Federal" or "Hornady" for our ammunition information, unless otherwise stated. We will NOT mention special target ammunition. We will try to cover the more common ammunitions used in upland game bird, waterfowl, turkey and deer hunting. We will also use popularity as one of our targets as well as commonality. As an example, if you are going out upland game bird hunting what would you be more likely to use, and which types of rifles use what type of ammunition. You would not want to use a big game rifle and ammunition if you are only mostly going out to hunt quail and doves. Depending on what ammunition it was, you might blow them to pieces. In other words "overkill." Bare that in mind as you read on through the section.

Now if all this is not enough to confuse you, there is the question of what type of ammunition do you use. Shotgun ammunition is referred to as shells and not bullets. In the United kingdom (UK) they are referred to as cartridges.   The size of the shell is called it's gauge. The gauge is a system of measurement for the internal bore diameter of a smooth-bore firearm. Shotgun ammunition is different from rifle bullets because you use shells filled with shot (many smaller round balls), or you can have sabot slugs which are more like bullets, or it can be a solid projectile called a slug. The solid ammunition is basically used by the Police or Military. We won't go into that in this book. What you use kind of depends on what you are going out to hunt for. You will mostly use the shells filled with shot for hunting upland game birds, waterfowl, or sometimes deer, turkey and varmint's. Some states will not let you use plain lead shot any more because of the lead poisoning debate, in some cases only steel. However, shotgun ammunition does come in other types such as lead with a hard copper plate or a tungsten base, and one Company makes a "bismuth" ammunition.

NOTE: We will try to chart this out for you in handy tables to make it a little easier for you to overview and link the shotgun, ammo and game together, for a quick overview. This will give you a general idea of what shotgun, ammo, small game, upland game bird, turkey, deer, or waterfowl are generally in the different classes . There are more shotguns used in the different classes, but in the tables we are going to only list the more common and popular shotguns in the different classes. The information we are showing comes from the manufacturers stated information, which may or may not be true. The muzzle velocity on shotguns is shown only to give you some idea of the ammunitions force out of the barrel.

Shotgun Ammo Types

There are a lot of ammo types for shotguns because there are many uses such as target shooting as well as hunting game. We will only go into the ammunition for hunting small game, deer, turkey and waterfowl. There are basically three types of shotgun ammunitions. Basically, the smaller the shot, the more pellets in a shell, which is for hitting smaller, faster moving game:

- Birdshot (100 to 200 small lead pellets)
- Buckshot (10 large lead pellets)
- Slug or Sabot (1 large lead projectile)

Here is an interesting fact. Some states and areas do NOT allow rifles for hunting larger game animals such as deer because of the danger of the bullet traveling much further than the target. So what has happened is many shotgun manufacturers have redesigned and adapted their shotguns for larger game. This is where buckshot comes in for a larger pellet or shot size. Generally there are four standard shell lengths; the standard 2-3/4 inch, the 2-3/4 inch magnum, the 3 inch magnum and the 3-1/2 inch magnum. You can decide power levels and charge weight, even within the same shot size. As an example there are "dove loads" which are usually #8 and # 7-1/2, or #5 and #6 for squirrels and rabbits. They have a low brass base and a mild recoil, in a standard 2-3/4 inch shell. Having a variety of ammunition makes the shotgun a very adaptable firearm, which spans shotguns for sporting hunting purposes all the way to law enforcement and military usages for them. Some states have outlawed the use of plain lead shot altogether because of the lead poisoning debate. They will only let you use steel or non-toxic shot. However, now shotgun ammunition is available in other types of material; such as lead with a hard copper plate, tungsten or bismuth.

Table Issues

There is the issue of how far away from the target should you be? Depending on the animal or bird, you don't want to be so close for the shot that you tear up what little meat there is, such as quail, doves, squirrels or rabbits. Otherwise you may be spending a lot of time cleaning the shot out of the meat. Some experts believe the shorter barrel lengths are important, especially for young kids, but this is more of a carry weight issue. That's why we put it in the tables. The "relative cost" we are showing is just general, and may be above or under what you may be able to purchase the shotgun for. It's just to give you a better idea of the different shotgun costs. The shot size we are showing is what is generally recommended for shotgun hunting activities by "internetarmory.com." Chokes are recommended to keep the shot pattern from spreading out

Bobwhite Quail

to much on longer shots. We added the shotgun's weight to show the lighter weight shotguns which may be better for 6, 7, and 8 year olds.

Other Issues

We believe that young kids can get into the double barrel type shotguns when they get a e older, and have more experience with shotguns. At closer distances, which is where most young hunters are to the target, double barrel shotguns will blow away small birds and game. That's OK for varmint's, but in case you are hunting for game to eat, you don't need that much power. Some game birds such as quail and doves only weigh 6 or 7 ounces. So it does not take much to blow them to pieces.

We have come up with two tables below to help classify game birds and waterfowl by weight. This is addition to our "CPX" table on page 97 for all sizes of game animals. This will help you match the shotguns and the ammunition to the target game or bird. As with rifles, in the tables we have the links to help you match the shotguns to the shells and the game, all in one convenient place.

Game Bird Classification Table	
GBX Class	**Weight and Birds Covered in this Classification**
GB1 This class calls for shells with a smaller shot size that will kill without blowing birds to pieces.	Composed of Very Small Game Birds: That weigh up to .50 pounds (8 Oz.). Birds like Quail, Mourning Doves, Wild Pigeons, and Snipe.
GB2 This class calls for shells with a shot size that will kill birds without blowing them to pieces.	Composed of Small Game Birds: That weigh from .50 pound (8 Oz.) up to 3.0 pounds. Birds like Partridges, Willow & Rock Ptarmigan, Prairie Chickens, Woodcocks, Chukar, and Crows.
GB3 This class calls for shells and shot size that will kill mid size birds without blowing them to pieces	Composed of Medium Size Game Birds: That weigh from 3.0 pounds up to 8.0 pounds. Birds like Ringneck Pheasants, and Golden Pheasants.
GB4 This class calls for shells and shot size that will kill larger birds without blowing them to pieces	Composed of the Larger Game Birds: That weigh from 8.0 pounds up to 40.0 pounds. Birds like Ruffed Grouse, Guinea Fowl, and Wild Turkeys.

Note: This table only considers game birds hunted somewhere in the USA.

Water Fowl Classification Table	
WFX Class	**Weight and Waterfowl Covered in this Classification**
WF1 This class calls for shells and shot size that.will kill small birds without blowing them to pieces	Composed of the smaller waterfowl Birds: That weigh up to 1 pound. Birds like the Teal family, and Bufflehead Ducks
WF2 This class calls for shells and shot size that will kill medium birds without blowing them to pieces	Composed of Medium Sized Waterfowl Birds: That weigh from 1 pound up to 5 pounds. Birds like Wigeons, Shovelers, Mergansers, and most of the Duck family.
WF3 This class calls for shells and shot size that will kill larger birds without blowing them to pieces	Composed of Larger Size Waterfowl Birds: That weigh from 5 pounds up to 13 pounds. Ducks like Pekin's (FR), Muscovey's (FR), and hybrid Moulard's (FR). Geese like Canada, Lesser Snow, and Greater Snow.

Note: This table only considers water fowl hunted or farm raised in the USA. FR = Farm raised.

Chukar

Small Game Birds (GB1)

Small game birds are usually quail and doves *(SEE TABLE 15, 16)*. We will cover the "single shot," the "pump action," and the "semi-automatic action." The birds in this class barely get up to half a pound in weight. So it does not take much to blow them to pieces up close. Some are very good eating when fixed right, so you may want to take that head shot if at all possible when you are up to 10 yards away, and the bird is not flying. However, when they are flying, you need to just make sure you lead them and hit them.

Small Game Birds (GB2)

This classification is for other small game birds which are usually partridges, ptarmigans, prairie chickens, woodcocks, chukars, and crows *(SEE TABLE 17)*. The birds in this class barely get up to 3 pounds in weight. So it does not take much to blow them to pieces up close. Some are very good eating when fixed right, so you may want to take a head shot if at all possible when you are up to 10 yards away, and the bird is not flying. However, when they are flying, you need to just make sure you lead them and hit them.

Ring Neck Pheasant

MFR Muzzel Velocity MV (FPS) →	Ammunition Caliber [1]					Shot Size [2]	Choke Type	Game Class	Barrel Length	Weight (Lbs)	Relative Cost
TABLE 15 SHOTGUNS FOR SMALL GAME & VERY SMALL GAME BIRDS	.410 Ga.	28 Ga.	20 Ga.	16 Ga. CPL	12 Ga.						
	1400	1350	1425	1425	1375						
BREAK OPEN SINGLE SHOT SHOTGUNS											
	Where to Take the Shot on Game [4]										
Remington Model SPR100	Head Shots Up To [3] 10 Yds.	—	Head Shots Up To [3] 10 Yds.	—	Anywhere on Body Up To 30 Yds.	5, 6	M	CPX1	29 Inch	6.5	Rea
						7.5, 8	M, IC	GB1			
NEF Pardner Youth	Head Shots Up To [3] 10 Yds.	Anywhere on Body Up To 30 Yds.	Head Shots Up To [3] 10 Yds.	—	Anywhere on Body Up To 30 Yds.	5, 6	M	CPX1	26-32 Inch	5.5	Very Rea
						7.5, 8	M, IC	GB1			
Winchester Model 37	Head Shots Up To [3] 10 Yds.	Anywhere on Body Up To 30 Yds.	Head Shots Up To [3] 10 Yds.	Anywhere on Body Up To 30 Yds.	Anywhere on Body Up To 30 Yds.	5, 6	M	CPX1	26-30 Inch	5.5	Very Rea
						7.5, 8	M, IC	GB1			
H & R Topper Model	Head Shots Up To [3] 10 Yds.	—	Head Shots Up To [3] 10 Yds.	—	Anywhere on Body Up To 30 Yds.	5, 6	M	CPX1	26-32 Inch	5 - 6	Very Rea
						7.5, 8	M, IC	GB1			
H & R Topper Jr, Jr Classic	Head Shots Up To [3] 10 Yds.	—	Head Shots Up To [3] 10 Yds.	—	—	5, 6	M	CPX1	26-32 Inch	5 - 6	Very Rea
						7.5, 8	M, IC	GB1			
Savage Model 94, Stevens	Head Shots Up To [3] 10 Yds.	—	Head Shots Up To [3] 10 Yds.	—	—	5, 6	M	CPX1	26 Inch	5 - 8	Very Rea
						7.5, 8	M, IC	GB1			
PUMP ACTION SHOTGUNS											
Browning BPS Model	Head Shots Up To [3] 10 Yds.	—	Head Shots Up To [3] 10 Yds.	—	Anywhere on Body Up To 30 Yds.	5, 6	M	CPX1	24-28 Inch	5 - 6	Mid
						7.5, 8	M, IC	GB1			
Mossberg Models 500, 505, 535, 835	Head Shots Up To [3] 10 Yds.	—	Head Shots Up To [3] 10 Yds.	—	Anywhere on Body Up To 30 Yds.	5, 6	M	CPX1	20-24 Inch	5.25 - 8.5	Very Rea
						7.5, 8	M, IC	GB1			
Remington Model 870, 1300	Head Shots Up To [3] 10 Yds.	Anywhere on Body Up To 30 Yds.	Head Shots Up To [3] 10 Yds.	Anywhere on Body Up To 30 Yds.	Anywhere on Body Up To 30 Yds.	5, 6	M	CPX1	18-28 Inch	7 - 7.5	Mid
						7.5, 8	M, IC	GB1			
Benelli Super Nova 37, ComfTech	—	—	Head Shots Up To [3] 10 Yds.	—	Anywhere on Body Up To 30 Yds.	5, 6	M	CPX1	24-28 Inch	6.6 - 8	Mid
						7.5, 8	M, IC	GB1			
Winchester Model 42, 12, 1300	Head Shots Up To [3] 10 Yds.	—	Head Shots Up To [3] 10 Yds.	Anywhere on Body Up To 30 Yds.	Anywhere on Body Up To 30 Yds.	5, 6	M	CPX1	20-30 Inch	6.5 - 7.75	Mid
						7.5, 8	M, IC	GB1			
Ithaca Model 37	—	—	Head Shots Up To [3] 10 Yds.	Anywhere on Body Up To 30 Yds.	Anywhere on Body Up To 30 Yds.	5, 6	M	CPX1	18.5-30 In.	6.5	Mid
						7.5, 8	M, IC	GB1			

Abbreviation Definitions:
Rea = Reasonable, Mid = Mid Range, Exp = Expensive, FPS = Feet Per Second, M = Modified, IC = Improved Cylinder, HBL = Hi-Brass Load,
[1] = Based on steel load specifications, [2] = Recommended by internetarmory.com, Ga. = Ammunition Gauge, [3] = Still Target,
[4] = Otherwise a Flying or Still Target

Medium Size Game Birds (GB3)

This classification is for medium size game birds which are usually the ring neck, golden, and the rest of the pheasant family (**SEE TABLE 17**). The birds in this class barely get up to 8 pounds in weight. So it does not take much to blow them to pieces up close. Some are very good eating when fixed right, so you may want to take a head shot if at all possible when you are up to 10 yards away. However, when they are flying, you need to just make sure you lead them and hit them.

Large Size Game Birds (GB4)

This classification is for larger size game birds which are usually the ruffled grouse, guinea fowl, and wild turkey (**SEE TABLE 19**). The birds in this class only get up to about 40 pounds in

MFR Muzzel Velocity MV (FPS) →	Ammunition Caliber [1]					Shot Size [2]	Choke Type	Game Class	Barrel Length	Weight (Lbs)	Relative Cost
	.410 Ga. 1400	28 Ga. 1350	20 Ga. 1425	16 Ga. CPL 1425	12 Ga. 1375						
SEMI - AUTOMATIC SHOTGUNS											
	Where to Take the Shot on Game [4]										
Browning Gold, A5 Models	—	—	Head Shots Up To [3] 10 Yds.	Anywhere on Body Up To 30 Yds.	Anywhere on Body Up To 30 Yds.	5, 6	M	CPX1	25.5-30 In.	6.5-7.9	Exp
						7.5, 8	M, IC	GB1			
Baretta AL391 Urica, 391	—	—	Head Shots Up To [3] 10 Yds.	—	Anywhere on Body Up To 30 Yds.	5, 6	M	CPX1	28-30 Inch	6.2-7.2	Exp
						7.5, 8	M, IC	GB1			
Benelli Super Black Eagle	—	—	—	—	Anywhere on Body To 30 Yds.	5, 6	M	CPX1	26-30 Inch	7.2-7.3	Exp
						7.5, 8	M, IC	GB1			
Remington Model 1100	Head Shots Up To [3] 10 Yds.	Anywhere on Body Up To 30 Yds.	Head Shots Up To [3] 10 Yds.	Anywhere on Body Up To 30 Yds.	Anywhere on Body Up To 30 Yds.	5, 6	M	CPX1	18-30 Inch	6.5-8	Exp
						7.5, 8	M, IC	GB1			
Mossberg Model 935	—	—	—	—	Anywhere on Body Up To 30 Yds.	5, 6	M	CPX1	22-28 Inch	7.5-7.75	Rea
						7.5, 8	M, IC	GB1			
Winchester Super X2 Model	—	—	—	—	Anywhere on Body Up To 30 Yds.	5, 6	M	CPX1	22-30 Inch	6.5-8.25	Mid
						7.5, 8	M, IC	GB1			

TABLE 16 SHOTGUNS FOR SMALL GAME & VERY SMALL GAME BIRDS

Abbreviation Definitions:
Rea = Reasonable, Mid = Mid Range, Exp = Expensive, FPS = Feet Per Second, M = Modified, IC = Improved Cylinder, HBL = Hi-Brass Load, [1] = Based on steel load specifications, [2] = Recommended by internetarmory.com, Ga. = Ammunition Gauge, [3] = Still Target, [4] = Otherwise a Flying or Still Target

weight. With the exception of turkeys it does not take much to blow them to pieces up close. However, turkeys are so wary that it's hard to get up that close to them anyway. So you may want to take a head shot if at all possible when you are close enough. However, when they are flying, you may need to just make sure you lead them and hit them.

Small Waterfowl Birds (WF1)

This classification is for the small size waterfowl birds which are usually the teal family of ducks, and bufflehead ducks (*SEE TABLE 20,21*). The birds in this class barely get up to 1 pound in weight. It does not take much to blow them to pieces up close. So you may want to take a head shot if at all possible when you are close enough. However, when they are flying, you may need to just make sure you lead them and hit them.

Medium Size Waterfowl Birds (WF2)

This classification is for the medium size waterfowl birds which are usually the wigeons, shovelers, mergansers, and most of the duck family (*SEE TABLE 20,21*). The birds in this class barely get up to 5 pounds in weight. It does not take much to blow them to pieces up close. So you may want to take a head shot if at all possible when you are close enough. However, when they are flying, you may need to just make sure you lead them and hit them. The shot size is what is generally recommened for shotgun hunting activities by "internetarmory.com" and "Federal Ammunition."

Mallard Duck

131

TABLE 17 SHOTGUNS FOR SMALL TO MEDIUM SIZE GAME BIRDS										
MFR Muzzel Velocity MV (FPS) →	Ammunition Caliber [1]					Shot Size [2]	Choke Type	Game Class	Barrel Length Range	Weight Range (Lbs)	Relative Cost
	.410 Ga. 1400	28 Ga. 1350	20 Ga. 1425	16 Ga. HBL 1295	12 Ga. 1375						
SINGLE SHOT & PUMP SHOTGUNS											
	Where to Take the Shot on Game [4]										
Remington Model 870 Express	Head Shots Up To [3] 10 Yds.	Anywhere on Body Up To 30 Yds.	Head Shots Up To [3] 10 Yds.	——	Anywhere on Body To 30 Yds.	6, 7.5, 8, 9	M, IC	GB2 GB3	18-28 Inch	6-8	Rea
Mossberg Model 500	Head Shots Up To [3] 10 Yds.	——	Head Shots Up To [3] 10 Yds.	Anywhere on Body Up To 30 Yds.	Anywhere on Body To 30 Yds.	6, 7.5, 8, 9	M, IC	GB2 GB3	20-31 Inch	6.5-7.5	Rea
H & R Ultra Slug, Topper	Head Shots Up To [3] 10 Yds.	——	Head Shots Up To [3] 10 Yds.	——	Anywhere on Body Up To 30 Yds.	6, 7.5, 8, 9	M, IC	GB2 GB3	22-28 Inch	5-9	Very Rea
Ithaca DS II, Ds III, Model 37	——	——	Head Shots Up To [3] 10 Yds.	Anywhere on Body Up To 30 Yds.	Anywhere on Body To 30 Yds.	6, 7.5, 8, 9	M, IC	GB2 GB3	20-26 Inch	6-7.6	Rea
NEF Pardner Youth	Head Shots Up To [3] 10 Yds.	Anywhere on Body Up To 30 Yds.	Head Shots Up To [3] 10 Yds.	——	Anywhere on Body To 30 Yds.	6, 7.5, 8, 9	M, IC	GB2 GB3	26-32 Inch	5.5	Very Rea
SEMI - AUTOMATIC SHOTGUNS											
	Where to Take the Shot on Game [4]										
Beretta Extrema2 Model	——	——	——	——	Anywhere on Body To 30 Yds.	6, 7.5, 8, 9	M, IC	GB2 GB3	26-28 Inch	7.5	Exp
Browning Gold Model	——	——	Head Shots Up To [3] 10 Yds.	——	Anywhere on Body To 30 Yds.	6, 7.5, 8, 9	M, IC	GB2 GB3	26-28 Inch	6.75-7.5	Exp
Benelli Super Black Eagle	——	——	——	——	Anywhere on Body To 30 Yds.	6, 7.5, 8, 9	M, IC	GB2 GB3	24-28 Inch	7.1-7.3	Exp
Winchester Modle SX2, SX3	——	——	Head Shots Up To [3] 10 Yds.	——	Anywhere on Body To 30 Yds.	6, 7.5, 8, 9	M, IC	GB2 GB3	24-30 Inch	6.38-8	Mid
Remington Model 11-87	——	——	Head Shots Up To [3] 10 Yds.	——	Anywhere on Body To 30 Yds.	6, 7.5, 8, 9	M, IC	GB2 GB3	21-30 Inch	8.25	Mid
Franchi Model 912	——	——	——	——	Anywhere on Body To 30 Yds.	6, 7.5, 8, 9	M, IC	GB2 GB3	24-30 Inch	7.38-7.6	Rea
Mossberg 935 Model	——	——	——	——	Anywhere on Body To 30 Yds.	6, 7.5, 8, 9	M, IC	GB2 GB3	22-28 Inch	7.5-7.75	Rea

Abbreviation Definitions:

Rea = Reasonable, Mid = Mid Range, Exp = Expensive, FPS = Feet Per Second, M = Modified, IC = Improved Cylinder, HBL = Hi-Brass Load, [1] = Based on steel load specifications, [2] = Recommended by internetarmory.com, Ga. = Ammunition Gauge, [3] = Still Target, [4] = Otherwise a Flying or Still Target

Snow Goose

Large Waterfowl Birds (WF3)

This classification is for the larger size waterfowl birds which are usually the pekin ducks, muscovey ducks, hybrid moulard ducks (all farm raised), canada geese, and snow geese (***SEE TABLE 22***). We will only list the more common and popular shotguns in the "single shot/pump action," and the "semi-automatic action" types. The birds in this class can get up to 13 pounds in weight. However, it does not take much to blow a lot of meat away if you get up close. So you may want to take a head shot if

TABLE 18 SHOTGUNS FOR MEDIUM SIZE GAME ANIMALS (DEER)

Buckshot (Lead) Ammunition [1]

MFR	20 Ga. 2.75	20 Ga. 3	16 Ga. 2.75	12 Ga. 2.75	12 Ga. 2.75	12 Ga. 2.75	12 Ga. 2.75	12 Ga. 2.75	12 Ga. 3	12 Ga. 3	12 Ga. 2.75 [3]	Choke Type [2]	Game Class	Barrel Length Range	Weight Range (Lbs)	Relative Cost
Shot Size →	3 Buck	2 Buck	1 Buck	4 Buck	00 Buck	4 Buck	00 Buck	000 Buck	4 Buck	00 Buck	00 Buck					
Muzzle Velocity MV (FPS) →	1200	1100	1225	1250	1290	1325	1325	1325	1210	1210	1140					

SINGLE SHOT & PUMP SHOTGUNS
Where to Take the Shot on Game

MFR	20 Ga. 2.75	20 Ga. 3	16 Ga. 2.75	12 Ga. 2.75	12 Ga. 2.75	12 Ga. 2.75	12 Ga. 2.75	12 Ga. 2.75	12 Ga. 3	12 Ga. 3	12 Ga. 2.75 [3]	Choke Type [2]	Game Class	Barrel Length Range	Weight Range (Lbs)	Relative Cost
Remington Model 870 Express	Head Shots Up To [4] 10 Yds.	Head Shots Up To [4] 10 Yds.	—	Anywhere on Body [5] To 40 Yds.	Anywhere on Body [5] To 40 Yds.	Anywhere on Body [5] To 40 Yds.	Anywhere on Body [5] To 40 Yds.	Anywhere on Body [5] To 40 Yds.	Anywhere on Body [5] To 40 Yds.	Anywhere on Body [5] To 40 Yds.	Anywhere on Body [5] To 40 Yds.	M, IC	CPX2	18-28 Inch	6-8	Rea
Mossberg Model 500	Head Shots Up To [4] 10 Yds.	Head Shots Up To [4] 10 Yds.	Anywhere on Body [5] To 40 Yds.	Anywhere on Body [5] To 40 Yds.	Anywhere on Body [5] To 40 Yds.	Anywhere on Body [5] To 40 Yds.	Anywhere on Body [5] To 40 Yds.	Anywhere on Body [5] To 40 Yds.	Anywhere on Body [5] To 40 Yds.	Anywhere on Body [5] To 40 Yds.	Anywhere on Body [5] To 40 Yds.	M, IC	CPX2	20-31 Inch	6.5-7.5	Rea
H & R Pardner, Topper	Head Shots Up To [4] 10 Yds.	Head Shots Up To [4] 10 Yds.	—	Anywhere on Body [5] To 40 Yds.	Anywhere on Body [5] To 40 Yds.	Anywhere on Body [5] To 40 Yds.	Anywhere on Body [5] To 40 Yds.	Anywhere on Body [5] To 40 Yds.	Anywhere on Body [5] To 40 Yds.	Anywhere on Body [5] To 40 Yds.	Anywhere on Body [5] To 40 Yds.	M, IC	CPX2	22-28 Inch	5-8	Very Rea
Ithaca DS II, Ds III, Model 37	Head Shots Up To [4] 10 Yds.	Head Shots Up To [4] 10 Yds.	Anywhere on Body [5] To 40 Yds.	Anywhere on Body [5] To 40 Yds.	Anywhere on Body [5] To 40 Yds.	Anywhere on Body [5] To 40 Yds.	Anywhere on Body [5] To 40 Yds.	Anywhere on Body [5] To 40 Yds.	Anywhere on Body [5] To 40 Yds.	Anywhere on Body [5] To 40 Yds.	Anywhere on Body [5] To 40 Yds.	M, IC	CPX2	20-26 Inch	6.0-7.6	Rea
NEF Pardner, & Pardner Youth	Head Shots Up To [4] 10 Yds.	Head Shots Up To [4] 10 Yds.	—	Anywhere on Body [5] To 40 Yds.	Anywhere on Body [5] To 40 Yds.	Anywhere on Body [5] To 40 Yds.	Anywhere on Body [5] To 40 Yds.	Anywhere on Body [5] To 40 Yds.	Anywhere on Body [5] To 40 Yds.	Anywhere on Body [5] To 40 Yds.	Anywhere on Body [5] To 40 Yds.	M, IC	CPX2	26-32 Inch	5.5-7.5	Very Rea
Winchester 37, Black Shadow	Head Shots Up To [4] 10 Yds.	Head Shots Up To [4] 10 Yds.	Anywhere on Body [5] To 40 Yds.	Anywhere on Body [5] To 40 Yds.	Anywhere on Body [5] To 40 Yds.	Anywhere on Body [5] To 40 Yds.	Anywhere on Body [5] To 40 Yds.	Anywhere on Body [5] To 40 Yds.	Anywhere on Body [5] To 40 Yds.	Anywhere on Body [5] To 40 Yds.	Anywhere on Body [5] To 40 Yds.	M, IC	CPX2	26-28 Inch	7.0-7.25	Rea

SEMI-AUTOMATIC SHOTGUNS

MFR	Smoothbore Barrel, Sabot Slugs [1]							Fully Rifled Barrel [1]		Choke Type [2]	Game Class	Barrel Length Range	Weight Range (Lbs)	Relative Cost
Shell Size →	.410 Ga. 2.50	20 Ga. 2.75	16 Ga. 2.75	12 Ga. 2.75	12 Ga. 2.75	12 Ga. 3	10 Ga. 3.50	20 Ga. 2.75	12 Ga. 2.75					
Slug Weight →	.25 Oz.	.75 Oz.	.80 Oz.	1.25 Oz.	1.00 Oz.	1.25 Oz.	1.75 Oz.	.875 Oz.	1.00 Oz.					
Muzzle Velocity MV (FPS) →	1775	1600	1600	1520	1610	1600	1280	1450	1500					

Where to Take the Shot on Game

MFR	.410 Ga.	20 Ga.	16 Ga.	12 Ga.	12 Ga.	12 Ga. 3	10 Ga.	20 Ga.	12 Ga.	Choke Type	Game Class	Barrel Length Range	Weight Range	Relative Cost
Browning Gold, A5 Models	—	Body Kill Areas To 50 Yds. [5]	Body Kill Areas To 50 Yds. [5]	Body Kill Areas To 75 Yds. [5]	Body Kill Areas To 75 Yds. [5]	Body Kill Areas To 75 Yds. [5]	[6]	Body Kill Areas To 75 Yds. [5]	Body Kill Areas To 75 Yds. [5]	M, IC	CPX2	25.5-30 In.	6.5-7.9	Exp
Baretta 391, AL391 Urika	—	Body Kill Areas To 50 Yds. [5]	—	Body Kill Areas To 75 Yds. [5]	Body Kill Areas To 75 Yds. [5]	Body Kill Areas To 75 Yds. [5]	[6]	Body Kill Areas To 75 Yds. [5]	Body Kill Areas To 75 Yds. [5]	M, IC	CPX2	28-30 Inch	6.2-7.2	Exp
Benelli Super Black Eagle	—	—	—	Body Kill Areas To 75 Yds. [5]	Body Kill Areas To 75 Yds. [5]	Body Kill Areas To 75 Yds. [5]	[6]	Body Kill Areas To 75 Yds. [5]	Body Kill Areas To 75 Yds. [5]	M, IC	CPX2	26-30 Inch	7.2-7.3	Exp
Remington Model 1100	Head Shots Up To [4] 25 Yds.	Body Kill Areas To 50 Yds. [5]	Body Kill Areas To 50 Yds. [5]	Body Kill Areas To 75 Yds. [5]	Body Kill Areas To 75 Yds. [5]	Body Kill Areas To 75 Yds. [5]	[6]	Body Kill Areas To 75 Yds. [5]	Body Kill Areas To 75 Yds. [5]	M, IC	CPX2	18-30 Inch	6.5-8	Exp
Mossberg Model 935	—	—	—	Body Kill Areas To 75 Yds. [5]	Body Kill Areas To 75 Yds. [5]	Body Kill Areas To 75 Yds. [5]	[6]	Body Kill Areas To 75 Yds. [5]	Body Kill Areas To 75 Yds. [5]	M, IC	CPX2	22-28 Inch	7.5-7.75	Rea
Winchester Super X2 Model	—	—	—	Body Kill Areas To 75 Yds. [5]	Body Kill Areas To 75 Yds. [5]	Body Kill Areas To 75 Yds. [5]	[6]	Body Kill Areas To 75 Yds. [5]	Body Kill Areas To 75 Yds. [5]	M, IC	CPX2	22-30 Inch	6.5-8.25	Mid

Abbreviation Definitions & Notes:
Rea = Reasonable, Mid = Mid Range, Exp = Expensive, FPS = Feet Per Second, M = Modified, IC = Improved Cylinder, [1] = Based on Sabot Slug Hollow Point Specs,
[2] = Recommended by internetarmory.com, Ga. = Ammunition Gauge, [3] = Low Recoil, [4] = Still Target, [5] = Running or Still Target
[6] = Probably Not Available in this Gauge

at all possible when you are close enough. However, when they are flying, you may need to just make sure you lead them and hit them. The shot size is what is generally recommended for shotgun waterfowl hunting activities by "internetarmory.com" and "Federal Ammunition."

Summation of Shotguns

The shotgun is a very versatile firearm. Use it right, take care of it, and it will last many years. And who knows what new kind of new ammunition will be available for it in 20 or 30 years. Think about it? How many rifles can you get that will shoot small quail all the way up to a deer at shorter ranges without blowing a hole right through them, and that you can get shotguns with two barrels instead of just one.

White Tailed Deer

Firearms | Shotguns | Muzzleloaders

TABLE 19 SHOTGUNS FOR LARGER SIZE GAME BIRDS (TURKEY)

| MFR ↓ | 20 Ga. FP 2.75 #4 (Lead) 1175 | 20 Ga. FP 2.75 #5 (Lead) 1350 | 20 Ga. WS 3.0 #4 1185 | 20 Ga. HS 3.0 #7 1090 | 20 Ga. RN 3.0 #5 (Lead) 1185 | 12 Ga. WXT 2.75 #6 (Lead) 1225 | 12 Ga. RP 2.75 4x6 CPL 1260 | 12 Ga. HS 2.75 #5 1090 | 12 Ga. RN 3.0 #4 (Lead) 1210 | 12 Ga. FP 3.0 #6 (Lead) 1300 | 12 Ga. HS 3.0 #4 1090 | 12 Ga. WSE 3.0 #4/5/6 1225 | 12 Ga. RN 3.5 #6 (Lead) 1300 | 12 Ga. HS 3.5 #4 1090 | 12 Ga. WSE 3.5 #4 1225 | Choke Type | Game Class | Weight Range (Lbs) |

(Shell Size, Shot Size, Muzzle Velocity MV (FPS) shown in header rows above.)

SINGLE SHOT & PUMP SHOTGUNS

Where to Take the Shot on Game

MFR	20 Ga. FP #4	20 Ga. FP #5	20 Ga. WS #4	20 Ga. HS #7	20 Ga. RN #5	12 Ga. WXT #6	12 Ga. RP 4x6	12 Ga. HS #5	12 Ga. RN #4	12 Ga. FP #6	12 Ga. HS #4	12 Ga. WSE #4/5/6	12 Ga. RN #6	12 Ga. HS #4	12 Ga. WSE #4	Choke	Class	Wt
Remington Model 870 Express	Head Shots Up To 10 Yds. [3]	Head Shots Up To 10 Yds. [3]	Head Shots Up To 10 Yds. [3]	Head Shots Up To 10 Yds. [3]	Head Shots Up To 10 Yds. [3]	Body Kill Areas To 75 Yds. [4]	Body Kill Areas To 75 Yds. [4]	Body Kill Areas To 75 Yds. [4]	Body Kill Areas To 75 Yds. [4]	Body Kill Areas To 75 Yds. [4]	Body Kill Areas To 75 Yds. [4]	Body Kill Areas To 75 Yds. [4]	Body Kill Areas To 75 Yds. [4]	Body Kill Areas To 75 Yds. [4]	Body Kill Areas To 75 Yds. [4]	M, IC	GB4	6-8
Mossberg Model 500	Head Shots Up To 10 Yds. [3]	Head Shots Up To 10 Yds. [3]	Head Shots Up To 10 Yds. [3]	Head Shots Up To 10 Yds. [3]	Head Shots Up To 10 Yds. [3]	Body Kill Areas To 75 Yds. [4]	Body Kill Areas To 75 Yds. [4]	Body Kill Areas To 75 Yds. [4]	Body Kill Areas To 75 Yds. [4]	Body Kill Areas To 75 Yds. [4]	Body Kill Areas To 75 Yds. [4]	Body Kill Areas To 75 Yds. [4]	Body Kill Areas To 75 Yds. [4]	Body Kill Areas To 75 Yds. [4]	Body Kill Areas To 75 Yds. [4]	M, IC	GB4	6.5-7.5
H & R Pardner, Topper	Head Shots Up To 10 Yds. [3]	Head Shots Up To 10 Yds. [3]	Head Shots Up To 10 Yds. [3]	Head Shots Up To 10 Yds. [3]	Head Shots Up To 10 Yds. [3]	Body Kill Areas To 75 Yds. [4]	Body Kill Areas To 75 Yds. [4]	Body Kill Areas To 75 Yds. [4]	Body Kill Areas To 75 Yds. [4]	Body Kill Areas To 75 Yds. [4]	Body Kill Areas To 75 Yds. [4]	Body Kill Areas To 75 Yds. [4]	Body Kill Areas To 75 Yds. [4]	Body Kill Areas To 75 Yds. [4]	Body Kill Areas To 75 Yds. [4]	M, IC	GB4	5-8
Ithaca DS II, Ds III, Model 37	Head Shots Up To 10 Yds. [3]	Head Shots Up To 10 Yds. [3]	Head Shots Up To 10 Yds. [3]	Head Shots Up To 10 Yds. [3]	Head Shots Up To 10 Yds. [3]	Body Kill Areas To 75 Yds. [4]	Body Kill Areas To 75 Yds. [4]	Body Kill Areas To 75 Yds. [4]	Body Kill Areas To 75 Yds. [4]	Body Kill Areas To 75 Yds. [4]	Body Kill Areas To 75 Yds. [4]	Body Kill Areas To 75 Yds. [4]	Body Kill Areas To 75 Yds. [4]	Body Kill Areas To 75 Yds. [4]	Body Kill Areas To 75 Yds. [4]	M, IC	GB4	6.0-7.6
NEF Pardner, & Pardner Youth	Head Shots Up To 10 Yds. [3]	Head Shots Up To 10 Yds. [3]	Head Shots Up To 10 Yds. [3]	Head Shots Up To 10 Yds. [3]	Head Shots Up To 10 Yds. [3]	Body Kill Areas To 75 Yds. [4]	Body Kill Areas To 75 Yds. [4]	Body Kill Areas To 75 Yds. [4]	Body Kill Areas To 75 Yds. [4]	Body Kill Areas To 75 Yds. [4]	Body Kill Areas To 75 Yds. [4]	Body Kill Areas To 75 Yds. [4]	Body Kill Areas To 75 Yds. [4]	Body Kill Areas To 75 Yds. [4]	Body Kill Areas To 75 Yds. [4]	M, IC	GB4	5.5-7.5
Winchester Model 37, 37A	Head Shots Up To 10 Yds. [3]	Head Shots Up To 10 Yds. [3]	Head Shots Up To 10 Yds. [3]	Head Shots Up To 10 Yds. [3]	Head Shots Up To 10 Yds. [3]	Body Kill Areas To 75 Yds. [4]	Body Kill Areas To 75 Yds. [4]	Body Kill Areas To 75 Yds. [4]	Body Kill Areas To 75 Yds. [4]	Body Kill Areas To 75 Yds. [4]	Body Kill Areas To 75 Yds. [4]	Body Kill Areas To 75 Yds. [4]	Body Kill Areas To 75 Yds. [4]	Body Kill Areas To 75 Yds. [4]	Body Kill Areas To 75 Yds. [4]	M, IC	GB4	7.0-7.25

SEMI-AUTOMATIC SHOTGUNS

Where to Take the Shot on Game

MFR	20 Ga. FP #4	20 Ga. FP #5	20 Ga. WS #4	20 Ga. HS #7	20 Ga. RN #5	12 Ga. WXT #6	12 Ga. RP 4x6	12 Ga. HS #5	12 Ga. RN #4	12 Ga. FP #6	12 Ga. HS #4	12 Ga. WSE #4/5/6	12 Ga. RN #6	12 Ga. HS #4	12 Ga. WSE #4	Choke	Class	Wt
Baretta 391, AL391, Extrema2	Head Shots Up To 10 Yds. [3]	Head Shots Up To 10 Yds. [3]	Head Shots Up To 10 Yds. [3]	Head Shots Up To 10 Yds. [3]	Head Shots Up To 10 Yds. [3]	Body Kill Areas To 75 Yds. [4]	Body Kill Areas To 75 Yds. [4]	Body Kill Areas To 75 Yds. [4]	Body Kill Areas To 75 Yds. [4]	Body Kill Areas To 75 Yds. [4]	Body Kill Areas To 75 Yds. [4]	Body Kill Areas To 75 Yds. [4]	Body Kill Areas To 75 Yds. [4]	Body Kill Areas To 75 Yds. [4]	Body Kill Areas To 75 Yds. [4]	M, IC	GB4	6.2-7.5
Browning Gold, A5 Models	Head Shots Up To 10 Yds. [3]	Head Shots Up To 10 Yds. [3]	Head Shots Up To 10 Yds. [3]	Head Shots Up To 10 Yds. [3]	Head Shots Up To 10 Yds. [3]	Body Kill Areas To 75 Yds. [4]	Body Kill Areas To 75 Yds. [4]	Body Kill Areas To 75 Yds. [4]	Body Kill Areas To 75 Yds. [4]	Body Kill Areas To 75 Yds. [4]	Body Kill Areas To 75 Yds. [4]	Body Kill Areas To 75 Yds. [4]	Body Kill Areas To 75 Yds. [4]	Body Kill Areas To 75 Yds. [4]	Body Kill Areas To 75 Yds. [4]	M, IC	GB4	6.5-7.9
Benelli Super Black Eagle	Head Shots Up To 10 Yds. [3]	Head Shots Up To 10 Yds. [3]	Head Shots Up To 10 Yds. [3]	Head Shots Up To 10 Yds. [3]	Head Shots Up To 10 Yds. [3]	Body Kill Areas To 75 Yds. [4]	Body Kill Areas To 75 Yds. [4]	Body Kill Areas To 75 Yds. [4]	Body Kill Areas To 75 Yds. [4]	Body Kill Areas To 75 Yds. [4]	Body Kill Areas To 75 Yds. [4]	Body Kill Areas To 75 Yds. [4]	Body Kill Areas To 75 Yds. [4]	Body Kill Areas To 75 Yds. [4]	Body Kill Areas To 75 Yds. [4]	M, IC	GB4	7.1-7.3
Winchester Super X2, SX3 Models	Head Shots Up To 10 Yds. [3]	Head Shots Up To 10 Yds. [3]	Head Shots Up To 10 Yds. [3]	Head Shots Up To 10 Yds. [3]	Head Shots Up To 10 Yds. [3]	Body Kill Areas To 75 Yds. [4]	Body Kill Areas To 75 Yds. [4]	Body Kill Areas To 75 Yds. [4]	Body Kill Areas To 75 Yds. [4]	Body Kill Areas To 75 Yds. [4]	Body Kill Areas To 75 Yds. [4]	Body Kill Areas To 75 Yds. [4]	Body Kill Areas To 75 Yds. [4]	Body Kill Areas To 75 Yds. [4]	Body Kill Areas To 75 Yds. [4]	M, IC	GB4	6.38-8.25
Remington Model 1100, 11-87	Head Shots Up To 10 Yds. [3]	Head Shots Up To 10 Yds. [3]	Head Shots Up To 10 Yds. [3]	Head Shots Up To 10 Yds. [3]	Head Shots Up To 10 Yds. [3]	Body Kill Areas To 75 Yds. [4]	Body Kill Areas To 75 Yds. [4]	Body Kill Areas To 75 Yds. [4]	Body Kill Areas To 75 Yds. [4]	Body Kill Areas To 75 Yds. [4]	Body Kill Areas To 75 Yds. [4]	Body Kill Areas To 75 Yds. [4]	Body Kill Areas To 75 Yds. [4]	Body Kill Areas To 75 Yds. [4]	Body Kill Areas To 75 Yds. [4]	M, IC	GB4	6.5-8.25
Franchi Model 912	Head Shots Up To 10 Yds. [3]	Head Shots Up To 10 Yds. [3]	Head Shots Up To 10 Yds. [3]	Head Shots Up To 10 Yds. [3]	Head Shots Up To 10 Yds. [3]	Body Kill Areas To 75 Yds. [4]	Body Kill Areas To 75 Yds. [4]	Body Kill Areas To 75 Yds. [4]	Body Kill Areas To 75 Yds. [4]	Body Kill Areas To 75 Yds. [4]	Body Kill Areas To 75 Yds. [4]	Body Kill Areas To 75 Yds. [4]	Body Kill Areas To 75 Yds. [4]	Body Kill Areas To 75 Yds. [4]	Body Kill Areas To 75 Yds. [4]	M, IC	GB4	7.38-7.6
Mossberg Model 935	Head Shots Up To 10 Yds. [3]	Head Shots Up To 10 Yds. [3]	Head Shots Up To 10 Yds. [3]	Head Shots Up To 10 Yds. [3]	Head Shots Up To 10 Yds. [3]	Body Kill Areas To 75 Yds. [4]	Body Kill Areas To 75 Yds. [4]	Body Kill Areas To 75 Yds. [4]	Body Kill Areas To 75 Yds. [4]	Body Kill Areas To 75 Yds. [4]	Body Kill Areas To 75 Yds. [4]	Body Kill Areas To 75 Yds. [4]	Body Kill Areas To 75 Yds. [4]	Body Kill Areas To 75 Yds. [4]	Body Kill Areas To 75 Yds. [4]	M, IC	GB4	7.5-7.75

Abbreviation Definitions & Notes:

FPS = Feet Per Second, M = Modified, IC = Improved Cylinder, CPL = Copper Plated Lead, FP = Federal Premium Wing-Shok Magnum Ammo, WS = Winchester Supreme Double-X Magnum Ammo, HS = Hevi-Shot Turkey Ammo, RN = Remington Nitro Ammo, WXT = Winchester Xtended Range Ammo, RP = Remington Premier Duplex Magnum Ammo, WSE = WinchesterSupreme Elite Xtended Range HD Ammo, Ga. = Ammunition Gauge, [1] = Based on Turkey Shotshell specifications, [2] = Recommended by internetarmory.com, [3] = Still Target, [4] = Flying or Still Target

Muzzleloaders

Explanation

This is an introduction into muzzleloaders. They are quite different from rifles and shotguns, in that they shoot bullets or sabot slugs which are similar to bullets, but fire them in a different way. A charge a black powder is packed down at the bottom of the barrel behind the bullet. Then a hammer device comes down when you pull the trigger, and ignites the charge which causes an explosion of the charge in the barrel and the force of the explosion pushes the bullet out of the end of the muzzle. They are called muzzleloaders because the bullets are loaded in from the muzzle end instead of chamber or breech end.

Types of Muzzleloaders

Muzzleloading rifles have been around since the 14th century. Modern muzzleloaders fall into two types: "Primitive" and "In-Line." Both types are based on the idea that the shooter pours powder down the end of the gun barrel, then rams a slug or ball down on top of it to load the gun. While

TABLE 20 SHOTGUNS FOR SMALL TO MEDIUM SIZE WATERFOWL BIRDS (20 Ga.)

Non-Toxic Shell Ammunition [1]

MFR ↓ Shell Size→ Shot Size→ Shot Oz.→ MV (FPS)→	20 Ga. FHV 2-3/4 #4 (STL) 3/4 1450	20 Ga. FHV 3.0 1,2,3,4 (STL) 1.0 1350	20 Ga. FHD 3.0 #2,4 (STL) 1.0 1350	20 Ga. BIS 3.0 4,5,6 (BIS) 1.0 1200	20 Ga. BIS 3.0 4,5,6 (BIS) 1-1/8 1250	20 Ga. KF 2-3/4 2,3,4 (BIS) 7/8 1550	20 Ga. KT 2-3/4 #5 (TUNG) 1.0 1350	20 Ga. KT 3.0 3.5 (FUNG) 1-1/8 1360	20 Ga. RHS 3.0 2,4 (STL) 3/4 1425	20 Ga. RHS 3.0 #2 (STL) 3/4 1330	20 Ga. RHSS 3.0 1,2,4 (STL) 1-1/4 1330	20 Ga. RHSS 3.0 #7 (STL) 3/4 1425	20 Ga. WXS 2-3/4 #7 (STL) 3/4 1300	20 Ga. FS 2-3/4 3,4,6,7 (STL) 3/4 1470	20 Ga. FS 3.0 2,3,4 (STL) 7/8 1500	Choke Type [2]	Game Class	Gun Weight Range (Lbs)
SINGLE SHOT & PUMP SHOTGUNS — Where to Take the Shot on Game																		
Remington Model 870 Express	20 Yds [3] / 40 Yds [4]	20 Yds [3] / 40 Yds [4]	20 Yds [3] / 40 Yds [4]	20 Yds [3] / 40 Yds [4]	20 Yds [3] / 40 Yds [4]	20 Yds [3] / 40 Yds [4]	20 Yds [3] / 40 Yds [4]	20 Yds [3] / 40 Yds [4]	20 Yds [3] / 40 Yds [4]	20 Yds [3] / 40 Yds [4]	20 Yds [3] / 40 Yds [4]	20 Yds [3] / 40 Yds [4]	20 Yds [3] / 40 Yds [4]	20 Yds [3] / 40 Yds [4]	20 Yds [3] / 40 Yds [4]	M, IC	WF1 WF2	6-8
Mossberg Model 500	20 Yds [3] / 40 Yds [4]	20 Yds [3] / 40 Yds [4]	20 Yds [3] / 40 Yds [4]	20 Yds [3] / 40 Yds [4]	20 Yds [3] / 40 Yds [4]	20 Yds [3] / 40 Yds [4]	20 Yds [3] / 40 Yds [4]	20 Yds [3] / 40 Yds [4]	20 Yds [3] / 40 Yds [4]	20 Yds [3] / 40 Yds [4]	20 Yds [3] / 40 Yds [4]	20 Yds [3] / 40 Yds [4]	20 Yds [3] / 40 Yds [4]	20 Yds [3] / 40 Yds [4]	20 Yds [3] / 40 Yds [4]	M, IC	WF1 WF2	6.5-7.5
H & R Pardner, Topper	20 Yds [3] / 40 Yds [4]	20 Yds [3] / 40 Yds [4]	20 Yds [3] / 40 Yds [4]	20 Yds [3] / 40 Yds [4]	20 Yds [3] / 40 Yds [4]	20 Yds [3] / 40 Yds [4]	20 Yds [3] / 40 Yds [4]	20 Yds [3] / 40 Yds [4]	20 Yds [3] / 40 Yds [4]	20 Yds [3] / 40 Yds [4]	20 Yds [3] / 40 Yds [4]	20 Yds [3] / 40 Yds [4]	20 Yds [3] / 40 Yds [4]	20 Yds [3] / 40 Yds [4]	20 Yds [3] / 40 Yds [4]	M, IC	WF1 WF2	5-8
Ithaca DS II, DS III, Model 37	20 Yds [3] / 40 Yds [4]	20 Yds [3] / 40 Yds [4]	20 Yds [3] / 40 Yds [4]	20 Yds [3] / 40 Yds [4]	20 Yds [3] / 40 Yds [4]	20 Yds [3] / 40 Yds [4]	20 Yds [3] / 40 Yds [4]	20 Yds [3] / 40 Yds [4]	20 Yds [3] / 40 Yds [4]	20 Yds [3] / 40 Yds [4]	20 Yds [3] / 40 Yds [4]	20 Yds [3] / 40 Yds [4]	20 Yds [3] / 40 Yds [4]	20 Yds [3] / 40 Yds [4]	20 Yds [3] / 40 Yds [4]	M, IC	WF1 WF2	6.0-7.6
NEF Pardner, & Pardner Youth	20 Yds [3] / 40 Yds [4]	20 Yds [3] / 40 Yds [4]	20 Yds [3] / 40 Yds [4]	20 Yds [3] / 40 Yds [4]	20 Yds [3] / 40 Yds [4]	20 Yds [3] / 40 Yds [4]	20 Yds [3] / 40 Yds [4]	20 Yds [3] / 40 Yds [4]	20 Yds [3] / 40 Yds [4]	20 Yds [3] / 40 Yds [4]	20 Yds [3] / 40 Yds [4]	20 Yds [3] / 40 Yds [4]	20 Yds [3] / 40 Yds [4]	20 Yds [3] / 40 Yds [4]	20 Yds [3] / 40 Yds [4]	M, IC	WF1 WF2	5.5-7.5
Winchester Model 37, 37A	20 Yds [3] / 40 Yds [4]	20 Yds [3] / 40 Yds [4]	20 Yds [3] / 40 Yds [4]	20 Yds [3] / 40 Yds [4]	20 Yds [3] / 40 Yds [4]	20 Yds [3] / 40 Yds [4]	20 Yds [3] / 40 Yds [4]	20 Yds [3] / 40 Yds [4]	20 Yds [3] / 40 Yds [4]	20 Yds [3] / 40 Yds [4]	20 Yds [3] / 40 Yds [4]	20 Yds [3] / 40 Yds [4]	20 Yds [3] / 40 Yds [4]	20 Yds [3] / 40 Yds [4]	20 Yds [3] / 40 Yds [4]	M, IC	WF1 WF2	7.0-7.25
SEMI-AUTOMATIC SHOTGUNS — Where to Take the Shot on Game																		
Baretta 391, AL391, Extrema2	20 Yds [3] / 40 Yds [4]	20 Yds [3] / 40 Yds [4]	20 Yds [3] / 40 Yds [4]	20 Yds [3] / 40 Yds [4]	20 Yds [3] / 40 Yds [4]	20 Yds [3] / 40 Yds [4]	20 Yds [3] / 40 Yds [4]	20 Yds [3] / 40 Yds [4]	20 Yds [3] / 40 Yds [4]	20 Yds [3] / 40 Yds [4]	20 Yds [3] / 40 Yds [4]	20 Yds [3] / 40 Yds [4]	20 Yds [3] / 40 Yds [4]	20 Yds [3] / 40 Yds [4]	20 Yds [3] / 40 Yds [4]	M, IC	WF1 WF2	6.2-7.5
Browning Gold, A5 Models	20 Yds [3] / 40 Yds [4]	20 Yds [3] / 40 Yds [4]	20 Yds [3] / 40 Yds [4]	20 Yds [3] / 40 Yds [4]	20 Yds [3] / 40 Yds [4]	20 Yds [3] / 40 Yds [4]	20 Yds [3] / 40 Yds [4]	20 Yds [3] / 40 Yds [4]	20 Yds [3] / 40 Yds [4]	20 Yds [3] / 40 Yds [4]	20 Yds [3] / 40 Yds [4]	20 Yds [3] / 40 Yds [4]	20 Yds [3] / 40 Yds [4]	20 Yds [3] / 40 Yds [4]	20 Yds [3] / 40 Yds [4]	M, IC	WF1 WF2	6.5-7.9
Benelli Super Black Eagle	20 Yds [3] / 40 Yds [4]	20 Yds [3] / 40 Yds [4]	20 Yds [3] / 40 Yds [4]	20 Yds [3] / 40 Yds [4]	20 Yds [3] / 40 Yds [4]	20 Yds [3] / 40 Yds [4]	20 Yds [3] / 40 Yds [4]	20 Yds [3] / 40 Yds [4]	20 Yds [3] / 40 Yds [4]	20 Yds [3] / 40 Yds [4]	20 Yds [3] / 40 Yds [4]	20 Yds [3] / 40 Yds [4]	20 Yds [3] / 40 Yds [4]	20 Yds [3] / 40 Yds [4]	20 Yds [3] / 40 Yds [4]	M, IC	WF1 WF2	7.1-7.3
Winchester Super X2, SX3 Models	20 Yds [3] / 40 Yds [4]	20 Yds [3] / 40 Yds [4]	20 Yds [3] / 40 Yds [4]	20 Yds [3] / 40 Yds [4]	20 Yds [3] / 40 Yds [4]	20 Yds [3] / 40 Yds [4]	20 Yds [3] / 40 Yds [4]	20 Yds [3] / 40 Yds [4]	20 Yds [3] / 40 Yds [4]	20 Yds [3] / 40 Yds [4]	20 Yds [3] / 40 Yds [4]	20 Yds [3] / 40 Yds [4]	20 Yds [3] / 40 Yds [4]	20 Yds [3] / 40 Yds [4]	20 Yds [3] / 40 Yds [4]	M, IC	WF1 WF2	6.38-8.25
Remington Model 1100, 11-87	20 Yds [3] / 40 Yds [4]	20 Yds [3] / 40 Yds [4]	20 Yds [3] / 40 Yds [4]	20 Yds [3] / 40 Yds [4]	20 Yds [3] / 40 Yds [4]	20 Yds [3] / 40 Yds [4]	20 Yds [3] / 40 Yds [4]	20 Yds [3] / 40 Yds [4]	20 Yds [3] / 40 Yds [4]	20 Yds [3] / 40 Yds [4]	20 Yds [3] / 40 Yds [4]	20 Yds [3] / 40 Yds [4]	20 Yds [3] / 40 Yds [4]	20 Yds [3] / 40 Yds [4]	20 Yds [3] / 40 Yds [4]	M, IC	WF1 WF2	6.5-8.25
Franchi Model 912	20 Yds [3] / 40 Yds [4]	20 Yds [3] / 40 Yds [4]	20 Yds [3] / 40 Yds [4]	20 Yds [3] / 40 Yds [4]	20 Yds [3] / 40 Yds [4]	20 Yds [3] / 40 Yds [4]	20 Yds [3] / 40 Yds [4]	20 Yds [3] / 40 Yds [4]	20 Yds [3] / 40 Yds [4]	20 Yds [3] / 40 Yds [4]	20 Yds [3] / 40 Yds [4]	20 Yds [3] / 40 Yds [4]	20 Yds [3] / 40 Yds [4]	20 Yds [3] / 40 Yds [4]	20 Yds [3] / 40 Yds [4]	M, IC	WF1 WF2	7.38-7.6
Mossberg Model 935	20 Yds [3] / 40 Yds [4]	20 Yds [3] / 40 Yds [4]	20 Yds [3] / 40 Yds [4]	20 Yds [3] / 40 Yds [4]	20 Yds [3] / 40 Yds [4]	20 Yds [3] / 40 Yds [4]	20 Yds [3] / 40 Yds [4]	20 Yds [3] / 40 Yds [4]	20 Yds [3] / 40 Yds [4]	20 Yds [3] / 40 Yds [4]	20 Yds [3] / 40 Yds [4]	20 Yds [3] / 40 Yds [4]	20 Yds [3] / 40 Yds [4]	20 Yds [3] / 40 Yds [4]	20 Yds [3] / 40 Yds [4]	M, IC	WF1 WF2	7.5-7.75

Abbreviation Definitions & Notes:

FPS = Feet Per Second, M = Modified, IC = Improved Cylinder, FHV = Federal Ultra-Shok High Velocity Ammo, FHD = Federal Ultra-Shok High Density, BIS = Bismuth, KF = Kent Faststeel, KT = Kent Tungsten Matrix, RHS = Remington Hevi-Shot, RHSS = Remington Hi-Speed Steel, WXS = Winchester Xpert Steel, FS = Fiocchi Steel, NEF = New England Firearms, H & R = Harrington & Richardson, STL = Steel, TUNG = Tungsten, MV = Muzzle Velocity, Ga. = Ammunition Gauge, [1] = Based on Waterfowl Shotshell specifications, [2] = Recommended by internetarmory.com, [3] = Head Shot On Still Target Up To, [4] = Flying or Still Target Shot Up To.

traditional or "Primitive" muzzleloaders *(SEE FIGURE 104-A)* are still available, the modern "In-Line" muzzleloaders *(SEE FIGURE 104-B)* account for about 95% of today's market. We will cover where guns of each type can be found, for purchasing purposes. However, the traditional models (Primitive) can be expensive because they are more rare and outdated for use today. If you want to get into actual muzzleloading hunting, I suggest you get one of the newer In-Line versions. You can find many of the old traditional guns, but they are listed as "Antique," so I'm not sure you would want to take it out and ac-

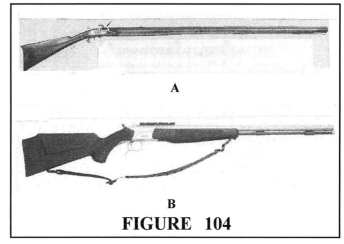

A

B

FIGURE 104

| TABLE 21 SHOTGUNS FOR SMALL TO MEDIUM SIZE WATERFOWL BIRDS (16 Ga. & 12 Ga.) | | | | | | | | | | | | | | | | | |

Non-Toxic Shell Ammunition [1]

MFR ↓ / Shell Size→ / Shot Size→ / Shot Oz.→ / MV (FPS)→	16 Ga. FHV 2-3/4 / #2,4 (STL) / 15/16 / 1350	16 Ga. BIS 2-3/4 / #4,6 (BIS) / 1.0 / 1350	16 Ga. HS 2-3/4 / 4,5,6 (ENV) / 1.0 / 1350	12 Ga. FHV 2-3/4,3 / BB,2,4 (STL) / 1-1/4 / 1375,1450	12 Ga. FHV 3-1/2 / BB,2,4 (STL) / 1-1/2 / 1500	12 Ga. BIS 2-3/4-3-1/2 / 2,4,5 (BT) / 7/8 / 1280,1400	12 Ga. KF 3.0 / BB,2,4 (STL) / 1-1/4 / 1300	12 Ga. KF 2-3/4,3-1/2 / BB,2,4 (Tung) / 1-1/4 / 1300,1625	12 Ga. KT 3.0 / BB,2,4 (Tung) / 1-1/8 / 1560	12 Ga. KT 3-1/2 / 1,3 (Tung) / 2.0 / 1260	12 Ga. HHSS 3.0,3-1/2 / BB,2,4 (STL) / 1-1/4,3-3/8 / 1400,1525	12Ga. WXS 2-3/4 / 6,7 (STL) / 1-1/8 / 1700	12Ga. FS 2-3/4,3.0 / BB,2,4 (STL) / 1-1/8 / 1375,1475	12 Ga. FS 3-1/2 / BB,2 (STL) / 1-3/8 / 1520	Choke Type [2]	Game Class	Gun Weight Range (Lbs)

SINGLE SHOT & PUMP SHOTGUNS — Where to Take the Shot on Game

Remington Model 870 Express	20Yds[3] / 40Yds[4]	20Yds[3] / 40Yds[4]	20Yds[3] / 40Yds[4]	20Yds[3] / 40Yds[4]	20Yds[3] / 40Yds[4]	20Yds[3] / 40Yds[4]	20Yds[3] / 40Yds[4]	20Yds[3] / 40Yds[4]	20Yds[3] / 40Yds[4]	20Yds[3] / 40Yds[4]	20Yds[3] / 40Yds[4]	20Yds[3] / 40Yds[4]	20Yds[3] / 40Yds[4]	20Yds[3] / 40Yds[4]	M, IC	WF1 WF2	6-8
Mossberg Model 500	20Yds[3] / 40Yds[4]	20Yds[3] / 40Yds[4]	20Yds[3] / 40Yds[4]	20Yds[3] / 40Yds[4]	20Yds[3] / 40Yds[4]	20Yds[3] / 40Yds[4]	20Yds[3] / 40Yds[4]	20Yds[3] / 40Yds[4]	20Yds[3] / 40Yds[4]	20Yds[3] / 40Yds[4]	20Yds[3] / 40Yds[4]	20Yds[3] / 40Yds[4]	20Yds[3] / 40Yds[4]	20Yds[3] / 40Yds[4]	M, IC	WF1 WF2	6.5-7.5
H & R Pardner, Topper	20Yds[3] / 40Yds[4]	20Yds[3] / 40Yds[4]	20Yds[3] / 40Yds[4]	20Yds[3] / 40Yds[4]	20Yds[3] / 40Yds[4]	20Yds[3] / 40Yds[4]	20Yds[3] / 40Yds[4]	20Yds[3] / 40Yds[4]	20Yds[3] / 40Yds[4]	20Yds[3] / 40Yds[4]	20Yds[3] / 40Yds[4]	20Yds[3] / 40Yds[4]	20Yds[3] / 40Yds[4]	20Yds[3] / 40Yds[4]	M, IC	WF1 WF2	5-8
Ithaca DS II, Ds III, Model 37	20Yds[3] / 40Yds[4]	20Yds[3] / 40Yds[4]	20Yds[3] / 40Yds[4]	20Yds[3] / 40Yds[4]	20Yds[3] / 40Yds[4]	20Yds[3] / 40Yds[4]	20Yds[3] / 40Yds[4]	20Yds[3] / 40Yds[4]	20Yds[3] / 40Yds[4]	20Yds[3] / 40Yds[4]	20Yds[3] / 40Yds[4]	20Yds[3] / 40Yds[4]	20Yds[3] / 40Yds[4]	20Yds[3] / 40Yds[4]	M, IC	WF1 WF2	6.0-7.6
NEF Pardner, & Pardner Youth	20Yds[3] / 40Yds[4]	20Yds[3] / 40Yds[4]	20Yds[3] / 40Yds[4]	20Yds[3] / 40Yds[4]	20Yds[3] / 40Yds[4]	20Yds[3] / 40Yds[4]	20Yds[3] / 40Yds[4]	20Yds[3] / 40Yds[4]	20Yds[3] / 40Yds[4]	20Yds[3] / 40Yds[4]	20Yds[3] / 40Yds[4]	20Yds[3] / 40Yds[4]	20Yds[3] / 40Yds[4]	20Yds[3] / 40Yds[4]	M, IC	WF1 WF2	5.5-7.5
Winchester Model 37, 37A	20Yds[3] / 40Yds[4]	20Yds[3] / 40Yds[4]	20Yds[3] / 40Yds[4]	20Yds[3] / 40Yds[4]	20Yds[3] / 40Yds[4]	20Yds[3] / 40Yds[4]	20Yds[3] / 40Yds[4]	20Yds[3] / 40Yds[4]	20Yds[3] / 40Yds[4]	20Yds[3] / 40Yds[4]	20Yds[3] / 40Yds[4]	20Yds[3] / 40Yds[4]	20Yds[3] / 40Yds[4]	20Yds[3] / 40Yds[4]	M, IC	WF1 WF2	7.0-7.25

SEMI-AUTOMATIC SHOTGUNS — Where to Take the Shot on Game

Baretta 391, AL391, Extrema2	20Yds[3] / 40Yds[4]	20Yds[3] / 40Yds[4]	20Yds[3] / 40Yds[4]	20Yds[3] / 40Yds[4]	20Yds[3] / 40Yds[4]	20Yds[3] / 40Yds[4]	20Yds[3] / 40Yds[4]	20Yds[3] / 40Yds[4]	20Yds[3] / 40Yds[4]	20Yds[3] / 40Yds[4]	20Yds[3] / 40Yds[4]	20Yds[3] / 40Yds[4]	20Yds[3] / 40Yds[4]	20Yds[3] / 40Yds[4]	M, IC	WF1 WF2	6.2-7.5
Browning Gold, AS Models	20Yds[3] / 40Yds[4]	20Yds[3] / 40Yds[4]	20Yds[3] / 40Yds[4]	20Yds[3] / 40Yds[4]	20Yds[3] / 40Yds[4]	20Yds[3] / 40Yds[4]	20Yds[3] / 40Yds[4]	20Yds[3] / 40Yds[4]	20Yds[3] / 40Yds[4]	20Yds[3] / 40Yds[4]	20Yds[3] / 40Yds[4]	20Yds[3] / 40Yds[4]	20Yds[3] / 40Yds[4]	20Yds[3] / 40Yds[4]	M, IC	WF1 WF2	6.5-7.9
Benelli Super Black Eagle	20Yds[3] / 40Yds[4]	20Yds[3] / 40Yds[4]	20Yds[3] / 40Yds[4]	20Yds[3] / 40Yds[4]	20Yds[3] / 40Yds[4]	20Yds[3] / 40Yds[4]	20Yds[3] / 40Yds[4]	20Yds[3] / 40Yds[4]	20Yds[3] / 40Yds[4]	20Yds[3] / 40Yds[4]	20Yds[3] / 40Yds[4]	20Yds[3] / 40Yds[4]	20Yds[3] / 40Yds[4]	20Yds[3] / 40Yds[4]	M, IC	WF1 WF2	7.1-7.3
Winchester Super X2, SX3 Models	20Yds[3] / 40Yds[4]	20Yds[3] / 40Yds[4]	20Yds[3] / 40Yds[4]	20Yds[3] / 40Yds[4]	20Yds[3] / 40Yds[4]	20Yds[3] / 40Yds[4]	20Yds[3] / 40Yds[4]	20Yds[3] / 40Yds[4]	20Yds[3] / 40Yds[4]	20Yds[3] / 40Yds[4]	20Yds[3] / 40Yds[4]	20Yds[3] / 40Yds[4]	20Yds[3] / 40Yds[4]	20Yds[3] / 40Yds[4]	M, IC	WF1 WF2	6.38-8.25
Remington Model 1100, 11-87	20Yds[3] / 40Yds[4]	20Yds[3] / 40Yds[4]	20Yds[3] / 40Yds[4]	20Yds[3] / 40Yds[4]	20Yds[3] / 40Yds[4]	20Yds[3] / 40Yds[4]	20Yds[3] / 40Yds[4]	20Yds[3] / 40Yds[4]	20Yds[3] / 40Yds[4]	20Yds[3] / 40Yds[4]	20Yds[3] / 40Yds[4]	20Yds[3] / 40Yds[4]	20Yds[3] / 40Yds[4]	20Yds[3] / 40Yds[4]	M, IC	WF1 WF2	6.5-8.25
Franchi Model 912	20Yds[3] / 40Yds[4]	20Yds[3] / 40Yds[4]	20Yds[3] / 40Yds[4]	20Yds[3] / 40Yds[4]	20Yds[3] / 40Yds[4]	20Yds[3] / 40Yds[4]	20Yds[3] / 40Yds[4]	20Yds[3] / 40Yds[4]	20Yds[3] / 40Yds[4]	20Yds[3] / 40Yds[4]	20Yds[3] / 40Yds[4]	20Yds[3] / 40Yds[4]	20Yds[3] / 40Yds[4]	20Yds[3] / 40Yds[4]	M, IC	WF1 WF2	7.38-7.6
Mossberg Model 935	20Yds[3] / 40Yds[4]	20Yds[3] / 40Yds[4]	20Yds[3] / 40Yds[4]	20Yds[3] / 40Yds[4]	20Yds[3] / 40Yds[4]	20Yds[3] / 40Yds[4]	20Yds[3] / 40Yds[4]	20Yds[3] / 40Yds[4]	20Yds[3] / 40Yds[4]	20Yds[3] / 40Yds[4]	20Yds[3] / 40Yds[4]	20Yds[3] / 40Yds[4]	20Yds[3] / 40Yds[4]	20Yds[3] / 40Yds[4]	M, IC	WF1 WF2	7.5-7.75

Abbreviation Definitions & Notes:

FPS = Feet Per Second, M = Modified, IC = Improved Cylinder, FHV = Federal Ultra-Shok High Velocity Ammo, FHD = Federal Ultra-Shok High Density, BIS = Bismuth, KF = Kent Faststeel, KT = Kent Tungsten Matrix, RHS = Remington Hevi-Shot, RHSS = Remington Hi-Speed Steel, WXS = Winchester Xpert Steel, FS = Fiocchi Steel, HS = Hevi-Shot Environ Metal, NEF = New England Firearms, H & R = Harrington & Richardson, STL = Steel, TUNG = Tungsten, MV = Muzzle Velocity, BT = Bismuth-Tin Alloy, Ga. = Ammunition Gauge, [1] = Based on Waterfowl Shotshell specifications, [2] = Recommended by internetarmory.com, [3] = Head Shot On Still Target Up To, [4] = Flying or Still Target Shot Up To.

tually use it for hunting. However, there are a few companies still making them, new and as kits, as reproductions of the old original models.

Primitive

We are going to list 8 of these for you to see what's out there:

1. Kulls Old Town Station " Percussion Muzzleloaders

This is about all you can find out there for the old traditional muzzleloaders, and they are talking some serious money for them. They are listed as antique.

2. Traditions- Shenandoah Model Muzzleloader

These are imported. They are both functional working rifles. The Shenandoah comes in either a .36 caliber percussion, or a 50 caliber Flint-lock version. Both have walnut stocks accented by a solid brass, and both have a curved buttplate.

TABLE 22 SHOTGUNS FOR LARGE SIZE WATERFOWL BIRDS

Non-Toxic Shell Ammunition [1]

MFR ↓	12 Ga. FHV 2-3/4 1-1/4 1375	12 Ga. FHV 3.0,3-1/2 1-1/4 1450,1500	12 Ga. FHD 3.0,3-1/2 1-3/8,1-5/8 1450	12 Ga. BIS 2-3/4,3.0 1-3/8,1-5/8 1280,1250	12 Ga. KF 2-3/4,3.0 1-1/16,1-1/8 1550,1560	12 Ga. KF 3-1/2 1-1/4 1625	12 Ga. KT 3.0(Tung) 1-1/4,2.0 1525,1250	12 Ga. RHSS 3.0,3-1/2 1-1/4,1-3/8 1700	12 Ga. WSX 2-3/4,3.0 1-9/16 1300	12 Ga. WSX 3.0,3-1/2 1-1/4,1-3/8 1300,1400	12 Ga. FS 2-3/4,3.0 1-1/4 1375,1475	10 Ga. FS 3-1/2 1-3/8 1520	10 Ga. FHV 3-1/2 1-1/2 1450	10 Ga. FHD 3-1/2 1-5/8 1400	10 Ga. WSXD 3-1/2 1-5/8 1350	Choke Type [2]	Game Class	Gun Weight Range (Lbs)

SINGLE SHOT & PUMP SHOTGUNS

Where to Take the Shot on Game

MFR		Shot distances														Choke	Game	Weight
Remington Model 870 Express	20 Yds [3] / 40 Yds [4] (all gauge columns)															M, IC	WF3	6-8
Mossberg Model 500	20 Yds [3] / 40 Yds [4] (all gauge columns)															M, IC	WF3	6.5-7.5
H & R Pardner, Topper	20 Yds [3] / 40 Yds [4] (all gauge columns)															M, IC	WF3	5-8
Ithaca DS II, Ds III, Model 37	20 Yds [3] / 40 Yds [4] (all gauge columns)															M, IC	WF3	6.0-7.6
NEF Pardner, & Pardner Youth	20 Yds [3] / 40 Yds [4] (all gauge columns)															M, IC	WF3	5.5-7.5
Winchester Model 37, 37A	20 Yds [3] / 40 Yds [4] (all gauge columns)															M, IC	WF3	7.0-7.25

SEMI-AUTOMATIC SHOTGUNS

Where to Take the Shot on Game

MFR																Choke	Game	Weight
Baretta 391, AL391, Extrema2	20 Yds [3] / 40 Yds [4] (all gauge columns)															M, IC	WF3	6.2-7.5
Browning Gold, A5 Models	20 Yds [3] / 40 Yds [4] (all gauge columns)															M, IC	WF3	6.5-7.9
Benelli Super Black Eagle	20 Yds [3] / 40 Yds [4] (all gauge columns)															M, IC	WF3	7.1-7.3
Winchester Super X2, SX3 Models	20 Yds [3] / 40 Yds [4] (all gauge columns)															M, IC	WF3	6.38-8.25
Remington Model 1100, 11-87	20 Yds [3] / 40 Yds [4] (all gauge columns)															M, IC	WF3	6.5-8.25
Franchi Model 912	20 Yds [3] / 40 Yds [4] (all gauge columns)															M, IC	WF3	7.38-7.6
Mossberg Model 935	20 Yds [3] / 40 Yds [4] (all gauge columns)															M, IC	WF3	7.5-7.75

Abbreviation Definitions & Notes:

FPS = Feet Per Second, M = Modified, IC = Improved Cylinder, FHV = Federal Ultra-Shok High Velocity Ammo, FHD = Federal Ultra-Shok High Density, BIS = Bismuth, KF = Kent Faststeel, KT = Kent Tungsten Matrix, RHSS = Remington Hi-Speed Steel, WSX = Winchester Super-X Magnum, FS = Fiocchi Steel, WSXD = Winchester Super-X Drylok, NEF = New England Firearms, H & R = Harrington & Richardson, STL = Steel, TUNG = Tungsten, MV = Muzzle Velocity, BT = Bismuth-Tin Alloy, Ga. = Ammunition Gauge, [1] = Based on Waterfowl Shotshell specifications, [2] = Recommended by internetarmory.com, [3] = Head Shot On Still Target Up To, [4] = Flying or Still Target Shot Up To.

3. Traditions- Pennsylvania Model Muzzleloader

These are imported. This is a functional working long rifle. It comes in either a 50 caliber percussion or flint-lock version, with a walnut stock and a solid brass patch box.

4. Traditions- Springfield Hawken Model Muzzleloader

Not imported. This is a functional working rifle. It comes in a 50 caliber percussion with a beech hardwood stock and brass appointments.

5. Traditions- Crocket Model Muzzleloader

These are imported. This is a functional working rifle. It comes in a 32 caliber, with a hardwood stock and brass appointments. Does not give the type of igniting mechanism.

6. Thompson Center- Hawken Model Muzzleloader

Made in the USA. This is a functional working rifle *(SEE FIGURE 105)*. It comes in either 50 or 54 caliber, flintlock action, with a Walnut stock and brass appointments,

137

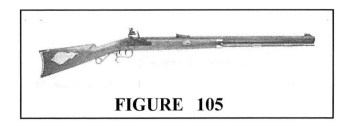

FIGURE 105

7. **CVA- St. Louis Hawken Model Muzzleloader**

Not imported. This is a functional working rifle. It comes in a 50 caliber, with wood stock and brass appointments, but does not give the type of igniting mechanism.

8. **Traditions- Deerhunter Model Muzzleloader**

These are imported. This is a functional working rifle. It comes in a percussion-lock, 50 caliber, with black composite stock, oversized trigger guard for winter glove use, sling swivels, adjustable hunting sights, and a nickel barrel with a 1 in 48" twist.

In-Line

We are going to list 10 of these for your consideration. To give you some idea of what's out there in the In-Line Muzzleloader family:

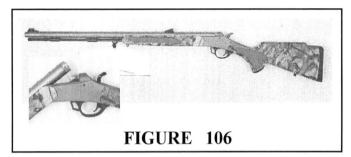

FIGURE 106

1. **Traditions- Vortek Muzzleloader**

This is a new, 50 caliber, modern in-Line muzzleloader, 25 inch ported barrel, removable breech plug, and with mossy oak camo finish stock *(SEE FIGURE 106)*.

2. **Traditions- Thunderbolt Model Muzzleloader**

This is a used, in very good condition rifle, 50 caliber, modern In-Line replica, percussion muzzleloader, with a synthetic stock.

3. **Thompson Center- Black Diamond Stainless Model Muzzleloader**

This is a used, in very good condition rifle, 50 caliber, modern In-Line replica, percussion muzzleloader, with a black synthetic stock, and a Leupold scope.

4. **Knight Extreme Model Muzzleloader**

This will be used now if you can find one. Excellent rifle, 50 caliber, bolt action, disc, centerfire, modern in-Line muzzleloader,

5. **Longhunter's Mercantile- Southern Mountain Model Muzzleloader**

This is a kit build it yourself. This has maple stock. Does not give any other information. You will have to inquire. Reasonably priced.

6. **White Super-91 Model Muzzleloader**

These were custom made and you look for them as used now. Great rifle. They come in a number of calibers, probably more available in a 50 or 45 caliber. You will have to inquire.

7. **Longhunter's Mercantile- Sir Hale .451 Whitworth Model Muzzleloader**

This is a used near new original. This has a hex bore, ladder sight, and the original tang aperature sight. Does not give any other information. You will have to inquire.

8. **Thompson Center- Triumph Model Muzzleloader**

Not imported. This is a functional working rifle. It comes in a 50 caliber, fiber optic sight, speed breech XT and toggle lock action for easy priming and cleaning. Does not give any other information. You will have to inquire. Reasonably priced.

9. **Thompson Center- Triumph Bone Collector Model Muzzleloader**

Not imported. This is a functional custom designed working rifle. It is part of the Triumph Magnum Muzzleloader family of rifles. Does not give any other information. You will have to inquire. Reasonably priced.

10. **Thompson Center- Omega Z5 Model Muzzleloader**

Not imported. This is a functional working rifle. It is a 50 caliber, and features a sealed pivoting breech design for simple operation. It does have user ratings. Does not give any other information. You will have to inquire. Very reasonably priced.

Muzzleloader Safety Rules

For muzzleloaders hunter safety rules follow the "10 Commandments" general gun rules found on page 26. However, there are additional hunter safety rules that apply only to muzzleloaders because they operate different than rifles, and require there own special rules:

1. NEVER smoke while you are using a muzzleloader or while you are near any quantity of black powder or PYRODEX.
2. ONLY use black powder or a black powder substitute in muzzleloading firearms.
3. ALWAYS store black powder and black powder substitutes away from heat, sparks, and static electricity.
4. ALWAYS store percussion caps and powder separately, and in a cool, dry place.
5. Before loading, ALWAYS make sure the firearm is not already loaded.
6. ALWAYS use a marked ramrod to see if a muzzleloader is loaded. NEVER look down into the barrel.
7. NEVER pour black powder or a black powder substitute directly into a muzzleloader from a "flask," powder horn, or a can. ALWAYS use a powder measure.
8. ALWAYS be sure to seat the ball, bullet, or wad, and the shot charge directly on top of the powder charge. A gap between the projectile(s) and the powder charge could damage the firearm, and injure the shooter and bystanders.
9. ALWAYS have a qualified gunsmith inspect older/antique muzzleloading firearms before using them.
10. ALWAYS check and clear the flash hole through the nipple before shooting.
11. NEVER exceed the maximum recommended powder charge contained in the instruction book for your muzzleloader.
12. NEVER use the wrong ammunition components specified for your muzzleloader.
13. ALWAYS use only cotton patching.
14. NEVER pound the ramrod. ALWAYS keep the ramrod directly away from your face or body.
15. ALWAYS know the range of your muzzleloader.
16. If your muzzleloader fails to fire, ALWAYS be prepared for a hangfire.
17. ALWAYS render your muzzleloader inoperable whenever you are not shooting (walking).
18. NEVER use the weather shroud for repeated shooting. It is intended for single shot usage ONLY.
19. NOTE: Black powder leaves a heavy corrosive residue. A thorough cleaning and lubing are an absolute necessity for your muzzleloader.

20. DO NOT fire Damascus-barreled shotguns (similar) unless they have been inspected If they are safe to use, load them ONLY with black powder or a black powder substitute like muzzleloaders require.

Handling Your Muzzleloader

Explanation
We will cover handling your muzzleloader out in the field and at home. When we talk about handling, we mean when you are just carrying out in the field, or on the couch at home. We will talk about firing, shooting, loading and unloading later in this section. NOTE: We are not going to cover muzzleloading pistols.

Handling In the Field Position and at Home
There are several ways to handle or carry a gun so that it is never a threat to other hunters, yet it is ready for instant use. While carrying in the field, basically follow the safety rules on page 139. In addition, basically do the same as with a rifle found on pages 76 and 77 *(SEE FIGURE 41)*. Also see handling your shotgun found on pages 115 and 116.

Firing Your Muzzleloader

Firing a Muzzleloader In the Field
Firing a muzzleloader is not like firing a rifle or shotgun. First of all read your manual. If you don't have one, get one. Many of them are free on the Internet, all you need to do is print them out. If that don't work, contact the company. Even if you need to pay for one, spend the money because you really need one. When you pull the trigger, make sure you are wearing shatterproof shooting glasses and ear protection, because both percussion and flintlock rifles may shower sparks and bits of caps/flint around when fired. Pre-1840's style round lensed safety glasses (best) are available from several suppliers. And there will be a puff of smoke. First thing, before firing check the area for other hunters, and observe what's behind your target. There are five basic standard positions to fire from, prone, standing, sitting, and kneeling, leaning. However, most of the time you may be standing or sitting in a boat. You also need to know how to sight and aim, and pull the trigger.

Table 23
Muzzleloader Shooting Distance vs Ammunition

Ammunition Caliber ↓	0 Yards	100 Yds	200 Yds	250 Yds	300 Yds	500 Yds	600 Yds	800 Yds	1000 Yds	3 Miles	5 Miles
Flintlocks											
FEDF .45 Bullet	1850 FPS MV										
EE .50 Bullet	1796 FPS MV										
HXTP .44 In .50 Sabot	2225 FPS MV										
HXTP .45 In .50 Sabot	2375 FPS MV										
Percussion											
FEDF .45 Bullet	1850 FPS MV										
EE .50 Bullet	1796 FPS MV										
HXTP .44 In .50 Sabot	2225 FPS MV										
HXTP .45 In .50 Sabot	2375 FPS MV										
In-Line											
FEDF .45 Bullet	1850 FPS MV										
EE .50 Bullet	1796 FPS MV										
HXTP .44 In .50 Sabot	2225 FPS MV										
HXTP .45 In .50 Sabot	2375 FPS MV										

NOTE:
Some data taken from "Long Range Muzzleloading" by Doc White. FPS = Feet Per Second, MV = Muzzle Velocity, FEDF = Federal Fusion, HXTP = Hornady XTP, EE = Extreme Elite, ▮▮▮▮▮ = Effefctive Range, ▒▒▒▒▒ = Leave Clear Behind Target

What's Behind Your Target
Find out ahead of time what's behind your intended target(s). There are state maps for their hunting areas, showing what is in these areas like state parks, firing ranges, hunting clubs, or homes. Know which nearby area your hunting partners might be in. Use Table 23 as a guide to see approximately how far your ammunition will actually travel in the air. These are not exact, but they will give you an idea how far they will go at line of sight (flat trajectory). The tables will not work though for shooting up in the air at an angle.

140

The information we do have is taken from "Long Range Muzzleloading" by Doc White. Once you have an idea what is behind your target, act responsibly and choose not to fire if their is any question about safety in your mind.

Getting Ready to Fire

Get familiar with your muzzleloader, know what it's capable of doing. If you have never used the gun before, read the manual ahead of time. If you bought your gun used, go on line at the manufacturers web site and print out a manual. Most guns have a manual on-line that you can print out. If not, buy one from the manufacturer. It will be worth the money. Before you shoot the gun, especially a new gun, follow the same steps as getting ready to fire a rifle on page 78. Make absolutely sure you have the right amount of black powder or Pyrodex in the barrel, and the right amount of powder in the pan. And make sure the charge and bullet or sabot is packed all the way down the barrel, not just part way!

After Loading

We will cover more information on muzzleloader ammunition later in this section where we cover "Loading and Unloading," and "Ammunitions" for muzzleloaders. After you have loaded your muzzleloader check the distance to your target, and know what lies beyond your target. Are you within the range of your gun? Have an idea before you leave, or take a copy of our distance tables out hunting with you. Check out our table for muzzleloaders *(SEE TABLE 23)*. As you can see in the table, your ammunition goes a long way past your intended target, especially if you miss. You need to be aware of where your hunting partners, and people living nearby, are located for miles in all directions. When you are sure of your target and what's beyond, then go ahead and sight in on the target, unlock the safety, try to stay relaxed, then pull the trigger. And make sure you have on your safety glasses and hearing protection.

Positions for Firing

There are a number of different firing positions you can get into before firing *(SEE FIGURE 44)* on page 80. You may end up using any one of them on a hunting trip.

Shooting Your Muzzleloader

Sighting and Aiming

See "sighting and aiming" in the rifle section on page 81. However, most of this information would apply when you might be deer hunting with your muzzleloader over a longer distances. Most muzzleloader hunters will be hunting deer or larger game. Most muzzleloader shooting is over a longer distance than with a rifle. So, another factor to consider is does your state let you use a scope during muzzleloader season. If they don't you will need to learn how to use the sights you have on your rifle, or find some special peep sight, tube sight, ghost ring sight or fiber optic sight. And some states won't let you use a fiber optic sight during muzzleloader season. Many primitive hunters won't use a scope. However, a scope may be better for long range shooting, especially if you don't have a lot of experience, and you are shooting at 200 or 300 yards. If you are any good with a muzzleloader a scope will not be much better up to 100 yards because the regular sight will be good enough. So, save your money when you are just starting out. Scopes may only be just a tiny bit better on the shorter distances than the sights that came with the rifle.

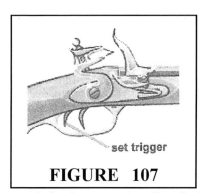

FIGURE 107

Pulling the Trigger

See "pulling the trigger" in the rifle section on page 82. However, most of this information would apply when you might be deer hunting with your muzzleloader over a longer distances. Many muzzleloader triggers are a hard pull. If that is not in your comfort level, then adjust the pull yourself (If you know how) or take it to a gunsmith to adjust it to a lighter pull for you. Some primitive muzzleloaders have double set triggers *(SEE FIGURE 107)*. You will need to look at a manual to see exactly how the double trigger works. Basically pull the back trigger to set the front trigger for a very light (hair-trigger) pull. Pull the front trigger first for a normal pull. Some in-line trigger pulls are long and kind of a hard pull, others are a regular smooth pull. It depends on the manufacturer. However, if you don't like the trigger pull, you can take it into a gunsmith and possibly have it adjusted to your liking. It's important that you are comfortable with your trigger pull. It could be the difference in that big trophy buck getting away.

Taking Care Of Your Muzzleloader (Maintenance)

Now, lets say you just got your muzzleloader and fired it. The next step is taking care of it. In other words, maintenance. This is all part of *"hunter safety"*. If your muzzleloader fails because of a malfunction due to the lack of maintenance, you or someone near you could get hurt. First, be absolutely sure your gun is UNLOADED. When the season is over, or after being used, it is recommended that you disassemble your rifle, clean it, re-lubricate it, oil the stock, then return it to it's storage place. Before you start to clean, check your owners manual that came with the rifle, for it's specific maintenance instructions. If you bought a used weapon, and don't have a manual, check on the internet for one. You can usually print them out for free if your muzzleloader is new, and even on some of the older primitive types. Or contact the manufacturer for a manual. If you need to pay for it, they are not very expensive, it's worth the money.

Cleaning And Lubricating

Caution. Our information in generalized, and may not match the parts on your muzzleloader. ALWAYS read your manual. There are a number of slightly different ways to clean and lubricate your muzzleloader. You can clean them basically the same standard way as a rifle *(SEE PAGES 83-84)*. A couple of "*TIPS*." Get a bore light so you can see better down the barrel. Use "Prolix" to clean with instead of using any gun oil. And last get a "Outer Fowl Out Kit." This is the ultimate in cleaning; it is an automatic electro chemical process that takes from 1/2 to 2 hours depending on how dirty the bore is, and it works with all kinds of firearms not just muzzleloaders.

NOTE: We will show some general diagrams for the different types of muzzleloaders. This is so that you can familiarize yourself with the general part names of the different parts of the muzzleloader, and see basically where they are located. Of course if you have a manual, it will show you where the parts are on your particular muzzleloader even better than our generalized pictures.

Primitive Percussion Cap Muzzleloader

Typical Basic Parts Location:

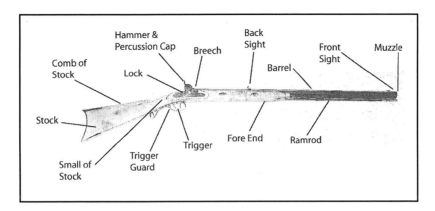

Primitive Flintlock Muzzleloader

Typical Basic Parts Location:

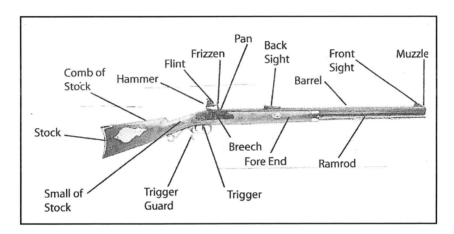

Modern In-Line

Typical Basic Parts Location:

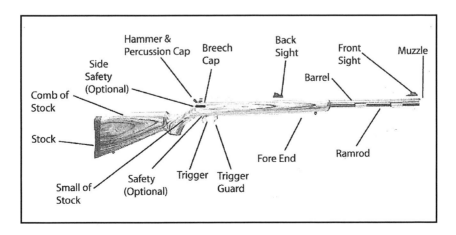

Muzzleloader Storage

Storage for muzzleloaders is the same as for rifles *(SEE PAGES 26, 27, 86)*. Basically it's under lock and key in a cabinet or safe. The closed door safe may be better because it is out of the sight of young inquisitive and prying eyes.

Transporting Your Muzzleloader

Transporting muzzleloaders is the same as for rifles *(SEE PAGES 27, 103-105)*. Basically it's under lock and key, and out of sight, in your truck or van. Minimum is in the trunk of your car with a trigger lock. If it's in plain sight you need to worry about theft. Keep that in mind if it's on a gun rack behind the front seat of your truck.

Loading and Unloading Your Muzzleloader

Loading a Muzzleloader

First, you need to realize there are basically two types of muzzleloaders, the "primitive" and the newer "in-line." Loading each one is similar in some ways but still a little different.

Loading Primitive Muzzleloaders

There are basically four types of locks on primitive muzzleloader rifles. They are the "matchlock," the "wheel lock," the "flintlock," and the "percussion lock." Matchlock and wheel lock muzzleloaders are rare and valuable, but generally speaking they be unsafe to use, especially for beginners. Flintlocks and percussion locks are the muzzleloaders typically used for hunting. So we will cover only the flintlock and percussion lock rifles in this book. Both are based on the premise that the shooter pours powder down the end of the gun barrel, then rams a slug or ball down on top of it to load the gun. Basically you use just "black powder" or a substitute called "pyrodex." We will go over these more in the "Ammunition" section of the book. **NOTE**: Here are some things you will need for loading your muzzleloader. 1. The proper amount and type of powder. 2. A lubricated precut patch. 3. A ramrod.

Loading a Flintlock Muzzleloader

This is how you load your flintlock muzzleloader. For safety purposes, here are some tips and warnings before you start:

- Position the rifle butt on the ground between your feet. You should be facing the underside of the barrel. The muzzle should be pointed upward in a safe direction, and away from your body. NEVER work directly over the muzzle.
- Next determine if the gun is already loaded by checking the barrel with a marked ramrod, which has an "unloaded" or "empty marking." If you are not sure, consult an experienced muzzleloader user or gunsmith.
- Measure out the proper amount and type of powder using the calibrated powder measure. Replace the powder horn's cap, then swing the horn to the other side of your body. Pour the powder into the barrel from the measure. Now tap the barrel to make sure all the powder falls to the breech end.
- Make sure your ramrod is marked to show when the ball, bullet, or sabot is properly seated over a specific load, such as 70 grains of FFFg powder.
- **CAUTION**: NEVER use modern-day smokeless powders in black powder firearms. Smokeless powders can cause serious injury if used in muzzleloading rifles.

Instructions *(SEE FIGURE 108)*:

1. Measure a powder charge. 2. Pour the measured powder down the barrel. 3. Place a patch and ball on the muzzle. 4. Tap the ball into the barrel with a starter. 5. Take out the ramrod. 6. Ram the ball down the barrel. 7. Be sure the ball is completely seated. 8. Clear the vent hole with a pick if necessary. 9. Pour powder in the pan and close the frizzen. The muzzleloader is now ready to fire.

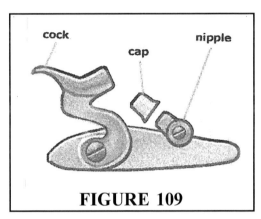

FIGURE 108

Unloading a Flintlock or Percussion Lock Muzzleloader

To unload either one of the primitive muzzleloaders just fire it at a target, but not into the air or ground, which may cause the bullet to ricochet. To determine if the rifle is still loaded, you can also check the barrel with a marked ramrod, which will have an "unloaded" or empty marking.

Loading a Percussion Lock Muzzleloader

This is how you load your percussion lock muzzleloader. For safety purposes, follow the same tips and warnings as for the "flintlock" muzzleloader.

Instructions *(SEE FIGURE 109)*:

Follow the same loading instructions as for the "flintlock" muzzleloader, except for step 9. On step No. 9 place the cap on the nipple. Now with the hammer cocked the muzzleloader is ready to fire.

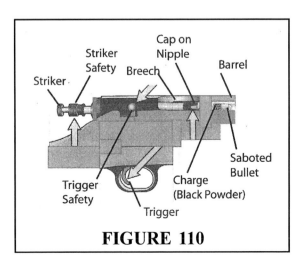

FIGURE 109

Loading a Modern In-Line Muzzleloader

This is how you load your in-line muzzleloader. For safety purposes, follow the same tips and warnings as for the "flintlock" muzzleloader. Your in-line muzzleloader may NOT be work exactly like the instructions, but it will be similar. Always check your manual.

Instructions *(SEE FIGURE 110)*:

1. Check for a load, then swab the bore dry. 2. Open the breech block to install the cap on nipple or primer. 3. Point in a safe direction and close the block. 4. Clear a channel by firing a cap. 5. Drop in the pellets or black powder. 6. Place a bullet in the muzzle. 7. Use a starter to push the bullet or saboted bullet into the muzzle. 8. Use a ramrod to seat the bullet completely. 9. Open the breechblock. 10. Install another cap or primer. 11. Close the block and put on "SAFE" or "FIRE." The muzzleloader is now ready to fire when the trigger and striker safety is on "FIRE."

FIGURE 110

145

Unloading an In-Line Muzzleloader

To unload an in-line muzzleloader just fire it at a target, but not into the air or ground, which may cause the bullet to ricochet. Or the alternative is removing the breech, dumping the powder out, then pushing the bullet out through the muzzle end of the barrel while keeping all parts of your body clear of the muzzle and breech.

Summation for Loading and Unloading all the Muzzleloaders

Muzzleloaders can be even more dangerous that rifles or shotguns. So, make sure you check your muzzleloader manual very carefully before you attempt to load or unload your muzzleloader. This can be for a number of reasons. One reason could be because your muzzleloader may be slightly different than the ones we show (basic muzzleloaders). Or maybe you have a "matchlock" or a "wheel lock" muzzleloader which we are not covering for hunting. Follow all the directions for loading and unloading, and make double sure you are loading the correct type of ammunition and powder for your muzzleloader. Anytime you have open powder involved, you have the possibility of an explosion. The information we have is in general, and only here to give you an idea how to load and unload in case you don't have a manual or even a clue how it operates. You can, in most cases, go on line and download a manual for your exact muzzleloader model, and print it out for the type of muzzleloader you have and how to operate it, and in most cases it is free.

Ammunition for Your Muzzleloader

Explanation

Now that you understand a little better of how to handle, load and unload your muzzleloader, you need to have some idea of what ammunition to use. We will NOT cover every possible ammunition that can be used in your muzzleloader. There is just too many types of ammunition sources out there, especially when you add in the newer in-line models, to try and cover them all. We will basically use "Federal" or "Hornady" for our ammunition information, unless otherwise stated. We will NOT mention special target ammunition. We will try to cover the more common ammunitions used in deer hunting. We will also use popularity as one of our targets as well as commonality. As an example, if you are going out deer hunting what would you be more likely to use, and which types of rifles use what type of ammunition, for the best results.

Now if all this is not enough to confuse you, there is the question of what type of ammunition do you use. Some primitive muzzleloader hunters may still use the large size ball. The newer in-line muzzleloader hunters are going to the saboted bullet. Some hunters may use the sabot slug which are more like a bullet, or it can be a solid projectile called a slug. The solid ammunition is basically used more by the Police or Military. We won't go into that in this book. What you use kind of depends on what you are going out to hunt for. You will probably start out hunting varmint's or deer. Many states will not let you use plain lead slugs any more because of the lead poisoning debate, in some cases only steel or a non-toxic material. Be sure you check your states muzzleloader hunting regulations because some states have strict regulations on the ammunition that can be used.

NOTE: We will try to chart this out for you in handy tables to make it a little easier for you to overview and link the muzzleloader, ammo and game together, for a quick overview. This will give you a general idea of what muzzleloader, ammo, small game, or medium size game are generally in the different classifications. There are more muzzleloaders used for the different types, but in the tables we are going to only list the more common and

146

popular muzzleloaders in the different types. The information we are showing comes from the manufacturers stated information, which may or may not be true. The muzzle velocity on the muzzleloaders is shown only to give you some idea of the ammunitions force out of the barrel.

Muzzleloader Ammo Types

There are several of ammo types for muzzleloaders because there are many uses such as target shooting and demonstration shooting as well as hunting game. We will only go into the ammunition for hunting game and waterfowl. There are basically five types of muzzleloader munitions. They are:

- Bullets
- Bullets with Sabot
- Powerbelt Bullets
- Shot Pellets
- Round Ball and Patch

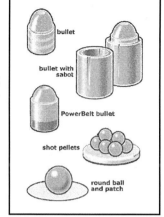

Munition Types

They are all really projectiles for muzzleloaders. The round ball, the shot, and the bullet are melted and cast from pure lead. The Power Belt bullet is actually pure lead coated with copper. It comes in a hollow point or an aero tip which gives you more penetration. Either one puts the target (deer) down quickly and in a more humane manner. The round balls are mostly used for target practice or demonstrations, but they can be used for hunting. The bullets and sabots are preferred for hunting because they are usually more accurate at hunting game distances. The shot pellets are used for a hunting spread shot, just like with shotguns. Most states now have a ban on the use of lead shot pellets though. Black powder is used to accelerate the munitions out of the barrel. Black powder is made of potassium nitrate (saltpeter), sulfur, and charcoal. When it is ignited, it makes a dense cloud of white smoke. Black powder comes in four sizes of granulations:

- **Fg**. This is a coarse grain typically used in cannons, rifles larger than .75 caliber, and 10 Ga. or larger shotguns.
- **FFg**. This is a medium grain typically used in larger rifles between .50 and .75 caliber, 20 to 12 Ga. shotguns, and pistols larger than ,50 caliber.
- **FFFg**. This is a fine grain typically used in smaller rifles and pistols under .50 caliber and smaller shotguns.
- **FFFFg**. This is extra fine grain typically used as a priming powder in flintlock rifles.

Primitive Muzzleloader Rifle Coverage

We are going to briefly cover the primitive "flintlock" and "percussion" muzzleloader rifles and ammunition because there are a few young kids that may want to try them. My advice is don't even attempt to shoot them though until you get some excellent training from someone who has been firing them for years, and is willing to mentor you until you learn, and you pass the hunter safety test. We will chart out the primitive firearms for you in a handy table *(SEE TABLE 24)* to make it a little easier for you to overview and link these rifles, the ammo, and game.

In-Line Muzzleloader Rifle Coverage

Since approximately 95% of muzzleloader hunters today use the newer "in-line" version, we will focus more on that type. However, even with all the rage over the in-line version, They may not be as effective as the primitive versions. They may be easier to load, unload, handle and re-fire though. There is a lot of different types of ammunition for the in-lines *(SEE TABLE 25)*. And there are a

TABLE 24 PRIMITIVE MUZZLELOADERS FOR MEDIUM SIZE GAME ANIMALS (DEER)

FLINTLOCK MUZZLELOADING RIFLES

MFR	45 Cal HORN 240 XTP SAB 2225	45 Cal BARN 195 EXP MZ 2600	45 Cal DC 340 SAB 1795	45 Cal DC 360 DUPLEX 1795	45 Cal EE 360 BUL 1500A	45 Cal FED 260 FUS BUL 1525A	50 Cal HORN 300 XTP SAB 2375	50 Cal BARN 250 EXP MZ 1940	50 Cal DC 340 SAB 1650	50 Cal DC 300 DUPLEX 2144	50 Cal EE 360 BUL 1450A	50 Cal KN 450 SC 1400A	50 Cal FED 300 FUS BUL 1895	Black Powder Grain [2]	Game Class	Barrel Length (In.)	Weight Range (Lbs)
	Ammunition [1] [6] — Where to Take the Shot on Game (each cell: 50 Yds [3] / 200 Yds [4])																
Traditions Pa Pellet	50 Yds [3] / 200 Yds [4]	50 Yds [3] / 200 Yds [4]	50 Yds [3] / 200 Yds [4]	50 Yds [3] / 200 Yds [4]	50 Yds [3] / 200 Yds [4]	50 Yds [3] / 200 Yds [4]	50 Yds [3] / 200 Yds [4]	50 Yds [3] / 200 Yds [4]	50 Yds [3] / 200 Yds [4]	50 Yds [3] / 200 Yds [4]	50 Yds [3] / 200 Yds [4]	50 Yds [3] / 200 Yds [4]	50 Yds [3] / 200 Yds [4]	FFFg	CPX2	26 OCT	7
J. Chambers Little Feller RK-13	50 Yds [3] / 200 Yds [4]	50 Yds [3] / 200 Yds [4]	50 Yds [3] / 200 Yds [4]	50 Yds [3] / 200 Yds [4]	50 Yds [3] / 200 Yds [4]	50 Yds [3] / 200 Yds [4]	50 Yds [3] / 200 Yds [4]	50 Yds [3] / 200 Yds [4]	50 Yds [3] / 200 Yds [4]	50 Yds [3] / 200 Yds [4]	50 Yds [3] / 200 Yds [4]	50 Yds [3] / 200 Yds [4]	50 Yds [3] / 200 Yds [4]	FFFg	CPX2	34	7
Lyman Deer-Stalker	50 Yds [3] / 200 Yds [4]	50 Yds [3] / 200 Yds [4]	50 Yds [3] / 200 Yds [4]	50 Yds [3] / 200 Yds [4]	50 Yds [3] / 200 Yds [4]	50 Yds [3] / 200 Yds [4]	50 Yds [3] / 200 Yds [4]	50 Yds [3] / 200 Yds [4]	50 Yds [3] / 200 Yds [4]	50 Yds [3] / 200 Yds [4]	50 Yds [3] / 200 Yds [4]	50 Yds [3] / 200 Yds [4]	50 Yds [3] / 200 Yds [4]	FFFg	CPX2	24	7.5
Traditions Deer-Hunter	50 Yds [3] / 200 Yds [4]	50 Yds [3] / 200 Yds [4]	50 Yds [3] / 200 Yds [4]	50 Yds [3] / 200 Yds [4]	50 Yds [3] / 200 Yds [4]	50 Yds [3] / 200 Yds [4]	50 Yds [3] / 200 Yds [4]	50 Yds [3] / 200 Yds [4]	50 Yds [3] / 200 Yds [4]	50 Yds [3] / 200 Yds [4]	50 Yds [3] / 200 Yds [4]	50 Yds [3] / 200 Yds [4]	50 Yds [3] / 200 Yds [4]	FFFg	CPX2	24	6
T/C Fire Storm	50 Yds [3] / 200 Yds [4]	50 Yds [3] / 200 Yds [4]	50 Yds [3] / 200 Yds [4]	50 Yds [3] / 200 Yds [4]	50 Yds [3] / 200 Yds [4]	50 Yds [3] / 200 Yds [4]	50 Yds [3] / 200 Yds [4]	50 Yds [3] / 200 Yds [4]	50 Yds [3] / 200 Yds [4]	50 Yds [3] / 200 Yds [4]	50 Yds [3] / 200 Yds [4]	50 Yds [3] / 200 Yds [4]	50 Yds [3] / 200 Yds [4]	FFFg	CPX2	26	7
T/C Hawken	50 Yds [3] / 200 Yds [4]	50 Yds [3] / 200 Yds [4]	50 Yds [3] / 200 Yds [4]	50 Yds [3] / 200 Yds [4]	50 Yds [3] / 200 Yds [4]	50 Yds [3] / 200 Yds [4]	50 Yds [3] / 200 Yds [4]	50 Yds [3] / 200 Yds [4]	50 Yds [3] / 200 Yds [4]	50 Yds [3] / 200 Yds [4]	50 Yds [3] / 200 Yds [4]	50 Yds [3] / 200 Yds [4]		FFFg	CPX2	28 OCT	8.5

PERCUSSION MUZZLELOADING RIFLES

MFR	45 Cal HORN 240 XTP SAB 2225	45 Cal BARN 195 EXP MZ 2600	45 Cal DC 340 SAB 1795	45 Cal DC 360 DUPLEX 1795	45 Cal EE 360 BUL 1500A	45 Cal FED 260 FUS BUL 1525A	50 Cal HORN 300 XTP SAB 2375	50 Cal BARN 250 EXP MZ 1940	50 Cal DC 340 SAB 1650	50 Cal DC 300 DUPLEX 2144	50 Cal EE 360 BUL 1450A	50 Cal KN 450 SC 1400A	50 Cal FED 300 FUS BUL 1895	Black Powder Grain [5]	Game Class	Barrel Length (In.)	Weight Range (Lbs)
	Where to Take the Shot on Game (each cell: 50 Yds [3] / 200 Yds [4])																
Traditions Hawkens Woodsman	50 Yds [3] / 200 Yds [4]	50 Yds [3] / 200 Yds [4]	50 Yds [3] / 200 Yds [4]	50 Yds [3] / 200 Yds [4]	50 Yds [3] / 200 Yds [4]	50 Yds [3] / 200 Yds [4]	50 Yds [3] / 200 Yds [4]	50 Yds [3] / 200 Yds [4]	50 Yds [3] / 200 Yds [4]	50 Yds [3] / 200 Yds [4]	50 Yds [3] / 200 Yds [4]	50 Yds [3] / 200 Yds [4]	50 Yds [3] / 200 Yds [4]	FFFg	CPX2	28 OCT	7.68
T/C Hawkens Model	50 Yds [3] / 200 Yds [4]	50 Yds [3] / 200 Yds [4]	50 Yds [3] / 200 Yds [4]	50 Yds [3] / 200 Yds [4]	50 Yds [3] / 200 Yds [4]	50 Yds [3] / 200 Yds [4]	50 Yds [3] / 200 Yds [4]	50 Yds [3] / 200 Yds [4]	50 Yds [3] / 200 Yds [4]	50 Yds [3] / 200 Yds [4]	50 Yds [3] / 200 Yds [4]	50 Yds [3] / 200 Yds [4]	50 Yds [3] / 200 Yds [4]	FFFg	CPX2	28	8.5
T/C Renegade	50 Yds [3] / 200 Yds [4]	50 Yds [3] / 200 Yds [4]	50 Yds [3] / 200 Yds [4]	50 Yds [3] / 200 Yds [4]	50 Yds [3] / 200 Yds [4]	50 Yds [3] / 200 Yds [4]	50 Yds [3] / 200 Yds [4]	50 Yds [3] / 200 Yds [4]	50 Yds [3] / 200 Yds [4]	50 Yds [3] / 200 Yds [4]	50 Yds [3] / 200 Yds [4]	50 Yds [3] / 200 Yds [4]	50 Yds [3] / 200 Yds [4]	FFFg	CPX2	26	8
Traditions Deer-Hunter	50 Yds [3] / 200 Yds [4]	50 Yds [3] / 200 Yds [4]	50 Yds [3] / 200 Yds [4]	50 Yds [3] / 200 Yds [4]	50 Yds [3] / 200 Yds [4]	50 Yds [3] / 200 Yds [4]	50 Yds [3] / 200 Yds [4]	50 Yds [3] / 200 Yds [4]	50 Yds [3] / 200 Yds [4]	50 Yds [3] / 200 Yds [4]	50 Yds [3] / 200 Yds [4]	50 Yds [3] / 200 Yds [4]	50 Yds [3] / 200 Yds [4]	FFFg	CPX2	24	6
Lyman Deer-Stalker	50 Yds [3] / 200 Yds [4]	50 Yds [3] / 200 Yds [4]	50 Yds [3] / 200 Yds [4]	50 Yds [3] / 200 Yds [4]	50 Yds [3] / 200 Yds [4]	50 Yds [3] / 200 Yds [4]	50 Yds [3] / 200 Yds [4]	50 Yds [3] / 200 Yds [4]	50 Yds [3] / 200 Yds [4]	50 Yds [3] / 200 Yds [4]	50 Yds [3] / 200 Yds [4]	50 Yds [3] / 200 Yds [4]	50 Yds [3] / 200 Yds [4]	FFFg	CPX2	24	7.5
Lyman Great Plains	50 Yds [3] / 200 Yds [4]	50 Yds [3] / 200 Yds [4]	50 Yds [3] / 200 Yds [4]	50 Yds [3] / 200 Yds [4]	50 Yds [3] / 200 Yds [4]	50 Yds [3] / 200 Yds [4]	50 Yds [3] / 200 Yds [4]	50 Yds [3] / 200 Yds [4]	50 Yds [3] / 200 Yds [4]	50 Yds [3] / 200 Yds [4]	50 Yds [3] / 200 Yds [4]	50 Yds [3] / 200 Yds [4]	50 Yds [3] / 200 Yds [4]	FFFg	CPX2	32	11.6

Abbreviation Definitions & Notes:
HORN = Hornady Mfg Co, BARN = Barnes Bullets, DC = Dead Center Ammo Co, EE = Extreme Elite Ammo Co, KN = Keith Nose Ammo Co, FED = Federal Premium Ammunition, SAB = Sabot, EXP = Expander, BUL = Bullet, SC = Solid Conical, OCT = Octagonal Shaped, MV = Muzzle Velocity, FUS = Fusion, CAL = Caliber, [1] = Based on Manufacturers Bullet & Sabot Specs, [2] = Use Only Black Powder in Flintlocks for Igniting, use FFFFg for priming in the pan, [3] = Still Target, head shots up to, [4] = Running or Still Target, anywhere on a body kill area up to, [5] = Can Use Black Powder or Pyrodex, [6] = MV No. with XXXXA is Approximate, T/C = Thompson Center

number of slightly different opinions as to which is the best to use for deer. Most hunters seem to be focusing on the 50 caliber. This is interesting, you can use a 45 caliber sabot type bullet in a 50

Powder Types

caliber rifle. This is because the sabot has a sleeve that fits around it. The sleeve is 50 caliber size, and the bullet inside is 45 caliber size. The experts say there are several things to look for in a bullet. The energy or muzzle velocity of the sabot or bullet coming out of the barrel is what gives it the power and energy to drop a deer quickly. Selecting the right bullet weight and matching it to the right barrel and twist rate is what gives you the most accuracy. Trying different weight bullets with a variety of powder types and charges in your specific barrel, will help you determine the best bullet weight to use. You can also try this at a target range before you go out hunting. Check your rifle manual if you just bought your muzzleloader. It should give you the information on how much powder to use, and how to load it. If not, check with your local

148

TABLE 25 IN-LINE MUZZLELOADERS FOR MEDIUM SIZE GAME ANIMALS (DEER)

MFR	Ammunition [1] [7]													Black Powder Grain [2]	Game Class	Barrel Length (In.)	Twist Rate (Ratio)	Weight Range (Lbs)
Bul Grain→ Bul Type→ MV (FPS)→	35 Cal REM 200 Whelan 2700	45 Cal HORN 240 XTP SAB 2225	45 Cal BARN 195 EXP MZ 2600	45 Cal DC 340 SAB 1795	45 Cal EE 360 BUL 1500A	45 Cal FED 260 FUS BUL 1525A	50 Cal HORN 300 XTP SAB 2375	50 Cal BARN 250 EXP MZ 1940	50 Cal DC 340 SAB 1650	50 Cal DC 300 DUPLEX 2144	50 Cal EE 360 BUL 1450A	50 Cal KN 450 SC 1400A	50 Cal FED 300 FUS BUL 1895					
IN-LINE MUZZLELOADING RIFLES																		
	Where to Take the Shot on Game																	
Austin & Halleck 320 Scout	—	50 Yds [3] / 200 Yds [4]	50 Yds [3] / 200 Yds [4]	50 Yds [3] / 200 Yds [4]	50 Yds [3] / 200 Yds [4]	50 Yds [3] / 200 Yds [4]	50 Yds [3] / 200 Yds [4]	50 Yds [3] / 200 Yds [4]	50 Yds [3] / 200 Yds [4]	50 Yds [3] / 200 Yds [4]	50 Yds [3] / 200 Yds [4]	50 Yds [3] / 200 Yds [4]	50 Yds [3] / 200 Yds [4]	FFg	CPX1 CPX2	20	1:28	7
Remington 700-ML Model	—	50 Yds [3] / 200 Yds [4]	50 Yds [3] / 200 Yds [4]	50 Yds [3] / 200 Yds [4]	50 Yds [3] / 200 Yds [4]	50 Yds [3] / 200 Yds [4]	50 Yds [3] / 200 Yds [4]	50 Yds [3] / 200 Yds [4]	50 Yds [3] / 200 Yds [4]	50 Yds [3] / 200 Yds [4]	50 Yds [3] / 200 Yds [4]	50 Yds [3] / 200 Yds [4]	50 Yds [3] / 200 Yds [4]	FFg	CPX1 CPX2	24	1:28	7.75
Savage 10 ML-II Model	—	50 Yds [3] / 200 Yds [4]	50 Yds [3] / 200 Yds [4]	50 Yds [3] / 200 Yds [4]	50 Yds [3] / 200 Yds [4]	50 Yds [3] / 200 Yds [4]	50 Yds [3] / 200 Yds [4]	50 Yds [3] / 200 Yds [4]	50 Yds [3] / 200 Yds [4]	50 Yds [3] / 200 Yds [4]	50 Yds [3] / 200 Yds [4]	50 Yds [3] / 200 Yds [4]	50 Yds [3] / 200 Yds [4]	[5] FFg	CPX1 CPX2	24	1:24	7.75
T/C Encore	—	50 Yds [3] / 200 Yds [4]	50 Yds [3] / 200 Yds [4]	50 Yds [3] / 200 Yds [4]	50 Yds [3] / 200 Yds [4]	50 Yds [3] / 200 Yds [4]	50 Yds [3] / 200 Yds [4]	50 Yds [3] / 200 Yds [4]	50 Yds [3] / 200 Yds [4]	50 Yds [3] / 200 Yds [4]	50 Yds [3] / 200 Yds [4]	50 Yds [3] / 200 Yds [4]	50 Yds [3] / 200 Yds [4]	FFg	CPX1 CPX2	26	1:28	7
T/C Omega	—	50 Yds [3] / 200 Yds [4]	50 Yds [3] / 200 Yds [4]	50 Yds [3] / 200 Yds [4]	50 Yds [3] / 200 Yds [4]	50 Yds [3] / 200 Yds [4]	50 Yds [3] / 200 Yds [4]	50 Yds [3] / 200 Yds [4]	50 Yds [3] / 200 Yds [4]	50 Yds [3] / 200 Yds [4]	50 Yds [3] / 200 Yds [4]	50 Yds [3] / 200 Yds [4]	50 Yds [3] / 200 Yds [4]	FFg	CPX1 CPX2	28	1:28	7
CVA Scout	50 Yds [3] / 200 Yds [4]	—	—	—	—	—	—	—	—	—	—	—	—	FFg	CPX1 CPX2	22	1:28	5.8
Knight Disc Extreme	—	—	—	—	—	—	50 Yds [3] / 200 Yds [4]	50 Yds [3] / 200 Yds [4]	50 Yds [3] / 200 Yds [4]	50 Yds [3] / 200 Yds [4]	50 Yds [3] / 200 Yds [4]	50 Yds [3] / 200 Yds [4]	50 Yds [3] / 200 Yds [4]	FFg	CPX1 CPX2	26	1:28	8
Traditions Buck-Stalker	—	—	—	—	—	—	50 Yds [3] / 200 Yds [4]	50 Yds [3] / 200 Yds [4]	50 Yds [3] / 200 Yds [4]	50 Yds [3] / 200 Yds [4]	50 Yds [3] / 200 Yds [4]	50 Yds [3] / 200 Yds [4]	50 Yds [3] / 200 Yds [4]	[6] FFg	CPX1 CPX2	24	1:28	6

Abbreviation Definitions & Notes:
HORN = Hornady Mfg Co, BARN = Barnes Bullets, DC = Dead Center Ammo Co, EE = Extreme Elite Ammo Co, KN = Keith Nose Ammo Co, FED = Federal Premium Ammunition, SAB = Sabot, EXP = Expander, BUL = Bullet, SC = Solid Conical, OCT = Octagonal Shaped, MV = Muzzle Velocity, FUS = Fusion, CAL = Caliber, [1] = Based on Manufacturers Bullet & Sabot Specs, [2] = Can Use Black Powder or Pyrodex, [3] = Still Target, head shots up to , [4] = Running or Still Target anywhere in target kill area up to, T/C = Thompson Center [5] = Can use Smokeless Powder, [6] = Uses 209 for Ignition, [7] = MV No. with XXXXA is Approximate, information not Available

gun shop, or gunsmith. The experts say barrel twist rates from 1:20" to 1:38 work the best. Heavier bullets generally require the slower twist rates. 26" barrel lengths seems to be the optimum size for 100 grain FFg powder charges. And always use black powder unless your specific rifle allows otherwise. There are a lot of possible combinations, so keep checking and testing until you get the best one. And remember, what is hyped and what sells is not always the best choice.

Summation of Muzzleloaders

Muzzleloaders can be very dangerous because you are dealing with gunpowder. As an example, lets say you light up a cigarette while holding your muzzleloader. Some how it gets too close to some powder residue on you or the rifle. Them boom you have a mini explosion. Oh well, maybe you were not going to need that hand or those fingers anyway. Get the idea. Muzzleloaders are also going to have a few different cleaning problems. Black powder and Pyrodex are very corrosive. Therefore, careful cleaning of your muzzleloading firearm is extremely important. Make sure you read our muzzleloader maintenance section very carefully before you start. If left unclean for any length of time the fouling will cause rust, pits, and degradation of the rifle metal, and your barrel.

SECTION 3 Archery

Explanation

This is an introduction into archery. The art of shooting bows and arrows for food goes back a long ways in time. It started with hand thrown spears, and then at some level of evolution someone got the idea that a tree branch with some type of string material could propel an arrow farther than by hand throwing. Then as time went on the bow material developed into stronger laminated wood and then to composite metals. So, now we have two branches of the bow family, "traditional" bows and "compound" bows. Compound bows are the state of the art of where we are today. Bows always were very accurate for hunting game. Now they are even more accurate and powerful, and over a longer distances. Arrows developed right along with the bows to where we are now. Along with wood, arrows at now made out of metals and composite materials. The broadhead tips have also developed into some very deadly types that really penetrate when they hit their target. I've seen a video where a hunting broadhead penetrated an old steel car door hanging on a clothes line. We will start with bows and then go to crossbows.

Choosing a Bow

This is an introduction into bows and arrows. First here is some general advice on choosing a bow. Choosing the right bow is very important. The two big choices are "draw weight" and bow "length."

Draw Weight

This is more important than any other factor. One of the biggest reasons shooters give up archery prematurely is they attempt to shoot a bow with too much draw weight. As an example, don't get fooled into thinking that you need to have a traditional bow that pulls with 75 pounds to get lots of arrow speed. Accuracy is far more important than arrow speed. Starting out with a draw weight of 35 to 45 pounds is good enough. Here is a little test you can try. Pick up the bow, hold it out in front of you, then try to draw the bowstring straight back to the corner of your mouth. If you need to point the bow up or down, or go through some kind of gyrations to get the bowstring back, then the weight is too much. You should be able to draw the bowstring back smoothly and comfortably for several times without any discomfort, this is especially true with traditional bows.

Bow Length

However, bow length is also an important factor to consider. Bows come in a wide variety of lengths; your physical stature and draw length will help you to determine which bow to get. As an example, if you are 6 feet, 2 inches tall with a 30 inch draw length, you should not be shooting a little 52 inch recurve bow. At your draw length, a bow that size and that short would cause a severe angle in the bowstring, and would pinch the fingers of your drawing hand. A more suitable bow would be a long bow or recurve in the 64 to 68 inch range, which would give you a less severe bowstring angle and give you a smoother draw. The opposite would be if you are 4 feet 8 inches tall, it would be very awkward for you to attempt to shoot a 68 inch long bow. To purchase a bow, go for a good well known bow manufacturing company. Find manufacturers back in the reference section. When you have more experience, you can invest in a custom-made bow, or make your own.

How Much Draw to Use

We have a Table 26 to give you some general guidelines for choosing an appropriate draw weight. Each individual is different though. So you need to apply your common sense here and interpret this table with respect to your own age, general physical condition, and body mass index (BMI). If you are new though to the sport of hunting there are other considerations.

Draw Weights Effect on Arrow Velocity

Higher poundage bows require

Table 26 Recommended Draw Weight Ranges		
The Bow Hunter	Your Weight (Lbs.)	Draw Weight (Lbs.)
Very Small Child	55 - 70	10 - 15
Small Child	70 - 100	15 - 25
Larger Child	100 - 130	25 - 35
Small Frame Women	100 - 130	25 - 35
Medium Frame Women	130 - 160	30 - 40
Athletic Older Child (Boys)	130 - 150	40 - 50
Small Frame Men	120 - 150	45 - 55
Large Frame Women	160 +	45 - 55
Medium Frame Men	150 - 180	55 - 65
Large Frame Men	180 +	65 - 75

heavier, stiffer arrow shafts. Even though they will certainly generate more energy at the target, they may not generate much faster arrow speeds at IBO standards. Lower poundage bows can use lighter, more limber arrow shafts. IBO standards allow 5 grains of arrow weight per pound of draw weight. As an example, a 70 Lb. bow can shoot an arrow (safely) as light as 350 grains. And a bow set for 60 Lbs. can shoot an arrow for down to 300 grains. Actually, when set for IBO minimum standards, many bows are only fractionally faster in the 70 Lb. version vs the 60 Lb. version. Since the 70 Lb. bow must shoot the heavier arrow, the savings in arrow weight offsets the loss of energy storage during the power stroke. So properly set up for the best speed, the 60 Lb. version of most bows will perform within 10 FPS of the heavier 70 Lb. version.

How Much Draw Weight is Necessary

Some states will require a compound bow to meet certain draw weight minimums in order to hunt larger game like Whitetail Deer. So ALWAYS observe the rules and regulations for legally harvesting game in your state. However, it should be noted that some of these rules have been in effect for many years, and do not necessarily consider the recent technological advances in archery manufacturing. 15 years ago the average bow was struggling to shoot at 230 FPS, and even at those speeds many bow hunters got clean pass thru's on large game like White-tailed Deer. Today the average bow is shooting at 300 FPS at 70 Lb. draw weight and 30 inch draw length. This means that even bows with shorter draw lengths and lower draw will still provide plenty of velocity to penetrate the rib cage of a White-tailed Deer and other large game. A modern single cam compound bow with a 50 Lb. peak draw weight and just a 26 inch draw length will still shoot arrows at well over 220 FPS. However, if you plan to hunt larger game like Elk or Moose, or if you plan to take shots at longer distances, you will need additional kinetic energy for complete penetration and the best chance for a humane harvest. As a general rule, a 40-50 Lb. draw weight will provide sufficient energy to harvest larger elk size game. Unless you are planning to hunt huge animals like Cape Buffalo or Musk Ox, a 70 Lb. bow isn't really necessary. You can be just as effective with a more moderate draw weight.

The Basics of Draw Length

A compound bow, unlike a traditional recurve bow that can be drawn back to just about any length, will only draw back a specific distance before it stops (hits the wall so to speak). They are designed to be shot from the full draw position. If a compound bow is set for a 29 inch draw length, it should ALWAYS be shot from the full 29 inch draw position. The bow can not be over drawn, to say 30 or 31 inches, without modifying the set-up on the bow. So the draw length on your compound bow must be set to match your particular size. Most compound bows use a series of interchangeable or sliding cam modules, which allow the bow to be adjusted to fit a given range of draw lengths. If you don't know your draw length, you should determine that before shopping for a new bow. Most men's bows adjust within a typical 26 -30 inch draw length range, which fits shooters from roughly 5'-5" to 6'-3." But that's not true for every bow. Some bows have a narrow range of adjustment, or in some cases, no adjustment at all. So the first step in selecting your new bow is finding a model that will adjust to suit your particular draw length. However, if you have an unusually long or short draw length, your choices may be limited. What this means is you need pay particular attention to the bow's advertised draw length range

The Draw Length will Effect Power

The longer draw length you have, the longer your bow's power stroke will be, and the faster your bow will shoot. As a general rule, 1 inch of draw length is worth about 10 FPS of arrow velocity. So, if your particular bow has an IBO speed of 300 FPS, and you intend to shoot the bow at a 27 inch draw length, you should then expect an approximate 30 FPS loss in speed right off the top. However, this is one area where speed should be a secondary concern. As an example, if you are 5'-9" tall, it would seem ridiculous to buy a size 13 shoe for your size 10 foot. Similarly, it's not such a good idea to buy a 30 inch draw length bow, when a 27 or 28 inch draw length would fit you much better.

Excessively Long Draw Lengths

Long draw lengths will earn you more speed, but to get that extra speed your likely to give up a considerable amount of control and comfort. We recommend that you NOT shoot a draw length that's too long for your particular body size. Accuracy should never be sacrificed for a little more speed. Think about it, a fast miss is no more impressive than a slow miss. Some experts say that the majority of compound bow owners set their bows for too much draw length, which results in poor shooting form, inaccuracy, and painful string slap on the forearm. You will be more successful, and enjoy your new bow, when it is fitted properly to your body. Remember this rule, if in doubt choose a little less draw length rather than a little more.

Other Draw Considerations

There are other things to consider in determining draw length, such as arm span and height. The primary method for increasing the amount of stored energy during the power stroke is to shoot a bow with a higher maximum draw weight. All other things being equal, a 70 pound bow will store more energy and shoot faster than a 60 pound bow. However this is a complicated issue you should consider carefully when selecting your new COMPOUND bow. The maximum draw weight of the bow is typically determined by the stiffness of the bow's limbs. COMPOUND bows come in a variety of maximum draw weights, but the most common are the 50-60 pound and the 60-70 pound versions. Although you may purchase a bow with 70 pound limbs, you can generally adjust the draw weight 1-10 pounds down from the maximum weight. So a 70 pound bow could actually be adjusted for 61 pounds, 64 pounds, 67 pounds, or any draw weight within the allowable range. However, it should be noted that a 70 pound bow, turned down to 60 pounds, will not perform as well as the same bow in a 60 pound version operating at it's maximum draw weight. Bows are generally more efficient at or near their maximum draw weight.

We have some more information on choosing a draw weight for a Compound bow. Unlike a traditional recurve bow that can be drawn back to virtually any length, a COMPOUND bow will draw back only a specific distance. Compound bows are designed to be shot from the full-draw position. If a compound bow is set for a 29 inch draw length, it should always be shot from the full 29 inch draw position. A bow that is set for a 29 inch draw can not be drawn back to 30 or 31 inches, without modifying the setup on the bow (forcibly overdrawing the bow is a dangerous practice). Similarly, a compound bow should not be shot from a position less than a full draw either. Where the bow stops, you stop. So if you are a 29 inch draw, then your bow should be a 29 inch draw.

Measuring Draw Length

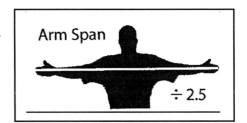

To measure your draw length, determine the length of your arm span in inches. Stand with your arms out and palms facing forward. Don't stretch when measuring. Just stand naturally. Have someone else help you, and measure from the tip of one middle finger to the other. Then simply divide that number by 2.5. The quotient is your approximate draw length (in inches) for your body size. The majority of COMPOUND bow owners set their bows for too much draw length, which results in poor shooting form, inaccuracy, and painful string snap on the forearm. You will better enjoy, and be more successful with your compound bow when it is fitted properly to your body. And if in doubt, choose a little less draw length rather than a little more. If you have heard that longer draw length bows shoot faster, you have heard right. But don't even think of shooting an excessively long draw length just for the sake of generating more speed. That's a very poor trade off which you will regret. Shooting your bow at an overly long draw length won't make you more macho. It will just make you miss the target. So don't do it. Just shoot at the correct draw length.

Height vs Draw Length

If you are a person of average proportions, your arm span will be roughly equal to your height (in inches). So there is often a direct correlation between a person's height and their draw length as well. Once you have computed your draw length using the method

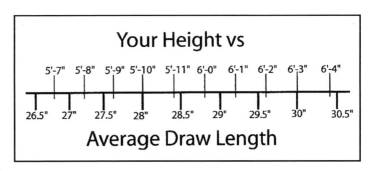

above, you can double check yourself by using this scale, to see if your draw length number is within the expected range. This data was taken from "Huntersfriend.com- Carbon Arrow University" on the web.

Types of Bows

Now that you know the draw weight and length of the bow you need, what type of bow do you buy. Their are more types of bows than you would expect. Each on has a special use. Bows break into two types now, "traditional" and "compound."

Traditional

- The Recurve
- The Relex
- The Self
- The Straight
- The Long bow
- The Composite
- The Takedown

Compound
- Single Cam ■ Dual Cam ■ Hybrid Duo Cam ■ Single Limb
- Quad Limb

Traditional Bows

Note: This is not a complete total in depth description of these types of bows, just enough so that you have an idea of what they are like, and what they do best.

Recurve

This is a special type of bow. It gets it's name from the opposite direction curves on each end of the bow limb *(SEE FIGURE 111)*. The recurve is better know for it's arrow speed. Make sure you handle and draw back a recurve before you buy one. This way you will know how it feels to you. Long bows will have a slightly different feel to them. The differences in grip area and the differences in weight of the bow can help you make your decision.

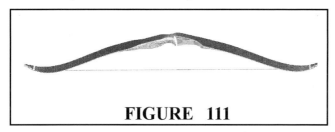

FIGURE 111

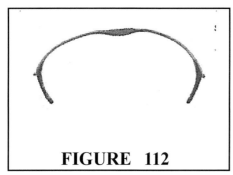

FIGURE 112

Reflex

This is a special type of bow. It sometimes is confused with the Recurve Bow. It curves completely away from the archer when unstrung. The most common one makes a "C" shape *(SEE FIGURE 112)*. The original reflex bow is not usually used in modern hunting. The newer Compound reflex bow is used more in hunting now.

Self Bow

This is a special type of bow. It is self made by the hunter. It is made from just one material, usually wood, and it is fairly straight like the straight bow when unstrung.

Usually there is an experienced bowmaker that helps young kids and adults get started *(SEE FIGURE 113)*. They show them what to do, then they do their own finish work. I just came back from a "Selfbow Jaboree," and watched them do this. It was very interesting There are some bow hunters that make their own bow because it gives them a good feeling, then they go out and hunt with it. It's not too bad at 20 yards.

FIGURE 113

Straight Bow

This is a special type of bow. It is straight in the profile view when unstrung as opposed to being slightly curved. Usually made of laminated fiberglass or carbon composite material. The difference is the straight bow is purchased. Not always, but usually the straight bow is not as long in length as a long bow.

Long Bows

This is another special type of bow. It gets it's name from the fact that it is for shooting longer distances *(SEE FIGURE 114)*. Make sure you handle and draw back a recurve before you buy a long bow.

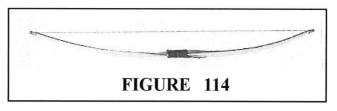

FIGURE 114

This way you will know how it feels in comparison to you. Long bows will have a slightly different feel to them, and they are to long for young kids to use. Typically new long Bows are 60 to 66 inches in length. The differences in grip styles to hold on to, and the differences in weight of the bow, can help you make your decision. There are five different grip holding styles you can find.

Composite Bow

This bow gets it's name because it is made out of more than one material: it is usually a wooden core, molded fiberglass and carbon composite on the outside, then all laminated together. Aside from being laminated, it may be a number of different bow types, styles and shapes, but made from the composite material.

The Takedown Bow

This is a special type of bow. This could also be a number of different bow style types. The "Grip," and the "Limbs" come apart to make it handy for traveling *(SEE FIGURE 115)*. This way they can fit in a suitcase or duffle bag. You just disassemble the bow, then when you get to your shooting destination, you can reassemble the bow and you are ready to shoot. It has some other features. As your strength increases, you can purchase increasingly heavier sets of limbs to set on the riser, and save yourself the cost of an entirely new bow with a heavier draw weight.

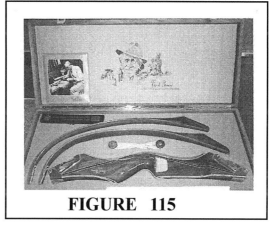

FIGURE 115

Picture Courtesy of Bear Archery Products

Traditional Bow Center Grip Styles

There are basically 5 different traditional bow center grip *(SEE FIGURE 116)* styles:

- The Straight
- The Reverse Handle
- The Locator
- The R.W. Style
- The Takedown Riser

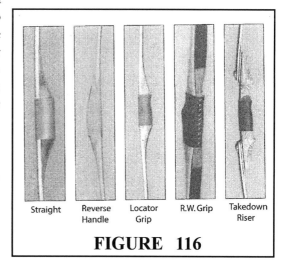

Straight | Reverse Handle | Locator Grip | R.W. Grip | Takedown Riser

FIGURE 116

Compound Bows

How They Work

This is a special type of bow. They come in a number of different types and styles. They are generally similar to a take down bow, except the basic bow has pulleys and cams that aid in the bows efficiency, and make the limbs adjustable. However, remember this bow does not necessarily mean it will give you an edge in getting more deer or turkeys. It just gives you a more adjustable

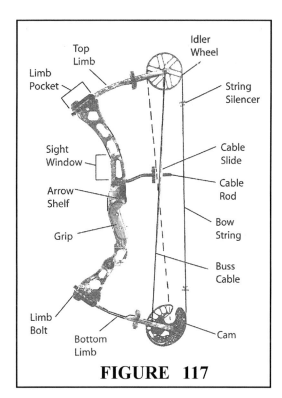

Top Limb
Idler Wheel
Limb Pocket
String Silencer
Sight Window
Cable Slide
Cable Rod
Arrow Shelf
Bow String
Grip
Buss Cable
Limb Bolt
Bottom Limb
Cam

FIGURE 117

bow. It's how you use that adjustability to make your shot easier and more accurate. So, before you run right out and get one of these, make sure you try it, and feel comfortable drawing it. Have the salesman show you exactly how it works, and all it's features. We are showing a typical single cam model *(SEE FIGURE 117)*, just so that you can get a feel for what they are like. The basic parts are shown to help you understand what they are, and where they are located. There are many companies that make them now. Bows are made to a standard by the way. The industry uses an "Apples-to-Apples" method of comparison.

The Standard

Companies generally rate their bow using the same IBO (International Bowhunting Organization) standard. To get an accurate IBO speed rating, manufacturers must test their bows under the same pre-set conditions: setting the bow for exactly 70 pounds "Peak Draw Weight," exactly a 30 inch draw length, and they must shoot a test arrow that weighs precisely 350 grains. This levels the playing field on bow characteristics. So, also check out the IBO numbers.

Types of

Compound bows come in basically 5 different styles:
- Single Cam
- Dual Cam
- Hybrid Duo Cam
- Single Limb
- Quad Limb

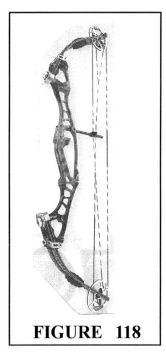

FIGURE 118

The Single Cam

The single cam has basically a cam on one end and a pulley on the other end. What that basically means is you have adjustability on one end and not the other *(SEE FIGURE 117)*.

The Dual Cam

The dual cam has basically a cam on both ends. What that basically means is you have even more adjustability from both ends *(SEE FIGURE 118)*.

The Hybrid Duo Cam

The hybrid duo cam basically has a special designed cam on both ends. What is gives you is greatly reduced cam lean and improved cable tracking. It is designed for those situations that call for either shorter draws or longer bows. If you are a bow hunter that has a shorter draw and want added speed, this is the type for you *(SEE FIGURE 118)*.

The Single Limb

This is your basic compound bow, with one limb on each end *(SEE FIGURE 119-A)*. Both limbs, on each end, pivot on the maim body of the bow, or the riser.

The Quad Limb

This is special designed compound bow, with two limbs on each end *(SEE FIGURE 119-B)*. Both limbs, two on each end, pivot on the maim boby of the bow. These maximum pre-loaded limbs give you maximum power without the bow stacking up during the draw.

Handling Your Bow

Explanation

We will cover handling your bow out in the field and at home. When we talk about handling, we mean when you are just carrying out in the field, or on the couch at home. We will talk about shooting, loading and unloading later in this section.

Handling a Bow In the Field Position

Handling a bow out in the field can be a problem. If you are holding it with your hand, and you are moving for any length of time, your arm may get tired. I see several ways you could carry your bow. The old time way of carrying a long bow was to just put your arm through the bow string and move the bow around over your back. The problem is if you need to get it ready in a hurry, it's not going to be quick. And if you have a quiver on your back, it's liable to get tangled with the bow. Another way is a "bow rest" that fits on a belt around your waist, and rides on your hip *(SEE FIGURE 120)*. Then there is what looks like the best way. That is to use the Altus "Crossfire Bow Sling *(SEE FIGURE 121)*. What I like about it is that when you need to quickly get ready to shoot, it never needs to be removed to shoot, just swing it around to the front and it's ready. And it leaves your hands free to call game, stalk, or load arrows while walking.

Handling a Bow At Home

When handling your bow at home whether just sitting and holding it, or working on it:

- First ALWAYS make sure it is unloaded without an arrow nocked.
- NEVER point the end of the limbs at your head or somebody elses head either.
- NEVER pull the bow string back and dry fire it. Eventually you will get a string burn, and it won't do the bow any good.
- Always use a bowstringer and unstring your bow in the house, especially when you won't be using it for a while.
- If you are cleaning it or repairing it, put it on a weapon holder of some kind if possible. It's easier to work on that way as opposed to holding it in your lap.

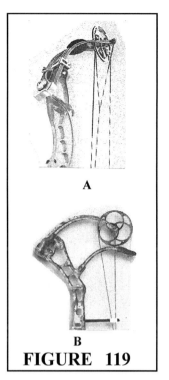

A

B

FIGURE 119

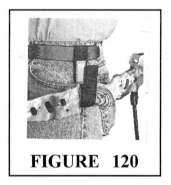

FIGURE 120

FIGURE 121

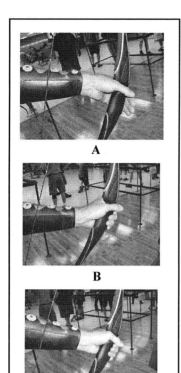

A

B

C

FIGURE 122

Bow Holding Grips

There are three different bow holding grip styles. They are:
- High Wrist
- Low Wrist
- Medium Wrist

My suggestion is try as many bows as you can before you make a choice. Until you do, you won't know which is the most comfortable to grip and hold.

High Wrist Grip

This grip places the pressure of the grip in the web of the hand because your hand points down *(SEE FIGURE 122-A)*. This causes your wrist to come up, which gives it the name.

Low Wrist Grip

This grip *(SEE FIGURE 122-B)* places the pressure of the grip closer to the heel of the hand; the bones in your wrist and forearm are more in alignment with this grip, which allows the pressure of drawing the bow to be more evenly distributed through your joints.

Medium Wrist Grip

This grip *(SEE FIGURE 122-C)* falls somewhere in between the other two with the angle varying in different degrees on different bows.

Bow and Arrow Hunter Safety

Following these simple archery safety rules at all times will make bow and arrow hunting a pleasant experience for you:

1. NEVER point a bow and arrow at another person.
2. NEVER shoot an arrow straight up into the air. You may end up hitting yourself or another person as it comes down.
3. NEVER shoot an arrow off into the distance where you cannot see where it will land. You could end up hitting another person.
4. ONLY use bows in places that are especially set up for target practice, such as indoor *(SEE FIGURE 123)* or outdoor target ranges. Targets should be set up to insure that no one can accidentally be hit by a stray arrow. Allow at least 20 yards behind the target, and a 30 degree "cone of safety" on each side of the shooting lane. Try to place targets against a hill or rising ground as an additional safety measure.

FIGURE 123

5. If you are looking for your lost arrow behind the target, ALWAYS leave your bow leaning against the target face so that it will be seen by other archers coming up. And if possible, have one archer from your group stand in front of the target to prevent anyone from shooting.
6. On field archery or 3-D courses, be sure to stay on the marked path and travel ONLY in the direction in which the targets are laid out while shooting is in progress. Go

ing backwards on the trail or going across an unmarked area could place you in a path of a flying arrow, resulting in a serious injury.

7. NEVER shoot arrows with broad heads at standard targets. Set up broad head pits for this.

8. If you are shooting wooden arrows, check them regularly for cracks. If one is found cracked, break it immediately to insure that it will NOT be accidentally used. Shooting a cracked arrow can result in it's breaking and causing a painful injury to the shooter.

9. ALWAYS use a bowstringer for long Bows and recurve bows. This will reduce the possibility of damage to the bow and injury to the hunter.

10. ALWAYS check your bow regularly for cracks or twisting. If in doubt, have it checked by a professional before shooting it any more.

11. ALWAYS check the condition of your bow string regularly. It's cheaper to install a new string than to replace the bow.

12. NEVER draw a bowstring back further than the length of the arrow from which it is intended. Overdrawing can break the bow and injure the shooter in the process.

13. NEVER draw the bowstring back except with an arrow on it and, especially, don't release the bowstring without an arrow on it. This is called dry firing and can damage the bow.

14. At practice ranges, the only safe place is behind the shooting line. NEVER shoot an arrow until you are positive that no one is in front of you or behind the targets. Also NEVER stand in front of a bow while it is being shot, even if you are to one side of the shooter.

15. ALWAYS wait for a verbal approval from the range captain or their designee before starting to shoot.

16. Arrows should ONLY be nocked on the shooting line and pointed in the target direction.

17. After you are done shooting, ALWAYS wait for the word "CLEAR" from the range captain or their designee before going toward the targets to retrieve your arrows.

18. ALWAYS walk, don't run towards the targets. Remember that arrows are sticking out of the target and can injure you if you trip and fall into them.

19. When pulling arrows out of a target, ALWAYS stand to one side and look to insure that no one is directly behind you.

20. If other archers will be shooting concurrently at varying distances, stagger the targets not the shooters. This goes back to rule No.14 about having ONLY one shooting line and everyone stays behind it.

21. If you are using broadheads, be sure that they are ALWAYS adequately covered when not in use. Treat it with the same caution you would with a razor blade. It's very sharp.

Loading Your Bow

Loading a Traditional Bow
First, you need to realize there are basically three traditional types of bows, the "standard or regular size," the "recurve," and the "long bow." As far as loading they are all very similar.

Loading an Arrow into a Traditional Bow
The nocking (loading) begins when you have assumed your stance facing the target. To load a bow means placing or nocking the back end of the arrow into the bow string. Nock the arrow by placing the nock (groove in the shaft) of the arrow onto the bowstring under the nocking point locator or mark on the bowstring *(SEE FIGURE 124)*. The first thing you need to do is place a "nocking point" on your bowstring. The most common nocking point is a small brass band with a plastic lining that clamps around the bowstring with pliers *(SEE FIGURE 125)*. They have special

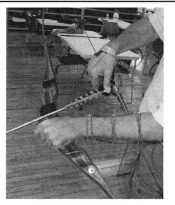

FIGURE 124

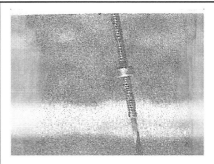

FIGURE 125

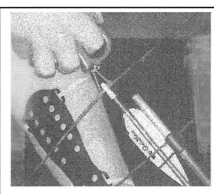

FIGURE 126

nocking point pliers to accomplish this in a round uniform manner. Start out with the nocking point about 3/4 of an inch above the arrow shelf. You can eyeball the measurement or use a bow square.

Suggestion For Locating a Nocking Point:
By starting out with the nocking point too high, the arrow will leave the bow with the nock above the field point and impact the target the same way. If the nocking point is too low, the arrow will fly with the nock of the arrow below the field point, or it may cause the nock end of the arrow to bounce off the arrow shelf and travel downrange with the nock high. This is very deceptive, causing you to think your nocking point is too high when, in reality it is too low. That's the reason for starting out with the nocking point in a location you know is too high, to avoid being fooled. First work on getting the shaft to the correct length to get it to fly and stick in the target fairly straight in the horizontal plane, then you gradually lower the nocking point to get rid of the nock up to high problem. More on the "arrow" size and type in the "ammunition" section.

Aligning the Fletch
Next make sure the index fletch, on a 3 fletch arrow, is facing horizontally towards you *(SEE FIGURE 126)*, and the knock is pushed firmly into the bowstring. Now place the front end of the arrow shaft on the "arrow rest." If you have a new bow, it may not have an arrow rest. In that case you will need to go out and buy one. You can find on at an archery store or shop. Now all you need to do to be fully loaded is pull the bowstring back to your draw point next to your cheek.

Loading a Compound Bow
Loading a compound bow is very similar to a traditional bow, except it is a little more complicated.

Loading the Arrow into a Compound Bow
To load a bow means placing or nocking the back end of the arrow in the bow string. The first thing you need to do is place a nocking point on your bowstring. Then nock the arrow by placing the nock (groove in the shaft) of the arrow onto the bowstring under the nocking point locator or mark on the bowstring *(SEE FIGURE 124)*.

Nocking Point Placement
Finger Shooters:
For the initial setting, install the nocking point on the bowstring approximately 5/16 of an inch plus an arrow width above a point where a horizontal line from the "arrow rest" intersects the bowstring *(SEE FIGURE 127)*.

Release Aid Shooters:
Install the nocking point the width of an arrow above a point where a horizontal line from the "arrow rest" intersects the bowstring. When the arrow is in position on the "arrow rest" the arrow nock should fit snug against the bottom of the knocking point. *(SEE FIGURE 126)*.

Arrow Rest Adjustment
The in/out position of the arrow rest should be adjusted so that the arrow is in alignment with the bowstring when shooting with a release aid. The arrow tip should be 1/2 a shaft diameter left of center on a right handed bow, and opposite for a left handed shooter, when shooting with your fingers *(SEE FIGURE 128)*.

Cable Guard Adjustment and Installation
Adjusting the "cable guard" is important. If you have one to install, follow the manufacturers instructions or install it as shown *(SEE FIGURE 129-A)*. Adjust the cable guard so that the cables just clear the arrow vanes. On bows using an offset cable guard rod, adjustments must be done with the rod in the up position at about approximately 1 o'clock *(SEE FIGURE 129-B)*. Or at the 11 o'clock position for left handed bows. Excessive arrow clearance may cause the cable to track incorrectly on the wheels and cause personal injury and/or damage to the bow itself.

Drawing Hand Finger Placement
Finger Shooters:
The index finger is placed above the arrow nock, and the second and third fingers are placed below the arrow nock. Curl the fingers around the bowstring so that the first joint of all three fingers are aligned on the bowstring. Keep a space clear between the index and second fingers and the arrow nock so that the fingers do not touch the arrow nock. This will prevent pinching of the arrow. Keep the back of the hand as flat as possible, and relaxed.

Thumb Placement
The thumb is tucked into the palm so that it can be placed against the neck at the full draw *(SEE FIGURE 130)*. Place a slight pull on the bowstring to set the fingers in position ready for the draw back. During the draw and anchor maintain an even amount of pressure on all three fingers. Your compound bow is now loaded and ready to draw back and shoot.

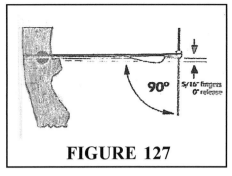

FIGURE 127

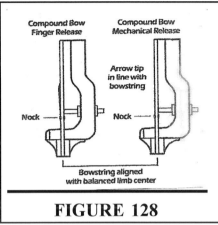

FIGURE 128

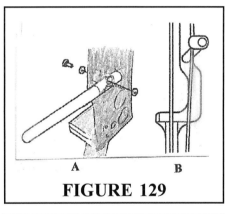

FIGURE 129

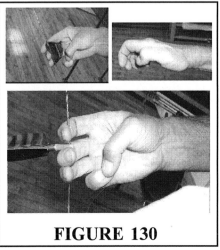

FIGURE 130

Shooting Your Traditional Bow

Shooting Standard and Long Bows In the Field

There are several stable ways to shoot bows out in the field so that it is never a threat to other hunters. First thing, before firing check the area for other hunters, and observe what's behind your target. Flat line regular bow shots drop over 9 feet in 50 yards, but if you are making long up in the air shots you better allow for 100 yards behind your target just to be safe. However, today long bow arrows have been known to travel 200 yards. So I would allow for at least that far behind your target to be safe. There are four basic standard shooting positions. They are standing, sitting, kneeling, and prone *(SEE FIGURE 131)*.

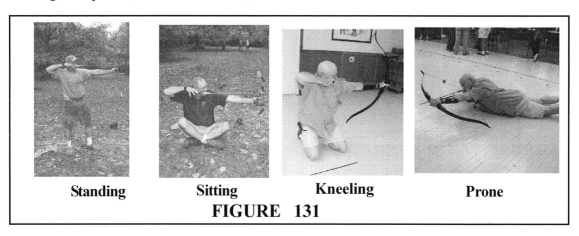

Standing   **Sitting**   **Kneeling**   **Prone**
FIGURE 131

A   **B**
FIGURE 132

Variations of Shooting Positions Standing

There are several positions to shoot a bow standing up *(SEE FIGURE 132)*. One is standing holding the bow as vertical as possible *(SEE FIGURE 132-A)*. The other is standing holding the bow canted or tilted to the side *(SEE FIGURE 132-B)*. This gets the upper bow limb out of the line of sight for normal shooting. In addition to the positions, you have 4 different stances to consider. The stances are important because the proper stance means the shooter will be able to distribute their body weight better. The proper stance keeps the shooter's shot consistent. Look at the stances and notice how each stance is different in feet placement *(SEE FIGURE 133)*. Each one has it's Pro's and Con's:

Standing Even Stance
Pro's Are: It's a natural Position, and easy to reproduce.
Con's Are: It has a small base of support in the front-To-back plane. The body isn't sturdy, so it can move if in a high wind. It lowers area for string clearance, especially for large chested shooters.
Standing Open Stance
Pro's Are: It's gives a stable support base. It reduces the tendency to lean back from the target.

Con's Are: It tends to make the upper body twist. towards the target. It tends to use arm muscles more than back muscles to draw the string back.

Closed Standing Stance

Pro's Are: It's gives a stable support base. It gives good alignment of the arm and shoulder in a direct line to the target.

Con's Are: It reduces string clearance, so the string may strike against the body. It tends to make the shooter lean away from the target and overdraw the bow.

Oblique Standing Stance

Pro's Are: It's gives the greatest amount of clearance for the bowstring when arrows are released. The body is in total equilibrium. The target can be seen clearly.

Con's Are: It's a hard stance to maintain, so it's mainly used by expert archers, not beginners.

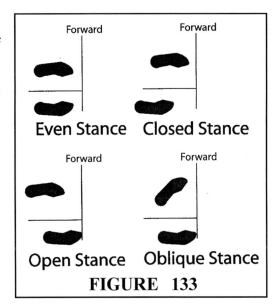

FIGURE 133

Kneeling

Rise Up Kneeling Stance *(SEE FIGURE 134-A)*.

Pro's Are: It lets you see the target a little better.

Con's Are: If you can see the target better (deer) then they may see you better when you raise up then take off.

Kick Out Balanced Kneeling Stance *(SEE FIGURE 134-B)*.

Pro's Are: Extending one leg way out to one side on uneven terrain can add balance and stability to your shot.

Con's Are: If not done right, or you have very shaky or bad balance, you could fall over on uneven terrain and miss the shot.

Beginning Target Practice

When you begin target practice, the exact placement of your feet on your shooting line should be marked. Some shooters will tell you that a stance deviation of even a few inches can cause sighting and aiming problems, which in turn could lead to accuracy problems. Based on only the scientific criteria, the

FIGURE 134

open and oblique stances are better. However, don't base your decision on just that. Individual choice is the pleasure of shooting. Feel comfortable in your stance. Many shooters prefer the even stance. In this stance, the shooter's body weight is evenly distributed between both feet, and the heels and toes are aligned. The middle of the instep of your foot is aligned with the center of the target. After all that, the open stance is recommended by the experts for the beginning shooter during their initial learning period. In this stance, your feet should be shoulder width apart. They also recommend that you distribute your body weight between both feet. The left foot should be moved back about 6 inches. In the closed stance the shooting line is straddled, and your weight is evenly distributed between both feet. Your left foot is moved forward a few inches so that a heel to instep alignment exists between the left and right foot respectively. Again try them all and see which one you are more comfortable in. Being comfortable will be an advantage.

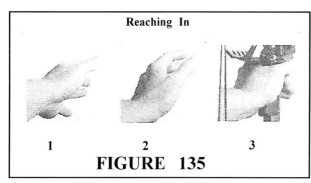

Reaching In

1   2   3

FIGURE 135

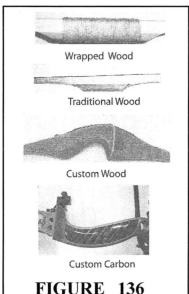

Wrapped Wood

Traditional Wood

Custom Wood

Custom Carbon

FIGURE 136

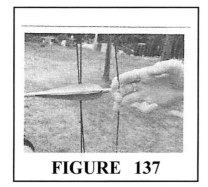

FIGURE 137

Holding to Draw and Aim

Once you have your position the next step is holding the bow handle in the right place. Grab the bow down low with your right hand (right handers), then reach out with your left hand, and grab the bow grip where your left hand is placed around the grip between the thumb and index finger *(SEE FIGURE 135)*. The index finger may wrap around the bow, but it should not grip it too tight. Exactly how you hold it may depend on it's shape. There are many kinds of grip shapes *(SEE FIGURE 136)*. Try them all, see which one feels more comfortable to you. Keep all your fingers relaxed as you grip the handle.

Nocking Your Arrow

Once you have your grip on the bow, the next step is nocking your arrow. Place the arrow on the shelf, then nock the back end to the string with your right hand. This is the proper placement of the arrow in it's shooting position. We will go more into nocking further on in the section under "loading and unloading" your bow.

Placing Fingers on String to Draw

Once you have made your grip and the arrow nocked, the next step is placing your fingers on the bowstring with the nocking end of the arrow between the index finger and the second finger *(SEE FIGURE 137)*. The traditional grip is three fingers with the index finger above the arrow, and second and third fingers below. Next you draw the bowstring back to your cheek or chin, aim, and then shoot.

Sighting

The first thing to do is align the sight level and level the bow. To sight align the bow, move your bow gripping arm and you body until the sight pin is in the center of the target *(SEE FIGURE 138)*. As the sight pin is moved into the center of the target, check the string alignment. String alignment is the alignment of the bowstring with the vertical alignment of the bow, and the alignment of the sight pin. Note: As the bowstring is just in front of the eye, it will appear blurred. When the bow is held in the correct vertical position, then the bowstring and the edge of the bow will be parallel. If not, then the bow is tilted away from vertical. Just before you give your full concentration to shooting, all the previous steps should be checked to make sure that everything is in the correct position. If any part of your body feels out of place, then it is best to stop, let the bowstring down and re-start again, rather than make a bad shot.

Aiming

When you are aiming into the center of the target, it's natural for the sight pin to move around a little, as the muscles try to hold it steady. With practice, aiming will become more steady. Move the sight pin up if the arrow lands high, move it down if the arrow lands low, move left if the arrow lands left, and move it right if the arrow lands right. Leveling means the tilt up and down with respect to the ground. When the bow is drawn, the sight level and bow level must be aligned properly to achieve the maximum accuracy. Poor alignment can occur due to fatigue or possibly a bad habit from practice. To minimize this problem, beginners should rehearse the correct bow alignment, and choose the bow weight that best suits them.

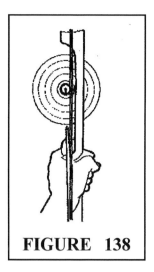

FIGURE 138

Release

The release of the bowstring is the most critical step in the whole shooting sequence. This is because if it's not done correctly, then all the efforts in the previous steps are cancelled out. To release the arrow correctly, the fingers holding the bowstring must allow the string to slip off the fingers. All three fingers must release at the same time. This lets the bowstring pull away from the fingers with the least amount of deflection. When the release is done correctly, the hand should move backwards, as the back muscles will pull the arm backwards and the fingers should come to rest beside the neck. If the finger muscles are flexed open to release the bowstring, then the hand will usually come to rest about 4 inches backwards from the anchor position *(SEE FIGURE 139)*. Flexing the finger muscles will deflect the bowstring sideways and the arrows will have a horizontal spread across the target.

FIGURE 139

Follow Through

The follow through is maintaining the position of the bow arm on release until the arrow hits the target. As the arrow slides along the arrow rest any movement of the bow will move the arrow. The position of the head and body should remain steady, while the drawing hand moves backward after the release of the arrow. It is important to not let the bow arm fall after the release, because this can become a problem when the bow arm actually starts to fall on the release, making some arrows land low on the target. Also by moving the head too soon after the release, to see where the arrow went, can make the bow arm move sideways. Make sure you relax after each shot to let the muscles recover from their effort.

Shooting Your Compound Bow

Shooting Compound Bows In the Field

Shooting a compound bow in the field is very similar to a regular or long bow. But there are differences. Make sure that your shooting is never a threat to other hunters. First thing, always check the area for other hunters, and observe what is behind the target. Here is the first big difference. A compound bow has more power and the arrows go farther. The compound bow weighs on an average about the same as your average traditional bow. It weighs less than your average wood long bow. It also weighs less than some combination laminated wood and fiberglass recurve bows. So even with all the mechanical adjustment features, it still is light weight to carry around.

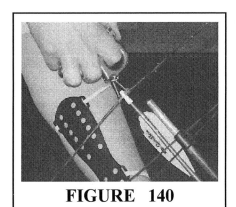

FIGURE 140

Position and Stance

The position and stance is basically the same as for traditional and long bows *(SEE PAGES 162-163)*. However, some coaches are only recommending an "Even" or an "Open" stance.

Nocking the Arrow.

When it comes to nocking the arrow, the compound bow has some advantages. Some come with a special hand grip release and a loop on the bowstring *(SEE FIGURE 140)*. This takes some of the finger problems away at the release because your fingers are not touching the arrow.

The Draw Back

When it comes to drawing back the bowstring, the compound bow has a big technical advantage. It has a feature called "Let-Off" which means the holding the bowstring back weight pull decreases when the bow is at a full draw. This lets you release the string almost like the squeeze of a trigger. And this also gives you a more consistent release every time than with your fingers. So if you are not very strong, this will help you hold the bowstring back while you go through the aiming process, which for some can be a problem.

Other Technical and Circumstantial Advantages Using a Compound Bow

The compound bow is resilient to temperature and humidity changes giving it superior accuracy, velocity, and distance in comparison to bows that are made of natural materials. The pulley system gives you a solid "wall" to draw against. This helps you achieve a consistent anchor point and a consistent amount of force imparted to the arrow on every shot, which further increases you accuracy. You can get them in a variety of cams which control the acceleration of the arrow. They go all the way from soft (gentle acceleration) to hard (to gain speed). Some pulley systems use a single cam at the bottom, and a balance wheel at the top, instead of two cams. This design eliminates the need for buss cables and instead uses a single string that begins at the cam on the bottom, then travels over the wheel on the top, around the bottom cam again, and ends up attaching at the top limb. They have stabilizers and dampers which let you shoot even more accurately, by reducing the movement of the bow when the string is released.

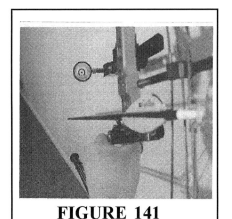

FIGURE 141

Circumstantial Disadvantages

They do have one disadvantage. The low holding weight of the compound bow compared to a recurve bow makes the compound bow more sensitive to certain form faults when you are at a full draw. This is because it's easier for the shooter to torque the bow around the vertical axis, leading to left or right errors.

Sighting

You can get these bows with a magnifying sight *(SEE FIGURE 141)* which can really help your aiming ability.

Traditional Bow (Maintenance)

Explanation

Now, lets say you just got your bow and shot it. The next step is taking care of it. In other words, maintenance. This is all part of "*hunter safety*". If your bow fails because of a malfunction due to the lack of maintenance, you or someone near you could accidentally get hurt.

General Cleaning and Waxing

First, be absolutely sure your bow has no arrows nocked when you start your maintenance. When the season is over, or after being used, it is recommended that you clean it, and put it away in storage if you won't be using it for a while. Before you start to clean, check your "Owners Manual" that came with the bow, for the manufacturers maintenance instructions. If you bought a used bow, and don't have a manual, check on the "Internet" for one that covers your particular bow. You can usually print them out for free if your bow is new, and even on some of the older bow types. Or contact the manufacturer for a manual. If you need to pay for it, they are not very expensive, it's worth it.

Bows

Here are some "*TIPS*" to help you preserve your bow: Never lay it on the ground. It can get dust and dirt on it and possibly moisture on the grass. If your bow is extra dirty use a cleaner especially designed for wood, such as Millennium cleaner. DO NOT use any old wax or an oil base cleaner. If your bow gets wet dry it off as fast as possible even if the finish is waterproof. This is because if it has any metal in it, then it will rust. Preserve the finish by using bow wax, and rub it in.

Bow String

Use bow string wax to keep it waterproof. It also helps it from becoming tangled.

Arrows

Always keep the feathers dry. If they get wet, then spread the arrows out until they all dry completely. This lets them expand back to their original shape. If the shaft has been badly damaged, and can not be fixed, the point may be removed and used again.

Nock

Check the nock for damage. It's plastic, so if it's damaged replace it.

Points (Tip)

Hitting hard objects can blunt the arrow point. You can sharpen it by filing. If it's severely damaged, then the tip should be replaced.

Arrow Rest

If it's worn down or broken, it needs to be replaced.

Sight

Check it periodically to make sure it's not damaged, and it's mounted on straight and aligned correctly.

NOTE: We will show some general diagrams for the different types of bows. This is so that you can familiarize yourself with the general part names of the different parts of the traditional bow and the compound bow, and see where they are located. Of course if you have a manual, it will show you where the parts are on your particular bow even better than our generalized pictures.

Typical Traditional Standard, Recurve, Long, Take Down Bow Common Parts Locations

Typical Compound Bow Common Parts Locations

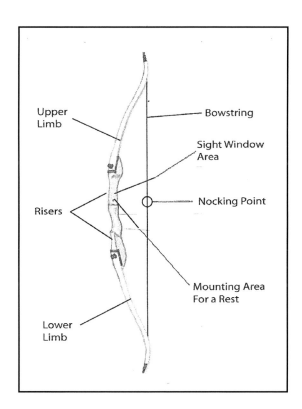

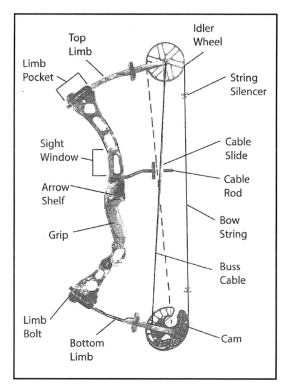

Compound Bow Maintenance

This is going to be a little different. Clean and take care of the bow parts the same way you would a traditional bow (free of dirt and dust). DO NOT leave your compound bow out anywhere where it will be exposed to temperatures of 150 degrees or more. Never put it away wet or store it in a damp place. Lightly oil all steel parts (axels, mounting screws) to prevent rust. You can relax the limbs if you are going to store your bow for more than a year. Wipe the cable guard periodically with a dry cloth to keep the cable slide running smoothly and free of dust. Usually the cam and idler wheel bearings do not require lubrication. Check your bows manual to make sure though. If any part does need lubricating, use white lithium grease or teflon lubricants. Avoid excessive lubrication of any item, as it can attract dirt. And on bows used for hunting, avoid lubricants with obvious odors because game like deer can SMELL it. Apply the bowstring wax to the string and synthetic cable system. Smear the wax into position, then rub it gently with your fingers or a soft piece of leather to work the wax into the strands. Some companies recommend replacing the bowstring and cable annually.

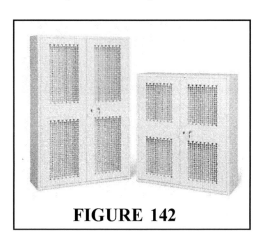

FIGURE 142

Bow and Arrow Storage

Storage for bow and arrows is best under lock and key in a cabinet *(SEE FIGURE 142)* if you have kids in the house. The closed door cabinet may be better because the bow is out of the sight of young inquisitive and prying eyes. Kids will want to take it out and shoot it when you are out of sight or not home. If you don't have kids there are alternatives. They can be stored on a bow rack *(SEE FIGURE 143-A)*, or in a case *(SEE FIGURE 143-B)*. Arrows can be stored in a quiver *(SEE FIGURE 143-C)*.

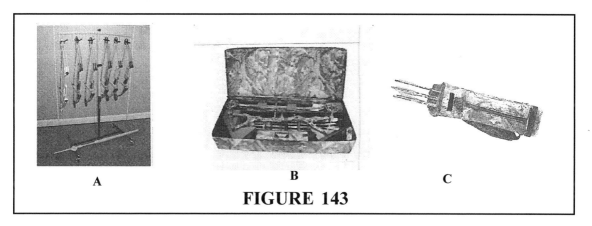

A   B   C

FIGURE 143

Transporting Your Bow and Arrows

The best place to transport your bow and arrows while in your car is in the trunk, where it can be locked. In a pick-up the best place is a lockable storage compartment built into the bed of the truck *(SEE PICTURE 5 and PAGE 27)*. You can't "carry on" bows and arrows in airplanes. They need to be packed and shipped as checked luggage. Check with the Airline for their particular rules.

Arrows

This is an introduction into arrows. Arrows are the ammunition for bows. They come in different types and materials. We will only explore the basics for beginners, not every possible technical explanation for their parts or materials.

Arrow Basics

There are four basic types of material for arrows: wood, aluminum, fiber glass, and metal composites *SEE CHART ON Pg. 170*. We are going to point out their use in hunting. Arrows break down into many parts. Basically they are: the point, the insert, the shaft, the fletching, the bushing and the nock *(SEE FIGURE 144 ON Pg. 170)*. Most modern arrows are in the 2-1/2 to 3 feet long range. The main thing to remember on arrows is make sure the shaft is as straight as possible. The arrowhead or point is the key. Broadheads are for hunting. Their function is to deliver a wide cutting edge so it will kill game as quickly as possible by cutting major blood vessels, and killing the game rather than only wounding. Some arrows have an insert on the end that lets you change tips when necessary. Fletchings are traditionally made from feathers, but most modern arrows are plastic, and are called vanes. They are bound or attached towards the end of the arrow shaft. With standard 3 fletching arrows, (most common) one feather is called the "cock feather." It is placed at a right angle to the knock. Then it is nocked (placed) so that it faces outside and will not hit the bow when the arrow is shot. Four fletching arrows, that are sometimes used, are symmetrical to the nock, and their is no preferred orientation when the arrow is nocked.

TYPES OF MODERN ARROWS			
Type	Pros	Cons	Generally Used For
Wood	Cheap	Each one has flaws, no matter how perfectly it was created. Has to be custom made for serious archers, to match their draw length and weight.	Longbows/Men Beginners
Aluminum	Can be manufactured privately. Wide range of sizes in the market. Durable, with inter-changeable arrowheads.	Expensive	Tournaments and Hunting
Fiber Glass	Can be fitted to draw length and weight. Easy to have more consistancy among arrows.	Brittle and break easily	Hunting, and Informal
Carbon, Aluminum Carbon. Composites	Fast. Can maintain shape pretty easily.	Very Expensive. Carbon layer breaks down on hits.	Serious Tournaments and Hunting

Parts (Anatomy) of an Arrow

The parts of a modern arrow are shown **(SEE FIGURE 144)**:

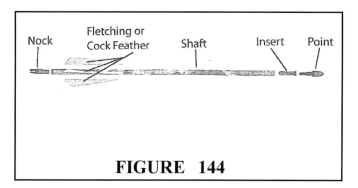

FIGURE 144

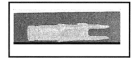

Nock

The "*Nock*" is the part of the arrow that the bowstring hooks into to propel the arrow and keep it launching straight. They are made of precision molded plastic, and pressfitted into a bushing or pin on the back end of the shaft.

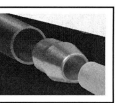

Bushing

The "*Bushing or Pin*" is a precision metal alloy part that fits into the back end of the shaft, and mates the nock to the shaft.

Fletching

The "*Fletching or Vanes*" are located around the shaft and provide stability for the shaft as it travels through the air on the way to it's target. The modern arrow fletching is made out of plastic. Some old wood arrows may actually have feathers for fletching. Generally there is 3 vanes equally spaced around the shaft, and in some cases there may be 4 vanes equally spaced around the shaft and nock.

Shaft

The "*Shaft*" is the main body of the arrow. The shaft can be made from a number of different materials (see arrow materials). They are manufactured to be very straight, and you can get them in different weights of grains per inch.

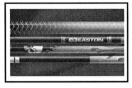

Insert

The "*Insert*" is a precision metal part that goes on the front end of the shaft, and is used to screw the point into the shaft to make them interchangeable. They come in different types depending on what the end of the point requires to mate to the shaft.

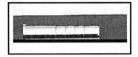

Points (Tips)

The "*Point*" is on the end of the arrow. It screws into the insert, which allows the points to be interchanged. Broadhead points are used just for hunting. Various types of field points are mainly used for target practice.

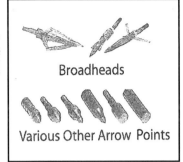

Broadheads

Various Other Arrow Points

Arrow Materials

There are basically four types or categories of arrow material:
- Wood
- Fiber Glass
- Aluminum
- Alloy Metal Composites

Wood Arrows

Wood arrows are the cheapest arrows, especially for beginners because they lose so many. The best wood arrows are made out of cedar. If you are going to use wood arrows, pick out the ones with the straightest shaft, and that are matched to each other and your bow. Each wood arrow will have flaws, no matter how perfectly it was created. Another problem is that for serious archers, wood arrows have to be custom made to match your particular draw length and weight.

Fiber Glass Arrows

Fiber glass arrows are more durable than wood arrows. They have another good quality; they can be fitted to each archer in various lengths and strengths. In addition, fiber glass arrows of any size are manufactured more consistently than wood arrows. This tends to keep the cost down, but they break more easily than wood arrows. However, generally they are still more durable.

Aluminum Arrows

Aluminum arrows are manufactured more consistently than both the wood and fiber glass types. This means you can purchase more arrows that match up with your originals. They come in a wide variety of sizes and in different types of aluminum alloys. All of this makes them more accessible to most anyone. These arrows can be straightened easily and the points replaced. This means you can keep a set of these arrows for a long time. Unfortunately, they are more expensive, but on the other hand, you may not have to keep buying them over and over like some of the other kinds. This is why many advanced experienced archers and hunters choose them.

Alloy Metal Composite Arrows

ALUMINUM CARBON; these arrows are made from an aluminum core with a carbon coat. They are smaller and lighter than pure aluminum arrows, making them fly faster. The major drawback of these arrows is their cost. If you are going to pack your arrows in one spot on a target while practicing, then these may not be the ones to buy. If they are struck by another arrow, then the wrapping or the coating may break down. However, they are still mostly used for target practice.

CARBON FIBER COMPOSITE; the newer arrows are made from high strength composite carbon fibers and wrapped in layers (not pultruded). They have exceptional durability and hoop strength. They have a unidirectional carbon fiber core. They have a thicker wall of unidirectional high strength carbon fibers for superior durability and deeper penetration. A micro smooth finish on the outside layer reduces wear on the arrow rest, gives you a quiet draw release, and makes target removal easier. The major drawback of these arrows is their cost. These newer arrows are used more now for hunting, because of less splintering. Usually when they break, they break cleanly.

Fletching (Vanes)

Fletching may be plastic or they may be feathers. They come in different colors, lengths, heights, and weights in grains. They are glued to the shaft with a special adhesive just developed for vanes and arrows.

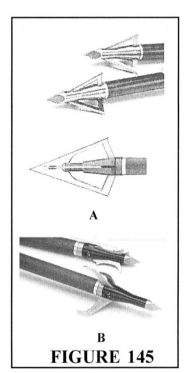

A

B

FIGURE 145

Types of Arrow Points (Tips)

They come in different types of points *(SEE FIGURE 145)*. Some are more for target practice, and others are for hunting. The "*Broadheads*" have razor-sharp edges, and are made from alloy Carbon. They are all interchangeable, and screw into the insert on the end of the arrow shaft. Many hunters use a "broadhead" type points on their arrows for hunting game like deer or turkey. *(SEE FIGURE 145-A)*. There is a newer kind now being used called a cut broadhead. These have cutting blades that stay folded in place while cutting through the air until contact with the target is made, then they deploy or expand out cutting a big hole in the game as they go through *(SEE FIGURE 145-B)*. Regular field tips will work fine when you are just practicing on targets *(SEE PICTURE on Page 171)*.

Arrow Standards

In order to standardize in arrows the "Archery Manufacturers Organization" (AMO) has come up with standards so that when you see their logo on an arrow, you know it has been made to their standards. Basically for all practical purposes arrow length and draw length may be considered the same. You can go on line and print out a copy of their standards, or write to them and request a copy. The arrow weight is important. The AMO has proposed a standard minium arrow weight of roughly six grains for each pound of your bow's maximum draw weight. As an example: a 20 pound bow = 120 grain arrow. The standard also covers the inserts on the end of the shaft so that the threads on your points will fit. Arrows that weigh between 6 and 8 grains per pound offer a good compromise between quiet shooting, long term durability and flat trajectory.

Choosing Your Arrows

Ways to Choose

We are going to give you several ways to choose your arrows. One is a computer program from Easton, the other is for using data to make your choice of length, diameter and weight:

Choosing the recommended aluminum arrows for a given bow is a complex process because the shafts are made in many sizes, diameters, and with different alloys. Easton Archery provides a free downloadable program for choosing arrows for your bow at:

Program Picture

> http://www.eastonarchery.com

Basically you enter the data that is relative to your bow and the program shows in shades of grey and black the proper arrow shaft to use relative to their weight *(SEE PROGRAM SAMPLE PICTURE)*. It covers aluminum, carbon and fiberglass type arrows. Then if you find a bargain on arrows that are NOT quite right it is better to err on the side of too stiff an arrow rather than one that is too flexible. WARNING: carbon arrows can become damaged, yet at first glance appear OK. However, under the stress of shooting they may splinter causing injury to the shooter. Carbon arrows should be examined each time before shooting them.

Information Marking Printed on the Arrow

Most arrows are marked with the bow weight for which they are recommended. If they are not, check the box or ask a knowledgeable bow sales person to advise you on this information. As an example, if you are shooting a bow with a 30 pound draw weight, you will need an arrow spined to shoot well with this weight.

Arrow Length Data Sizing

Here is how to get the hunting length of your arrows. However, I would like to mention something. If you are a young 10 or 12 year old beginning hunter, you may want to think about not getting too many arrows using this sizing because in say 3 years you may move to a bigger draw weight bow. Then you will need longer arrows. Referring to the picture chart to get your arrow length for bows without a cut out window, take a longer arrow and draw it back to your full draw. Then have someone mark the arrow 1 to 2 inches out from where the arrow contacts the most forward portion of the arrow rest. For bows with a cut out window refer to the chart picture, then have someone mark the arrow 1 to 2 inches in front of where the arrow contacts the most forward edge of the arrow rest or bow handle.

For Bows without a Cut Out Window

For Bows with a Cut Out Window

Arrow Sizing Charts

Diagram Courtesy of Easton Archery Co.

EXAMPLE CASE:

Lets say you are 8 years old, and you have just bought one of these youth archery bow sets. It will probably have a draw length of 20 to 22 inches. You are strong so you want to use the full 22 inches for your draw length. Next you look at table

26 on page 151. Lets say you weigh 70 pounds. The table says your recommended draw weight is 15 to 25 pounds. Lets say the bow you just bought has a 17 to 22 pound draw weight range. Now lets say you can comfortably draw the bow back to the 22 inches. Your bow has no cut out windows, so you nock in a 30 inch or longer arrow. Next set the arrow on the rest and have mom or dad measure out 2 inches past the most forward portion of the arrow rest or bow grip and mark the arrow there. Allowing about 2 inches for the bow handle width, your mark should be at about 26 inches. Adding another 1 to 4 inches for the insert and point, you are looking at a 27 to 30 inch, tip to tip, arrow length. And I just looked it up, and that is a pretty standard length fiberglass or wood arrow.

Calculated Peak Bow Weight

Using the Easton Catalog Selection chart data, a single or hard cam, a compound bow, a 75 grain point weight, 26 inch correct hunting arrow length and group "B" medium weight, you get a 35-39 pound "peak bow weight." Your suggested arrow size is "1913." It has a weight of 8.3 grains per inch. Your shaft weight would then be 26 x 8.3 or 216 grains. Looking at "Easton" youth or junior arrows, this means you can get a 17/64 or 9/32 diameter shaft arrow in fiberglass, aluminum or carbon ST composite material in a standard length of 28 inches.

Miscellaneous Arrow Data

Matching Arrows

When you go out hunting, you should try to have all your arrows matched as close as possible in type and weight. There are several good reasons for this. If you mix types then one arrow might hit your target using the same aim, and the next will miss. Then while you stop to figure out which arrow to try next, your target game is going to take off out of range. Point weight is an important factor in choosing the correct arrow stiffness, especially if you release using your fingers. Determine your broadhead hunting weight, then use field points of the same weight when target shooting.

Price vs Straightness

Most arrows are manufactured in grades. This the manufacturers way to charge more money for the higher grade product. In most cases, there is only one difference that separates the categories: straightness. The top grade arrows have straightness tolerances of +/- .001 to +/- .002 of an inch. Lower grade arrows have straightness tolerances of +/- .003 to +/- .006 of an inch. At most typical deer hunting distances there is no difference in accuracy between the various shaft grades. So, unless you are buying additional features such as a better nock system or a camo finish on the shaft, there is no reason to spend extra for arrows that are only a few thousandths of an inch straighter because you won't notice the difference. For adults, one of the best values in arrows are found in "Easton's" Yukon shafts.

Making Your Arrows

Many hunters now favor Aluminum arrows for their crossbow. However, Carbon and Carbon fiber composites with a jacket of Aluminum is starting to gain some favor with bow hunters. Whatever arrow shaft you buy, make sure the front end has threads so that your arrowheads can be interchangeable. The Archery Manufacturers Organization (AMO) has standards for the threads so that your arrowheads will always fit. Many hunters like to buy their own materials, cut it to their particular personal size, then build the rest of the arrow themselves. If you take care of an arrow it can last several years. When using metal arrows, you can get a metal detector to find your arrows and recover them. There are a number of sites on the InterNet that will instruct you exactly how to make arrows.

TABLE 27 BOWS FOR SMALL TO MEDIUM SIZE GAME

BOW ↓ MFR / Matl Type →	Ammunition Arrows [1]							Draw Length, Draw Wt (lbs)	Game Class	Type of Bow, Ht	Relative Bow Cost
	3-Rivers Youth Archery [6] Wood	Port Orford Cedar [6]	[6] Norway Pine	Easton GameGt XX75 Al	Bear Thund FiberG [6]	SportG GoldT-Th Carbon	Easton AxFMJ Alum Carbon				
TRADITIONAL, RECURVE, AND LONG BOWS											
	Suggested Distance to Take the Shot [5]										
Bear Arch Crusader Pkg	10 to 30 Yds.	10 to 30 Yds.	10 to 30 Yds.	20 to 40 Yds.	10 to 30 Yds.	20 to 40 Yds.	20 to 40 Yds.	20-28" 10-20	CPX1	Trdt [2] - [4]	Very Rea
Bear Arch Goblin Pkg	10 to 30 Yds.	10 to 30 Yds.	10 to 30 Yds.	20 to 40 Yds.	10 to 30 Yds.	20 to 40 Yds.	20 to 40 Yds.	22-24" 15-18	CPX1	Trdt [3] [4]	Very Rea
Bear Arch Lil' Brave2	10 to 30 Yds.	10 to 30 Yds.	10 to 30 Yds.	20 to 40 Yds.	10 to 30 Yds.	20 to 40 Yds.	20 to 40 Yds.	16-24" 8-12	CPX1	Recur [2]	Rea
Bear Arch Kodiak Cub	10 to 30 Yds.	10 to 30 Yds.	10 to 30 Yds.	20 to 40 Yds.	10 to 30 Yds.	20 to 40 Yds.	20 to 40 Yds.	24-48" 20-30	CPX1 CPX2	Trdt [4]	Mid
PSE Legacy	10 to 30 Yds.	10 to 30 Yds.	10 to 30 Yds.	20 to 40 Yds.	10 to 30 Yds.	20 to 40 Yds.	20 to 40 Yds.	28" 40-55	CPX1 CPX2	Long 68"	Mid
Martin Venom	10 to 30 Yds.	10 to 30 Yds.	10 to 30 Yds.	20 to 40 Yds.	10 to 30 Yds.	20 to 40 Yds.	20 to 40 Yds.	21-26" 45-55	CPX1 CPX2	Long 66"	Exp
Martin Jaguar	10 to 30 Yds.	10 to 30 Yds.	10 to 30 Yds.	20 to 40 Yds.	10 to 30 Yds.	20 to 40 Yds.	20 to 40 Yds.	25-31" 40-80	CPX1 CPX2	Trdt	Mid
TAKE DOWN BOWS											
	Suggested Distance to Take the Shot [5]										
Martin Jaguar	10 to 30 Yds.	10 to 30 Yds.	10 to 30 Yds.	20 to 40 Yds.	10 to 30 Yds.	20 to 40 Yds.	20 to 40 Yds.	Adj 35-55	CPX1 CPX2	Tdrec	Very Rea
Bear Supreme	10 to 30 Yds.	10 to 30 Yds.	10 to 30 Yds.	20 to 40 Yds.	10 to 30 Yds.	20 to 40 Yds.	20 to 40 Yds.	Adj 45-60	CPX1 CPX2	Tdrec	Exp
SR Swift Blackhawk	10 to 30 Yds.	10 to 30 Yds.	10 to 30 Yds.	20 to 40 Yds.	10 to 30 Yds.	20 to 40 Yds.	20 to 40 Yds.	Adj 45-65	CPX1 CPX2	Tdrec 56"	Exp
Great Plains 20th Aniv	10 to 30 Yds.	10 to 30 Yds.	10 to 30 Yds.	20 to 40 Yds.	10 to 30 Yds.	20 to 40 Yds.	20 to 40 Yds.	Adj Adj-60	CPX1 CPX2	Tdrec 58"	Exp
Polaris Youth	10 to 30 Yds.	10 to 30 Yds.	10 to 30 Yds.	20 to 40 Yds.	10 to 30 Yds.	20 to 40 Yds.	20 to 40 Yds.	24-28 20-36	CPX1 CPX2	Tdrec [2]-[4]	Very Rea
Sky Arch Skyhawk	10 to 30 Yds.	10 to 30 Yds.	10 to 30 Yds.	20 to 40 Yds.	10 to 30 Yds.	20 to 40 Yds.	20 to 40 Yds.	Adj 65-70	CPX1 CPX2	Tdrec 56-60"	Mid
Hoyt Dorado	10 to 30 Yds.	10 to 30 Yds.	10 to 30 Yds.	20 to 40 Yds.	10 to 30 Yds.	20 to 40 Yds.	20 to 40 Yds.	Adj 35-65	CPX1 CPX2	Tdrec 60"	Rea
PSE Razorback	10 to 30 Yds.	10 to 30 Yds.	10 to 30 Yds.	20 to 40 Yds.	10 to 30 Yds.	20 to 40 Yds.	20 to 40 Yds.	Adj 15-30	CPX1 CPX2	Tdrec 62"	Very Rea

Abbreviation Definitions and Notes:
Rea = Reasonable, Mid = Mid Range, Exp = Expensive, Arch = Archery, Trdt = Traditional, Recur = Recurve, [1] = Based on Arrow Specifications, [2] = Fits Kids 7-10, [3] = Fits Kids 10-12, [4] = Fits Kids 16 and Up, Pkg = Youth Bow Package, Ht = Height of Longbow or bow, Thund = Thunderglass shaft, Long = Longbow, Tdrec = Take down recurve, Adj = Adjustable, Aniv = Anniversary, GameGt = Eastons Gamegetter, Al = Aluminum Alloy, Matl = Material made from, FiberG = Fiberglass, GoldT-Th = Gold Tip - Trophy Hunter HP, SportG = Sportsman's Guide, AxFMJ = Axis Full Metal Jacket Arrow, [5] = Higher probility of hitting Humane vital area, [6] = Won't last as long

Bow and Arrow Ammunitions

NOTE: We will try to help you decide on arrows, by charting them out for you in handy tables, to make it a little easier for you to overview and link the game with what arrows to use. This will at least give you a general idea of which arrows might work best for the different types

BOW ↓ MFR / Matl Type →	Ammunition Arrows [1]							Draw Length, Draw Wt (Lbs)	Game Class	Axle to Axle Ht	Relative Bow Cost	IBO Speed/Velocity (FPS)
	3-Rivers Youth Archery [6] Wood	Port Orford Cedar [6]	Norway Pine [6]	Easton GameGt XX75 Al	Bear Thund FiberG [6]	SportG GoldT-Th Carbon	Easton AxFMJ Alum Carbon					
TABLE 28 BOWS FOR SMALL TO MEDIUM SIZE GAME (DEER)												
COMPOUND BOWS												
	Suggested Distance to Take the Shot [5]											
Bear Arch Apprentice Set	10 to 30 Yds.	10 to 30 Yds.	10 to 30 Yds.	20 to 40 Yds.	10 to 30 Yds.	20 to 40 Yds.	20 to 40 Yds.	15-27" 20-50	CPX1 CPX2	27.5" [2][3]	Mid	265
Bear Arch Young Gun Set	10 to 30 Yds.	10 to 30 Yds.	10 to 30 Yds.	20 to 40 Yds.	10 to 30 Yds.	20 to 40 Yds.	20 to 40 Yds.	14-27" 15-50	CPX1 CPX2	29.75" [2][3]	Mid	270
PSE Ranger Set	10 to 30 Yds.	10 to 30 Yds.	10 to 30 Yds.	20 to 40 Yds.	10 to 30 Yds.	20 to 40 Yds.	20 to 40 Yds.	24-25" 14-24	CPX1 CPX2	36" [2][3]	Rea	125
Mathews Genesis Mini	10 to 30 Yds.	10 to 30 Yds.	10 to 30 Yds.	20 to 40 Yds.	10 to 30 Yds.	20 to 40 Yds.	20 to 40 Yds.	14-25" 6-12	CPX1 CPX2	29.13" [2][3]	Mid	N/A
Hoyt Trykon Jr Set	10 to 30 Yds.	10 to 30 Yds.	10 to 30 Yds.	20 to 40 Yds.	10 to 30 Yds.	20 to 40 Yds.	20 to 40 Yds.	10-40" 17-25	CPX1 CPX2	29.5" [2][3]	Mid	255
Alpine Micro Bow	10 to 30 Yds.	10 to 30 Yds.	10 to 30 Yds.	20 to 40 Yds.	10 to 30 Yds.	20 to 40 Yds.	20 to 40 Yds.	21-28" 30-50	CPX1 CPX2	32" [2][3]	Mid	280
Browning Micro Adren	10 to 30 Yds.	10 to 30 Yds.	10 to 30 Yds.	20 to 40 Yds.	10 to 30 Yds.	20 to 40 Yds.	20 to 40 Yds.	28" 40-50	CPX1 CPX2	31" [2][3]	Mid	273
CROSSBOWS												
	Suggested Distance to Take the Shot [5]											
Horton Scout Set	10 to 30 Yds.	10 to 30 Yds.	10 to 30 Yds.	20 to 40 Yds.	10 to 30 Yds.	20 to 40 Yds.	20 to 40 Yds.	10.5 PS 125	CPX1 CPX2	25" Width	Mid [2]-[4]	250
Barnett Phantom Jr Set	10 to 30 Yds.	10 to 30 Yds.	10 to 30 Yds.	20 to 40 Yds.	10 to 30 Yds.	20 to 40 Yds.	20 to 40 Yds.	10.0 PS 60	CPX1 CPX2	26.75" Width	Rea [2][3]	157
Excalibur Pixel Set	10 to 30 Yds.	10 to 30 Yds.	10 to 30 Yds.	20 to 40 Yds.	10 to 30 Yds.	20 to 40 Yds.	20 to 40 Yds.	PS N/A 30-40	CPX1 CPX2	N/A	Exp [2][3]	N/A
PSE Copperhead Set	10 to 30 Yds.	10 to 30 Yds.	10 to 30 Yds.	20 to 40 Yds.	10 to 30 Yds.	20 to 40 Yds.	20 to 40 Yds.	10.5 PS 150	CPX1 CPX2	28.5" Width	Mid [2]-[4]	265
Parker Buckbuster 150	10 to 30 Yds.	10 to 30 Yds.	10 to 30 Yds.	20 to 40 Yds.	10 to 30 Yds.	20 to 40 Yds.	20 to 40 Yds.	12.4 PS 150	CPX1 CPX2	24.5" A to A	Exp [2]-[4]	315
Carbon Express X-Force 300	10 to 30 Yds.	10 to 30 Yds.	10 to 30 Yds.	20 to 40 Yds.	10 to 30 Yds.	20 to 40 Yds.	20 to 40 Yds.	12.0 PS 165	CPX1 CPX2	27" Width	Mid [2]-[4]	300
Ten Point Titan HLX W/ Scope	10 to 30 Yds.	10 to 30 Yds.	10 to 30 Yds.	20 to 40 Yds.	10 to 30 Yds.	20 to 40 Yds.	20 to 40 Yds.	11.1 PS 175	CPX1 CPX2	25.8" A to A	Exp [2]-[4]	300

Abbreviation Definitions and Notes:
Rea = Reasonable, Mid = Mid Range, Exp = Expensive, Arch = Archery, FPS = Feet Per Second, [1] = Based on Arrow and Bolt Specifications, [2] = Fits Kids 7-10, [3] = Fits Kids 10-12, [4] = Fits Kids 16 and Up, Ht = Height, Thund = Thunderglass shaft, Adj = Adjustable, Aniv = Anniversary, Adren = Adrenaline, GameGt = Eastons Gamegetter, Al = Aluminum Alloy, Matl = Material made from, FiberG = Fiberglass, GoldT-Th = Gold Tip Trophy Hunter HP, SportG = Sportsman's Guide, AxFMJ = Axis Full Metal Jacket Arrow, [5] = Higher probility of hitting Humane vital area, [6] = Won't last as long, IBO = International Bowhunting Organization, N/A = Not Available, PS = Power Stroke, A to A = Axel to Axel

of game classifications. Much of the information we are showing comes from the manufacturers stated information, which may or may not be true. We have no way of testing all the data. The data we are giving you is so that you can see some of the different draw lengths and bow heights of the more popular bows being used these days, and what they are being used for. We added the bow cost to kind of give you a ballpark idea of what these bows might cost. We are also giving you a suggested distance to take the shot from, depending on whether you are going for the meat, or trophy antlers.

TABLE 29 BOWS FOR LARGER GAME BIRDS (TURKEY)

BOW ↓ MFR / Matl Type →	Ammunition Arrows [1]							Draw Length, Draw Wt (Lbs)	Game Class	Axle to Axle Ht	Relative Bow Cost	IBO Speed/ Velocity (FPS)
	3-Rivers Youth Archery [6] Wood	Port Orford Cedar [6]	Norway Pine [6]	Easton GameGt XX75 Al	Bear Thund FiberG [6]	Xcalibur Firebolt Carbon	Easton AxFMJ Alum Carbon					
COMPOUND BOWS												
Bear Arch Apprentice Set	10 to 30 Yds.	10 to 30 Yds.	10 to 30 Yds.	20 to 40 Yds.	10 to 30 Yds.	20 to 40 Yds.	20 to 40 Yds.	15-27" 20-50	GB4	27.5" [2][3]	Mid	265
Bear Arch Young Gun Set	10 to 30 Yds.	10 to 30 Yds.	10 to 30 Yds.	20 to 40 Yds.	10 to 30 Yds.	20 to 40 Yds.	20 to 40 Yds.	14-27" 15-50	GB4	29.75" [2][3]	Mid	270
PSE Ranger Set	10 to 30 Yds.	10 to 30 Yds.	10 to 30 Yds.	20 to 40 Yds.	10 to 30 Yds.	20 to 40 Yds.	20 to 40 Yds.	24-25" 14-24	GB4	36" [2][3]	Rea	125
Mathews Genesis Mini	10 to 30 Yds.	10 to 30 Yds.	10 to 30 Yds.	10 to 40 Yds.	10 to 30 Yds.	20 to 40 Yds.	20 to 40 Yds.	14-25" 6-12	GB4	29.13" [2][3]	Mid	N/A
Hoyt Trykon Jr Set	10 to 30 Yds.	10 to 30 Yds.	10 to 30 Yds.	20 to 40 Yds.	10 to 30 Yds.	20 to 40 Yds.	20 to 40 Yds.	10-40" 17-25	GB4	29.5" [2][3]	Mid	255
Alpine Micro Bow	10 to 30 Yds.	10 to 30 Yds.	10 to 30 Yds.	20 to 40 Yds.	10 to 30 Yds.	20 to 40 Yds.	20 to 40 Yds.	21-28" 30-50	GB4	32" [2][3]	Mid	280
Browning Micro Adren	10 to 30 Yds.	10 to 30 Yds.	10 to 30 Yds.	20 to 40 Yds.	10 to 30 Yds.	20 to 40 Yds.	20 to 40 Yds.	28" 40-50	GB4	31" [2][3]	Mid	273
CROSSBOWS												
Horton Scout Set	10 to 30 Yds.	10 to 30 Yds.	10 to 30 Yds.	20 to 40 Yds.	10 to 30 Yds.	20 to 40 Yds.	20 to 40 Yds.	10.5 PS 125	GB4	25" Width	Mid [2]-[4]	250
Barnett Phantom Jr Set	10 to 30 Yds.	10 to 30 Yds.	10 to 30 Yds.	20 to 40 Yds.	10 to 30 Yds.	20 to 40 Yds.	20 to 40 Yds.	10.0 PS 60	GB4	26.75" Width	Rea [2][3]	157
Excalibur Pixel Set	10 to 30 Yds.	10 to 30 Yds.	10 to 30 Yds.	20 to 40 Yds.	10 to 30 Yds.	20 to 40 Yds.	20 to 40 Yds.	PS N/A 30-40	GB4	N/A	Exp [2][3]	N/A
PSE Copperhead Set	10 to 30 Yds.	10 to 30 Yds.	10 to 30 Yds.	20 to 40 Yds.	10 to 30 Yds.	20 to 40 Yds.	20 to 40 Yds.	10.5 PS 150	GB4	28.5" Width	Mid [2]-[4]	265
Parker Buckbuster 150	10 to 30 Yds.	10 to 30 Yds.	10 to 30 Yds.	20 to 40 Yds.	10 to 30 Yds.	20 to 40 Yds.	20 to 40 Yds.	12.4 PS 150	GB4	24.5" A to A	Exp [2]-[4]	315
Carbon Express X-Force 300	10 to 30 Yds.	10 to 30 Yds.	10 to 30 Yds.	20 to 40 Yds.	10 to 30 Yds.	20 to 40 Yds.	20 to 40 Yds.	12.0 PS 165	GB4	27" Width	Mid [2]-[4]	300
Ten Point Titan HLX W/ Scope	10 to 30 Yds.	10 to 30 Yds.	10 to 30 Yds.	20 to 40 Yds.	10 to 30 Yds.	20 to 40 Yds.	20 to 40 Yds.	11.1PS 175	GB4	25.8" A to A	Exp [2]-[4]	300

Suggested Distance to Take the Shot [5]

Abbreviation Definitions and Notes:
Rea = Reasonable, Mid = Mid Range, Exp = Expensive, Arch = Archery, FPS = Feet Per Second, [1] = Based on Arrow and Bolt Specifications, [2] = Fits Kids 7-10, [3] = Fits Kids 10-12, [4] = Fits Kids 16 and Up, Ht = Height, Thund = Thunderglass shaft, Adj = Adjustable, Aniv = Anniversary, Adren = Adrenaline, GameGt = Eastons Gamegetter, Al = Aluminum Alloy, Matl = Material made from, FiberG = Fiberglass, GoldT-Th = Gold Tip Trophy Hunter HP, SportG = Sportsman's Guide, AxFMJ = Axis Full Metal Jacket Arrow, [5] = Higher probility of hitting Humane vital area, [6] = Won't last as long, IBO = International Bowhunting Organization, N/A = Not Available, PS = Power Stroke, A to A = Axel to Axel

Crossbows

Explanation

This is an introduction into crossbows. In Archery the Crossbow is usually not considered, and the purest don't like it. I am including it in this section because hunters do use it, and it is partially in the bow family. It's like a cross between a bow and a firearm with a trigger. This is a special type of bow, although the purists don't classify it as archery. It definitely has a fan base in hunting though.

177

In some states it is not allowed for turkey hunting, but is allowed for deer hunting. Before you run out and buy a crossbow, make sure they are allowed for hunting in your state for the game you intend to use it on. If you are disabled, check the rules and regulations for your state because some states have NO provisions for disabled crossbow hunters.

Types of Crossbows

Crossbow features and safety mechanisms may differ; so refer to the manufacturer's instructions for specific information on your model crossbow. Crossbows come in regular curved limbs models, recurve limb models, and compound Crossbow models.

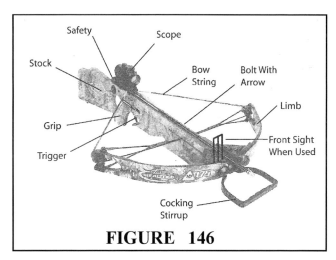

FIGURE 146

Regular Curved Limb Crossbow

The regular curved limb crossbow has been around a long time. The more modern versions just have improved parts and scopes. Also the modern versions have higher shooting speeds getting up to 375 FPS (feet per second). Some of their newer features include cheek pads, safety mechanisms, cocking stirrups, and improved trigger mechanisms *(SEE FIGURE 146)*.

Regular Recurve Limb Crossbow

The recurve limb crossbow has also been around a long time. They are almost the same as a regular curved limb crossbow, except for the recurve shape out at the ends of the limbs. They are more quiet when fired when compared to a regular curved limb crossbow. Something to consider if you are using your crossbow to hunt deer. The more modern versions have improved parts and scopes. Also the modern versions have higher shooting speeds getting up to 345 FPS (feet per second). Some of their newer features include cheek pads, safety mechanisms, cocking stirrups, and improved trigger mechanisms.

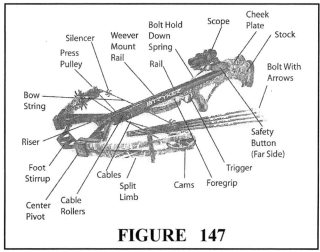

FIGURE 147

Curved Limb Compound Crossbow

We are going to show a parts breakdown for a typical curved limb compound crossbow so that you can see what features they have *(SEE FIGURE 147)*. If you look at the two pictures you can see the differences between them. The compound bow is much more complicated, with it's pulleys, cams and cables.

Crossbow Manufacturers

Go to the reference section in the back of the book under resources to find manufacturers.

Crossbow Bolts (Arrows)

Types of Crossbow Bolts

I know it's kind of hard to understand, but crossbow arrows are called bolts. Crossbow bolts are a little different than traditional bow arrows. They need to be very straight because they set in a rail groove. To be accurate they are matched to the shooters draw weight. There are basically three types of bolts for crossbows:

- Special Wood
- Aluminum
- Carbon Fiber

Special Wood Bolts

Wood is not usually used for crossbow arrows because it is prone to warping, and not easily straightened. However, there is one company called "Hexshaft" that makes an extremely tough wooden laminate arrow. The shaft is made from 6 individually machined triangles, all from the same piece of wood. Then they are laminated together to produce a superior shaft strength, which is higher than that achieved with a standard wood-dowel type bolt shafting.

Aluminum Bolts

There are aluminum arrows that are manufactured especially for crossbows. They are matched to the draw weight of the crossbow to ensure their accuracy. Some of most popular alloys that they are made from is 2018, 2117, 2213, 2216 and 2219. The 2219 is by far the most popular among crossbow hunters.

Carbon Fiber Bolts

Carbon fiber arrows are very strong, light weight, and fly faster and flatter than aluminum arrows. They became very popular in the 1990's. As with any new product though they had their share of problems. However, with advancements in carbon fiber composite technology, they now find themselves pulling away from the rest of the (bolts) in the crossbow field.

Plastic Bolts

Hard to believe, but true. They do make plastic arrows for 50 to 80 pound "pistol type" crossbow use. They have PVC shafts and metal tips. They are mostly only used for target practice though, but they could be used for varmint's and small game.

The Anatomy (Parts) of a Bolt

For the parts of a crossbow bolt **SEE FIGURE 144 ON Pg. 170**. There is one exception though, crossbow bolts don't normally use the insert section. Points screw right into the front of the bolt.

Handling Crossbows

Handling a Crossbow In the Field Position

Handling a crossbow out in the field can be a problem. If you are holding it just with your hand, and you are moving or walking for any length of time, your arm will get tired, even more than with a long bow because it is heavier. Because it's a little more complicated the crossbow can't be just slung over your shoulder and around to your back, unless you use a special sling **(SEE FIGURE 148)**. The "Claw Non-Slip Bow Sling" takes care of that problem by hanging down on your hip ready to swing up, load, and

FIGURE 148

FIGURE 149

fire. Another way to carry your crossbow is the "Crossbow" backpack *(SEE FIGURE 149)*. It is designed so that you can get the crossbow off your back without taking the backpack off. There is another alternative way to handle your crossbow in the field. If you are going to be hunting in a blind, or out on the edge of a woodline, you could use the "Archery Stand-By" *(SEE FIGURE 150)*. This is a stand to set you bow on while you wait. It has a sand filled base and will not tip over indoors or out. It's rugged because it's made of high-density molded plastic making it resistant to all kinds of weather. It also works well at shooting ranges, while you go out to retrieve your arrows.

FIGURE 150

Handling a Crossbow At Home

When handling your crossbow at home you can also use the "Archery Stand-By," except maybe when you have small children around. Not so much that they would be able to use it, but they might accidentally damage it because they are inquisitive and pick it up then accidentally drop it, or knock it over. And it's probably a good idea to keep the arrows in another place than where the crossbow is located. If it's setting across your lap don't have an arrow in it, and if there is an arrow in it, don't point it at anyone near you. When you work on it, use some type of holding device instead of setting it across your lap.

Crossbow Hunter Safety

Following these simple archery safety rules at all times will make crossbow hunting a pleasant experience for you:

1. NEVER fire your crossbow until you are 100% sure of your target, and what is beyond.
2. ALWAYS use an adequate backstop and target when target shooting.
3. ALWAYS unload your crossbow when climbing and descending from an elevated platform, and when traveling to and from hunting areas. A cocked crossbow loaded with a bolt should never be carried to and from an elevated tree stand.
4. When hunting from an elevated stand ALWAYS:
   a. Be sure you are firmly attached to the tree with a full body harness at all times. It could save your life.
   b. Use a haul line to bring gear to and from the ground, keeping the line away from trigger mechanisms while hauling the unloaded crossbow stock first.
   c. Make sure that the limbs of the crossbow are clear of any tree branches when taking a shot. If the crossbow's limbs strike a tree branch upon firing, the shooter could get knocked out of the stand.
5. NEVER point your crossbow at anything other than a lawful target, and ALWAYS keep the safety engaged until you are ready to shoot.
6. When cocking a crossbow, ALWAYS be sure that your foot is firmly planted in the cocking stirrup. If your foot slips out during cocking, the crossbow will fly up into your chest and face and cause a serious injury.
7. ALWAYS make sure your equipment is in good working order by inspecting it before use.
8. ALWAYS read your owner's manual and follow the manufacturer's recommended operating procedures before you use your crossbow.

Loading and Unloading Crossbows

Loading a Crossbow
Loading a crossbow is very similar to a traditional and compound bow, except a little more complicated.

Loading a Bolt into the Crossbow

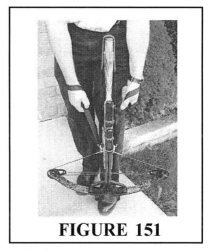

FIGURE 151

To load a crossbow means placing or nocking the bolt in the bowstring. A "Bolt" by the way is just another name for a slightly shorter arrow designed especially for the crossbow. First the crossbow needs to be cocked *(SEE FIGURE 151)*, then the safety moved to "ON." Next place the point of the bolt forward under the sight bracket until it lies flat on the flight groove with the cock feather down. Then, slide the bolt back under the bolt retainer until it contacts the bowstring. The bolt retainer should exert enough downward pressure to the rear of the bolt to hold it in place, but should not lift the front of the bolt off of the groove. The bolt should now be lying directly parallel with the flight groove. The crossbow is now loaded and ready to shoot.
CAUTION: The bolt must be long enough to clear the front of the flight groove.

Unloading a Crossbow
The easiest way to unload a loaded crossbow is to shoot the bolt into a hay bale target or the ground. But make sure the ground is free of rocks. Shooting into the ground should only be done with a field tip or a blunt point, not a broadhead bolt. However, the crossbow can be unloaded manually if desired. First, remove the bolt, then grasp the bowstring firmly with both hands and place your foot in the cocking stirrup. Then release the trigger with your thumb and let the bowstring down slowly using both hands.

Shooting a Crossbow

Shooting Crossbows In the Field
Shooting a crossbow in the field is a little different than a regular or long bow. Actually it's about like shooting the compound bow as far as the effective range goes. First thing, always check the area for other hunters, and observe what is behind the target. A crossbow has an effective range of up to about 50 yards for hunting. However, a bolt can travel out about 1000 feet (333 yards) and still be lethal. So you need to allow for about 400 yards behind your target, just to be sure.

Cocking the Crossbow
The first thing you need to do is cock the crossbow. Place the cocking stirrup in the front of the bow on the ground. Next insert your foot into the stirrup, with the stock end resting against your midsection *(SEE FIGURE 151)*. It's best to use a strap harness or rope to help you pull the bowstring up into the trigger mechanism. Place both hands on the harness and secure the other end to the bowstring. Now pull the string up into the trigger mechanism until it locks and you hear an audible "click." Next slowly release hand pressure on the string until you are sure it is locked securely into the mechanism. The crossbow should now be cocked with the safety on. Keep the crossbow pointing down just in case the string is not locked, and accidentally snaps back.

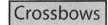

Loading the Crossbow

The next step is loading a bolt into the crossbow. Once it is loaded with a bolt, the crossbow needs to be handled with extreme caution by not pointing it at anyone or anything.

Sighting the Crossbow

To sight the crossbow, you need to first shoot it at a close range. If the rear sight is adjustable, remember that lowering the rear sight will lower the point of impact. Moving the rear sight left or right moves the point of impact in the same direction. Just the opposite applies for adjustable front sights.

Firing or Shooting the Crossbow

After getting your crossbow sighted in, the next step is firing or shooting it. On most crossbows the safety must be released to fire the bolt. The safety release button is usually located near the trigger mechanism. To release the safety, you need to point the crossbow down or in a safe direction, and in most cases push a button forward. The crossbow will then fire when the trigger is pulled. The safety must be disengaged this same way before every shot. Hold the crossbow under the forestock with your non trigger hand. But be sure to keep your fingers away from the top of the flight groove while shooting *(SEE FIGURE 152)*. This prevents your hand or fingers from being struck by the string as it travels forward. Now pull the trigger.

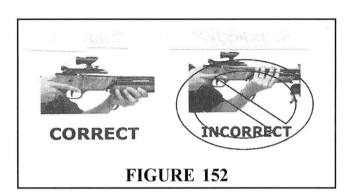

CORRECT   INCORRECT

FIGURE 152

Crossbow Maintenance

Taking care of your crossbow will make it last longer and improve your safety. A poor working crossbow could cause you to be injured. Here are some maintenance "Tips."

- First, ALWAYS check your manual for your crossbow's specific maintenance.
- Check that all screws are tight.
- Check batteries if you have any.
- Keep the bolt (arrow) carriage and all bolts clean.
- ALWAYS check your crossbow for wear and tear before you shoot. This means axles, bushings, cables, cable slides, e-clips, and especially the bow string. If any of these items show excessive wear, contact your authorized dealer for check and repair if needed. This also keeps from voiding your warranty.
- Keep your crossbow in a dry environment, and be sure to keep it lubricated. Proper lubrication of axles, bearings, and chain limits wear and tear. Add enough lubricant to these areas to create a barrier between each working part and to optimize the performance. NOTE: A 10 to 15 weight oil is recommended. DO NOT use WD-40.
- Rail Lubrication is recommended. Occasionally apply a light coating of string wax or silicone lube to the top of the flight rail. This will keep your crossbow operating smoothly and free from rust.
- Grease the eyes of your bow string and apply bow string wax. With proper maintenance your string should last a minimum of 100 shots. However, lasting several hundred shots is not uncommon if you take care of your crossbow.

- If your stock is hardwood, keep it wiped off with a clean cloth and periodically oil it with "Formsby" lemon oil or "Milisek" furniture cleaner and polisher. A word of caution: try a little spot on the bottom of the stock first though to make sure the oil does not remove any camouflaging or finish on the wood.

- A word of caution; if you add extra accessories to your crossbow it could cause it to lose some of it's speed.

Crossbow Transporting and Storage

Taking care of your crossbow while transporting, and proper storage, will make it last longer and improve your safety. See the sections on "transporting and storage" of bow and arrows" on page 169. Crossbows can be stored on wall racks *(SEE FIGURE 153*, in cases *(SEE FIGURE 154)*, or in a locking weapons storage cabinets *(SEE FIGURE 142 On Pg 168)* for safety reasons, especially if you have young kids around the house. Everybody is a lot safer that way.

FIGURE   153

Crossbow Ammunition

Crossbow ammunition is called bolts (arrows). I know it's confusing, but that's the way it is. The main thing to remember is that bolts must be much straighter than regular bow arrows. This is because they slide across a groove in the crossbow. Bolts are sized much like arrows. It's going to depend on the draw length. Lets say you have a 22 inch draw length, then your bolt will need to be a little longer. Just enough so that the tip clears out over the front end. Weight also is important. 400 grains is recommended for Aluminum bolts. However, carbon bolts will give you better performance. Check with your manual and make sure you have the proper diameter and weight for your particular crossbow.

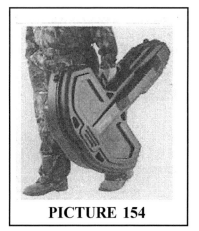

PICTURE 154

NOTE: We will try to help you decide on bolts, by charting them out for you in handy tables 28 and 29 *(SEE Pgs.176-177)*, to make it a little easier for you to over view and link the game with what bolts to use. This will at least give you a general idea of which bolts might work best for the different types of game in the different game classifications that you may be hunting. Much of the information we are showing comes from the manufacturers stated information, which may or may not be true. We have no way of testing the data to find out. The data we are giving you on the crossbows is just so that you can see some of the different draw lengths, weights and heights of some of the more popular crossbows being used these days, and what they are being used for. We added the crossbow cost to kind of give you a ballpark idea of what these crossbows might cost. We are also giving you a sug`gested distance to take the shot from, depending on whether you are going for the meat, or trophy antlers.

SECTION 4 Misc. Hunting Devices

Explanation

This is an introduction into miscellaneous legal hunting devices for hunting game. These are "slingshots" and "atlatls." Slingshots, while only accurate at shorter distances compared to firearms, are good for shooting small game and varmint's (rats, rabbits and squirrels). Atlatls are becoming legal in a few states, with others looking into it. Atlatls are one of the oldest shooting devices on the planet for killing game for food. They are legal in almost all states for non-listed game such as varmint's and animals not covered by any game regulations. It looks like atlatls best use, as they gain acceptance, will be in hunting deer.

Slingshots

Explanation

This is an introduction into slingshots. And believe it or not there are people who hunt with devices like "Slingshots." A slingshot is powerful enough to hunt game such as small rodents and birds at ranges up to 25 meters (about 27 yards). A typical heavy band slingshot should be used with 9 mm (3/8") to 12 mm (1/2") diameter steel balls. Using lighter ammunition does not increase the speed of the projectile very much. But remember slingshots can be very dangerous, and you can certainly kill someone if you are not careful and accidentally hit another hunter out in the field. ALWAYS wear "hunter orange" and "eye protection." Actually hunting with a slingshot can be a great way to improve your skills with traditional hunting as well."

FIGURE 155

Types of Slingshots

There are basically two different types of slingshots, the ones with a wrist support holding *(SEE FIGURE 155)*, which are most hunting slingshots, and traditional slingshots without the arm support *(SEE FIGURE 156)*. There are all kinds of each. Some are just a lot more accurate than others, or made better and last longer. Whichever kind you decide to get, you will need to go out and do a lot of target practice (Plinking) for accuracy. Here is some general advice on choosing a slingshot. Make sure you try different types and see which is the most comfortable when you shoot it. I think if you are not comfortable with your slingshot, you probably won't be accurate with it either. We will show a bunch of different types and let you decide. They are all not that expensive, ranging from $10 to $20. Then you can always build your own. All you need is some wood, or a "Y" tree limb, some rubber strips or surgical tubes, and some leather.

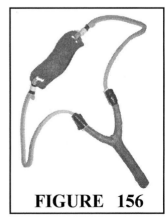

FIGURE 156

Wrist Held Only Slingshots

American Made

We will list the manufacturers of some of the better ones, not in any particular order or popularity:

1. Trumark, S9T, Aluminum frame slingshot. Comes with built in ammo holder in the handle.
2. Trumark, S9FO, Aluminum frame slingshot. Comes with built in ammo holder, and fiber optic sights.
3. Trumark, BAT-007, Nylon frame slingshot. Comes with a night light holder, fiber optic sights with rotating prongs. The adjustable stabilizer counteracts and reduces the recoil when the slingshot is shot. Effective up to a 185 yard range.
4. Crossman, Cyclone, metal frame slingshot. Comes with finger grip, rubber handle.
5. Marksman, Classic II 3027, tempered steel yoke slingshot. Comes with black plastic handle.
6. Marksman, Laserhawk 3030, tempered steel yoke slingshot. Comes with black plastic handle, Talon grip pouch, magnet holds ammo in place.
7. Barnett, Strike 9, metal yoke, contoured handle.

Imported

We will list the manufacturers of some of the better ones, not in any particular order:

1. Feiyun, FY-AB3, steel frame slingshot (Chinese)
2. Oriental Trading, IN-27/967, 7-1/4" wood handle, jute wrapped
3. Dankung, Jungle Hunter ll USA Model, steel yoke, jute wrapped. (Chinese)
2. Siping Bailong, Handicraft, carved wooden handle (Chinese)

Wrist Held Braced Slingshots

American Made

We will list the manufacturers of some of the better ones, not in any particular order or popularity:

1. Trumark, FS-1, Aluminum frame slingshot. Comes with folding wrist brace, ammo storage.
2. Barnett, Black Widow, metal yoke slingshot. Comes with a fold away brace.
3. Marksman, 3055, Laserhawk, steel yoke slingshot. Comes with brace support, Talon grip pouch, and a magnet holds steel ammo in place.
4. Beeman, MS3060K Laserhawk, steel yoke adjustable slingshot. Comes with brace sup port, Talon grip pouch, and a magnet holds ammo in place.
5. Crossman, 10990 Firestorm, metal yoke slingshot. Comes with a folding brace sup-port, and a push button shot feeder.
6. Chief AJ, HFX *(SEE FIGURE 157-A)*, shoots arrows, or can be adapted to use a reel "slingbow" fishing setup. Very good for hunting or fishing.
7. Robert Blair, ComBow *(SEE FIGURE 157-B)*, metal yoke slingshot. Comes with a stabilizer, and shoots full length arrows, short arrows, and bearings.
8. Daisy, Powerline P51, metal yoke slingshot. Comes with a flexible wrist support, and a molded pistol grip handle.

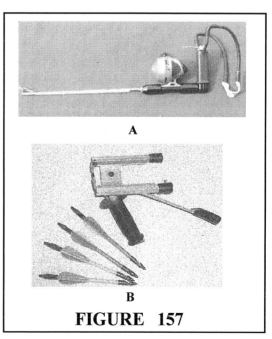

A

B

FIGURE 157

Imported

We will list the manufacturers of some of the better ones, and not in any particular order or popularity:

1. Armex, Black Shadow, steel chrome finished yoke slingshot. Comes with a folding brace. (UK)
2. Dankung, Sniper Model Mo11, stainless steel yoke slingshot. Comes with a folding brace. (Chinese)
3. Australian, Model 271201AUS, black metal yoke slingshot. Comes with wrist brace and molded handle. (Australia)

Help In Choosing Your Slingshot

Helpful Information

When talking about how to choose a slingshot, you need to decide first whether it's going to be used for just hunting small game and varmint's, or for just going out "plinking," or both. I suspect most slingshot buyers are planning to do both. Here are some factors to consider:

- ■ *SIZE*, what is it's height.
- ■ *FIT*, how does it fit into your hand.
- ■ *COMFORT*, is it comfortable in your hand.
- ■ *DURABILITY*, how and what is it made from, will it last.
- ■ *POWER,* is it powerful enough for your intended uses.

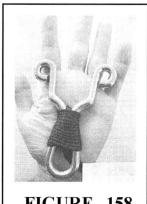

FIGURE 158

Size

Many companies have tested slingshots for hunters, and they seem to have an average height of around 5.0 Inches. You can get them in different total heights from about 4-7/8" (124mm) high to 5-3/4" (146mm) high.

Fit

I have an average size hand, and 5 Inches fits pretty good *(SEE FIGURE 158)*. If you have a bigger hand, you can find heights up to around 6 Inches, or get them custom made for you.

Comfort

How does it feel in your hand? It should feel comfortable in your hand. You may need to try out several slingshots to see how they actually feel when you grasp them.

Durability

Slingshots come in many different yoke materials, from wood to metal, to plastic. I suspect that Stainless Steel may last the longest. It would take some serious handling to ruin a Stainless Steel yoke slingshot. However, you can get them in Aluminum, plated Steel and a material like Pot Metal.

Power

Each company talks about how powerful their brand is. Some studies have shown that a 1/4 " diameter steel ball can get up to speeds of 309 feet per second in certain types of slingshots, just to give you an idea. Tapered bands will also speed up the shot. You may need to shoot at some targets and see what kind of penetration you can get using different types of ammunition. However, don't choose a slingshot with too much power for what you are hunting (overkill). It's not going to take too much to kill some sparrows that are being a nuisance. Just about any slingshot with a BB will do the job if you can hit them. Same with Doves and Quail.

Handling Your Slingshot

Handling a Slingshot In the Field Position
Handling a slingshot out in the field is not a big problem. However, if you are holding it in your hand, and you are moving for any length of time, your arm will get tired. I see several ways you could carry your slingshot. The old time way of carrying it in your back pocket might work, especially if it's the fold up type. Another way is to carry it in a backpack if you will be traveling a long way to where you will be hunting. If you are out fishing the fold up type fits in a fishing tackle box.

Handling a Slingshot At Home
When handling your slingshot at home make sure it is not loaded with the ball bearing or any other ammunition. It's too big of a temptation, and too dangerous, to raise it up, draw it back and pretend to shoot. And if there are any little kids around don't let them handle it either for the same reason. Keep it locked up in one place, and the ammunition locked up in another place. And if you do bring it out for some reason to look at it, don't bring out the ammunition with it.

Slingshot Safety Rules
Purchased slingshots are designed to be a safe and fun product. However, as with any shooting style weapon, certain safety rules must be observed because they are NOT toys. The slingshot is a legal hunting weapon to use for wildlife, except deer and turkey (Missouri). Following these simple sling-shot safety rules at all times will make hunting a more pleasant experience for you:
1. NEVER aim or draw the slingshot in the direction of a person. Aim and draw ONLY in the direction of an appropriate target or the game you are hunting.
2. ALWAYS have a full view of the path to your target and beyond when shooting.
3. ALWAYS wear safety glasses when shooting a slingshot.
4. ALWAYS treat your slingshot as if it were loaded.
5. ALWAYS keep your slingshot on safety by not drawing it back until you intend to shoot.

Loading and Unloading a Slingshot

Loading a Slingshot
Loading a slingshot is really pretty simple. First you grip the slingshot handle in the middle with your non-shooting hand. If it has a wrist hold (recom-mended), then hold the handle of the slingshot by in-serting your hand up and through the wrist hold, which should come to rest on the top of your forearm. Next, choose your ammunition and place it in the center of the leather pouch using your shooting hand. More on ammunition in the "Ammunition" section. Now fold the pouch over the ammunition and clutch the outside of the pouch firmly using your thumb, and middle in-dex finger. Then keep a firm, but steady, grip on the projectile. Now your slingshot is loaded *(SEE FIGURE 159)*.

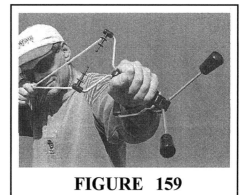

FIGURE 159

Unloading a Slingshot

Unloading your slingshot is even more simple. You just reach in and take the ammunition out, or just un-grip the pouch, turn the pouch upside down and dump out the ammunition.

Shooting Your Slingshot

Shooting the Slingshot In the Field

There are several stable ways to shoot a slingshot out in the field so that it is never a threat to other hunters. First thing, before firing check the area for other hunters, and observe what's behind the target. There are several ways to stand, and several ways to hold the slingshot. I suggest you use goggles to protect your eyes because at times, the ammunition ricochets after hitting the target. It might be a good idea to use a glove or a forearm guard to protect your slingshot holding arm in case the leather pouch hits it when you shoot.

What's Behind Your Target

Find out ahead of time what's behind your intended target(s). I have heard of slingshots shooting out in the 225 yard range. So it's probably a good idea to allow 300 yards clear behind your target. Since most of your slingshot shooting is going to only be up to 25 yards, you just need to be sure that the area behind your target is clear.

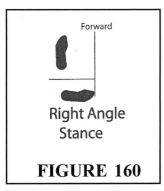

Forward

Right Angle Stance

FIGURE 160

Standing Positions

There are several stable ways to shoot a slingshot out in the field so that it is never a threat to other hunters. First thing, before firing check the area for other hunters, observe what's behind the target and who is standing nearby watching. The basic standing position is at a right angle to the target with the front foot pointing at the target *(SEE FIGURE 160)*. The arm holding the slingshot handle is extended straight out in front towards the target. Most shooters like the handle straight up and down vertically. Others like to turn the slingshot over on it's side 45 -90 degrees because their eyes sight the target better *(SEE FIGURE 161)*. Still others say straight up and down has more overall accuracy. I think it's really doing a lot of practice with your slingshot and getting a better feeling of what it can do.

FIGURE 161

Gripping the Handle

Grip the handle of the slingshot in the middle using your non-dominate hand. If your slingshot has a wrist support hold, then hold the handle by inserting your hand up and through the wrist hold *(SEE FIGURE 161)* which will come to rest on the top of your forearm. Try to keep a constant wrist position on each shot for more accurate shooting. Twist your wrist slightly so that the center of the slingshot lines up with your arm. However, DO NOT bend your wrist because this puts extra strain on the lower power band(s), then when the pellet or ball is released you will have a tendency to twist the slingshot which will cause a miss on the target. Once your arm is extended out and you wrist is set you want to shoot with a relaxed grip because a tight grip can cause the "U" frame to work off the handle.

Placing the Ammunition (Loading)

Place the ammunition, then fold the pouch over it and then grasp the outside of the pouch firmly with the fingers of your dominant hand. Then keep a firm, but steady, grip on the ammunition while sighting in the target. This is gone over in detail in the "loading and unloading" section.

Drawing Back

Your non-dominant arm is extended out towards the target now. Try to keep it straight. While holding the handle, pull the pouch back smoothly taking a deep breath. Practice this to try and develop a smooth rhythm to the movement.

Anchoring

Try to ALWAYS keep the pouch in the same position in relation to the aiming eye. Anchor the draw back hand with the joint of your thumb and fingers sunk into the hollow of your cheek.

Aiming

Using the anchor method, the top prong of the fork should be brought approximately on the target. Now, vary the position with each shot until you are hitting the target consistently. If you have one of the newer technical slingshots with fiber optic sighting, you will need to go to your owners manual for directions on how to use it.

Release

Gently let the pouch slip between your finger and thumb without jerking or moving.

Follow Through

Hold your position momentarily without swinging your sling hand. Try to see the path the projectile has taken. This will help you make adjustments for the next shot, especially if you miss the target.

Slingshot Maintenance

Taking Care of Your Slingshot

Taking care of your slingshot is part of "hunter safety." Many slingshots are made out of high quality aircraft aluminum, which does not rust. You can polish the frame with an aluminum cleaner to make it look like new. "Flitz" brand polish does wonders and you can find it at hardware stores. Also the slingshot's surgical, latex powerbands, leather pouch, and sponge rubber wrist-brace recoil-padding can be made to last longer by applying some high quality "303 Aerospace Protectant." It's the same stuff used on car dashboards to give them maximum protection from the elements. Just one application will give you many months of protection.

CAUTION: **Don't use any protectants too near the slingshot's powerband ends where they are attached to the fork prongs. This might cause the bands to eventually slip off the prongs when you pull back on the bands to shoot. This can happen if the cloth is too wet when you rub the protectant on the bands as you get close to the bands ends. This is because some of the liquid might creep under the rubber where they are attached to the prongs if you are not careful.**

NOTE:

Latex rubber is a "live" organic material so it will naturally deteriorate and lose it's flexibility over time. It's a good idea to give the latex bands some extra protection, especially when you first buy the slingshot, or put it into storage for long periods of time. Restoring/protecting rubber is a good idea because natural latex is very unstable chemically and highly sensitive to environmental factors such as oxygen, pollutants, and especially ultraviolet rays in visible light like fluorescents and daylight.

Powerband Replacement

If your powerbands break too soon after you have purchased the slingshot, you might have nicked, hit, or scratched the end of the fork prong and rubber tubing with a jagged rock (If you do use stones it's a good idea to take a little time to pick up some good round ones that are not too large). **Very Important:** Repairing the aluminum prong ends is easy, and only takes a few minutes. First, remove the bands by rolling them off the prongs with the thumb or heel of your hand. Then carefully examine the round ends of the slingshot prongs for any nicks or scratches. Usually you can see the nick with your eyes, but you can also feel with your fingers for any roughness. Any knicks can be fixed by using fine steel wool or #320 grit sandpaper to "polish" the nicks away to a smooth finish. Since aluminum is a rather soft metal, this is not hard to do. If your prong tips are "perfectly" smooth your slingshot will be like new, and the powerbands will last a lot longer. Even new bands will break very quickly if they are installed on prongs that have been damaged. Use a similar smoothing technique for steel yokes if necessary.

Installing the Powerbands

1. Dip the band ends into approximately 1/8 inch of ordinary rubbing alcohol that does not contain any glycerin or lotion. **DO NOT use soap** anywhere on the bands, as soap will cause the bands to deteriorate.
2. Slip the bands on about one inch, not less, onto the sling shot prong-ends. Be sure that both bands are slipped on an equal distance. Then check to see if the pouch is aligned properly to the prongs so that the pouch sits straight in the non-shooting position (See the picture on the left). If it is not aligned correctly then proceed to step 3 below.
3. Immediately, before the alcohol starts to dry, turn the entire one inch of the rubber on both prongs until both sides of the leather pouch are adjusted so that they are held straight by the prongs and rubbers like the picture on the left. It is necessary to make these adjustments rather fast because the rubbers can become pretty hard to turn as the alcohol starts to dry. Your slingshot will shoot a lot straighter if this is done properly.

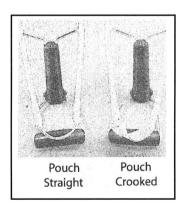

Pouch   Pouch
Straight   Crooked

4. **For Safety**, avoid shooting or pulling backwards on the sling shot powerbands for 12 hours to allow the alcohol to dry. **NOTE**: DO NOT let your slingshot lie in the sun or fluorescent light when not in use. Strong Ultra-Violet light makes latex tubing deteriorate pretty quickly by drying it out and causing it to crack. Once the surface begins to crack, even slightly, it doesn't take very long before the band will break, especially where it is attached to the prongs or leather pouch.

Slingshot Storage

Storing your slingshot in a safe place is also part of "hunter safety." If you need to put it into storage for long periods of time, a small metal cabinet with door locks, and no windows would work great. Restoring/protecting the rubber parts is a good idea because natural latex is very unstable chemically and highly sensitive to environmental factors such as oxygen, pollutants, and especially ultraviolet rays in visible light like fluorescents and daylight.

NOTE: Don't leave the slingshot in a cabinet for long periods of time though without checking the rubber surgical tubes for deterioration. It really should be under lock and key, but OUT OF any light and in a clean dry place. This will also keep your kids from getting it. Young kids are inquisitive, they will want to take it out and see how it works, especially if they have seen you using it.

Transporting Your Slingshot

Transporting your slingshot is also important. First, check the rules for transporting in your state if you are going to take your slingshot out with you. In many states, if you are carrying a slingshot in areas frequented by wild animals, you must be in possession of a licence for your slingshot. You can in most states transport your slingshot without a hunting license if it is enclosed in a case, or carried in a vehicle in a location that is not readily accessible to any occupant of the vehicle. A nice little case with a lock would work great. But then where to put it? Maybe there would be enough room under the drivers seat? I don't know whether the glove box would be considered accessible or not? You will need to ask someone or look into this issue yourself. When traveling to and from hunting trips, you could store it in the trunk of your car where it is locked, just as long as you can keep it cool and dry. It is considered a weapon, so if you have it setting on the seat next to you it's like a loaded gun. When you are out hunting, you could keep it in your back pocket until you are ready to use it, or in a back pack, so that your hands are free to do other things. You can not carry it on a plane, it has to go on as "checked baggage," in a case along with the ammunition.

Slingshot Ammunition

Types of Slingshot Ammunition

There are many possible types of ammunition for slingshots. There are 10 different types they mostly talk about. We will list them, and briefly give you the "Pro's" and "Con's" of each one.

- Stones (rocks)

    Pro's: They are free and cost you nothing. If you train exclusively with them you can become quite accurate.

    Con's: They are a poor choice for a slingshot. If they are jagged or irregular they can damage your bands. They also increase the chance of a fork hit.

- Clay

    Pro's: They are almost free, they leave no shards, they don't ricochet and they are totally biodegradable. Rain washes the remains away. Density is comparable to glass. Well suited to distances up to 15 meters. Easy to roll them by hand into a ball and let them dry. Use of a carp bait roller will let you make hundreds of little ball in no time. You can use them to see where you hit on a target because they leave a visible spot on a hard surface. They won't break to mess up your pouch.

    Con's: Not immediately available if any? It would take a little time to make them.

- Glass Shot and Marbles

    Pro's: They are common, cheap, and available in any supermarket. High visibility, they can be tracked during flight which helps you adjust your aim until you hit the target. They are easy to spot and recollect. Their round shape makes them perfectly accurate. Their 1/2" or more diameter makes them easier to hold than steel or lead with small calibers. Their price makes them better to use than 1/4" steel balls. Manufacturers glass has bright colors which makes them easy to see in flight, they have a guaranteed consistent size.

    Con's: Their low density compared to steel or lead makes them bad for long range shots when high power is needed. Glass ammo from slingshot manufacturers is usually expensive.

■ Steel Shot

Pro's: It is the most common type of ammo. It comes in different sizes, usually 1/4", 5/16", 3/8" and 1/2." It can be used for target sooting as well as hunting. It's almost impossible to destroy, so it can be used over and over again. A strong magnet makes them easy to recollect and handle.

Con's: Their ability to ricochet is a disadvantage, never shoot them against a hard surface.

■ Lead Balls

Pro's: They have the highest density of all the common materials, which is good when you need heavy ammunition. They have the power to down your quarry humanely. The cost can be lowered to almost zero if you can get a mold and cast them yourself. Because they are so dense, there is no need for calibers over .50, a .44 ball is considered a very good hunting ammo.

Con's: Their disadvantage is they have environmental and health problems. They deform quickly when the hit a hard surface.

■ Paintballs

Pro's: They are accurate for close range target shooting. They make visible splats on hard surfaces. They don't ricochet, and pose no big danger to bystanders.

Con's: They are not reusable and can be crushed in a pouch if you are not careful. Be aware that many slingshots have more power than paintball markers.

■ Cylindrical Pellets

Pro's: Accuracy is very good on short ranges. They are easy to hold and faster to reload. They can be made for almost free. You get 8 mm nails or iron rods and chop or saw off pieces of about one centimeter in length.

Con's: They are not accurate when you shoot them beyond 10-15 meters. You will find sharp edges on this ammo which will mess up your backstop or cut your hands. Time and work to make a fair amount of these pellets is a disadvantage. Using a saw is too much work. Using a bolt cutter you could make them a little faster.

■ Hex Nuts

Pro's: They are cheap when purchased in bulk. They are surprisingly accurate and powerful. If you want to keep your ammo cost low without sacrificing too much power, they are a great choice. Their non-aerodynamical shape is no problem for close distances.

Con's: Their shape takes its toll on how effective long range shots will be.

■ Chopped Wheel Weights (Lead)

Pro's: These car wheel balancing weights are cheap. You can get them for free at garages and car dumps. You can chop them in pieces with pliers and use them as heavy ammo. Their high density compensates for an uneven shape, even for medium range shots.

Con's: Disadvantages are they have environmental and health issues from the lead. The soft material will flatten easily and the edges may cut your backstop, your pouch and your hands.

■ Plastic Balls

Pro's: They are readily available. Manufactures sell these for their slingshots.

Con's: They are far too lightweight, relatively expensive and not biodegradable. They ricochet when they hit a hard surface. So there is probably no point in using them.

Slingshot Ammo Weights

We are adding an ammunition weight table so that you can evaluate the ammo all in one table. When you look at the table you can see the dramatic difference between say, a 1/4" steel ball and a .45 caliber lead ball. With some of the heavy pull slingshot bands, a 1/2" steel shot carries more than 4 times the power than a 1/4" steel pellet carries, and almost double the power of a 3/8" diameter projectile. But many hunters say forget about the power and focus more on the accuracy. A hunter or a long range shooter won't be happy with 1/4" steelie or a small marble. They won't be happy with a huge lead ball either because it gives them a bad trajectory bow, they would be better served using something like a 10mm steel bearing.

Dia. (mm)	Dia. (Inch)	Weight in Grams		
		Glass/Clay	Steel	Lead
4.5	.177 Cal	0,12	0,38	0,54
5		0,16	0,51	0,74
6		0,28	0,89	1,28
6.35	1/4"	0,33	1,05	1,51
7		0,45	1,41	2,03
8	5/16"	0,67	2,11	3,03
9		0,95	3	4,31
9.5	3/8"	1,12	3,53	5,07
10	.40 Cal	1,31	4,12	5,91
11	7/16" .45 Cal	1,74	5,48	7,87
12		2,26	7,12	10,22
12.7	1/2"	2,68	8,44	12,11
13		2,87	9,05	12,99
14		3,59	11,3	16,23
15		4.42	13,9	19,96
17.5	Paintball Marker Avg. 3,201g	—	—	—

Table 30 Common Slingshot Ammunition Weight

Atlatls

Explanation

This is an introduction into "Atlatls," pronounced **AT**'-lat-ul. The atlatl is the oldest hunting weapon discussed in this book. Basically it is a casting (throwing) stick for a long dart (spear). The atlatl is the oldest since we have archaeological evidence dating it to the Upper Paleolithic period in Europe. It is the youngest in the sense that it has only been about the last two decades that it has started to gain the attention of modern hunters. Most of the people who use an atlatl today participate in target competitions throughout the USA and Europe. It is only now beginning to become a legal hunting weapon or device in the USA. It was used for thousands of years in the Americas and started to be replaced by the bow and arrow about 2000 years ago. It was in use along with the bow and arrow by groups like the Aztec when Europeans first arrived, and is still used by a few traditional cultures today. It is also still used by some groups in New Guinea and by some Australian Aborigines. It has been legal foe deer hunting in Alabama now for several years, and it legal for deer hunting in Missouri starting in the fall of 2010. It is legal for fish, small game, and varmint's not covered by state regulations. However, check your state anyway before going out hunting large animals with an atlatl!

Anatomy of an Atlatl (Parts)

The atlatl parts break down into the handle area, the dart rest area, the mid part or shaft, the weight area and end hook area *(SEE FIGURE 162)*.

About the Atlatl

The "atlatl" is a carrier or casting device to propel a dart. By itself it is not a hunting device until you

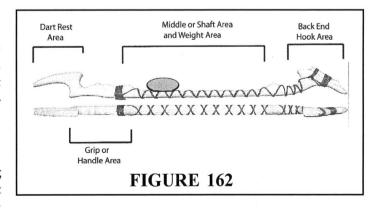

Dart Rest Area   Middle or Shaft Area and Weight Area   Back End Hook Area

Grip or Handle Area

FIGURE 162

attach the dart to it. They come in many different versions, styles and types. Maybe too many to try and show all of them in this book. Atlatls go back so far that almost every early society had their own version (20,000 plus years). So we are only going to show the modern available types that you can purchase. Many of the atlatls you can get are replicas of atlatls found in archaeological sites or replicas of those still used today by some traditional societies. Additionally, as more interest has grown in the atlatl over the last several decades, many atlatlists have modified traditional designs or developed unique new designs. Of course you can also always try to make your own. It's not that hard. Before you run out to buy one for hunting though, make sure they are legal in your state because in many they are not. Virtually all atlatls have a "hook" on the back end to engage the dart. Atlatls average from 18 to 24 inches in length, although some have been found as short as 6 inches in California, and as long as 48 inches in Australia. The length is probably a matter of personal preference with atlatl casting hunters. All atlatls have three basic sections; the grip, the shaft and the hook. In addition, some non-traditional atlatls incorporate a form of dart rest near the grip *(SEE FIGURE 162)*. In many cases atlatl sections are made from the same piece of wood, but in other cases they might consist of more than one piece of wood or other material like antler or bone that are attached to the main shaft. In addition to these sections, many atlatls incorporate a weight that is fastened to the shaft *(SEE FIGURE 162)*. The most important distinction regarding the kinds of atlatls is the grip styles.

Handle and Grip Styles

These break down into:

- Knuckle Styles ■ Finger Holes ■ Grip Wrappings

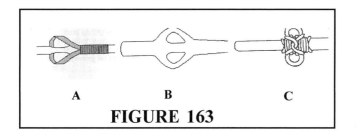

A   B   C

FIGURE 163

Knuckle Style Grips

These can be braided or leather loops *(SEE FIGURE 163-A)*, they can be single or double holes on the shaft, either drilled or carved in the wood *(SEE FIGURE 163-B)*, they can be cord formed finger holes *(SEE FIGURE 163-C)*, or they can be carved antlers or other material.

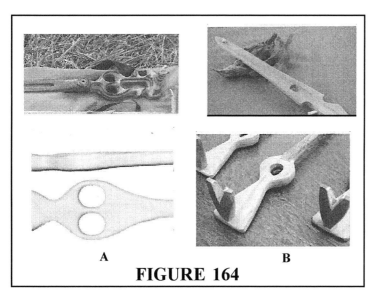

A   B

FIGURE 164

Finger Hole Style Grips

These can be two hole finger grips *(SEE FIGURE 164-A)*, or they can be a single hole finger grip *(SEE FIGURE 164-B)*. They are usually drilled into the Atlatl shaft, and in some cases carved out.

Wrapping Style Grips

The grip area can be wrapped with different types of material, or they can be unwrapped. One way is to wrap natural twine around the shaft grip area *(SEE FIGURE 165-A)*. Another way is to wrap leather around the grip area *(SEE FIGURE 165-B)*. Wrapping the grip area can make it easier to throw without your hand slipping off.

Hook Styles

All atlatls use a hook on the back end. The hook fits into an indentation or dimple on the back end of the dart. In many instances, such as the *Basketmaker Atlatl* of the American Southwest, the hook is simply carved into the wood shaft. However, in many other instances, the hook is made from separate materials such as antler, bone, or wood and then attached to the end of the shaft *(SEE FIGURE 166)*.

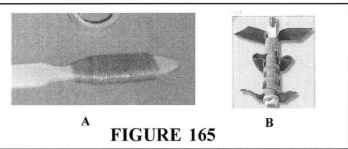

FIGURE 165

A   B

Shaft Styles

Atlatl shafts can be made from a wide variety of materials. By far the most common is wood. Almost any hardwood would work well *(SEE FIGURE 166)*, and some are made from other natural materials like bamboo or man made materials like fiberglass. Shafts can be found in round *(SEE FIGURE 166)* or flat *(SEE FIGURE 164)* shapes, or in some cases other shapes *(SEE FIGURE 162)*.

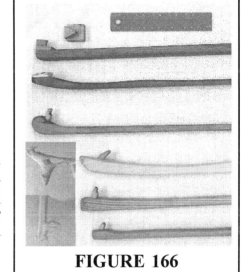

FIGURE 166

Picture Courtesy of World Atlatl Assoc.

Atlatl Darts (Ammunition)

Explanation

Darts are like spears, but in atlatl ammunition they are called "darts." Darts are typically 5 to 8 feet in length and can be made from a variety of natural materials including wood, bamboo, river cane (native bamboo), and a variety of reeds. Many American atlatlists prefer river cane or bamboo because they are very durable, and have a natural taper which allows the dart to flex (bend) during it's initial flight. This flex is necessary in order for the dart to work properly, and this flex should be mostly in the back two thirds area of the dart. Reeds such as arundo donax and phragmites also have natural tapers, but they are not as durable.

Darts can also be made from non-natural materials such as metals like aluminum or carbon fiber shafting. If these materials are used it might be necessary to insert a wood dowel or other material to stiffen the front of the dart. An advantage of aluminum or carbon darts is that they can be made to come apart for traveling more easily than darts of natural materials.

While darts made from natural materials such as river cane will usually also use a fore shaft, some wooden darts as well as aluminum or carbon darts will not use a fore shaft, and the point will be attached directly to the main shaft.

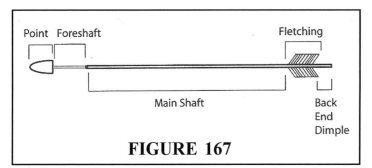

FIGURE 167

Anatomy of a Dart
The atlatl dart breaks down to the point area, the foreshaft, the main shaft, the fletching and the back end dimple to catch the hook *(SEE FIGURE 167)*.

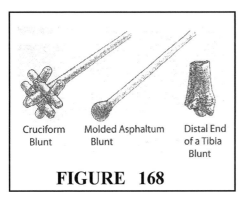

Cruciform Blunt   Molded Asphaltum Blunt   Distal End of a Tibia Blunt

FIGURE 168

Dart Points
Darts points are made from a variety of materials. Target points can use regular steel arrow target points called field points, or can be made of traditional materials such as flint (stone), bone *(SEE FIGURE 169)*, antler or wood. For hunting small game, any field point used for target casting can be used. In addition, a blunt point made of wood or other materials could be used *(SEE FIGURE 168)*. These were used to stun game by some early hunters.

For hunting large game such as deer it is critical to use a point that will both penetrate and cut. Traditionally, the main material used for hunting big game was stone such as flint or chert. While some present day big game hunters prefer to use stone points, modern arrow steel broadheads will work quite well *(SEE FIGURE 169)*. When used with an adapter glued to the foreshaft, steel target field points and broadheads can be easily interchanged. Traditional points such as those made of stone or bone would be attached by inserting them into a slit in the foreshaft, and then fastening them securely with natural or synthetic binding materials and glue.

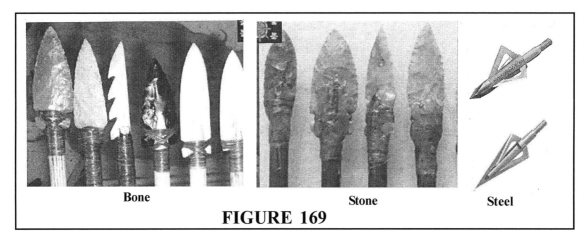

Bone   Stone   Steel
FIGURE 169

Dart Fletching
Fletching is the feathers that attach to the back end of the dart shaft *(SEE FIGURE 170)*. Most common is 3 feathers that attach to the shaft. However, there can also be 4 or 2 feathers. They are always equally spaced around the shaft. If you buy darts, they come with feathers, or if you make your own darts you can go out and find the feathers yourself in the woods or buy them. Turkey, duck and geese feathers are very popular. Actually bright colored feathers work good because you can see the dart easier as it flies through the air. And I'm not sure it would make any difference

while truly hunting because turkeys are very wary already, whether a color or black and white arrow is coming at them. If you want to make your own darts, you can buy a jig to help you locate and attach the feathers. This gets them located properly around the shaft. There are several sites on line that will give you full instructions on how to make your own darts, and how to attach the fletching. Check the back of the book in the reference section for sites.

FIGURE 170

Back End Indentation Dimple
Most atlatl and dart builders say you should wrap and reinforce the back end of the dart shaft, where the dimple is located, with natural materials. This protects it from splitting or other damage. Dart builders will use natural material, artificial sinew, thread or small diameter cord wrapped around the back end for about 1/2 an inch *SEE FIGURE 171)* for this process. Then they coat it with glue to keep it in place

FIGURE 171

Loading and Unloading Atlatls

Loading an Atlatl
Loading an atlatl is really pretty simple when compared to a firearm. One end has a hook of some sort, and the other end has some type of hand hold. The hook on the end is designed to connect to the back end of the dart by placing it in a dimple so that it won't easily come out. Each dart has a dimple on the end. The dart then lays parallel to the atlatl, and at the handle or grip end it is held in place either by your forefinger and thumb *(SEE FIGURE 172)*, or some type of "V" notch or rest. Some atlatls will have a rest for the dart, but others won't. The "V" rest tends to be easier for beginners so the dart stays in place during the arm casting motion *(SEE FIGURE 173)*. When the back end of your dart is pushed into the hook, is laying along parallel to the atlatl, and held with your fingers, your atlatl is loaded and ready to cast.

Unloading an Atlatl
Unloading your atlatl is even more simple. You just grasp the dart with your non-casting hand, then disengage the dart where it is pushed into the hook. There are so many varieties and types of atlatls that they are almost endless, and each one has some different features, but they all connect to the dart at it's back end with the hook in the dimple. When the two come apart you are unloaded.

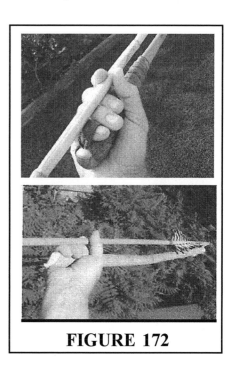

FIGURE 172

FIGURE 173

Casting (Throwing) Atlatls

Explanation
Throwing an atlatl is referred to as "casting." In casting an atlatl, the most important part is the grip you use. Depending on your natural abilities, they will effect your casting accuracy. Three different basic grips are used to cast an atlatl.

Atlatl Hand Holding Grip Styles
There are basically three different hand grips that are used to hold the atlatl. They are the "hammer," the "split (two) finger," and the "single finger" *(SEE FIGURE 174)*. As I talk to them, It seems that each atlatl caster has their own favorite grip. As the term implies, in using the hammer grip you hold the atlatl as you would a hammer. This may

Hammer Grip No.1

With-Loops Split Finger Grip

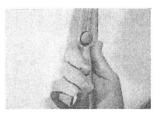

With-Single Hole Finger Grip No.1

Hammer Grip With "V"

Hammer Grip On Hide

No-Loops Split Finger Grip

With-Single Hole Finger Grip No.2

FIGURE 174
Atlatl Grip Styles

feel "more natural" than the other grips. However, many atlatlists prefer split finger or single hole grips because they allow for easier rotation of the wrist during the cast. For single hole grips, the hole is typically carved into the atlatl shaft or is made as a separate piece and is attached to the shaft. Split finger grips can also be carved into the shaft, but more typically the atlatl has a reduced diameter at the finger location, and then uses leather strips or other material to place the fingers in.

The grip can be either left unwrapped *(SEE FIGURE 164)* or wrapped with materials such as leather or twine *(SEE FIGURE 165)*. Atlatls have been found at archeological sites unwrapped and wrapped. Each grip seems to have it's advantages and disadvantages. Some grips will work with one atlatlist caster and not another. However, out of the ones I have tried, I personally had more control and straight ahead accuracy with the split finger grip atlatls. I think it's because of my baseball pitching. It's a lot like my two finger fastball pitch. I think what a beginner needs to do is try all the grips and see which one works the best for them.

Casting an Atlatl In the Field

There are several ways to cast (throw) an atlatl out in the field. First make sure that it is never going to be a threat to other nearby hunters. First thing, before casting always check the area for other hunters, and observe what's behind your target. Atlatl darts can be very dangerous. At 20 meters they could pass entirely through your body. I have heard of atlatl hunters throwing up to 70 meters at targets. So I suggest you make sure that about 100 meters behind your target is clear. Check your states hunting laws before you go out hunting with an Atlatl. It may not be legal in your state. There are several ways to cast an atlatl. Overhand, sidearm, and underhand. I would learn the overhand method, it's more accurate at 20 to 30 meters which is the effective range of an Atlatl.

Overhead Casting Stance

While it is not necessary to step out when casting, stepping is very popular with many atlatlists. You should try both ways and see which works best for you. For many beginning atlatlists, it takes a lot of practice to learn how to make an accurate cast. First stand up straight and tall, facing the target. Then the basic foot position for a cast is your non-casting side foot slightly out in front *(SEE FIGURE 175)*. The casting side foot is turned out a little towards the casting hand side so that you are not quite turned 90 degrees to the target . This is so that the left arm can be raised and pointed out towards the target if you are right handed *(SEE FIGURE 176-A)*. The dart is level or a little bit above horizontal, and at or above eye level depending on how far

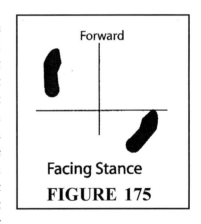

Forward

Facing Stance
FIGURE 175

away the target is. Then you visually align the spear with the target even though you can't sight down it like a gun barrel, then bring your arm and elbow back. If you are not taking the step, then this is your stance when you are ready to cast. Next you would lean back with your weight on your back foot on the casting side.

Taking a Step

The cast starts with a slight bend in the non-casting side foot knee as you rock back just a little, then you bring the non-casting foot forward in a full step *(SEE FIGURE 176-B)*, which brings your body, dart, and arm forward. You do this without moving the arm or rotating the torso until the full step is complete, with the left foot flat or almost on the ground.

The Arm and Body

As your step is completed, the upper arm flexes at the shoulder, which brings the hand and the atlatl forward until it is about even with the back of your head *(SEE FIGURE 176-C)*. All the way through this the atlatl remains horizontal. The shoulder flexion seems to be small at this point,

A   B

FIGURE 176

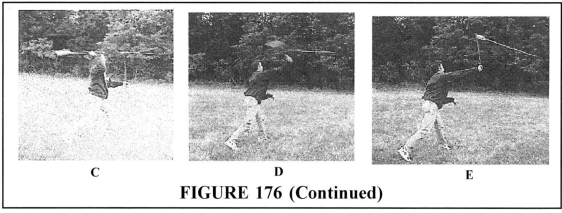

C   D   E

FIGURE 176 (Continued)

F

FIGURE 176 (Continued)

and the wrist must be rotating to keep the dart pointed at the target.

The Release

Just before the hand reaches the back of the head, the hand and forearm start to rise. Then as the hand passes the head, you give a vigorous snap of your wrist, swinging the atlatl up to near vertical and flicking the dart away *(SEE FIGURE 176-D)*. The dart will flex as the point remains aimed at the target, while at the same time the nock is rapidly raised by the atlatl. At this same time, the arm is extended straight out. Note: the wrist motion is about the same as throwing a baseball, with the only difference being that the fingers remained closed to the grip on the atlatl. Notice how far above the head the dart is as it is just about to leave the atlatl *(SEE FIGURE 176-E)*. With the atlatl in the vertical position, the dart has recovered from it's initial flexing, and is about to fly away from the atlatl while flexing in the opposite direction.

The Follow Through

As the dart leaves the atlatl, either horizontal or slightly past, continue your cast motion with a nice easy follow through. At this point there seems to be two different techniques for the follow through. *ONE*, you lean slightly forward, then swing the atlatl and your right arm down and across your body, ending outside of your left leg. *TWO*, as your hand comes down, imagine you are swatting a fly, with your palm facing straight down towards the ground *(SEE FIGURE 176-F)*.

Handling Atlatls and Darts

Handling an Atlatl In the Field Position

Handling an atlatl out in the field is not a problem as with a loaded firearm. There are two handling situations. One is out hunting and the other one is during target practice. If you are holding it just with your hand while out hunting, and you are moving or walking for any length of time, your arm may get tired. If it does you may want to get a hunting back pack *(SEE FIGURE 85)* and store it in a PVC tube in the back pack until you get close to where your target game (deer) is located. When you do get close, get it out and load a dart so that you will be ready to cast. If you are going to be waiting to hunt in a tree stand, then follow the applicable safety rules for hunting in a tree stand found on page 41. For target practice you can put your atlatl in a PVC tube so that nobody will accidentally step on it if you set it down while waiting your turn.

Handling an Atlatl At Home

When handling your atlatl at home, with kids around, just be sure it does not have a dart loaded. It's OK to show it to people. There is not much on it that can hurt anyone, just as long as they are careful and don't swing it around like a club. However, if it has a weight on it, it could hurt someone if it hits their head, or anywhere else on their body.

Handling a Dart In the Field Position

Handling a dart out in the field hunting is pretty simple. They are too long to put in a back pack, so you just carry one or two in your hand, always keeping the point down. This way if you drop it, the fletching won't get damaged. If you stop walking for a minute or two to rest, then lean it against a tree or branch, point down. When you are doing target practice, you store your darts in a ring *(SEE FIGURE 177)*, like the ones to support the tomatoes in your garden, point down . Hold it in your hand, point down, while you are waiting to cast.

Handling a Dart At Home

When handling your atlatl at home, with kids around, just be careful that the point does not cut anyone. Keep the point towards the floor, and try not to damage the fletching.

FIGURE 177

Atlatl Safety Rules

Basic Information

As with any shooting style weapon, certain safety rules must be observed because atlatls are not toys. The "Atlatl" is a casting device to launch a dart. It is mostly used for target practice now, and just beginning to be legal in some states for hunting. Following are some basic "atlatl" safety rules. Following them at all times will make using an atlatl a more pleasant experience for you:

General Safety Precautions

    1. NEVER aim, lob, or cast your dart (spear) in the direction of a person. Aim and draw
        ONLY in the direction of an appropriate target or the game you are hunting *(SEE FIGURE 178)*.

FIGURE 178

Picture Courtesy of the World Atlatl Assoc

2. If there is even any chance of a person coming into your casting (throwing) area, it should be marked with caution tape and warning signs.
3. ALWAYS peg or fasten your target to foam or hay bales to stop your darts from going through and beyond.
4. ALWAYS make sure there is enough space beyond your target to handle bounces and overcasts. Darts can glance off the target, or any other obstacle, and travel well beyond. In some cases the dart actually picks up speed after it glances off a target.
5. NEVER cast a dart for distance without an adequate marked off space.
6. NEVER cast darts over someone's head. No matter how high you aim, there is always a chance for a misfire. The result could be a serious, even fatal injury.
7. NEVER cast over an obstacle where you cannot see your target area.
8. NEVER stand behind someone when they are casting. Not only can you distract them, their casting motion could even injure you.

Safety Rules When Casting in a Group

1. A safety director, preferably an adult with atlatl safety experience, can be appointed to coordinate a group that is throwing.
2. When casting with another person in a group, it is necessary to make sure that all darts have been cast before you cross over the casting line to retrieve them. Having a safety director to give an "ALL CLEAR" signal to the group so they know that it is safe to cast or retrieve, is a good idea. If there is no safety director, you must ask each member of the group if they are ready to retrieve.
3. It is recommended that two people pull all the darts from the targets, then hand them to the others. One person can stand at each side of the target, way out to the side, starting at the outer edge then working towards the middle to pull the darts.
4. NEVER stand behind the darts as they are being pulled from the target.

Safety Rules Retrieving Darts

1. *From the ground*: The proper technique for pulling a dart from the ground is to clasp the dart in front of the fletching (feathers) and pull it out backwards at the same angle it is sticking into the ground.
2. Do NOT pull straight upward and do NOT grasp it at the fletching to pull it out. It could be damaged or broken this way.
3. *From the target*: The proper technique for pulling a dart from the target is to hold the target with one hand and grasp the dart with the other hand as close to the target as possible, then pull straight out the same direction it went in.

Safety Rules for Carrying Darts Properly

1. The point of the dart is the most dangerous end of this weapon. ALWAYS keep it pointed in a safe direction: the ground is the best choice.

2. ALWAYS be aware of how you, and others, are carrying the darts. Do NOT walk behind someone carrying their dart improperly as they may suddenly stop.

3. It is probably very unlikely that you will ever need to run with darts in your hand (possible hunting situations being an exception). However, ALWAYS have full control of your equipment, with dart points down.

4. DON'T twirl your darts around, especially when others are near.

5. DON'T stab at people, or any objects near people, when using a dart.

Safety Rules for Storing Equipment in Between Throws

1. Whether at a tournament or throwing in your backyard, sometimes you want to take a break. It is important for you to put your equipment in a safe place so that it does not get damaged. A dart stand placed outside any travel area can hold darts and atlatls better than leaning them against a tree or vehicle. If NOT properly stored, wind, people or other causes might knock them down to the ground, and make them more likely to be stepped on or run over. Putting them in a PVC tube is a good option to keep them safe.

Optional Atlatl Features

Dart Rests

Traditional atlatls do not use dart rests. Rather, the dart is typically rested on the fingers of the throwing hand and held in place by one or more fingers *(Five of Seven Pictures in FIGURE 174)*. In the last two decades or so, some atlatlists have incorporated dart rests into the atlatl. There are basically two types of rest areas. The dart either sits on an upward protrusion in front of the grip *(SEE FIGURE 179-A)* or rests in a "V" shaped piece of wood *(SEE FIGURE 179-B)* often lined with soft leather for gripping the dart.

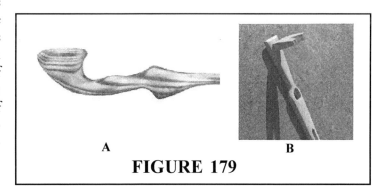

A   B

FIGURE 179

Atlatls Weights

While many atlatls found throughout the world did not use weights, most atlatls in ancient America used some form of weight that was attached to the shaft, many modern day atlatlists prefer using weights. While there is some debate regarding the advantages of using weights, most modern day atlatlists would agree that the weight helps balance the atlatl when hooked to a dart, and may also allow a smoother and more controlled cast. Weights can come in a variety of sizes and shapes *(SEE FIGURE 180)*. As illustrated some weights such as the Type I single and double weights are simple in shape and are often just a stone with some modification for attaching to the atlatl shaft. Others, such as Type II are more elaborately shaped and the Type III bannerstones found throughout the eastern United States were the most elaborately shaped. Some modern atlatl makers have come up with a classification system to describe the weight placement. I think this is a good idea if for no other reason than to discuss atlatl weights. There are four classifications of weights they have set up for atlatls in this system *(SEE FIGURE 180)*:

- Type I Single Weight
- Type I Double Weight
- Type II Boatstone Weight
- Type III Banner Stone

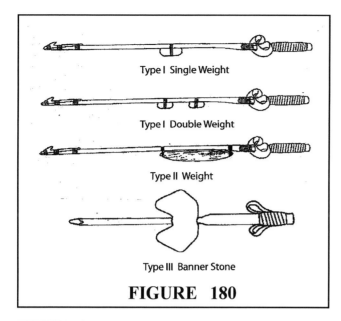

Type I Single Weight

Type I Double Weight

Type II Weight

Type III Banner Stone

FIGURE 180

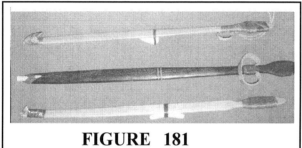

FIGURE 181

Examination and study have found that Type I single and Type I double are about the same weight whose mass adds up to 65g. This weight is usually found somewhere from center to more in the front half of the atlatls length. In Type I double, the weight is evenly distributed along the shaft in two places and centered near the same place as Type I single. In Type II the mass is still about 65g, but evenly distributed and spread out along the front half of the length. In type III the weight, commonly known as a Bannerstone, has a mass weight of about 80g. Atlatls from the western United States, which Type I and II represent, have been found to be approximately 60 cm in length including the attached weight *(SEE FIGURE 181)*.

Atlatl and Dart Maintenance

Maintenance on an atlatl is basically checking the cords and braids for damage that might let the weights or other tied on parts fall off or come loose, or the loops come loose or fray. You can keep your atlatl clean by wiping it off occasionally with a clean cloth or rag. Also check your darts for damage to the point fletchings, and indentation dimple. Replace as necessary. Check your wood, cane, or bamboo darts for cracks or fractures on the shaft, from being accidentally stepped on. Get a piece of PVC pie to place your atlatl in, it will keep it from accidentally being damaged. You can find replacement for the wood, cane or bamboo shafts. See the reference section in the back of the book for where to buy parts. If you are using Aluminum or Carbon Fiber dart shafts, you can buy replacements for them also. Check your hunting points after each use for damage. They can be replaced. Atlatl hunters should use a foreshaft. This way you can have different interchangeable points. If you are using metal darts, you can use threaded parts that interchange fairly quickly. You can even find replacement rocks or Bannerstone weights if you loose them. Replacement fletching (feathers) are also available. Just about anything you might need is available on line. If you want to repair your atlatl or darts yourself, which is usually inexpensive, you can go on line and find all kinds of printout instructions and videos to show you step by step how to do it. Go in the back of the book in the reference section for some web sites to get started in finding this information.

Carrying & Transporting Atlatls and Darts

Carrying and Transporting Atlatls

These are just some suggestions. You can get a special made for atlatls canvas bag to carry your atlatl in *(SEE FIGURE 182)*. However, maybe a better idea would be a bag used to carry fencing foils (swords) around in. It looks like they would be just about the right size *(SEE FIGURE 183)*. Just to make sure you don't get in any trouble by breaking any laws on your way out to a hunting trip, contact your state about their weapons carrying laws first. The law will be under transporting and carrying firearms or weapons. PVC Tubing is an inexpensive alternative.

Carrying and Transporting Darts

Carrying your darts might be a problem? The darts can average 6 to 8 feet or so long. One idea might be to use a track & field javelin carrying bag *(SEE FIGURE 184)*. They will hold about 10 to 15 darts. Or another alternative might be to get some heavy canvas and design your own bag, especially if you know someone who sews. You could have a handle sewn on also. PVC tubing may also be an inexpensive alternative for carrying your darts. If you need to transport your darts, or atlatls, by air then check with your airline as to what they require. You will not be able to do a "carry-on with atlatls or darts," only in checked baggage.

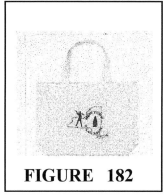

FIGURE   182

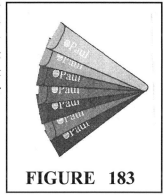

FIGURE   183

Storing Atlatls and Darts

If you can get an inexpensive metal cabinet with a lock on the door, that would work. The reason I am suggesting this is because small inquisitive kids might pick up the darts and hurt themselves, trying to see how it works or playing with it as kids will do. Remember though, the hunting points are razor sharp. I know some of the atlatls and darts may be easy to build or replace, so maybe you think you don't need a cabinet, but I would be more worried about the danger to young kids than the expense. A fairly inexpensive suggestion is get some 1/2 or 3/4" plywood, and build a 34" wide x 12" deep x 84" high (or higher) cabinet in the garage.

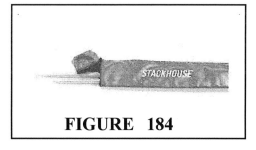

FIGURE   184

Atlatl 3-D Practice Course

Many archery clubs offer outside targets for practice, and a 3-D course to help improve on your hunting techniques and skills *(SEE FIGURE 185)*. They may have 10-12 stations in the woods with typical hunting animal targets to shoot at. These are real life looking type targets. They are made from a variety of E-Z pull type materials. Some even have a removable vital target area section for replacement.

FIGURE   185

Picture Courtesy of the World Atlatl Assoc.

SECTION 5 Game Hunting

Explanation

In this section we will cover some of the basic techniques and tips for youth hunting. Not every possibility, but some of the fundamental things you might consider when you first go out on a hunting trip. Many of you will be going with your dad, and some of you with your mom. What we will do is point out some of the skilled hunter techniques and tips that some of the skilled game, varmint, deer, turkey, waterfowl and upland game bird have come up with over the years. We are not going to cover big game hunting such as bear or elk. There will be time for that when you get older and more experienced at hunting. This book is basically for youth and beginners. It will help you get through some of your states yearly scheduled youth hunts that go on for deer, turkey and maybe waterfowl and upland game birds. One last point to make, be sure you have been through a hunter safety course first before you start out.

Varmint Hunting

What You Will Encounter

The definition of a varmint is: any animal considered to be a pest. They are classed as vermin and are usually unprotected by game laws. Theses could be animals like coyotes, bobcats, mountain lions, grey fox, red fox, badgers, raccoons, ring tailed cats, skunks, prairie dogs, porcupines, feral cats and jackrabbits. There is no closed season for predator hunting. Where required, hunting licenses are usually inexpensive and available over the counter. Under TEXAS law, hunters may shoot as many predators and varmint's as they choose per day, but they may only reduce one of each species of "fur bearer" animals (raccoon, fox, ring tail cat, badger) into possession per day, unless they have a furbearers license. There are other restrictions, so check your state if you want to hunt predators and varmint's. For serious predator hunters you need to learn how to call them. And you need to learn their habits and how to outwit them.

Night Hunts

You need to hunt predators and varmint's at night because that's when you will have the most success. Many states let you hunt these animals from a vehicle. Jeeps and pickups seem to be the favored vehicle. A technique they use is while making calls they shine a dim red light around, searching for the reflective red glow of incoming eyes. People that do a lot of this type of hunting will work in pairs. One partner holds the rifle ready while their partner shines the light and makes the calls. When a predator is located, the caller will tap the hunter on the shoulder to let them know the predator is on the way. When the predator is within gun range, the calling partner lights them up with a powerful spotlight so that the hunter can get a visible shot. Most shots are under 40 yards so shotguns work best. Longer shots may require a small centerfire caliber rifle such as a .222, .223 or 22-250.

Coyote

Daytime Hunts

Daytime hunts are very similar to any hunt where you

hunt early in the morning or late in the afternoon. These hunts usually have hunters wear their camouflage. Lots of you will live way out in the country or on the edge of the city. And you will encounter coyotes trying to get your chickens or even your small inside house dog out in the back yard. Make no mistake about it coyotes are a predator. I've heard stories where people living on the edge of cities will let their small house pet dog out in the backyard to do their business in the evening. Then along comes a female coyote in heat, they come up to your dog and lure them to the edge of the yard, or even out of the yard. Next their mate comes up, attacks, and kills your dog, then they drags it off to eat.

Varmint and Predators

Vermin or varmint's are animals that are regarded as pests or nuisances, and especially those associated with the carrying of disease. Disease carrying rodents (Rats) are usually the case. A predator (Coyote) is an animal that hunts or kills other animals, usually for food. A predator species kills and eats other animals known as prey. There is an hierarchy of predators; as an example, though small birds prey on insects, they in turn may be prey for snakes, which in turn may be prey for hawks. A predator at the top of the food chain is called an apex predator. Some predators specialize in certain classes of prey, not just a single species. Almost all will switch to other prey when the preferred target is extremely scarce.

Varmint Rifles

This is an American term for a small caliber firearm used for varmint hunting. They are primarily used for killing animals such as coyotes and rats, and occasionally ground hogs, ground squirrels, rabbits and grey squirrels that destroy gardens. For varmint and pest control in urban areas, air guns make suitable choices. While it's power is limited to small rodents or other animals at very close ranges, the limited penetration and low noise allows them to be

used in city areas where the use of firearms is normally not too practical. In bigger open areas like on urban farms, the use of centerfire rifles with a light, fast bullet gives a nice flat trajectory. This makes range estimation less vital for accurate shot placement. The smaller bullets also produce less noise that might scare the target animal. Smaller rounds like .25 caliber are most often used with specialized varmint rifles. .22 caliber bullets are the most common. Some varmint hunters swear by the .17 HMR bullet as the ultimate short range round. It has tremendous hitting power with a muzzle velocity of about 2550 feet per second (FPS). With the use of a scope on your rifle and some sand bags, you can pick off these varmint's out to about 200 to 300 yards.

Ground Hog

Varmint Shotguns

If you can get close enough to a coyote or bobcat, you can use a shotgun. Learn how to call them in. I have been reading stories of hunters calling in coyotes from out about 1000 yards, and they came in to about 100 yards before they stopped. The best story I read was where the coyote came running in from the backside of the caller and grabbed his flipping rabbit decoy and ran right past him with it before he could get a shot off. A 20 or 12 Ga. will work well, especially if you are up to 30 yards away. At that range a shell with #4 buckshot will do the job. At that distance the hitting power has a muzzle velocity of about 1207 feet per second (FPS). At about 100 yards out you may want to use Hornady's super accurate FXT bullet. These shotgun slugs can deliver a 2" group at 100 yards. It comes in 20 or 12 Ga. The 12 Ga. 300 Gr. FXT delivers about 1793 foot pounds of energy at the muzzle, and the 20 Ga. 250 Gr. FXT delivers about 1200 foot pounds of energy at the muzzle.

Organized Varmint Hunts

If you and a buddy decide to organize a varmint hunt, here are some ideas. You can go out at night as previously mentioned, or you can go out early in the morning. What you need to do for early morning hunts is scout out where the target animal will be located. Then set up with your jeep or pickup out about 100 to 200 yards away. Put your sandbags on a rail or fixed surface, set your rifle on the sand bags, sight out the area through the scope and get all set up to shoot. I would recommend the Hornady "V-Max" bullets or equivalent for the best results if you will be shooting out at 200 to 300 yards. Coyotes and foxes like the chickens, so you might want to set up with a good view of where the chickens are housed. Rats like to live in wood piles, so you might scout out any wood piles in the area ahead of time to see if any rats are around. Also you can ask any local farmer if they have any particular varmint's they would like to get rid of, and where they have been seen. That way you will know you have their permission to hunt the varmint's on their farm. Close in the city cotton tail rabbits can be a problem in the garden. They will eat and destroy lots of your vegetables. They can be good eating if fixed right. So you might want to look into that along with shooting grey squirrels. We have even caught the grey squirrels eating all our tomatoes just to get the seeds and moisture out, and leaving the rest of the tomato just sitting there on a stump.

Deer Hunting

What You Will Encounter

There is an organization called "Mid-America Hunting Assoc. (MAHA)." They offer private land hunting since 1965. They encourage all parents with children to participate in these youth hunts. It is my understanding that each state has a special deer hunting season now for kids 18 and under.

Picture Courtesy of Bear Archery

They ask that each youth deer hunter once having harvested a racked buck then work to harvest bucks with only larger racks. They also ask the hunters to grow up to the 130 class for archery and the 140 class and above for gun hunting. These class numbers are a way of scoring the size of a white tailed deer. When you see a buck, you have to very quickly ask yourself if you want to shoot it or not. First thing to look for is how many points it has and how long are they.

Next make sure you see both sides of the rack. Then look at the length of the main beams. If they are out past the middle of the nose, and turn inward, you know they have potential. The width of the rack is next. If the spread is out to or beyond the tips of their ears, that's good enough. Their mass and body weight can make a difference on a border line set of antlers. If you go to the "Boone and Crockett Club" web site it shows you how to score your buck. The "Pope and Young Club" also gives you information on how to score your buck. And they give you some minimums for scoring different big game animals.

Learning to Score your Buck

Before you ever start to hunt deer, first try to learn as much as you can about scoring them. First thing to realize is that bucks always look bigger than they really are. There are a lot of web sites on the internet that will help you to become a better judge of deer antlers, especially white tails.

There are groups such as the "Quality Deer Management Association" (QDMA), Buckmasters, North American Whitetail and others that will offer you a chance to view and practice scoring white-tails. They are interactive. You go on line, look at the video, then attempt to score what you see. Like many things, the more you try to score, the better you will get. And I'm sure mom or dad will help you if you ask them. This is very important because you don't want to shoot just any little old deer you come across. So invest the time and learn to do it right. You will glad you did.

Hunting by Moon Phase

This is an interesting bit of information. Animals like deer are in tune with their surroundings and shifts in natures natural forces can trigger corresponding responses in wild deer. Researchers have studied the reaction of wild life to changes in the position of the sun and moon. They have come up with some interesting observations in relation to hunting by the phases of the moon. So how could paying attention to moon phases possibly help you in hunting deer? First deer will tend to be less active during daylight hours. Because they feel safer under the cover of darkness, deer will increase their activity as dusk falls. These researchers have also noticed that deer activity is greater when the moon is full, and hunting during full moons can get hunters more success. In other words the more active deer are, the better your chances are for finding them. Even if you don't believe in this at first, try it because it might work for you. The various phases of the moon also seem to have a direct effect on deer mating patterns, which also helps you to locate them.

You need to be aware of when the breeding season begins because it helps in determining travel patterns and areas of increased activity. When the breeding period is at it's peak, finding them is easier, and finding more than one in a particular area is more likely. A female deer's reproductive cycle is influenced by the different phases of the moon. It peaks in the 3 or 4 days surrounding the second full moon after the autumnal equinox. When the does are in heat, bucks begin scraping and rubbing trees in an attempt to attract them. So if you know when the full moon occurs, you can be at the right spot, at just the right time, and have your best chance of luring bucks to your location. Also the moon phases can help you determine when not to hunt. You are not going to be very successful after the deer have mated, and even the phase where the bucks are chasing the does can be bad sometimes. By becoming familiar with the moons phases and planning ahead, hunting by moon phase could lead to your best season ever. You can find calendars that show the moon phase on certain days of each month. In the northern hemisphere the autumnal equinox occurs around the 22nd to 23rd of September.

Other Hunting Techniques

There are several basic techniques you can use. The obvious one is going out in the woods and stalk them. To do this you need to be in camouflaged clothing, with one difference. You need to be wearing a "hunter orange" vest. Otherwise you are taking a big risk of getting shot by one of the many other hunters out in the woods during deer season. The deer is color blind and can't tell orange from brown, so why take the chance. I would advise getting some binoculars also, to help in spotting and getting a closer look at what "class" they are. Another technique that is popular is waiting in tree stands. In this technique you sit in a stand way up in a tree in your camo gear and wait for the deer to come along. This is a usually a way shorter shot, so your chance of being successful is much better. Plus you will probably get a better look at the antlers. Don't forget to clear your shooting lanes. But do your trimming in such a way that nobody, including the deer, can tell you have trimmed. Don't forget the "scent" factor. Deer can smell multiple scents (7) at the same time. They can smell your sweat in your hat band, what's on the bottom of your shoes, and even the oil on your rifle. When they detect you they are going somewhere else to feed. What can you do? There are a number of good tips. Scent elimination is the first step. By removing a high percentage of your human smell from the mix, you make cover scents and attractants much more effective.

Cover Scents and Attractants

Cover scents are intended to confuse and distract the deer from your scent. Some examples are skunk or fox scent to cover your human scent with a strong odor of a varmint smell. Or confuse the deer with fresh earth fumes or the scent of a food source like apples or acorns (attractants). Also cedar, juniper and pine are good cover scents to use any time of the year. Attractants like muscadine (wild grapes), crab apples, corn, persimmons and honeysuckle are best used timed to their normal season. Other scents come in amber glass, spray bottles, wafers, smoke sticks that burn like incense, soaps, shampoos, breath mints and chewing gum. They can be applied to wicks, posted surrounding tree stands, or tied to your shoes and dragged on the trail behind you. One guy gathers the local vegetation himself, mixing it with water from a pond or mud puddle. Then he invented a portable electric blender. Then at the beginning of each hunt he grinds up the local vegetation to cover his scent and pours it in a bottle for use throughout the week. Then there is a company called "Buck Bomb." They make all kinds of scent sprays, from deer to bear. You can find them on line on the internet. You can even use clothing that has been specially treated.

Deer Hunting Regulations

Before you go on your first hunting trip, make sure to check with your state's deer hunting regulations to make sure you are in full compliance with all of them. Here are just a few of the things to remember: you can't hunt with the aid of bait, so make sure you know if the area you are hunting in has been baited. You can use food scents, but only as long as they are not used on or with grain and other feeding type products. Manipulating crops, such as mowing or knocking them down, is not considered baiting for deer. An area is considered baited for 10 days even after complete removal of the bait. It is illegal to place bait in a way that causes others to be in violation of the baiting rule. Mineral blocks, including salt, are not considered bait, however mineral blocks that contain grain or other feeding food additives are prohibited. In most states a legal buck must have a minimum of 4 points on one side, regardless of the number of points on the other side. Does, button bucks and bucks with spikes less than 3 inches are legal to take on antlerless or any deer permits. But for deer management it is better to take does. Protected deer include all antlered deer (defined as having at least one antler 3 inches or longer) that do not have a minimum of at least 4 points on one side. Letting these younger males mature will increase the number of adult bucks in the future.

You are required to wear a cap or hat and also a shirt, vest or coat of "*hunter orange*" so that the color is plainly visible from all sides. Camouflage orange does not satisfy this requirement. If you are a hunter using archery methods within municipal boundaries where discharge of firearms is prohibited, you are exempt from the hunter orange requirement. Hunter orange is recommended for archery hunters who are hunting close to areas open to firearms methods. Beware: When using a camouflaged blind, other hunters can't see you even if you are legally wearing hunter orange. To be safe, tie hunter orange on each side of the blind so that it can be seen from all sides. Deer may not be hunted, pursued or taken within any area enclosed by a fence greater than 7 feet high, except in licensed hunting preserves. Deer may not be perused or taken from or with a motor-driven vehicle. Deer may not be taken while they are in a stream or any body of water, or from any boat with a motor attached. There is a "purple paint" law; Landowners may post or define the boundaries of their property by marking trees and fence posts with purple paint. In a court of law, a property boundary marked with purple paint is the same as posting "No Trespassing" signs.

Harvesting Deer

All harvested deer, either whole or processed, must be labeled with the taker's full name, address and Telecheck confirmation number if it applies in your state. A hunter who takes a deer may give it to another person, but the game counts towards the taker's bag limit. Deer that are given away must be labeled with the taker's full name, address, Telecheck confirmation number if it applies, species and the date taken. Properly checked deer may be possessed by anyone if labeled with the takers full name, address, Telecheck confirmation number if it applies, and the date taken. The Telecheck confirmation number if it applies must remain attached to the carcass until a processor begins the act of processing the meat for packaging. For deer heads and/or antlers attached to skull plates, a dated bill of sale identifying the seller must be retained while the heads or antlers are in the buyers possession. Any person who finds a dead deer with antlers still attached to the skull plate may take the antlers, but must report the find to a conservation agent within 24 hours to receive authorization to possess the antlers.

Buckshot Information

This may be of interest if you decide to hunt for deer with your shotgun. These are the Standard Buckshot sizes *(SEE TABLE 31)*.

TABLE 31 Standard Buckshot Size		
Size	Diameter	Pellets/10g Lead
000 or LG (Triple-aught)	9.1mm (.36")	2.2
00 (Double-aught)	8.4mm (.33")	2.9
0 or SG (One-aught)	8.1mm (.32")	3.1
SSG	7.9mm (.31")	3.4
1-Buck	7.6mm (.30")	3.8
2-Buck	6.9mm (.27")	5.2
3-Buck	6.4mm (.25")	6.5
4-Buck	6.1mm (.24")	7.4

Turkey Hunting

What You Will Encounter

What you will find is a target that is very smart. They have very good eyesight and will test your hunting skills. You just need to learn their habits and outsmart them. Most states have now set aside special youth turkey hunting seasons. These are usually for young hunters age 11 to 15. Young firearm hunters, 6 to 15 who are not hunter education certified can still hunt with a mentor. The mentor must be at least 18 years old and be hunter education certified though unless they were born before a certain date. Many states have lots of restrictions, so check with the game or conservation department in your state first to be sure you will be in compliance with the regulations. Turkey can be hunted in most states using a firearm or a bow. However, in some states the firearm must be a shotgun, and with shot no larger than No.4. And in most states you can not have a bow and a firearm in your possession at the same time. Turkeys must be taken in most states without the use of dogs, bait, electronic calls or live decoys. And between 1/2 hour before sunrise to sunset. This means no night hunting after dark using flood lights and that sort of thing. And usually in the youth firearm seasons, you can only take one male turkey the first week. In most states you will be able to take 2 turkeys during a bow hunting season.

Turkey Hunting Techniques

First learn how to call that big tom turkey in. They are very smart, so you need to make sounds just like the hens. And in most states using an electronic device is prohibited. This means you need to learn how to do it using your voice, hands, and a tube or box. Once a tom hears your call, and he gobbles back, you have to have patience because it may take him up to 30 minutes to get to you in some cases. If you know turkeys are in the area, but you don't hear them gobbling, you might try a "shock" call.

FIGURE 186

One of the best is the "shock gobble" owl call. It requires you to create back pressure by loosely covering the end of the call with your cupped free hand. Or you might try a "turkey box" caller. Here is something to remember. Tom's like to investigate those hen yelps. When you hear them gobble back, and they sound close, you sit down with your back to the base of a tree and wait for them to come in *(SEE FIGURE 186)*. Here is a *TIP:* When the turkey is coming your way DO NOT stand up to see where he is. Be patient and stay sitting. And start your hunting at the crack of dawn, don't sleep in. Be prepared for rain. Wear appropriate clothing and snakeproof, waterproof, camouflaged boots are a good choice. And don't forget to bring a plastic bag to put your call box in if it starts to rain. If it does start to rain head for the open areas because that's where the turkey is headed. If you only wound the turkey you are obligated to hunt him down or finish him off. DO NOT leave him out in the woods to die. And last, make sure you know how to properly skin your turkey after the kill.

Bow Hunting Techniques

Bow hunting techniques are quite different from shotgun techniques. The turkeys body is different from a deer. When they get hit, many times the arrow goes all the way through, then they can manage to escape. There are several solutions for this. First you can pick an arrow and arrow head that will stick in the turkey and not pass through. Or you can pick one of these newer type of

Wild Turkey

cutting heads that expands and tears up the inside when it hits. When an arrow hits and stays in the turkey it will cause severe internal impairment, then this will give you a better chance at recovery. Because of this many hunters prefer to use a less powerful bow in the range of only 45 pounds. An advantage to these less powerful bows is their ability to remain at full draw for an extended period of time. Oftentimes, a bow hunter will need to stay at a full draw for a long period of time while waiting for the turkey to come nearer. However, there could be a problem with the draw poundage in your state. So be sure and check first. Huge broadheads are recommended to guarantee the stay of the arrow in the turkey. Some hunters even use arrow stoppers to avoid full penetrations. Other hunters have even soldered 2 fishhooks to the back of the broadhead which helps keep the arrow inside of the turkey. In addition some hunters attach string trackers to the arrowhead to help them track and grab hold of the turkey. Decoys also help bring the tom in closer.

Turkey Hunting Regulations and Restrictions

Different states have a lot of regulations and restrictions. So, again make sure you first check with your states conservation or game department. Restrictions will more than likely involve types of calling devices, and the type of shotgun ammunition you can use. As an example many states will not let you use an electronic device caller. And in most states they will only let you use a 10 Ga. shotgun or smaller, No. 4 shot or smaller, and no semi-automatic shotguns (3 shots max). For archery most states only allow bow and arrows, no crossbows. However, the state of Texas does allow crossbows. Some states don't allow muzzleloaders, while others will allow muzzleloading shotguns, and still others any kind of muzzleloader is legal.

Taxidermy

If your going to save your turkey for taxidermy, make sure you take the right steps to preserve him for the taxidermist. Here are some steps to take before and after the hunt. The first step is shop around for the best taxidermist you can find before you even go on your hunt. Don't skimp on the taxidermy because later you may wish you had not. Take a large plastic bag, a cooler, paper towels, cotton balls and used panty hose to stuff him in. Go on line to see how to prepare the panty hose. Then put him in carefully head first. A big plastic bag is another alternative.

Waterfowl Hunting

What You Will Encounter

This is a "whole nother ballgame" as they say. First of all water is involved. This requires extra precautions. To be proficient at waterfowl hunting, must have the right equipment. You need to be able to accurately judge distances, an be a reasonably good shot. You need to know the shots you can make and the ones you should not take. A little practice before the season is advisable. When we say waterfowl what are we talking about? Basically it's ducks and geese. By the way don't forget to check out our "Waterfowl Classification Table on *PAGE 129*. The lead shot issue is still going on. However, most states won't let you use it. It has to be steel or some alloy that is not toxic. Here are some questions you need to ask yourself; are you going to be on a boat, are you going to be in a blind next to the water, and are you using a dog as the retriever. And if you are not planning on using a dog, I hope you are a good wader, swimmer or rower.

Duck Hunting Techniques, Tactics and Strategies

Learn to set out good decoy patterns, and learn how to be a good caller. Public hunting areas may be a good choice, and maybe not too far away for travel. Your state probably provides information on their websites about public hunting opportunities, including locations, site maps, special regulations and harvest figures. Check it out! Here are some *TIPS* by the experts. Go the first day after a rest period. As an example, if a public area is closed Monday and Tuesday to rest the birds, then reopens Wednesday, be there that morning early. Remember, hunting is usually better during weekdays when fewer hunters are out. Be ready to move with the birds. A boat blind is often helpful in hiding when you reach where the birds are working. Also consider using a ground blind in a waterproof liner for hunting large open areas where standing cover is sparse. Purchase and learn to use a GPS. This way you will

Waterfowl Hunting

213

always know where your located. Use as many decoys as feasible. Ducks and geese find reassurance in a spread that resembles a refuge group setting for them. Experiment with calling styles to determine which the birds like best on that particular day. Be patient. Birds will often trickle back to public hunting areas after most hunters have left. Be flexible in your hunting tactics because you will be rewarded if you have realistic expectations about hunting on public areas. One hunter says he carries only a mallard call, a Canada goose call, a diver duck call and a dog whistle on his lanyard. "That's it," he says.

Goose Hunting Techniques, Tactics and Strategies

Basically you are hunting either Canada Geese or Snow Geese, which are a little different than ducks. For successful hunting do your scouting first. Look for recently harvested fields. This is what the geese look for. Freshly cut silage fields and wheat fields are a great place to start. Geese seem to find them within a day or two after a harvest. Notice what the birds are doing when they are down feeding. Then arrange your spread to mirror what the birds were doing when you were scouting them. Some hunters like to place their decoys in small family groups with some open space between them. However, the best plan is stick with what the real geese are doing in the field. Large groups may apply more to Canada Geese. The whole idea is get them to come in close so that you can get some good shots off. If you are working snow geese on the spring snowline, here is what you might want to do. Put your decoys out on water setups in flooded fields, sloughs or ponds. A flooded corn field works great because it provides a good food source as well. But find an area that's NOT surrounded by high vegetation because snow geese don't like to roost and feed where they are susceptible to predators or hunters. Because remember you are trying to bring them in to you. Pass shooting is a popular technique for harvesting snow geese. Birds are always coming and going from one feeding field to another. So what you do is get to the north side of a feeding field. Birds usually move to the next field to the north, then you get them when they pass overhead.

Hunting Boats

This is a just going to give you some ideas. The internet has many boats to look at. There are way too many boats to cover, and everyone you ask has a different opinion on which one to get. Many experienced waterfowl hunters like a small lightweight boat they can carry on a roof rack or in a pickup bed. Before you buy or design a blind for your boat, check out what your local waterfowl

Low Riding Layout Boat

guides are using. This will probably save you time and money. One of the best solutions for hunting shallow water is a shallow riding, what they call a layout boat. It is about 13-1/2 feet long, 50 inches wide and weighs just under 100 pounds. It floats only 8 inches above the water surface, but it is very stable and can haul two hunters and gear. Along with a camo cover, grass mats and recliner seat, you can go wherever the ducks or geese are, set up a small decoy spread, and become invisible.

Decoy Spreads and Layouts

This is just going to give you some ideas of how to set up decoys. The internet has a number of decoy setups, layouts and arrangements to look at. There is just too many! So we are not even going to attempt to show them. We advise you to first go on the Internet and look at them. What may be the best way though is take a pad of paper and pencil with you when you go out to scout feeding birds. Then sketch out how the birds are gathered. This can change depending on the time of year and the season. So just set your decoys up the way the birds were grouped when you scouted them. This will help you be more successful with your hunt.

Being a Good Caller

This is an art you need to learn if you are going to do much waterfowl hunting. One hunter had this comment on calling, "I try not to call too much for the early birds." He says quite often the September birds are not looking for a lot of calling. He prefers to let his scouting and decoys do most of the work. He says there is one exception to this rule though. After a shot, young birds, confused by the shooting, can often be called back around for another look at the decoys. Young birds don't always know what to do when adult birds are taken out of the flock. More often than not, you are able to bring the remaining birds back in with a heavy, insistent calling. Here is a *TIP*. When flying ducks see your decoys and start working on their own, don't call until they make their downwind swing. Then issue one quick comeback call to pull them around the corner and back towards the decoys. This is what real ducks do in the wild. You don't hear birds on the water call a lot while a flock is approaching, but it's common to hear a hen give a quick four-or-five note call after the birds pass overhead. This usually spins those downwind ducks right around.

Retrieving Dogs

A dog is not only good company on a waterfowl hunt, but a big help in retrieving the ducks out of the water so that you don't need to. I highly suggest you get one. If you don't already have a dog for this, what kind would you get? I know there is more than one breed, but I would personally get a Golden Labrador Retriever. Retrieve is what they do, in water or anywhere. They are at the top of the list. They are particularly valued for their willingness to please, intelligence, obedience, and having a soft mouth. However, Brittany's, German Shorthairs, and Spaniels can also be trained to retrieve. When I was a young boy, I had a mix dog. Part Golden Labrador and Spitz. "King," as I called him, was the best dog I ever had. Very friendly, got along with everyone, and was a good buddy to me. He used to jump the fence, then follow our mailman around the neighborhood every day and protect him from other dogs. When the mailman was done, King would come back home, jump the fence back in, and be waiting for me when I got home from school. Whichever dog you get, they do need to be trained to retrieve.

Regulations and Restrictions

First always check with your states Conservation or Game department to make sure you are up to date with your regulations and restrictions. Here are just a few to remember:
Migratory bird hunting does require a permit in most states. Be aware of any "conservation orders" from your state. In Missouri that would be snow, blue, or Ross's geese which takes a special permit because of conservation purposes. In most states migratory game bird hunting hours are from 1/2 hour before sunrise to sunset. Most states have a non-toxic-shot only restriction for hunting in conservation areas with a shotgun. The migratory bird hunting permit for waterfowl in most states is 16 years of age and older. Firearm must be a shotgun, and can be no larger than 10 ga.

Upland Game Bird Hunting

What You Will Encounter

This is a little different than waterfowl hunting. It's usually out in fields or rolling hills country. In most states these would be birds like quail, woodcock, pheasant and grouse. But there are also others because of the type of habitat in a state and which game birds it will support. In some states doves are very popular. By the way don't forget to check out our "Game Bird Classification Table" on *PAGE 129*. Game bird hunting is mostly shotgun hunting. Most states restrict the size to not larger than 10 Ga. The smaller gauges like 20 and 28 Ga. are becoming more and more popular. Electronic calls are not legal. No shooting from land based motor vehicles. In California mostly partridges, ptarmigan and chukar are hunted. You can't use bait to draw in birds, and birds may NOT be taken within certain distances of "baited areas" such as not closer than 400 yards. You may NOT hunt at night, which in most states is usually from 1/2 hour after sunset to 1/2 hour before sunrise. And always check the bag and possession quantities for your state. These are just a few things you will encounter.

Game Bird Hunting Techniques, Tactics and Strategies

One of the problems is getting a good pointer dog to find the game birds for you. Next which are the best areas to look for certain game birds. Quail stay most of the day time out on the edge of a corn or high grass field about 70 feet away from a woody cover. That's where to find them. Since woodcocks feed mostly on earthworms, they can be found during the day in moist soil in forest openings, alder bottoms, and aspen alder stands. That's where you find them. Pheasants like to feed on weed seeds. You can find them with your binoculars by glassing distant corn fields, hayfields. Wetland borders and fence rows. They like to feed right after sunrise. Partridges like to feed on wheat, oats, barley and small grain. They tend to feed on the edges of the fields, so that's where you glass for them. They only move about 60 feet from where their roosts and food are located. They prefer higher elevations so they can escape by flying down fast instead of up. Prairie chickens live in grasslands and adjacent cultivated fields. You can also find them in the draws, along the fence rows, or the edges of timber. That's where you glass for them. Stake out any of these birds with a partner and a dog. If there are ridges, one person at the top of the ridge and one below it. Then have your dog flush the birds from the middle area.

Pheasant Hunting

Conditioning

Stay in good physical shape because you may end up doing a lot of up and down walking along ridges while hunting. Some of the western habitats for theses game birds is pretty rough, rocky terrain. Avoid hunting these upland game birds alone, especially partridges. Experts warn that, due to the harsh environments and sometimes extreme weather, it is best to hunt partridges with a friend. And bring a survival kit with you because some of the habitat can be deadly for hunters.

Choice of Firearms

We are talking shotguns here. Use a 12 or 20 gauge shotgun. They are the favorites of upland game bird hunters because they are an affordable choice with good range. For a faster kill, choose the 20 Gauge. And it's best to use No. 6 or 7-1/2 shot because many times you have only longer distance shots. Most of these birds are very hardy, and using this gauge will help make sure the bird you shoot dies quickly.

Hunting Dogs

Depending on where you are hunting, you may want to use a pointer or a retriever, or a dog that can do both. In most cases, when hunting upland game birds, it's probably best to use a dog that works well at close range. A Brittany Gordon setter or a German short haired pointer are good options because they don't stray to far away from you. Make a good choice because dogs that are good at working large open spaces may work too far ahead and end up flushing the birds out of your range.

Archery Season

Some hunters do hunt upland game birds with bows and even in some states crossbows can be used. There are some archery restrictions. Usually states require that you don't use arrows with explosive heads or tips that have material that will tranquilize or poison birds. For the archery techniques and tips, check out bow hunting in the "Turkey Hunting" section starting on *Page 208*.

Regulations and Restrictions

First always check with your states Conservation or Game department to make sure you are up to date with your regulations and restrictions. Here are just a few to remember:

You can't use bait to lure in birds. In most states you must use non-toxic-shot ammunition with a shotgun. And in most states shotguns can be no larger than 10 ga. You can only hunt basically from sunrise to sunset. And be sure and check your states bag limits before you leave on your hunting trip, for whichever bird you are hunting. And NO hunting from your jeep, pick-up or car.

Improving Your Shotgun Techniques

We are adding these tables to give you a little insight into how you might improve your shotgun techniques, and your approach strategy. Looking at the tables you can see how many, and the size of, pellets are going out there towards the target. As an example, you can see by looking at the choke pattern diagram that if your target is out at 50 yards, and you have no choke in the cylinder, that the pellets will spread out too far to make many hits. Also, don't forget to practice your trap shooting.

TABLE 32	No. of Shotgun Pellets Per Ounce		
Shot Size	Lead	Steel	Bismuth/Tungsten [1]
8	585	– – –	585
7-1/2	410	– – –	428
6	225	316	255-297
5	170	243	170
4	135	191	120-140
2	87	125	87-97
1	– – –	103	77
BB	50	72	54
BBB	– – –	61	– – –
T	– – –	52	169(4T), 375(6T)
F	– – –	40	– – –

Note: [1] = About the same or similar to Lead

TABLE 33	American Standard Birdshot Size		
Size	Diameter	Pellets/10g Lead	Pellets/10g Steel
FF	5.84mm (.230")	8	12
F	5.59mm (.220")	10	14
TT	5.33mm (.210")	11	16
T	5.08mm (.200")	13	12
BBB	4.83mm (.190")	15	22
BB	4.57mm (.180")	18	25
B	4.32mm (.170")	21	30
1	4.06mm (.160")	25	36
2	3.81mm (.150")	30	44
3	3.56mm (.140")	37	54
4	3.30mm (.130")	47	68
5	3.05mm (.120")	59	86
6	2.79mm (.110")	78	112
7	2.41mm (.100")	120	174
8	2.29mm (.090")	140	202
9	2.03mm (.080")	201	290

Gateway Gun Club Trap Shooting

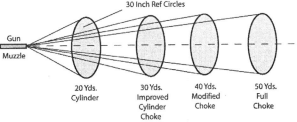

Shotgun Choke Pattern vs Range Diagram

SECTION 6 Reference Section

Explanation
In this section we will cover some useful information that may help you understand more about hunting and what is involved. We will have resources such as miscellaneous laws and regulations, miscellaneous hunting organizations and who to contact for information, diagrams and nutrition menus. We are not attempting to list all the possible firearm, bow and other hunting devices manufactures because there are just to many.

Miscellaneous Laws and Regulations

Who May NOT Possess Firearms
The catagories of persons NOT permitted to possess or transport firearms are; felons, minors, the mentally ill, and persons under court-ordered abuse or harassment injunctions.

Felons
Basically federal law prohibits felons from possessing firearms, but federal law allows individual states to determine what constitutes a restoration of civil rights for the purpose of firearm ownership. However, many states allow previously convicted felons to possess firearms after a certain number of years following completion of their sentences. Also some states require that the felon must generally receive a pardon from the governor before being given a permit to own a gun.

Minors
Generally, both federal and state law prohibit persons under the age of 18 from possessing firearms. However, some states (like Wisconsin) make exceptions for long guns used for hunting, or firearms used during adult-supervised activities such as target shooting. On the other hand, children adjudicated delinquent based on a felony may NOT own any type of gun, and school districts must suspend pupils found in possession of a firearm either on school property or while under the supervision of a school authority, such as on a field trip.

The Mentally Ill
Persons charged with a felony but found not guilty, or not responsible, for the crime due to mental illness may not possess firearms. This ban extends to a person who has been involuntarily commited for treatment of mental illness, drug dependency, or developmental disability if the court deems the person to be a threat to self or others. For those involuntarily commited, the court must order the person's firearms seized or stored until the person is judged to no longer suffer from the mental illness and is no longer likely to be a danger to the public.

Persons Under Abuse or Harassment Injunctions
Some states have a law that bars possession of a firearm in cases where a person is under a court-ordered injunction or restraining order for domestic abuse, child abuse, or harassment. Such persons are required to surrender their firearms to the county sheriff or a third party approved by the court. Federal law also prohibits a person under such a restraining order from possessing a firearm.

Safety of the Devices

Transporting safety of the equipment (firearms-Other Devices) is also important. First thing is CHECK on the laws in your STATE, and the AIRLINE you are flying with, because each one may have different transporting rules. The next thing to consider is where they will be stored while transporting. Since they are transported as "checked" baggage, they are in the bottom of the aircraft and may be shifted or banged around. To prevent damage to your equipment, pack them in approved cases and in an unloaded or uncocked position, such as with crossbows *(SEE FIGURE 154)*. Firearms are particulary important. You pay lots of money for some of these guns and compound bows, and you won't want to find out they have been damaged during transport.

Organization Resources

State or American National Hunting Organizations

Missouri Department of Conservation
2901 W. Truman Blvd
P.O. Box 180, 65102
Jefferson City, MO. 65109   (573) 751-4115

National Hunters Assoc.
560 Wendell Blvd.
Knightdale, NC. 27545
(916) 365-7157

Firearms Organizations

National Rifle Assoc. of America (NRA)
11250 Waples Mill Road
Fairfax, VA. 22030   1-800-672-3888
www.nraila.org

National Muzzle Loading Rifle Assoc.
(NMLRA) P.O. Box 67
Friendship, IN. 47021 1-800-745-1493
www.nmlra.org

Archery Organizations

North American Bow Hunters Coalition
NABC P.O Box 493
Chatfield, MN. 55923

Missouri Bow Hunters Assoc ·
1164 Decker Road
Labadie, MO. 63055   (636) 742-2531

Atlatl Sports Organizations

The World Atlatl Assoc, Inc.
5024 King Road
Jeffersonville, IN. 47130
theatlatl@1st.net

Missouri Atlatl Assoc
Ron Mertz (314) 628-9376

Deer Hunters Organizations

Buckmasters
10350 Highway 80 East
Montgomery, AL. 36117
(334) 215-3337

Whitetails Unlimited
P.O. Box 720
2100 Michigan Street
Sturgeon Bay, WI. 54235 1-800-274-5471

Upland Game Bird Organizations

Quail Unlimited
P.O. Box 610
Edgefield, SC. 29824 (803)637-5731

Pheasants Forever
1783 Buerkle Circle
St. Paul, MN. 55110   (651) 773-2070

The Ruffed Grouse Society
451 McCormick Road
Coraopolis, PA. 15108
1-800-JOIN-RGS

Big Game Organizations

    Rocky Mountain Elk Foundation
    5705 Grant Creek
    Missoula, MT. 59808
    1-800-CALL ELK

    Rocky Mountain Bighorn Society
    P.O. Box 8320
    Denver, CO. 80201
    (720) 201-3791

Waterfowl Organizations

    Ducks Unlimited
    One Waterfowl Way
    Memphis, TN. 38120
    1-800-45DUCKS

Turkey Hunters Organizations

    National Wild Turkey Federation
    P.O. Box 530
    Edgefield, SC. 29824

Slingshot Organizations

    National Slingshot Assoc.
    P.O. Box 131
    Tuscola, IL. 61953
    Go on line at www.chiefaj.com/national_slingshot_assocation.htm
    and contact your nearest state representative.

Mfrs/ Equipment Resources

Atlatl Equipment Sources

    The World Atlatl Assoc, Inc.
    5024 King Road
    Jeffersonville, IN. 47130
    www.worldatlatl.org

    List of Atlatl Manufacturers
    Go to www.flight-toys.com/atlatl/atlatl
    6 pages are listed

Firearm Equipment Sources (Rifles-Shotguns-Muzzleloaders-Pneumatic)

    Gunshots.Net (On-Line)
    www.gun-shots.net/gun-manufacturers

    Gunnerden.com (On-Line)
    www.gunnersden.com/index.htm.gun-manufacturers

Archery Equipment Sources

    Archery BassPro.com (On-Line)
    www.archeryequipmentinfo.com

    TradShops.com (Traditional On-Line Locator)
    www.tradshops.com/shop-list.php

Slingshot Equipment Sources

    Master List of Commercial Slingshot Mfr. (On-Line)
    www.slingshotforum.com/topic/15-master-list-of-commercial-slingshot-manufacturers/

Miscellaneous Diagrams

Bullet and Shotshell Anatomy 101

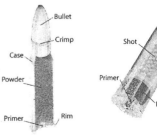

Centerfire Rifle
Bullet Anatomy

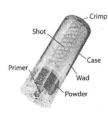

Shotshell
Anatomy

Basically bullets and shotshells are similar in how they work. When you pull the trigger a pin hits the primer cup and drives it into the powder charge and ignites it. Then it explodes, and because of the shell case containing it, the force goes forward driving either the bullet tip or the shot out the front of the shell case. The shotshell has a "wad", the bullet does not. The wad is a disc used to separate the powder from the shot. This is to seal propellant gases behind the shot or to hold the shot together in the barrel.

Nutrition Resources

Nancy Clark's Suggested Menus

Here are some menus from Nancy Clark's guidebook to get your kids started. I'm going to recommend the same things she does. Make your breakfast the most important meal of the day. A 500 calorie breakfast will keep your weight down *(SEE SAMPLE MENU No.1)*. This is especially true for young girls going through puberty, who seem to be the most vulnerable. For more menus and information than I have room for in this book, get a copy of Nancy Clark's "Sports Nutrition Book." It covers all kinds of options. We are showing just a few that you can use as examples. Check out the vegetarian menu we show *(SEE SAMPLE MENU No.2)*. It's based on a cook free menu for a sports active 150 pound vegetarian that drinks milk and eats dairy foods, who might need about 2800 calories per day. To take in the extra calories needed to "GAIN WEIGHT," you can eat frequently throughout the day if that fits your life-style. Plan on having food on hand for every eating opportunity or try these tips:

- Eat an extra snack, such as a bedtime peanut butter sandwich with a glass of milk.
- Eat larger than normal portions at mealtime.
- Eat higher calorie and carbohydrate foods.

I know it's not directly hunting related, but here is a sample menu for a boy or girl who is underweight, such as a boy that wants to play Football, but they have been told they are too small for their age, and to light in weight. These are healthful, high calorie, carbohydrate rich sports meals *(SEE SAMPLE MENU No.3)*.

Use these menus as a sample only. There are many more to choose from. "Nancy Clark's Guidebook" goes into nutrition, diets, and menus in much more depth for more specific situations.

Nutrition

Clark, N. 2003. *Sports Nutrition Guidebook*: A guidebook for all your nutritional needs. Champaign, IL.: Human Kinetics

Eating Disorders

Otis, C, and R. Goldingay. 2000. *The Athletic Woman's Survival Guide*: *How to Win the Battle Against Eating Disorders, Amenorrhea and Osteoporosis*. Champaign, IL.: Human Kinetics

Breakfast on the run

Bagel, medium Large	300
Vanilla yogurt	200
Total:	500

Nontraditional breakfast

2 slices of cheese pizza	500
Total:	500

Desk drawer breakfast

Instant oatmeal, 2 packets	250
Raisins, 1 small box (1.5 oz)	130
Powdered milk, 1/2 cup	120
Total:	500

Sample Menu 1 No.1

Food	Protein (g)	Calories
Breakfast		
1 cup orange juice	2	110
2 cups bran flakes	8	240
1 medium banana	1	100
1-1/2 cups low fat milk	12	150
Lunch		
2 peanut butter sandwiches	30	700
1 apple	1	100
2 cups milk	16	200
Snack		
1 cup fruit yogurt	10	250
Dinner		
1 medium pizza	70	1000
Total:	150	2850

Sample Menu 2

Approximate Calories		Approximate Calories	
Breakfast			
16 oz. orange juice	200	16 oz. pineapple juice	280
6 pancakes	600	1 cup granola	500
1/4 cup syrup	200	1/4 cup raisins	120
1 pat margarine	50	16 oz. low fat milk	200
8 oz. low fat milk	100	1 large banana	130
Total:	1,150	Total:	1,230
Lunch			
4 slices hearty bread	400	1- 7 inch pita pocket	240
1- 6.5 oz. can tuna	200	6 oz. turkey breast	300
4 tbsp lite mayo	150	2 tbsp lite mayo	80
1 bowl lentil soup	250	2 cups apple juice	250
16 oz. low fat milk	200	1 cup fruit yogurt	250
2 oatmeal cookies	150	1 medium muffin	300
Total:	1,350	Total:	1,420
Dinner			
1 medium cheese pizza	1400	1 breast chicken	300
16 oz. lemonade	200	2 large potatoes	400
Total:	1,600	2 pats margarine	100
		1 cup peas	100
		2 biscuits	300
		2 tbsp honey	100
		16 oz. low fat milk	200
		Total:	1,500
Second Lunch			
2 slices hearty bread	200	1 large N.Y. style bagel	450
2 tbsp peanut butter	200	3 oz. lite cheese	250
3 tbsp jelly	150	16 oz. crangrape juice	350
12 oz. low fat milk	150	Total:	1,050
2 tbsp chocolate powder	100		
Total:	800		
Total for day: 4,900 calories		Total for day: 5,200 calories	
● 60% carbohydrate (745 g)		● 65% carbohydrate (832 g)	
● 15% protein (193 g)		● 15% protein (180 g)	
● 25% fat (121 g)		● 20% fat (123 g)	

Sample Menu 3

221

Try these other excellent books for teaching, coaching, or learning more about sports fundamentals

These Jacobob Press LLC books are available at our web site jacobobpress.com, your local Borders bookstore, amazon.com, barnesandnoble.com, or by calling the publisher direct at (314) 843-4829

Teach'n Football (2nd Edition) - Have mom or dad help you learn all the basic fundamentals you need to play the game of football, and all in one book. They will have fun helping to teach you. You will have more fun playing the game because you will feel like you know what you are doing. This book is complete with everything you need to know. It covers all the positions, new parent orientation to the game of football (Football 101), equipment required, field size, glossary and general game rules.
ISBN 0-9772817-5-2, soft cover paperback, perfect bound, 8 x 10-1/2, 192 pages.

Teach'n Basketball (2nd Edition) - Have mom or dad help you learn all the basic fundamentals you need to play the game of basketball, and all in one book. They will have fun teaching you. You will have more fun playing the game because you will feel like you know what you are doing. This book is complete with everything you need to know. It covers all the positions, new parent orientation to the game of basketball (Basketball 101), equipment required, court size and general game rules.
ISBN 0-9705827-6-5, soft cover paperback, perfect bound, 8 x 10-1/2, 151 pages.

Teach'n Baseball & Softball (2nd Edition) -Have mom or dad help you learn all the basic fundamentals you need, to play the game of baseball or softball, and all in one book. They will have fun teaching you. You will have more fun playing the game because you will feel like you know what you are doing. This book is complete with everything you need to know. It covers all the positions, new parent orientation to the games of baseball and softball (Baseball/ Softball 101), equipment required, glossary, history, field size and rules.
ISBN 0-9772817-1-X, soft cover paper back, perfect bound, 8 x10-1/2, 204 pages.

Teach'n Track & Field - Have mom or dad help you learn all the basic fundamentals you need to excel in track & field events, and all in one book. And mom or dad, you will have fun teaching them, and they will have more fun learning the events because they will feel like they know more about what they are doing. This book is complete with everything you both need to know. It covers all the events, new parent orientation to track and field (Track & Field 101), equipment required, glossary, history, track size and rules.
ISBN 0-9705827-5-7, soft cover paperback, perfect bound, 8 x 10-1/2, 180 pages.

Teach'n Soccer - Have mom or dad help you learn all the basic fundamentals you need to play the game of soccer, and all in one book. They will have fun teaching you. You will have more fun playing the game because you will feel like you know what you are doing. This book is complete with everything you need to know. It covers all the positions, new parent orientation to soccer (Soccer 101), equipment required, glossary, field size and general game rules.
ISBN 0-9705827-3-0, soft cover paperback, perfect bound, 8 x 10-1/2, 138 pages.

Teach'n Volleyball - Have mom or dad help you learn all the basic fundamentals you need to play the game of volleyball, and all in one book. They will have fun teaching you. You will have more fun playing the game because you will feel like you know what you are doing. This book is complete with everything you need to know. It covers all the positions, new parent orientation to volleyball (Volleyball 101), equipment required, court size, glossary and general game rules.
ISBN 0-9705827-7-3, soft cover paperback, perfect bound, 8 x 10-1/2, 144 pages

Teach'n Rink Hockey - Have mom or dad help you learn all the basic fundamentals you need to play the games of ice hockey and roller hockey, and all in one book. They will have fun teaching you. You will have more fun playing the game because you will feel like you know what you are doing. This book is complete with everything you need to know. It covers all the positions, new parent orientation to rink hockey (Rink Hockey 101), equipment required, rink size, glossary and general game rules.
ISBN 0-9705827-8-1, soft cover paperback, perfect bound, 8 x 10-1/2, 181 pages.

Teach'n Field Hockey - Have mom or dad help you learn all the basic fundamentals you need to play the game of field hockey, and all in one book. They will have fun teaching you. You will have more fun playing the game because you will feel like you know what you are doing. This book is complete with everything you need to know. It covers all the positions, new parent orientation to field hockey (Field Hockey 101), equipment required, field size, glossary and general game rules.
ISBN 0-9705827-9-X, soft cover paperback, perfect bound, 8 x 10-1/2, 195 pages

Learn'n More About Skateboarding (2nd Edition) - You Young boys and girls can learn all the basic fundamentals you need to skateboard, and all in one book. And mom or dad can help you if needed. They will have fun teaching you. And you will have more fun learning because you will feel like you know more about what you are doing. This book is complete with everything you need to know. It covers the basic tricks plus many more, new parent orientation (Skateboarding 101), where you can skate, history, glossary, and staying safe.
ISBN 0-9772817-3-6, soft cover paperback, perfect bound, 8 x 10-1/2, 140 pages.

Learn'n More About Fencing - You young boys and girls can learn all the basic fundamental skills you need to fence, and all in one book. And mom and dad can help if needed. They will have fun teaching you. And you will have more fun learning because you will feel like you know more about what you are doing. This book is complete with everything you need to know. It covers foil, epee, saber, new parent orientation to fencing (Fencing 101), equipment required, history, glossary, strip size (for field of play, general rules and reference information section.
ISBN 0-9772817-4-4, soft cover paperback, perfect bound, 8 x 10-1/2, 196 pages.

Learn'n More About Boxing - You young boys and girls can learn all the basic fundamental skills you need to box, and all in one book. And mom and dad can help if needed. They will have fun teaching you. And you will have more fun learning because you will feel like you know more about what you are doing. This book is complete with everything you need to know. It covers punching, defending, counterpunching, new parent orientation to boxing (Boxing 101), equipment required, ring size, glossary, history, reference section and general rules.
ISBN 0-9820960-0-3, soft cover paperback, perfect bound, 8 x 10-1/2, 200 pages.

Learn'n More About Track & Field - You can learn all the basic fundamentals you need to get into a track & field event, and all in one book. And mom or dad can help if needed. They will have fun teaching you. And you will have more fun learning because you will feel like you know more about what you are doing. This book is complete with everything you need to know. It covers all the events, new parent orientation to track (Track & Field 101), equipment required, glossary, history, track size and general rules.
ISBN 0-9820960-1-1, soft cover paperback, perfect bound, 8 x 10-1/2, 216 pages.

Basketball Drills, Plays, and Games Handbook (2nd Edition) - You young coaches and assistant coaches will have all the drills, plays, an games you need to get started, and all numbered for easy reference. All your players will have more fun learning and playing because they will feel like they know more about what they are doing out on the court. This book is complete with 160 basic fundamental drills, plays, and games covering both the offensive and defensive phases of the game of basketball.
ISBN 0-9820960-3-8, soft cover paperback, perfect bound, 5-1/4 x 8-1/4, 102 pages.

Baseball & Softball Drills, Plays, and Situations Handbook - You young coaches and assistant coaches will have all the drills and plays you need to get started, and all numbered for easy reference. All your players will have more fun learning and playing because they will feel like they know more about what they are doing out in the field and at bat. This book is complete with 147 basic fundamental drills, plays and situations,covering all the offensive and defensive phases of the games of baseball and softball.
ISBN 0-9772817-8-7, soft cover paperback, perfect bound, 5-1/4 x 8-1/4, 108 pages.

Football Drills & Plays Handbook - You young coaches and assistant coaches will have all the drills and plays you need to get started, and all numbered for easy reference. All your players will have more fun learning and playing because they will feel like they know more about what they are doing out on the field. This book is complete with 156 basic fundamental drills and plays, covering all the offensive and defensive phases of the game of football.
ISBN 0-9772817-9-5, soft cover paperback, perfect bound, 5-1/4 x 8-1/4, 116 pages.

Soccer Drills & Plays Handbook - You young coaches and assistant coaches will have all the drills and plays you need to get started, and all numbered for easy reference. All your players will have more fun learning and playing because they will feel like they know more about what they are doing out on the field. This book is complete with 134 basic fundamental drills, plays,and alignments, covering all the offensive and defensive phases of the game of soccer.
ISBN 0-9772817-7-9, soft cover paperback, perfect bound, 5-1/4 x 8-1/4, 112 pages.

Lacrosse Drills, Plays, & Games Handbook - You young coaches and assistant coaches will have all the drills, plays, and games, you need to get started, and all numbered for easy reference. All your players will have more fun learning and playing because they will feel like they know more about what they are doing out on the field. This book is complete with 197 different fundamental drills, plays,and games, covering all the offensive and defensive phases of the game of lacrosse.
ISBN 0-9820960-5-4, soft cover paperback, perfect bound, 5-1/4 x 8-1/4, 130 pages.

Volleyball Drills, Plays, & Games Handbook - You young coaches and assistant coaches will have all the drills, plays, and games, you need to get started, and all numbered for easy reference. All your players will have more fun learning and playing because they will feel like they know more about what they are doing out on the court. This book is complete with 210 different fundamental drills, plays, and games, covering all the offensive and defensive phases of the game of Volleyball.
ISBN 0-9820960-7-0, soft cover paperback, perfect bound, 5-1/4 x 8-1/4, 106 pages.

Ice Hockey Drills, Plays, & Games Handbook - You young coaches and assistant coaches will have all the drills, plays, and games, you need to get started, and all numbered for easy reference. All your players will have more fun learning and playing because they will feel like they know more about what they are doing out on the rink. This book is complete with 155 different fundamental drills, plays, and games, covering all the offensive and defensive phases of the game of Ice Hockey.
ISBN 978-098209609-3, soft cover paperback, perfect bound, 5-1/4 x 8-1/4, 139 pages.

Index